Worship and in Context

in Context

*Studies and Case Studies in Theology
and Practice*

Edited by
Duncan B. Forrester & Doug Gay

scm press

© Duncan Forrester and Doug Gay 2009

Published in 2009 by SCM Press
Editorial office
13–17 Long Lane,
London, EC1A 9PN, UK

SCM Press is an imprint of Hymns Ancient and Modern Ltd
(a registered charity)
St Mary's Works, St Mary's Plain,
Norwich, NR3 3BH, UK

www.scm-canterburypress.co.uk

British Library Cataloguing in Publication data

A catalogue record for this book is available
from the British Library

978 0 334 04168 9

Typeset by Regent Typesetting, London
Printed in the UK by
CPI Antony Rowe, Chippenham, Wiltshire

Worship and Liturgy in Context

CONTENTS

PREFACE

The studies collected in this volume are authored by a wide range of academics and practitioners from Baptist, Episcopalian, Presbyterian and Roman Catholic backgrounds, who are variously based in England, Wales and Scotland. Their work combines historical and practical concerns, often within the same piece and, taken together, offers a rich, new, ecumenical and contextual resource for reflection on the past, present and future of Christian worship within and beyond Scotland.

Thanks are due to many people for their participation in this project. They are due above all to the contributors, who responded with enthusiasm and energy to our invitation to write and whose work provides a wealth of new insights and perspectives. They are due also to Natalie Watson, our editor at SCM Press, for her patience, skill and support.

Working on this book has been a labour of love and a journey of appreciative friendship for us in our conversations with contributors and with one another. We have learned much and been left with new and provocative questions. Our shared hope is that these studies may contribute towards increasing the understanding and enriching the practice of worship in many contexts, not least in Scotland.

Duncan Forrester, New College, University of Edinburgh
Doug Gay, Trinity College, University of Glasgow

CONTRIBUTORS

John L. Bell is a Church of Scotland Minister who works for the Iona Community and has an international ministry teaching and training in liturgy and worship.

Stuart Blythe is a Baptist Minister who lectures at the Scottish Baptist College in the University of the West of Scotland.

Stewart J. Brown is Professor of Ecclesiastical History at the University of Edinburgh.

Jeremy Crang is Senior Lecturer in History at the University of Edinburgh.

Jane Dawson is Professor of Reformation History at the University of Edinburgh.

Peter Donald is a Church of Scotland Minister.

Fiona Douglas is Chaplain to the University of Dundee.

Owen Dudley Edwards is Reader in Commonwealth and American History at the University of Edinburgh.

David Fergusson is a Church of Scotland Minister, Professor of Divinity at the University of Edinburgh and Principal of New College.

Duncan Forrester is a Church of Scotland Minister and Emeritus Professor of Practical Theology and Christian Ethics at the University of Edinburgh.

Doug Gay is a Church of Scotland Minister and Lecturer in Practical Theology at the University of Glasgow.

Alison Jack is a Church of Scotland Minister who is Editor of the *Expository Times* and Deputy Principal of New College Edinburgh.

David Lyall is a Church of Scotland Minister and former lecturer in Practical Theology at New College Edinburgh.

Donald Macleod is a Free Church of Scotland Minister and Principal of the Free Church College in Edinburgh.

Paul Nimmo lectures in Systematic Theology at the University of Edinburgh.

Ian Paton is Rector of Old St Paul's Scottish Episcopal Church in Edinburgh.

Michael Regan is a Roman Catholic priest who lectures at New College Edinburgh.

Norman Shanks is a Church of Scotland Minister and former Leader of the Iona Community.

Nigel Yates was, until his death in 2008, Professor of Ecclesiastical History at the University of Wales, Lampeter.

Introduction

IN SPIRIT AND IN TRUTH

Christian Worship in Context

Duncan B. Forrester

The Place for Worship

In the fourth chapter of John's Gospel we find the account of Jesus' conversation at the well with a Samaritan woman. Part of the conversation is about worship. The woman reminds Jesus that Jews regard Jerusalem, Mount Zion, as the proper place for worship, whereas Samaritans have always seen Mount Gerezim as the best place for the worship of God. Jesus responds, 'Woman, believe me, the hour is coming, and is now here, when you will worship the Father neither on this mountain [Gerezim] nor in Jerusalem [Mount Zion] ... The hour is coming and is now here, when the true worshippers will worship the Father in Spirit and in Truth, for the Father seeks such as these to worship him. God is Spirit, and those who worship him must worship in Spirit and in Truth.'[1]

Seeking *the* one proper place for worship is wrong, because authentic worship, worship in Spirit and in Truth, can take place anywhere. Yet the place or places for worship remain an important issue, because worship relates in fascinating and important ways to its various contexts – place, time, community, culture and so forth. This was true in the experience of God's people, Israel. When they were delivered from bondage in Egypt, they bore with them the Ark of the Covenant as a sign of God's presence with them as they journeyed to the Promised Land. Outside their main encampment they constructed, according to God's design, the Tabernacle, or Tent of Meeting. Here, in this place, the Israelites could meet with God and be sure of his presence with them as they journeyed onward.[2]

When they settled in the Promised Land they constructed, according to the design that had been given to them in great detail, a temple in Jerusalem, the holy city, as a place of sacrificial worship, of proclamation of the

---

1 John 4.20–21, 23–25.
2 See especially Exodus 25—28 and 36—40.

Law, and above all as a constant sign of God's presence with his people.[3] But although most Jews might have regarded the Temple as the *best* place to worship, it was certainly not the only place. Passover, for instance, was primarily a family festival, to be celebrated normally at home, although it was also felt by many that Jerusalem was an even better place to celebrate Passover.[4] In the Passover Haggada (ritual) the youngest child present asks why everything is different on this particular evening, and in this peculiar meal. In response the story of the exodus, of God's deliverance of his people from slavery in Egypt, is retold and celebrated once again. This story, retold and re-enacted in the context of worship, reminds God's people who they are, where they belong, and how God has guided them to this day, and will guide them in the future.

A third special place for Jewish worship – the synagogue or meeting house – was added when the Israelites were forced into exile, far from home, and from the Temple. The synagogue became the principal place for Jewish worship throughout the Diaspora until today. Synagogue worship centres on the Torah, God's law, but it also focuses on a story, the story of God's people. The synagogue is a place of meeting with God and with God's people.

Christianity, too, like Judaism, has had from the beginning the belief that there are three special contexts for Christian worship, although God may be worshipped anywhere and at any time. The three special contexts are the great church – cathedrals, pilgrimage centres and such like – the local church, which is used for worship by a local congregation and is in many ways like the synagogue, a meeting place for God's people, and, third, the home, which is again and again asserted as the context for regular family and private worship.

But of course in addition to those special places for Christian worship, worship relates to a great diversity of contexts. Worship in Spirit and in Truth needs far more than special places.

Christian Worship and Life

As we have seen, Christian worship is in many ways continuous with Jewish worship, the sacrificial and ceremonial worship of the Temple, the Scripture-centred worship of the synagogue, and the worship of the family at home. The worship of Passover in the home is the direct ancestor of the Lord's Supper, the Eucharist or the Mass, to give the central act of Christian worship a few of its many names. Above all, Christian worship is an encounter with the Triune God, the Father, the Son and the Holy

---

3 But according to Paul, God does not live in shrines made by human hands – Acts 17.24.
4 See especially Exodus 12—13 and the Gospel accounts of the Last Supper.

Spirit, and it is rooted in the history of God's dealings with humankind and with God's creation. Although there is a significant place for private worship and for the worship of families, Christian worship is essentially the worship of the Church, understood in the broadest sense, so that it includes the fellowship of the saints, and becomes part of the constant worship of heaven. Christian worship, as this book suggests, relates in complex and various ways to ethics, politics, theology, culture and the broader society.

Worship is expected to provide a kind of foretaste and appetizer for the joys of heaven, and a model of what human societies should be like, and how people should behave to one another and towards God. Christian worship is often, and properly, seen as the definitive and central activity of the people of God. It is something we do rather than observe, or listen to, or talk about. It is the strange practice, which is characteristic of Christians. In worship the Church manifests itself most clearly, and in worship Christians are nourished for the broader 'divine service' or 'liturgy after the liturgy' in the life of the world. In worship we are involved in the life of heaven, we experience in a fragmentary way the life that is to come, and we glimpse God's purposes for everyone and for the whole of creation. Worship expresses and creates community, *koinonia*, and in worship we find an ethic, a lifestyle, embodied and sustained.

Worship is thus seen as a kind of template of the Christian life. The worship of communities of expectant faith anticipates God's future and challenges the present. Those who sing God's song in a strange land are thereby disturbing the existing order and proclaiming an alternative. As they reappropriate the tradition in celebrating together the love and the justice of God, they discover that there are opportunities of renewal, witness, transformation and liberation offered to them. Eastern Orthodox Christians in particular have reminded us all that when we speak of worship we do not mean simply or exclusively set times of worship, the 'cult', a particular and rather odd compartment of life. The wholeness of the Christian life should be rooted in the times set apart; any sharp disjunction between worship and the Christian life is a distortion of each. 'Christ did not establish a society for the observance of worship, a "cultic society",' wrote the Orthodox theologian Alexander Schmemann, 'but rather the Church as the way of salvation, as the new life of re-created [hu] mankind.'[5]

Worship can indeed be understood as an anticipation of God's future. But all too often we have made of the worship which should sanctify and illumine the whole of life, which should be the leaven of the lump and the

---

5 Alexander Schmemann, *An Introduction to Liturgical Theology*, New York: St Vladimir's Seminary Press, 1986, p. 28.

sign of God's love for the world, a temporary escape from reality and a way of avoiding the ethical task. In fact, it is argued, worship ought to be a resource for the enrichment and humanization of the life of the world, a source, perhaps *the* source, of Christian ethics. Christian worship, in other words, is the heart of Christian practice and ethics. It expresses the significance of the whole, and sustains and illumines the Christian life. In worship and in action that flows from worship we learn how to be Christians; and in the doing we explore the nature and the claim of faith.

None of this is done in isolation. In worship we experience what it is to be 'Church'; together we encounter God in worship, and this is inseparable from our meeting and responding to our neighbours with their needs. In worship we find that together we are opened to God and to the world that God has made and redeemed in Christ.

This is heady stuff indeed – for Christians, at any rate. But even for them cautionary notes must be sounded, as when the great Archbishop Trevor Huddleston declared that it was a scandal that so many Christians were so obsessed with the real presence of Christ in the Eucharist that they couldn't see the real presence of Christ in the needy neighbour. It is good to be reminded that worship can be, and often is, an escape from reality, or a disguise for sin and immorality. It is worth remembering that Christian worship in its regular sequence took place within easy reach of Belsen, Auschwitz, Dachau and Buchenwald, the Nazi extermination camps. And one wonders, too, whether a theology that is entirely rooted in and expressed through the various elements of Christian worship can communicate prophetically or evangelically to those for whom Christian worship is not a vividly relevant activity at the centre of their lives.

Christian Worship in Context[6]

In this book we offer studies of Christian worship in some of the many forms that it has taken in Scotland. Contexts, like place and time and story, matter. Christian worship relates in many and diverse ways to the various contexts in which it finds itself. In this book we will be exploring some of the ways in which Christian worship in Scotland related, and relates, to its contexts, varying over space and time. We chose Scotland not because we felt that it was particularly important or interesting, but simply to focus the discussion in the hope that this book would stimulate people in quite different contexts to examine the changing interactions over time between worship and context.

---

6 Some of the material in this section is derived from Duncan B. Forrester, 'The Reformed Tradition in Scotland', in Geoffrey Wainwright and Karen Westerfield Tucker, eds, *The Oxford History of Christian Worship*, Oxford: Oxford University Press, 2006.

In this diversity of contexts and of places we will be especially interested in the outside forces that have influenced Christian worship in Scotland, and the diversity, development and conflicts that have shaped worship in Scotland. Scottish theology has often attempted to reshape Scottish worship, and has regularly been concerned with the relation of Word and sacrament, and especially with the integrity of preaching, and the pastoral care and discipline of the believing community. Particularly from the time of the Reformation, worship in Scotland has often been politically controversial, with persecution at times forcing Roman Catholic worship underground or causing large numbers of Covenanters to worship in secret conventicles in the open air. These Covenanters also believed that in worship they found a kind of proleptic embodiment of the kind of community that Scotland might and ought to be.

We will also be concerned with the influence of Scottish patterns of worship outside Scotland, and its ongoing and complex interaction with theology, ethics, society, politics and culture. And, finally, we discuss contemporary forms of worship in Scotland, and ask how in a radically secularized Scotland Christian worship in some of its many forms may be renewed and vigorous while other forms may decay and die.

Relevant to the whole discussion is H. Richard Niebuhr's classic work, *Christ and Culture* (1951). Niebuhr distinguishes five basic relationships between faith – or worship – and culture – Christ *against* Culture, the Christ *of* Culture, Christ *above* Culture, Christ and Culture *in Paradox*, and Christ *transforming* Culture. These are helpful in discussing some of the situations with which we deal in this book. Some Christian worship, such as that of the Amish people in Pennsylvania, seeks to be quite separate from the surrounding culture. Sometimes Christian worship may be a clear and public protest against the surrounding culture. Sometimes, on the other hand, worship enriches and affirms culture, supporting and shaping the whole contextual culture. Sometimes worship, as the Old Testament prophets knew so well, may support and dignify a highly oppressive political culture – for instance, the white Dutch Reformed Church in South Africa before the collapse of apartheid. Worship in many situations may be self-consciously archaic, perhaps in liturgical language or otherwise, or it may seek to relate constructively to recent developments, say in popular music. Worship may challenge its context, or reflect that context, or reshape the context, or evangelize its context, or offer an alternative. In a way it is encouraging that dictatorial regimes like that in the old East Germany, or the Soviet Union, saw Christian worship as a threat that had to be subdued, and secular alternatives to baptism and confirmation provided. Perhaps today too many people in the West regard worship as a quaint and irrelevant survival from a long past age.

WORSHIP IN SCOTLAND[7]

The Origins of Christian Worship in Scotland

Christian worship first came as a major force to Scotland in the fourth century when Ninian and his followers established a base at Whithorn in Galloway, while in the sixth century Columba and his followers moved from Ireland to the island of Iona, from which missionaries went throughout what is now Scotland, interacting with the existing Pictish and Celtic cultures and forms of devotion. Some people suggest that what is now known as 'Celtic spirituality' was shaped by these evangelistic movements. But others suggest that it is a product of a far later time. We in fact know very little about the early Celtic Church in Scotland, sometimes called the Culdees, so little in fact that some 'evidence', such as the so-called 'Dunkeld Litany', was designed to fill the gap! While currently attracting intense interest worldwide, the roots and history of Celtic spirituality are today much contested, as can be seen from Donald Macleod's essay in this book.[8]

Medieval Worship

The customs, traditions and forms of worship of the Celtic or Culdee Church in Scotland were in many ways different from the main traditions and practices of continental Europe. But by the mid eleventh century, partly under the influence of Malcolm Canmore's Hungarian wife, Margaret, the Scottish Church had by and large adopted the customs and liturgical practices of the Western Church in communion with Rome. There was still some diversity tolerated or even encouraged. Scotland, in general, followed the English Sarum Rite, and the 'Aberdeen Breviary' was in some significant ways distinctively Scottish, but there was also some persistent feeling that the English put steady pressure on Scotland, especially in times of war, to conform to an English pattern in their worship. The Reformers, and particularly George Buchanan, depicted the medieval Church in Scotland as a foreign imposed interlude until the Reformers restored the primitive purity of the Celtic Church. This interpretation of the religious history of Scotland was hugely influential for centuries, but it could hardly resist the questioning of historical scholarship.[9]

---

7 Some of the material in this section is derived from Duncan B. Forrester, 'The Reformed Tradition in Scotland', in Geoffrey Wainwright and Karen Westerfield Tucker, eds, *The Oxford History of Christian Worship*, Oxford: Oxford University Press, 2006.

8 See James Cooper, ed., *Reliques of Ancient Scottish Devotion*, Edinburgh: Foulis, 1913, pp. 13–38.

9 See James Galbraith, 'The Middle Ages', in Duncan Forrester and Douglas Murray, eds, *Studies in the History of Worship in Scotland*, 2nd ed. Edinburgh: T. & T. Clark, 1996.

Reformed Worship in Scotland[10]

The Reformation in Scotland was among the most radical and thorough-going of the Calvinist reformations in Europe. In relation to worship, doctrine and other matters as well, there was a strong sense of discontinuity, of sweeping away a sullied past, of making a new start with a return to the purity, integrity and simplicity of the worship of the early Church. The Bible, and the Bible alone, was to be normative for authentic Christian worship. All else was denounced as 'idolatrie', a dangerous distortion of the worship of the Triune God. Images and statues, stained glass windows, relics, pilgrimages, the cult of the saints, special feasts and festivals, and indeed the whole Christian year save for Sunday and Easter, were to be swept away. In order that 'Christ Jesus be truly preached and his holy sacraments rightly ministered', idolatry and the centres in which it had flourished, were 'to be utterly suppressed in all bounds and places of this Realme'. By idolatry was understood 'the Masse, invocation of Saints, adoration of images and the keeping and retaining of the same. And finally, all honouring of God not contained in his holy word.'[11]

A clean sweep with the past, a radical break, a new beginning was the intention. But inevitably there was a good deal of continuity. The same church buildings were used for congregational worship, although with major modifications in their layout. Many priests and monks conformed to the Reformation and were made readers or ministers. Some of them eagerly and intelligently embraced the new understanding of the faith; others were timeservers, and continued quietly with many old practices and customs. Popular feeling in many parts of lowland Scotland was inflamed against Romanism, and it was urban mobs that destroyed many friaries, shrines and images, and removed altars and the instruments of 'idolatrie'.

But sometimes the very same people were strongly attached to old practices which the leaders of the Reformation discountenanced, such as the celebration of saints' days, especially when associated with fairs or seasonal festivities. Funeral and birth rituals continued to fulfil an important role in society. Popular prejudices against, for instance, frequent reception of communion, died hard and triumphed over the Reformers' intentions and their theology of the Lord's Supper, which was to follow as closely as possible the precedent of Jesus' gathering with his disciples in the Upper Room to eat the Passover the evening on which he was arrested.

Such continuities are, by the nature of things, hard to demonstrate or document in detail. Even harder to substantiate is the suggestion, which goes back at least as far as the Reformation humanist George Buchanan

---

10 See Professor Jane Dawson's chapters in this book.

11 James K. Cameron, ed., *The First Book of Discipline*, Edinburgh: St Andrew Press, 1972, pp. 94–5.

(1506–82), that the Scottish Reformation restored the purity and the practices that had been characteristic of the ancient Celtic Church before it
was subordinated to Rome. Most of the specific suggestions – that Scottish Reformed worship inherited from the Eastern churches via the Celtic
Church the emphasis on the *epiclesis,* or the so-called 'Great Entrance'
at the offertory in the Lord's Supper – are no more than nineteenth- or
twentieth-century romantic fantasies.

Granted the fact that people in general tend to be more conservative in
matters of worship than in almost anything else, it would be surprising
had there not been some carry-over of worship practices from the medieval
Church. What is more surprising is that such radical religious change became generally accepted. In most of Scotland the old ways were laid aside
with remarkably little resistance, and new worship practices found a fairly
ready acceptance, perhaps because the corruption of the late medieval
Church had encouraged the development of widespread anti-clericalism.

Whatever continuities there may have been with the more immediate,
Roman, or more remote, Celtic, religious past of Scotland, it is abundantly clear that the patterns of worship established in the Reformation
period were greatly influenced by outside forces. These may, perhaps, be
summed up under three headings, in ascending order of significance: German Lutheranism, the English Reformation and Calvinism.

German Lutheranism

Early Scots Reformers such as Patrick Hamilton (martyred 1528) and
George Wishart (martyred 1546) were deeply influenced by the German
Reformation, and brought distinctively Lutheran doctrines with them. We
may assume that they also imported Lutheran understandings and practices
of worship. But the evidence that distinctively Lutheran worship ever took
root in Scotland is virtually non-existent. What is clear, however, is that
the Reformation in Scotland, as in Germany, was born in song, and much
of this song at the beginning came from German Lutheran sources.[12] This
is especially true of *The Gude and Godlie Ballates* compiled by the Wedderburn brothers, James, John and Robert, merchants from Dundee. This
was published in some shape or other between 1542 and 1546 (no copy of
the original edition is extant), and became immensely popular, being published in edition after edition until 1621.[13] This collection includes many

---

12 See references in John Bell's chapter in this book.

13 Modern editions are David Laing, ed., *A Compendious Book of Psalms and Spiritual
Songs, commonly known as 'The Gude and Godlie Ballates'* reprinted from the edition of
1578, Edinburgh: 1868; and Iain Ross, ed., *The Gude and Godlie Ballatis*, Edinburgh: Oliver
and Boyd, 1939 (a selection).

metrical psalms, metrical versions of the creed and the Lord's Prayer, a catechism in metre, ballads and popular spiritual songs set to ballad tunes, Christmas carols, and hymns. Numerous of these were translations from the German, and the doctrine of the catechism was distinctly Lutheran. It is not clear how far this book was used in public worship, and how much in the family circle. The fact that it included numerous examples of what can only be called 'taunt songs' against the Roman Catholics suggests that it was a popular rather than an officially sanctioned book for worship. In *The Gude and Godlie Ballatis* there is sublime devotion:

> Our Saviour Christ, King of grace,
> With God the Father maid our peace;
> And with his bludie woundis fell,
> Hes us redemit from the Hell.
> And he, that we suld not foryet,
> Gave us his body for to eit
> In forme of breid, and gave us syne
> His blude to drink in forme of wyne.[14]

And, at the other extreme, a lively attack on the Pope in the form of a folk song:

> The Paip, that pagane full of pryde,
> He hes us blindit lang;
> For where the blind the blind dois gyde,
> Na wonder baith ga wrang:
> Lyke prince and king he led the ring
> Of all iniquitie:
> Hay trix, tryme go trix,
> Under the greenwood tree.[15]

English Influence

The English and Scottish Reformations interacted closely with one another. The Reformation party in Scotland constantly sought an alliance with England. There was much movement of people, and especially ministers between the two countries. Knox himself spent much of his ministry in England. He was a court chaplain to Edward VI, and played some part in the production of the Second Prayer Book of 1552. He was prepared 'to think well of the Book', and advised his congregation in Berwick to use it.

---

14 Ross, *Ballatis*, p. 17.
15 Ross, *Ballatis*, p. 60.

There is evidence that this prayer book was widely used in Scotland, and it continued to be used in Scotland and among the Marian exiles long after it was abolished on Mary's accession in England. In 1557 the Protestant nobles of Scotland enjoined its use in every parish of the land. Only after 1560 did more radically Calvinist forms of worship gradually displace the second English Book of Common Prayer.

Calvinist Worship[16]

By the late 1550s it seemed to many people that the Reformation movement was getting out of control. *The First Book of Discipline* suggests that some treated the ordinances of religion with contempt, and it heads a section, 'For punishment of those that Profane the Sacraments and contemne the Word of God and dare to presume to minister them not being thereto lawfully called.'[17] In St Andrews a man informed one of the deacons, 'I shall buy a pint of wine and a loaf and I shall have as good a sacrament as the best of them all shall have.'[18] The *Book of Discipline* called for drastic punishment for 'idolaters', that is Roman Catholics, and also for 'those who despise the Sacrament'.

By 1560 there was a pressing need to bring order to the worship of the Reformed Kirk. It was Calvinism that gave this order, principally by way of two documents, both promulgated in 1560, the Scots Confession and *The First Book of Discipline.* In traditional Calvinist style, the Confession put the first two 'marks of the true Kirk' the faithful preaching of the Word of God, and the right administration of the sacraments of Jesus Christ, 'quhilk man be annexed unto the word and promise of God, to seale and confirme the same in our hearts'.[19] Word and sacrament together are the vital and essential components of Reformed worship. Word without sacrament lacks demonstrative power; sacraments without the Word are in danger of becoming magic or idolatry.

There is evidence that Knox insisted on frequent celebrations of the Supper and its centrality in worship from the earliest days of the Scottish Reformation.[20] The sacramental doctrine of the Scottish Reformation is clearly set out in the Scots Confession. Sacraments are not simply 'naked and bare signs'. Through the sacraments we are joined to Christ: 'be Baptisme we ar ingrafted in Jesus Christ, to be made partakers of his

---

16 See especially Professor Jane Dawson's chapters in this book.

17 *The First Book of Discipline,* p. 204.

18 Cited in William McMillan, *The Worship of the Scottish Reformed church, 1550–1638,* London: James Clark, 1931, p. 40.

19 G. D. Henderson, ed., *Scots Confession 1560 and Negative Confession 1581,* Edinburgh: Church of Scotland, 1937. Article XVIII, p. 75.

20 James S. McEwan, *The Faith of John Knox.* London: Lutterworth, 1961, pp. 56–9.

justice, be quilk our sins are covered and remitted. And alswa, that in the Supper richtlie used, Christ Jesus is so joined with us, that hee becummis very nurishment and fude of our saules.'[21] Transubstantiation is explicitly excluded, but through the working of the Holy Spirit who enables us to share now in the heavenly banquet, 'the faithful ... do so eat the bodie and drink the blude of the Lord Jesus, that he remaines in them and they in him'.[22] The real presence of Christ is conveyed to us in the elements of the Lord's Supper. Robert Bruce, in his remarkable sermons on the Lord's Supper, delivered in the High Kirk of Edinburgh in 1586, suggested that the Supper is a *verbum visibile*, the Word made visible. It 'exhibits and delivers the thing that it signifies to the soul and heart, as soon as the sign is delivered to the mouth'.[23] In and through the Supper, the Lord gives himself to us.

Knox's Liturgy

The practice of worship in the early years of the Reformation may be found in the *First Book of Discipline* and in the service book, which quickly displaced the Anglican Book of Common Prayer. This *First Book of Common Order*, popularly known as Knox's Liturgy, was largely derived from Geneva, where Knox and others had been in exile, and was authorized in Scotland in 1564. In it the Lord's Supper is 'commonly used once a month, or as oft as the Congregation shall think convenient'.[24] The practice of Jesus is to be followed as closely as possible. Accordingly, communicants are to receive communion sitting at the table, not on their knees before an altar. The communion service follows the usual Sunday service of prayers, psalm singing, Bible reading and preaching. It consists of the institution from 1 Corinthians 11, an exhortation, including the exclusion of all unrepentant sinners from the table, and calling on the congregation to 'consider, then, that this Sacrament is a singular medicine for all poor sick creatures, a comfortable help to weak souls, and that our Lord requireth no other worthiness on our part, but that we unfeignedly acknowledge our naughtiness and imperfection'.[25] The minister then, standing at the table, takes bread and gives thanks in words such as these:

---

21 *Scots Confession*, Article XXI, pp. 83–5.

22 *Scots Confession*, Article XXI, p. 85.

23 Robert Bruce, *The Mystery of the Lord's Supper*, ed. T. F. Torrance, London: James Clark, 1958.

24 The *First Book of Discipline* judges four times a year to be 'sufficient'.

25 George W. Sprott and Thomas Leishman, eds, *The Book of Common Order of the Church of Scotland and the Directory for the Public Worship of God*, Edinburgh: Blackwood, 1868, p. 125.

At the commandment of Jesus Christ our Lord, we present ourselves to this His Table, which he has left to be used in remembrance of His death until His coming again, to declare and witness before the world, that by Him alone we have received liberty and life, that by Him alone Thou dost acknowledge us Thy children and heirs, That by Him alone we have entrance to the throne of Thy grace, that by Him alone we are possessed in our spiritual Kingdom, to eat and drink at His Table, with whom we have our conversation presently in heaven , and by whom our bodies shall be raised up again from the dust, and shall be placed with Him in that endless joy, which Thou, O Father of mercy, hast prepared for Thine Elect before the foundation of the world was laid.[26]

After the prayer of thanksgiving, often called in Scotland the 'Action Prayer', the minister breaks the bread, and the people divide and distribute the elements among themselves. Then follows a prayer of thanksgiving, the singing of a psalm and the blessing. *The Book of Common Order* was much more than a directory, but it was not a book for the people, nor was the wording of its prayers mandatory. It use was authorized and usual in Scotland until it was replaced by *The Westminster Directory of Public Worship.*

The Westminster Standards

From as early as 1615 there was steady pressure from the crown to re-introduce into Scottish worship practices that had been abandoned in Scotland but had been retained in England, or reintroduced under Archbishop Laud. Charles I and Laud initially wanted Scotland to adopt the English Prayer Book. This met with deep-seated opposition in Scotland, and the next effort, to introduce in 1637 a substantially altered Scottish Prayer Book led to riots in Edinburgh and elsewhere. The crown's attempts to reform the worship of Scotland were overtaken by the civil war, and in practice abandoned without them having any significant effect on what actually happened in most churches. The Westminster Assembly of Divines was convened by the English Parliament in 1643 to reform the Church of England and its practices and, in the view of the Scots commissioners at least, to unite the two great churches of Britain 'in one forme of Kirk Government, one Confession of Faith, one Catechism, and one Directorie for the Worship of God'. This Directory was intended, in the words of Robert Baillie, one of the Scots commissioners, 'to abolish the great Idol of England, the Service Book, and to erect in all the parts of

---

26 *Book of Common Order*, p. 126.

worship a full conformitie to Scotland in all things worthie to be spoken of'. The English Parliament ordered the *Directory* to be observed throughout England, Ireland and Scotland in 1645, and in the same year, reflecting the different constitutional position, it was enacted by the General Assembly and approved by the Scottish Parliament.

The Westminster Directory of Public Worship should be read alongside the other documents of the Westminster Assembly. One the one hand, the Confession, the Larger and Shorter Catechisms, and the Form of Church Government outline the relatively new federal Calvinism which was now the orthodoxy of Presbyterian Scotland and which deeply shaped the understanding of worship and the sacraments in the Directory. On the other hand the General Assembly moved quickly to introduce, in 1647, *The Directory for Family Worship*, a reminder that 'the secret worship of each person alone, and private worship of families' should take place during the week; on the Lord's Day, the congregation gathered for public worship in the church.

The *Westminster Directory* starts with a quaint, and revealing, account of how the people should behave in times of worship. Apart from psalm singing, the people's part is very passive. They are not to read in church, and should abstain from 'all private whisperings, conferences, salutations ... as also from all gazing, sleeping and other indecent behaviour'! Normal Sunday worship is centred on Bible reading and the sermon. All the canonical books are to be read in order. What was called the 'lecture' – an exposition of the passages read – was allowed in addition to the sermon. Preaching was given a pre-eminent place, and the Directory's section on preaching is a classic account of biblical preaching: 'Preaching of the Word, being the power of God unto salvation, and one of the greatest and most excellent works belonging to the ministers of the Gospel, should be so performed that the workman need not be ashamed, but may save himself and those that hear him.' Thus the preacher should do his work 'painfully, ... plainly, ... faithfully, ... wisely, ... gravely, ...with loving affection, ... as taught of God, and persuaded in his own heart, that all that he teacheth is the truth of Christ; and walking before his flock as an example to them in it'. A model of a long prayer before the sermon and a shorter prayer afterwards is offered, and after a final psalm, the people are dismissed with a blessing.

Baptism is assumed to be baptism of infants into the covenant. It should be in public, usually as part of the ordinary Sunday service, and it should not be in 'popish fonts'! The Lord's Supper is 'frequently to be celebrated', although how often is not specified. It should take place after the sermon, reading of Scripture and the prayers, and it starts with an exhortation which is both an invitation and a 'fencing of the table', excluding notorious and unrepentant sinners from communion. There is to be no altar, but a table 'decently covered', and so placed that the communicants may 'orderly sit about it or at it'. This provision represented a compromise between the Scots and the English. The Scots believed that the biblical precedent required that communicants sit at long tables, as for a meal, while the English at the time were accustomed to tables set lengthways in the chancel with the minister at the centre of the north side, and the people gathered around. The minister begins what was called the Action 'with sanctifying and blessing the Elements of Bread and Wine set before him ... having first in a few words showed that these Elements, otherwise Common, are now set apart and sanctified to this holy use by the Word of Institution and Prayer'. After this 'Taking' and reading of the narrative from 1 Corinthians 11.23–27, the 'Prayer, Thanksgiving, or Blessing' is outlined in some detail. After thanksgiving for all God's goodness, there is a strong echo of Knox's Liturgy's Christological emphasis: 'There is no other name under heaven by which we can be saved, but the name of Jesus Christ, by whom alone we receive liberty and life, have access to the throne of grace, are admitted to eat and drink at his own table, and are sealed up by his Spirit to an assurance of happiness and eternal life.' There is a more explicit consecration, praying to God 'to vouchsafe his gracious presence and the effectual working of his Spirit in us, and so to sanctify these elements, both of bread and wine, and to bless his own ordinance, that we may receive by faith the body and blood of Jesus Christ, crucified for us, and so ... feed upon him, that he may be one with us, and we one with him; that he may live in us, and we in him, and to him who hath loved us, and given himself for us'. After this prayer, the minister breaks the bread and gives to the people. The mode of distribution was left unspecified. The Scots wanted communicants to pass the elements from hand to hand, each serving and being served by neighbours within the royal priesthood; the English wished to permit a variety of practices. After a brief post-communion prayer, the service concludes.

The *Westminster Directory* certainly influenced the worship of Presbyterian Scotland very profoundly, and only in modern times has it been effectively replaced with the various *Books of Common Order* and their like. Some later periods of history left their mark on the worship of Scotland, most notably the struggles between the Covenanters and the 'prelatists', supported by the government. Powerful and evocative stories of Covenanters worshipping in the open, and celebrating the Lord's Supper in the hills, with sentries in place to warn of coming dragoons were etched deeply in the Presbyterian psyche, and contributed to the shape of worship after the firm establishment of Presbyterianism in 1688.

The Communion Season[27]

Although Communion was in many Scottish parishes celebrated infrequently, commonly once a year, from the seventeenth century 'the communion season' was a great festival, attracting in some cases thousands of people, for services over a period of nearly a week climaxing in the great celebration of Communion on the Sunday. Burns wrote a poem, 'The Holy Fair', and at his time the Communion was just that – not simply a liturgical activity, but a great social occasion, attracting thieves, drunkards and 'whores' as well as the devout:

> How mony hearts this day converts,
>   O' sinners and o' lasses!
> Their hearts o' stane, gin night, are gane, as saft as any flesh is:
>   There's some are fou o' love divine;
> There's some are fou o' brandy.

The crowds were so large that services frequently spilled out of the church building into the surrounding fields, with hundreds of communicants sitting down at long trestle tables for each of the successive sittings. In the country areas the Communions were fixed at times in the summer when there was not much activity on the farms and when travel was easy. Teams of ministers led the various services, and the devout would travel a circuit of Communions in the course of the summer, thus receiving communion frequently. The communion season was exported to America and played for a time a major part in the spirituality of the camp meetings in America.[28]

Except in the West Highlands, where the communion season survives to some extent, the Lord's Supper is celebrated today in most Presbyterian parishes quarterly, and in an increasing number monthly or even weekly. The latest service book of the Church of Scotland, *Common Order* (1994) offers a range of orders for the Lord's Supper, ranging from one that is derived from Knox's Liturgy, to modern ones influenced by the Iona Community and the renewed interest in Celtic Christianity.

Church Music[29]

The Scottish Reformation was hostile to accompanied singing in church. Medieval organs were destroyed or removed. Despite the rich diversity

---

27 See Alison Jack's chapter in this book.

28 See Leigh Schmidt, *Holy Fairs: Scottish Communions and American Revivals in the Early Modern Period*, Princeton: Princeton University Press, 1989.

29 See especially John Bell's chapter in this book.

represented by *The Gude and Godlie Ballatis*, the steady practice from the early days was that only psalms should be sung in church, and in family worship. Each family was expected to have, for church and family use, a Bible and a psalm book. The latter often contained, in addition to psalms, metrical versions of the creed, and a number of prayers. The tunes should be 'plain tunes' so that the people could take a full part in this, their central role in worship. Many of these tunes were at the beginning imported from Geneva, but gradually a magnificent diversity of psalm tunes was composed. There were few choirs to lead the singing, but each church had a precentor instead, often using the practice of 'lining', whereby the precentor sings each line alone and the congregation then repeats it – a practice dating probably from the time when many in the congregation would be illiterate.

Successive versions of the metrical psalter were authorized by the General Assembly, the most recent in 1929. Some Scottish metrical psalms have passed into the treasury of the universal Church such as Psalm 23, 'The Lord's my shepherd', Psalm 100, 'All people that on earth do dwell', and Psalm 121, 'I to the hills will lift mine eyes'. The authorization, in 1781, of certain paraphrases of Scripture passages other than psalms caused much controversy; but a few of the paraphrases have become classics, for example:

I'm not ashamed to own my Lord,
or to defend his cause,
Maintain the glory of his cross,
and honour all his laws.

Hymns were introduced later in the nineteenth century, and the Scottish Presbyterian tradition has produced a number of distinguished hymn writers, among whom the Revd John Bell of the Iona Community is pre-eminent today.

Church Buildings[30]

From the time of the Reformation, churches have been regarded in Scotland as meeting places for God's people when they come to worship God together, rather than shrines. At the time of the Reformation most of the monastic chapels and chantries, and even the cathedral in a city like St Andrews were destroyed, or left to decay, stripped of their furnishings and ornaments. It was quite different with parish churches and college

---

30 See especially Nigel Yates's chapter in this book

chapels, which had to be adapted for the use of a Reformed congregation. Big city churches, after they had had altars and all the instruments of the old forms of worship removed, were often divided into two, three or even four churches for different congregations, each and every one with galleries and a high pulpit so that everyone could hear the preacher.

As Scotland was a poor country, there were relatively few splendid country kirks; most were very simple rectangular affairs, easily adapted to Reformed worship by putting the pulpit half way along the long wall. If expansion became necessary, an aisle and gallery could be added opposite the pulpit, thus giving the common T-shaped church design. The pulpit, with precentor's desk beneath, and often seats for the elders within an enclosure around the pulpit was the commonest plan. A baptismal bowl was often attached to the pulpit, but there was normally no fixed communion table; for communion trestle tables were erected in the centre of the church, or perhaps, if numbers were large, outside. When pews became common, many churches had an ingenious arrangement, still to be seen in some places, whereby pews could be adjusted so that they made long, narrow tables with seats at both sides.

Presbyterian city churches built in the eighteenth and nineteenth centuries tended to be built as auditoria, with huge pulpits, often in front of a display of organ pipes, and galleries around three sides. The Scoto-Catholic movement encouraged churches to be built in Gothic style. Also favoured were Romanesque basilica-type churches with the communion table in the apse so that minister and elders could sit behind it. There are a number of interesting modern churches, but on the whole little attention has been given for some time to the requirements for a church building to house contemporary Reformed worship.

Sectarian Conflicts

The seventeenth century was the era of struggle between prelatists and Presbyterians, with leaders such as James and Andrew Melville struggling for the independence of the Church from state control. Early on, during the Commonwealth, the Westminster Assembly sought to make the Church of England Presbyterian, and produced confessions and directories for public worship and for family worship, which for long remained standard in Scotland, despite Episcopalian attempts to introduce a prayer book. The dominant theology was a federal Calvinism, and there was much theological coming and going with the Continent, especially with the Netherlands.

The eighteenth and nineteenth centuries were a time of high Presbyterian dominance in worship forms, with Episcopalian, Methodist and Roman

Catholic forms discouraged. The new missionary movement meant that Scottish Presbyterian forms of worship were exported first to the American colonies and then to Africa and Asia.

Roman Catholic worship survived long after the Reformation in the remoter parts of the Highlands and in the Hebrides. In the nineteenth and early twentieth centuries there was considerable immigration of Irish Roman Catholics, bringing with them their traditional worship, which had been denounced by Reformed Christians since the Reformation as 'the idolatry of the Mass'.

In the north-east, especially in Aberdeenshire, considerable numbers of Episcopalians survived and continued to use the old and the new Scottish Prayer Books. Elsewhere in Scotland, the Episcopalian Church was the church of an Anglicized aristocracy, and commonly described, and dismissed, as the 'High English Church'. In recent times, however, the Scottish Episcopal Church in all its three groupings – high church, liberal and evangelical/charismatic – has shown considerable energy and imagination in the renewal of worship. The Roman Catholic Church in Scotland has over the course of the twentieth century moved into the mainstream of Scottish life, and has engaged creatively with the liturgical renewal that was sparked off by the Second Vatican Council.

Recent Developments[31]

From the early twentieth century onwards, two movements have had an increasing impact on the understanding and practice of Christian worship in Scotland – the ecumenical movement and the liturgical movement. In an increasingly secular Scotland there have also been various interesting experimental forms of worship, stemming from the Iona Community or involvement in the changing ecumenical scene, especially after the Second Vatican Council. Charismatic and Pentecostalist worship forms have influenced especially hymnody throughout the churches in Scotland.

Both worship and its contexts are changing in contemporary Scotland. The chapters that follow, in their exploration of history, theology and practice are concerned with understanding where these changes have come from, what they mean and where they might lead.

---

31 For recent developments in the Roman Catholic Church and in the Scottish Episcopal Church, see the chapters by Michael Regan, Owen Dudley Edwards and Ian Paton in this book Debates and controversies about baptism and the Lord's Supper among Presbyterians are discussed in the chapters by Peter Donald, Paul Nimmo, Donald Macleod and David Fergusson.

Further Reading

George B. Burnet, *The Holy Communion in the Reformed Church of Scotland, 1560–1960*, Edinburgh, 1960.

Duncan Forrester and Douglas Murray, eds, *Studies in the History of Worship in Scotland*, 2nd edition, Edinburgh: T&T Clark, 1996.

George Hay, *The Architecture of Scottish Post-Reformation Churches*, Oxford: Oxford University Press, 1957.

William Macmillan, *The Worship of the Scottish Reformed Church, 1550–1638*, London: James Clark, 1931.

William D. Maxwell, *A History of Worship in the Church of Scotland*, Oxford: Oxford University Press, 1955.

Miller Patrick, *Four Centuries of Scottish Psalmody*, Oxford: Oxford University Press, 1949.

Leigh Eric Schmidt, *Holy Fairs: Scottish Communions and American Revivals in the Early Modern Period*, Princeton: Princeton University Press, 1989.

Part One

WORSHIP AND CULTURE

I

AESTHETICS OF THE REFORMED TRADITION

David Fergusson

Is there a Reformed Aesthetic?

At least three problems confront any attempt to articulate a Reformed doctrine of the arts. Indeed some critics suggest that this task is almost oxymoronic, so radical has been the hostility of the Reformed Church to artistic work. The first problem concerns the scruples generated by a commitment to the second commandment.[32] The horror of idolatry, together with the fear of sensual distraction, provokes a suspicion of artistic forms. It is not difficult to find examples ranging from Calvin to Barth of this aesthetic ambivalence.

A second problem concerns the abstractness of the key aesthetic concept of 'beauty' when applied to God. Rather than expressing the theological setting of aesthetic properties, descriptions of the divine being often tend to rely on alternative terms that divert us to the intellectual and moral attributes of God. In this respect, discussions of the divine attributes are usually dominated by the predicates of wisdom, knowledge and goodness. Beauty, if it features at all, becomes subordinate to these.[33]

Third, the negative reception of Calvinism by many commentators, especially in the English-speaking world, renders any attempt to develop a Reformed aesthetics problematic. Castigated for its repressed attitudes to the visual arts, the theatre and dancing, the Reformed tradition, unlike the Catholic and the Orthodox, has suffered from an aesthetic deficit

---

32 The Reformed identification of the second commandment and the consequent renumbering of the Decalogue is itself testimony to this greater concentration on the theme of idolatry.

33 This is a complaint of Hans Urs von Balthasar, who laments Kierkegaard's disjoining of the aesthetic from the moral and the religious stages of existence in *Glory of the Lord: A Theological Aesthetics*, Vol. 1, Edinburgh: T&T Clark, 1982, p. 50. For a helpful overview of theological aesthetics see Patrick Sherry, *Spirit and Beauty*, 2nd edition, London: SCM Press, 2002.

in our cultural mindset. Several brief examples will suffice. In his celebrated history of Europe, Norman Davies rightly notes the contribution
of Lutheranism to the development of music in Europe. 'The genius of
J.S. Bach could have found no more fertile soil than in Lutheranism,' he
writes, before adding that 'one has only to compare the sterile music of
Calvinism whose ban on "Popish polyphony" reduced the Geneva Psalter
(1562) to a collection of metrical unisons, to see the felicity of Luther's
music-making'.[34] Or again, in the poetry of the Orcadian writer Edwin
Muir the evils of a repressed, cramped Scottish social order with its ersatz
artistic depictions of national identity are deplored. These are attributed
directly to the legacy of Protestantism that destroys a rich, life-affirming
culture with its censorious judgements. So the poet is 'crushed with an iron
text'.[35] Muir is not egregious among Scottish literati. Iain Crichton Smith
complains about the black-hatted and white-collared ministers of Lewis
– with their tight-lipped brilliance, they have suppressed the magic of the
theatre.[36] And to cite one further stock criticism, it is widely assumed that
the Reformed horror of images led to a widespread denigration of painting in Calvinist culture. One literary scholar (Ferdinand Brunetière) has
claimed that 'horror of art was and would remain one of the essential,
characteristic traits of the Reformation in general and the Calvinist Reformation in particular'.[37]

This reception of the tradition needs to be overcome not simply because
it contains significant elements of caricature but also on account of the
Church's need to recover the distinctive aesthetic that resides within the
Reformed tradition. Let us deal first with the second point before considering why this harsh portrait is a caricature. Although the beauty of
God is not a strongly recurrent theme in Scripture, there are significant
references to it alongside a plethora of related concepts. Divine beauty
is extolled in several places in the Psalms (27.4, 145.5) which also refer
to the beauty of the divine house (84.1, 96.6). Elsewhere the emphasis
upon the glory and majesty of God suggests that for the Old Testament
writers the revelation of the divine being is received and apprehended in
terms that are irreducibly aesthetic. The delight, attraction and desire for
God cannot be understood otherwise, and it is significant that when the
evangelists describe the transfiguration of Jesus there is recourse to Old
Testament categories of the divine glory, light and cloud. The weight and
splendour of God's glory make aesthetic notions constitutive of the divine
being. These are not limited to God, but in two ways may be perceived as

34 Norman Davies, *Europe: A History*, London: Pimlico, 1997, p. 487.

35 Edwin Muir, 'Scotland 1941', *Selected Poems*, London: Faber, 1965, p. 34.

36 Iain Crichton Smith, *Murdo: The Life and Works*, Edinburgh: Birlinn, 2001, p. 227.

37 Quoted by Philip Benedict, 'Calvinism as a Culture' in Paul Corby Finney, ed., *Seeing Beyond the Word: Visual Arts and the Calvinist Tradition*, Grand Rapids: Eerdmans, 1999, p. 21.

extended derivatively to creaturely realities. In the handiwork of creation, the divine beauty is displayed by the starry heavens (Ps. 19.1), all living forms (Ps. 104, Job 38—41) and the laws governing human conduct (Ps. 119). In examining the scriptural allusions to divine beauty, one finds moreover that many references are located in the Psalms and set in the context of divine worship. In our praise of God, true delight is found.

Assuming the various distinctives of the Reformed tradition, one can quickly see that these are accompanied by a theological aesthetic. With a renewed attention to the twin themes of the transcendence and immanence of God, there was stressed both divine majesty and its presence in the actions of the worshipping congregation. In the metrical psalms of the French-Genevan tradition (and later the Scottish paraphrases) there is a powerful sense of sovereignty and grace, passion without lapse into sentimentality, and a strength of conviction united with moments of tenderness.[38] These forms of worship were further determined by the emphasis upon the Word of God as preached and thereby heard, comprehended and applied by all present. The role of the minister, no longer that of the priest performing a sacramental act at the altar, is marked by the wearing of sober vestments and the requirement of a scholarly training for the task of interpreting Scripture. The building set apart for the worship of God is characterized by open spaces, the centrality of table and pulpit, and seating that gathers people together as a worshipping community. Music, instead of being banished, ceases to be the province of the choir by becoming the expression of the whole people in their praise of God and response to the Word. In all those respects Reformed theology and worship together express a particular set of aesthetic qualities.[39]

What emerges is not the denial of aesthetic qualities but their restatement in forms of simplicity, sobriety and measure. Donald Davie discerns these in Isaac Watts's paraphrase of Psalm 90, 'O God, our help in ages past'. The profound restraint, faithfulness to the text, and accommodation to the capacities of the primary audience offer an insight into the aesthetics of his Congregationalist tradition. By resisting and finally rejecting more expansive forms of expression an 'unusually frugal and therefore exquisite'[40] pleasure is produced. This is not an accidental development

---

38 One thinks here of that combination of paternal and maternal images of divine providence in the penultimate verse of 'O God of Bethel'.

39 Alec Cheyne's posthumously published collection of Scottish devotional writing provides a fitting testimony to the (largely neglected) aesthetic richness of the Scottish Reformed tradition. See A. C. Cheyne, *Scottish Piety: A Miscellany from Five Centuries*, Edinburgh: Dunedin Press 2007.

40 Donald Davie, *A Gathered Church: The Literature of the English Dissenting Interest, 1700–1930*, London: Routledge & Kegan Paul, 1978, p. 26. The pastoral setting of Watts's hymns is also noted by Davie. He 'was there in the congregation, hearing his hymns sung at sight by his neighbours, most of whom, no doubt, he knew and could name' (p. 30).

dependent solely upon Watts's creativity. It is a feature of a theological tradition marked by attention to the second commandment, divine sovereignty, pastoral care and the piety of each member of the congregation under the Word of God. The aesthetic qualities noted here are rooted in a doctrine of God and an account of the Christian life. Calvin speaks of 'integrity' as that quality commended by God as the chief part of worship.[41] This wholeness, order and sincerity characterize the Christian life and define what is beautiful alongside goodness and holiness. David Willis perceives this aesthetics to have close affinities with the classical tradition in defining goodness and beauty in terms of fittingness with that purpose for which something or someone has been created.[42] Perhaps not surprisingly, the mark of integrity, singled out by Calvin, is close to Thomas Aquinas's earlier account of beauty in terms of wholeness, harmony and radiance.[43] In the philosophies of art that flourished in the eighteenth century, writers emerging from the Reformed tradition would advance realist theories of artistic values. This aesthetic realism perceived works of art to represent moral and spiritual truths that derived ultimately from the Creator.[44]

Why then does there persist this impression of a Reformed hostility to the arts? In large part, it derives from a fear of visual images in the sanctuary, a fear that is not generally present in the Lutheran tradition. In the context of worship, painting or sculpture can too readily become the object of adoration, thus violating the second commandment. No human work can represent God without violence to the divine majesty. To this extent, what is intended merely as a likeness of the original can too easily function as an idol.[45] Against the argument that religious art may serve an instructive end for the uneducated, Calvin insists that this merely conceals the absence of sound teaching. No visual representation of the crucifixion should obscure Paul's testimony that by the true preaching of the gospel

---

41 *Institutes* III.6.5.

42 David Willis, *Notes on the Holiness of God*, Grand Rapids: Eerdmans, 2002, p. 120.

43 *Summa Theologiae* 1a.39.8. Aquinas appropriates these terms to the second person of the Trinity as the Word of the Father. The Reformed theologian whose work is most permeated with an expansive and intense sense of divine beauty is surely Jonathan Edwards. In his writings, the created beauty of the natural world is a compelling image of spiritual beauty. 'How great a resemblance of a holy and virtuous soul is a calm, serene day.' 'The Images or Shadows of Divine Things', *Basic Writings*, New York: New American Library, 1966, p. 252. A fuller treatment of this subject would require extensive consideration of his contribution. Cf. Robert W. Jenson, *America's Theologian: A Recommendation of Jonathan Edwards*, Oxford: Oxford University Press, 1988, pp. 15–22.

44 Cf. Thomas Reid, *Essays on the Intellectual Powers*, Essay 8, Chapter 4. For a discussion of other Scottish philosophers of the period see Alexander Broadie, 'Art and Aesthetic Theory' in *Cambridge Companion to the Scottish Enlightenment*, Cambridge: Cambridge University Press, 2003, pp. 280–97.

45 *Institutes* I.11.9.

'Christ is depicted before our eyes as crucified' (Gal. 3.1).[46] It is presumably this insistence upon the necessity and sufficiency of the Word of God that prevents Calvin from holding that the incarnation of the Son of God permits or even demands its artistic representation. This is implicit in his position, rather than tackled in a systematic fashion.[47] Zwingli argued that after the resurrection Christ could not be depicted corporally. This tendency is also apparent in Bullinger's *Second Helvetic Confession* with its rather doubtful claim that Christ's bodily presence is not profitable for the Church, only his nearness to us through the agency of the Spirit.

> Since God as Spirit is in essence invisible and immense, he cannot really be expressed by any art or image. For this reason we have no fear pronouncing with Scripture that images of God are mere lies ... Although Christ assumed human nature, yet he did not on that account assume it in order to provide a model for carvers and painters ... He denied that his bodily presence would be profitable for the Church, and promised that he would be near us by his Spirit forever.[48]

A similar argument appears in Karl Barth. The perfections of Christ being unique, complete and unrepeatable it appears that no visual representation should be attempted. (Given that Barth kept in his study a reproduction of Grünewald's painting of the crucified Christ, I have never quite understood this passage.) Like Zwingli, Calvin appears to have maintained the view that this prohibition is confined to the sanctuary as opposed to a domestic setting. This may conceal the relative weakness of the Reformed position with respect to depictions of Christ. In the *Second Helvetic Confession*, Calvin's north German followers recognized the right of believers to keep images of Christ in private homes where there was little danger of these becoming the source of an idolatrous cult.[49] It seems that even a rigorous pursuit of the original Reformed position left scope for the visual arts in Protestant societies. Art has a divinely appointed end through depicting histories or events; it can have a moral and pedagogical purpose while also being the source of pleasure.

---

46 *Institutes* I.11.7.

47 Cf. Sergiusz Michalski, *The Reformation and the Visual Arts: The Protestant image question in Western and Eastern Europe*, London: Routledge, 1993, p. 66.

48 *Second Helvetic Confession* (1566), Chapter 4. There is a rather different argument but to a similar conclusion in Karl Barth. On the principle that only through God can God be known, the face of Christ cannot be repeated or represented. 'This picture, the one true picture, both in object and representation, cannot be copied, for the express reason that it speaks for itself, even in its beauty.' *Church Dogmatics* II/1, Edinburgh: T&T Clark, 1957, p. 666. The argument here may adumbrate Barth's later refusal of sacramental status to baptism and the Lord's Supper.

49 *Second Helvetic Confession*, p. 71.

In any case, given the commitment to the distinctive aesthetic forms in the Reformed tradition, it would be surprising if its subsequent history had been one of remorseless hostility to the arts. It is not the burden of this chapter to defend the excesses of Reformation history; still less is it to deny the value of artistic achievements associated with other theological traditions and the need to learn from these. Nonetheless, the caricatures of repression and unrelenting iconoclasm need to be challenged. We can discern in the Reformed tradition a commitment to a range of artistic forms that produced some noteworthy work in several fields. Although opposed to the use of visual art inside church buildings, Calvin did not seek to deny its value as a divine gift.

In the Netherlands, Rembrandt painted biblical scenes with a new realism to striking effect. Though criticized for ugliness, his paintings, especially of women, display an awareness and compassion not only for biblical figures but also for the people of his own society and acquaintance. The honesty of his paintings is suffused with a sense of worth for their subjects that attests divine grace amid human weakness.[50] Portrait painting could also flourish in Presbyterian Scotland. The work of Henry Raeburn and David Wilkie has been noted for its sombreness, simplicity and austere compassion all of which are consonant with the religious culture in which they worked, albeit informed also by newer Enlightenment ideas.[51] What happens in the visual arts under the impact of Reformed criticism of idolatry is not so much the suppression of artistic work as its refraction. In the absence of ecclesiastic patronage and no longer required for the adornment of church buildings, works of art continued to be commissioned by private individuals and to be displayed in households and other more secular contexts. This led to a process of disenchantment by which the visual arts could be used for a wider range of functions. The laicization of the arts can be seen both in continuity with the Renaissance and also as a further application of the secularization of vocations in the Protestant tradition.[52] Subsequently, this facilitates an awareness that art has not one purpose but many. It functions not only or even primarily

---

50 'Rembrandt was the painter of the grace of God, exhibited to the unworthy, the unimportant, those without merit, in such a way that only the grace of God mattered.' John Dillenberger, *A Theology of Artistic Sensibilities: The Visual Arts and the Church*, London: SCM Press, 1987, p. 99.

51 Raeburn (1756–1823) is discussed by Duncan Macmillan, who considers his understanding of intuition to be derived from the realist account of perception offered by Thomas Reid. *Painting in Scotland: the Golden Age*, Oxford: Phaidon, 1986. Wilkie (1785–1841) was the son of a Presbyterian minister. His art rivalled that of his contemporary Joseph Turner. Murdo Macdonald, speaks of Wilkie's work as possessing 'an integrity of vision', *Scottish Art*, London: Thames & Hudson, 2000, p. 90.

52 This was argued by Abraham Kuyper, in his Princeton Stone lectures, *Calvinism*, Edinburgh: T&T Clark, 1898, pp. 189–230.

to elicit a sense of the divine presence. By amusing, shocking, warning, exposing, educating, inspiring and entertaining us, works of art do not do one thing but many.[53] The release of art from serving God in only an ecclesiastical milieu can, even if unintentionally, have a liberating effect in spawning a greater variety of forms and functions. Of course, the iconoclasm of the Reformation was not without serious defects and excesses. The destruction of cathedrals and abbeys, the loss of artistic treasures, and the general lawlessness that attended these actions are to be deplored. Indeed the vandalism of artefacts and theft of church property appalled Calvin in later life, his theological position notwithstanding.[54]

Leaving aside the visual arts, we should note also the promotion of other artistic forms. Some of these are central to worship, most notably church architecture, music and rhetorical styles. Furthermore, the Reformed accentuation upon Scripture promoted higher literacy rates and a heightened awareness of the vernacular, with Calvin's *Institutes* being regarded as one of the first classics in the French language. In England, the Book of Common Prayer and the King James Authorized Version of the Bible became landmarks in literary history. Elsewhere, Protestantism produced religious classics such as Bunyan's *Pilgrim's Progress* or devotional works of a surprising erotic intensity in the Puritans and Samuel Rutherford. The dedication to linguistic precision, scholarly attainment and intellectual understanding was later manifested in the production of dictionaries, lexicons and encyclopaedias, the *Encyclopaedia Britannica* first emerging on Presbyterian soil.[55] The qualities exhibited in such output again reflect something of the distinctive aesthetic of the Reformed tradition: a concern for clarity; the search for truth in every sphere; a scorn for pretentiousness; the importance of exactitude; and integrity, both moral and intellectual.

The Aesthetics of Worship

In concluding his discussion of the divine perfections, Karl Barth argues that beauty is to be attributed to God as a subordinate feature of the divine glory.[56] As beautiful, God can convince, delight and please us. Without this

---

53 This is a central theme of Nicholas Wolterstorff, *Art in Action: Toward a Christian Aesthetic*, Grand Rapids: Eerdmans, 1980. By resisting the modern assumption that the only legitimate function of art is the production and contemplation of 'high art', Wolterstorff shows how its function within the liturgy can be recovered.

54 Cf. Michalski, *The Reformation and the Visual Arts*, p. 74.

55 The first edition was published in Edinburgh in 1768. The connections between this aspect of Protestant culture and the development of literature are explored by Robert Crawford, 'Presbyterianism and Imagination in Modern Scotland' in *Scotland's Shame: Bigotry and Sectarianism in Modern Scotland*, Edinburgh: Mainstream, 2000, pp. 187–96.

56 *Church Dogmatics* II/1, pp. 650ff.

necessary aspect of glory, our apprehension of God would take an entirely different form from the one described in Scripture. This divine beauty cannot be demonstrated but is simply displayed to us through revelation. In this sense it is self-attesting, and Barth offers three examples of the divine attributes, tri-unity and the incarnation. These are the measure of beauty wherever it is found. What is significant in this context is the manifestation of that beauty in acts of human worship. '[I]f a different view of God's glory is taken and taught, then even with the best will in the world, and even with the greatest seriousness and zeal, the proclamation of God's glory will always have in a slight or dangerous degree something joyless, without sparkle or humour, not to say tedious and therefore finally neither persuasive nor convincing.'[57] Although we are dealing here only with the form of revelation, this is not to be neglected, Barth continues. Without proper attention to this beauty and the joy that it radiates, the glory of God will not fully be appreciated or perceived. This claim is crucial for any act of worship in which God is proclaimed and glorified. It has two principal implications. First, the forms of worship must be made subordinate to its essential content, namely divine revelation. Hence the being and action of God in relation to creatures determines the most appropriate forms of exchange that take place in worship. We have already noted how this gave rise in the Reformed tradition to standards of sobriety, order and measuredness. But, second, the assessment of public worship must include an aesthetic component by which the church service is evaluated for its capacity to glorify God. The claim that the efficacy of divine worship depends upon the agency of Holy Spirit does not release us from this task, any more than it abrogates human responsibility in ethical matters.

There is also a subsidiary reason for attending to the aesthetics of worship, perhaps one with which Barth would have been uneasy; for many people in today's culture the experience of beauty functions as the gateway to or surrogate for religion. A failure to recognize this will inevitably impede the church's evangelism and mission towards its host culture, to say nothing of the richness of its Scriptures. Simone Weil notes how the experience of the beauty of the world, though distorted and soiled, remains a preoccupation of secular life.[58] It is the most common way of approach to God since it is itself a finality with no objective. Lacking any instrumental function, the beauty of the world betokens the being of God which is desirable, loveable and transcendentally beautiful. Art takes us beyond ourselves, necessarily opening onto the transcendent.

The need for an aesthetic assessment of worship can be illustrated under several headings.

---

57 *Church Dogmatics* II/1, p. 655.
58 Simone Weil, *Waiting on God*, London: Collins, 1959, p. 115f.

Church architecture

Attention to church architecture in the Reformed tradition is not born of a loss of artistic sensibility but from a desire to create those forms that are most appropriate to divine worship. The gathering of the people, an uncluttered open space for audible speech, the centrality of table and pulpit, and a simplicity of style are all desiderata of Reformed church architecture in different cultural settings. Early examples of such architecture are not apparent largely for the reason that sixteenth-century congregations occupied existing buildings and merely modified them. But when new churches did emerge, for example in France, Puritan England and in territories colonized by Reformed Christians, especially New England, these distinctive ends were represented, although even here the different ways in which the Lord's Supper was administered made for significant variations in style. Cultural adaptation and development were inevitable but one can still observe at later periods the impact of this aesthetic. For example, in the work of the Glasgow architect, Alexander 'Greek' Thomson we find a self-conscious theological aesthetic wedded to classical forms. Critical of neo-Gothic fashions, for example that represented in the University of Glasgow at Gilmorehill, Thomson designed buildings – including St Vincent Free Church, reckoned to be one of the three finest buildings in the city – with an emphasis upon horizontal lines and stone lintels that betoken strength, simplicity, durability and eternity. Following the tradition of Thomas Reid and other Enlightenment thinkers, Thomson perceived these qualities in terms of an aesthetic realism – they represent, in architectural form, moral and spiritual laws that derive ultimately from God.[59] In response to the legitimate concern that this emphasis promotes a form of cultural elitism not always in the practical interests of worshipping congregations, it is worth recalling that utility is also a mark of architectural beauty. A building must be measured by its success in fulfilling the function for which it is appointed. Thomson himself displayed in his work an obvious concern for such matters as drainage, ability to withstand the prevailing climate, availability of raw materials, and the cost of construction and maintenance.

What lessons can be learned from this? The need for a sanctuary set apart for the worship of God with a capacity for facilitating its various elements should caution against the pragmatic assumption, apparent in some

---

59 'The simple unsophisticated stone lintel contains every element of strength which is to be found in the most ingeniously contrived girder, so that Stonehenge is really more scientifically constructed than York Minster.' Alexander 'Greek' Thomson, *The Light of Truth and Beauty*, ed. Gavin Stamp, Glasgow: Alexander Thomson Society, 1999, p. 67. For further discussion of Thomson's theological roots, see Sam McKinstry, 'Thomson's Architectural Theory', in Gavin Stamp & Sam McKinstry, eds, *'Greek' Thomson*, Edinburgh: Edinburgh University Press, 1994, pp. 63–71.

quarters, that congregations can worship equally well in multi-purpose buildings. The Reformed tradition does not indeed invest buildings or other places with a special sacral quality. Yet the effect on the Christian life of a building marked by a simple elegance and associated primarily with the regular worship of the people of God is not to be underestimated. Conversely, the patterns of dissociation that often accompany closure of a cherished building should hardly surprise us. Nevertheless, assessed according to aesthetic criteria including utility, many church buildings today must be judged seriously deficient. At least, this is true in Scotland where a significant proportion of Victorian and Edwardian church buildings are evidently too large for their congregations and too dominated by a didactic vision of worship focused on pulpit oratory and theatre. The abandonment of the practice of celebrating the Lord's Supper together at a long table positioned at the centre of the sanctuary has led to a detachment of the congregation from those ministers and elders gathered apart at the communion table.[60] The demoralizing effect of rows of empty pews, uncomfortable surrounds, dingy interiors, cluttered chancel areas, drab decor and bad acoustics needs to be faced with some degree of urgency for the sake of honouring God and serving the mission of the Church. The minister who once remarked that every Presbytery should employ an arsonist was not wholly wrong.

Music

Closely related to the atmospherics of the church building is the need to foster lively and enriching singing. Music is not the exclusive province of the choir; it has a capacity beyond the spoken word to inspire the congregation. For Calvin, the power of music was recognized for its almost unrivalled capacity to move and inflame human hearts. Since it was a gift from God intended for praise and worship, it was vital that music have a weight and majesty appropriate to this function. Music was to engage not only the heart but also the understanding. 'For a linnet, a nightingale or a popinjay will sing well, but it will be without understanding. But man's proper gift is to sing, knowing what he says; after understanding must follow the heart and the affection, something that can only happen when we have the song imprinted on our memory never to cease singing it.'[61] Singing was promoted by Calvin and Bucer as a corrective to the coldness of

---

60 This is perceptively explored by James Whyte, 'The Setting of Worship', in Duncan Forrester & Douglas Murray, eds, *Studies in the History of Worship in Scotland*, Edinburgh: T&T Clark, 1984, pp. 140–55.

61 John Calvin, 'The Form of the Prayers and Songs of the Church, 1542: Letter to the Reader', trans. Ford Lewis Battles, *Calvin Theological Journal*, 15 (1980), p. 164. For discussion of Calvin's theology of music in relation to the use of metrical psalms in worship see James

worship in other Reformed contexts. The concerted effort in their work to match word and music reflects earlier Renaissance traditions,[62] yet is also born of a desire to subordinate musical forms to the Word of God. However, as Jeremy Begbie has recently shown, this was not altogether successful in practice since the Genevan Psalter employs melodies that 'show a distinct rhythmic independence from the words they carry, giving them a character quite distinct from, say, the songs of the German Reformed regions'.[63] This mismatch of theory and practice is salutary in cautioning against an austere functionalism that may be discerned in Calvin's declared position. Art is not merely to be appropriated for theological ends. As a work of God's good creation, it has its own rules, standards and ends that are not determined exclusively by their ecclesiastical utility.[64] (Ironically, this may be more apparent in Calvin's comments on those visual arts that he perceives to have no function in Christian worship.) While the use of music in worship is to be regulated by the Word of God, its capacity to do this may require greater recognition of its distinctiveness and relative autonomy. This might enable us to justify the subsequent emergence of a much wider variety of musical forms than those prescribed by Calvin. This can be done without forsaking his essential claims about the need to blend word, understanding and melody, the weight and majesty of God's praise, and the inclusion of the whole congregation in singing.

Nonetheless, some prevalent aspects of the tradition can be faulted in light of earlier ideals. The reappearance of church choirs – itself a welcome development in enhancing congregational praise – has led to the preparation of modern hymnals designed primarily for four-part harmony singing. The pitch is thus appropriate to the register of the different sections of the choir. But the treble line has become unreachable for many male voices in the congregation, as is painfully obvious every week. Ian MacKenzie has spoken in this regard of the choir as the number one obstacle for good congregational singing and recommends that in some cases the pitch of psalm and hymn tunes be reduced by half an octave.[65] Furthermore, the musical tastes of the majority are probably folk rather than classical yet these are generally ignored in many Presbyterian hymnals. The

Hastings Nicols, *Corporate Worship in the Reformed Tradition*, Philadelphia: Westminster Press, 1968, pp. 35ff.

62 Cf. Jeremy Bebgie, 'Music, Word and Theology Today: Learning from John Calvin', in Lyn Holness and Ralf K. Wüstenberg, eds, *Theology in Dialogue: The Impact of the Arts, Humanities and Science on Contemporary Religious Thought*, Grand Rapids: Eerdmans, 2002, pp. 15–16.

63 Bebgie, 'Music, Word and Theology Today', p. 17.

64 Calvin's recommendation that all singing should be only psalm singing seems misguided and unnecessary in this connection.

65 'To spell it out in two words of one syllable: SING LOW. For this, a sweet chariot is not necessary.' Ian Mackenzie, *Tunes of Glory*, Edinburgh: Handsel Press, 1993, p. 149.

more recent retrieval of folk melodies in pentatonic form and the modern paraphrasing of psalms are welcome developments, particularly in the new fourth edition of the Church of Scotland Hymnary. These resonate with earlier ideals of broad participation and the animation of human lives by the Word of God expressed in musical form.[66]

Language

The commitment to felicitous expression and intellectual precision was noted earlier as a feature of Reformed scholarship. This has been manifested also in the language of prayer and preaching. The commitment to prayers that were accessible to the congregation and to devotional practices that could be developed in domestic settings necessitated a use of language that was clear, dignified and employed scriptural allusions. The pattern of the Lord's Prayer provided an obvious model. A commitment to extempore prayer has often been a feature of the same tradition, alongside a suspicion of prayer books that has only recently begun to disappear. How successfully this engages the minds and hearts of congregations is unclear. Some research suggests that the public prayers offered by the minister are listened to only fitfully; failing to be properly absorbed, too often they pass over bowed heads. This might suggest a need to reconsider the usefulness of set prayers, responses, and broader participation in the interests of a wider ownership of public prayer. It is beyond the scope of this chapter to address the theology of preaching, but suffice it to say that the recent dearth of theological reflection on this subject itself signals an uncertainty and loss of confidence in the sermon. The proper stress on rhetorical techniques and communication theory, necessary given the need to address aesthetic qualities, cannot substitute for an informed account of what makes the sermon necessary to divine worship. A prioritizing of form over content is a sheer inversion of the Reformed tradition's aim of establishing aesthetic standards that are determined by the subject matter of God's Word.

Towards the conclusion of his discussion of images, Calvin makes this interesting remark.

When I ponder the intended use of churches, somehow or other it seems to me unworthy of their holiness for them to take on images other than those living and symbolic ones which the Lord has consecrated by his Word. I mean Baptism and the Lord's Supper together with other rites by which our eyes must be too intensely gripped and too sharply affected to seek other images forged by human ingenuity.[67]

---

66 For example, *Common Ground*, Edinburgh: St Andrew Press, 1998.
67 *Institutes*, I.11.13.

The physical senses are to be engaged not merely by the spoken word but by the tangible and visible signs of baptism and Eucharist. This sacramental seriousness is set in a discussion of how the faith is to be communicated and appropriated. Whether Reformed habits confirm this conviction is doubtful. The presence of more Zwinglian elements in both theory and practice suggests otherwise. With infrequency of celebration, confusion over the custom of infant baptism, and the layout of buildings isolating congregations from the liturgical action and contributing to excessively long communion services, the sacramental life of the Reformed tradition needs some reassessment. The simplicity and measure that elsewhere inform worship are too often lacking in a sacramental context. Given Calvin's persuasion about the accommodation of sacraments to our sensory capacities, this is sadly ironic.

Visual arts

What of the visual arts? The prohibition on depictions of Christ is advanced on grounds that are not readily defensible. By conceding that these may be appropriate in private, domestic settings, the early Reformers may have been tacitly admitting the relative weakness of their argument on this point. If the incarnate Son of God made himself visible to his contemporaries then why should this not be recalled and celebrated pictorially? It is not clear why the prohibition on this should be absolute. *Abusus non tollit usum*. However, even conceding this point, we have still to reckon with the historical and moral functions of art inspired by the Holy Spirit and to enquire whether these may have a role in church buildings, worship and education. John de Gruchy's recent study is a powerful reminder of this, noting the early link between Isaiah's vision of God's beauty and his call to proclaim justice.[68] In this connection, the arts can make a strong contribution to the Christian life through their capacity to expose human suffering and social injustice, to recall the harmony of creation, and to celebrate the bonds of friendship and community. There is nothing within Reformed theology that should prevent this and much that ought to promote it. Judiciously used, even PowerPoint may enable an important visual contribution to the preaching of the Word and praising of God's name.

---

68 John W. de Gruchy, *Christianity, Art and Transformation: Theological Aesthetics in the Struggle for Justice*, Cambridge: Cambridge University Press, 2001. De Gruchy discusses the role of art in the life of the church, pp. 213–54.

2

CELTIC SPIRITUALITY

Donald Macleod

The world has long had a love–hate relationship with the Celt. Some have seen him as a primitive savage, fickle and sensuous. Others have seen her as a saint, dreamy and mystical. The great Cambridge New Testament scholar, J. B. Lightfoot, attributed the problems among the Galatians to the fact that (as he believed) they were Celts: a fiery people naturally addicted to drunkenness and revelling ('a darling sin of the Celtic people'[69]) and much given to fierce and rancorous self-assertion. By contrast, another Cambridge sage, the late Dr John Macquarrie, described the Celt as 'a God-intoxicated man whose life was embraced on all sides by the divine Being'.[70] It was this intoxication which seemed to be reflected in Alexander Carmichael's *Carmina Gadelica*, a collection of hymns and incantations gleaned from Gaelic oral tradition in the late nineteenth century. Carmichael claimed that his work afforded incontestable proof of Renan's observation that Celts everywhere were endowed with 'profound feeling and adorable delicacy in their religious instincts'.[71]

It is these instincts, and the practices bred by them, which are now lauded by the devotees of Celtic spirituality. But there is a problem of definition. Carmichael gathered most of his collection from the southern, Roman Catholic islands of the Hebridean archipelago. There, he was enchanted. But when he went north to Lewis, things were entirely different. Here, he was among Presbyterians, and savouring a very different religion. It might produce a notable degree of courtesy and hospitality, but there was little by way of music and lyric. Here, too, were Celts; and here, too, was spirituality. But it was not, according to Carmichael, 'Celtic spiritual-

---

69 J. B. Lightfoot, *St Paul's Epistles to the Galatians*, London: Macmillan, 1876, p. 13.

70 John Macquarrie, *Paths in Spirituality*, London: SCM Press, 1972, pp. 155–6.

71 Alexander Carmichael, *Carmina Gadelica: Hymns and Incantations Orally Collected in the Highlands and Islands of Scotland*, Edinburgh: Scottish Academic Press, reprint of 2nd edition, 1928 [1900], p. xxxix.

ity'. The Baptists of Tiree and the Presbyterians of Lewis must be covered by some other trademark. Why?

Clearly because 'the Celtic Way'[72] draws more or less arbitrarily on a very limited segment of the total Celtic experience: specifically on what we think we know of the Celtic Church as established by St Patrick in Ireland and St Columba in Scotland. That Church left significant traces of itself on the archaeological, political and ecclesiastical map of Britain. It also left its impress on our cultural heritage, particularly in such priceless illuminated manuscripts as the Book of Deer, the Book of Kells and the Lindisfarne Gospels. But for our knowledge of its beliefs and practices we have to rely on two main sources. One of these is the nine-stanza hymn known today as 'St Patrick's Breastplate'.[73] The other is Adomnán's *Life of St Columba*.[74]

Neither of these is without its complications. Few scholars today would ascribe 'The Breastplate' to St Patrick: the hymn belongs to the eighth century, the saint to the fifth. Similarly, Adomnán's *Life* was written a century after the saint's death; it is deliberate, unabashed hagiography; and its template of sainthood is such as no modern (we hope) would aspire to. Adomnán's Columba is a magician of Merlinesque proportions.

The other fascinating question is the relation between Patrick and Columba on the one hand, and Carmichael on the other. Carmichael's collection is a thousand years later than 'The Breastplate', and across such a divide the link with the ancient Celtic Church must be tenuous indeed. Carmichael's Gaelic is instantly accessible to the twenty-first-century Gaidheal;[75] the original text of 'The Breastplate' only to specialists in Old Irish.

But perhaps the most striking feature of the *Carmina* is that if you came to them cold, with no prior awareness of 'the Celtic Way', they would strike you simply as straightforward Catholicism. One clear symptom of this is the constant allusion to the Virgin Mary. The invocation, 'Failte dhuit, a Mhuire Mhathair' is typical:

Hail to thee, Mary, Mother!
Thou art full of loving grace,
The Lord God is always with thee,
Blessed art thou Mary among women,

---

72 See Ian Bradley, *The Celtic Way*, London: Darton, Longman and Todd, 1993.

73 See N. D. O'Donaghue, 'St Patrick's Breastplate', in James P. Mackey, ed., *An Introduction to Celtic Spirituality*, Edinburgh: T&T Clark, 1989, pp. 45–63. This article contains an excellent translation (pp. 46–9).

74 Adomnán of Iona, *Life of St Columba*, ed. Richard Sharpe, London: Penguin Books, 1995.

75 Gaelic speaker.

Blessed is the fruit of thy womb, Jesus,
Blessed art thou, Queen of grace[76]

In Adomnán, by contrast, there is not a trace of the invocation of Mary, even though three centuries had passed since the Council of Chalcedon had pronounced her, *Theotokos* (popularly, 'Mother of God'). This is not to say that the Columban Church had no affinities with the Roman: it clearly had. But even in Catholicism the formal cult of Mary did not develop till much later. It is this later cult that is reflected in Carmichael's *Carmina*.

On the other hand, the Celtic Church was by no means unaffected by the trends which eventually led to Marian devotion. The Book of Kells (probably early eighth century) contains a full page picture (Folio 7V) of the Virgin and her child, and in that picture Mary already wears a halo. By the time we come to *Carmina Gadelica* that halo has grown to its full proportions, and the chants and invocations bespeak a typical Roman Catholic spirituality with the *Ave Maria* at its heart. This, the Book of Kells being witness, was no erratic development, and it warns us not to accept too readily the idea of a Celtic spirituality radically different from European Christianity as a whole.

But though Carmichael is clearly irrelevant as a witness to Columban Christianity, he is essential reading when it comes to defining the modern Celtic Way. Along with Adomnán and the 'Breastplate' he forms its three-fold canon; and to the extent that the Way is faithful to that canon it will bear four clear characteristics: it will be orthodox; it will be profoundly aware of the need for spiritual protection; it will be hagiographical; and it will be monastic.

Celtic Orthodoxy

The orthodoxy shines through unmistakeably in both the 'Breastplate' and the *Carmina*. Both are strikingly Trinitarian. The 'Breastplate' was widely known by its Latin title, 'Lorica Sancti Patritii' ('The Shield of Saint Patrick'), and as Noel O'Donaghue points out it is a protection prayer,[77] the shield being 'the power of the Three' (*neart an triuir*, in modern Gaelic).

For my shield this day I call:
    A mighty power:
    The Holy Trinity!

---

76 Carmichael, *Carmina*, p. 111.
77 O'Donaghue, 'Breastplate', p. 49.

Affirming threeness,
Confessing oneness,
In the making of all
Through love.

This strikes one as almost catechetical, as if the hymn had been composed as an aid to learning, and this is equally true of the *Carmina*. Indeed, if these incantations were commonly sung they must have made a huge contribution to keeping orthodoxy alive. The tone is set by the very first hymn:

I am bending my knee
In the eye of the Father who created me,
In the eye of the Son who purchased me,
In the eye of the Spirit who cleansed me,
In friendship and affection.[78]

There is clearly more here than the charming song of the milkmaid. Some of the prayers have the formal structure of Collects, and almost all are theologically explicit. The ancient Celtic Way was certainly not one of doctrinal indifferentism. There may be no explicit mention of either Nicaea or Chalcedon, but the doctrines laid down by these councils provide the framework not only for the formal life of the church, but also for the daily life of the people. This is why among the dark powers from which the soul needs protection the 'Breastplate' includes, 'heretical lying and false gods all around me'. Heresy was to be dreaded, not courted.

But was Celtic spirituality Pelagian? The claim has become popular. Both Ian Bradley and M. Forthomme Nicholson speak with pride of Pelagius as a Celtic theologian, and Bradley even declares: 'In so far as there was a distinctive Celtic theology, it (too) stressed the essential good-ness of nature, including human nature, and saw Jesus Christ as the one who was sent not so much to rescue the world from the consequences of the fall as to complete and perfect it.'[79]

It is difficult to document such claims. What is clear, however, is that the presuppositions of *Carmina Gadelica* are those of Augustinian religion, including a clear sense of the guilt of sin, the reality of divine anger and the fact of atonement:

Thou it was who bought'st me with Thy blood
Thou it was who gavest Thy life for me[80]

---

78 Carmichael, *Carmina*, p. 3.

79 Bradley, *The Celtic Way*, p. 52. Cf. the more extended treatment in M. Forthomme Nichol-son, 'Celtic Theology: Pelagius', in Mackey, *Introduction to Celtic Christianity*, pp. 386–413.

80 Carmichael, *Carmina*, p. 85.

And would not the following satisfy the most pessimistic Augustinian?

> We are guilty and polluted, O God,
> In spirit, in heart, and in flesh,
> In thought, in word, in act
> We are hard in thy sight in sin.[81]

The Need for Protection

A second clear feature of Celtic spirituality was the deeply felt need for protection. Some of the perils are familiar enough: temptation, personal failings, enemies and natural calamities such as burning and drowning. Similar concerns are covered in the Litany of the Book of Common Prayer: 'From lightning and tempest; from plague, pestilence and famine; from battle and murder, and from sudden death, Good Lord, deliver us.' But the 'Breastplate' also reflects a world filled with dark spiritual forces: hence the need to be saved not only from snares of the demons, pagan devisings and false gods, but also from spells cast by women, blacksmiths and druids, and from occult knowledge that injures both body and spirit.

This thought-world pervaded ancient Celtic spirituality and survived down to the age of the *Carmina*. On occasion, indeed, the invocations in Carmichael's collection are unadulterated paganism:

> From every brownie and banshee
> From every evil wish and sorrow,
> From every nymph and water-wraith
> From fairy-mouse and grass-mouse
> (Oh! save me to the end of my day).[82]

Yet it would be a mistake to limit this belief in immanent evil spirits to the world view of the Columban Church. It is not unknown to the Book of Common Prayer, which asks for deliverance from 'all evil and mischief' and from 'the crafts and assaults of the devil'; and it appears with stark clarity in Hugh Miller's *Scenes and Legends*, set in the non-Celtic north-east of Scotland in the eighteenth century, but reflecting a culture equally convinced of the existence of evil spirits. Local folklore abounded with legends to this effect, one of the most graphic being the story retold by Miller of a young Cromarty fisherman returning home after nightfall. The stillness was suddenly broken by the baying of a pack of hounds, but when he went to pacify them, all he saw was the figure of a man, whom he assumed to be the keeper of the beasts. As he walked on, the man followed him, but when

---

81 Carmichael, *Carmina*, p. 23.
82 Carmichael, *Carmina*, p. 31.

he paused, waiting for the man to catch up, the figure grew taller and taller and then, suddenly falling on all fours, assumed the form of a horse.[83] It was for protection against similar evils that the Celts sought a shield.

But if these dark forms were immanent and ever-present, no less so were the forms of protection. In the *Carmina* these include personal guardian angels, the principal archangels (Michael, Gabriel, Raphael and Uriel), the apostles (especially Peter and Paul), saints and the Virgin. In the Breastplate, the approach is much more disciplined. The shield includes, certainly, seraphim, angels, the glorious company of 'the holy and risen ones' and the prayers of the fathers, but the true shield, as represented in the most famous stanza of the 'Breastplate' (VII), is the omni-dimensional presence of Christ:

Christ beside me, Christ before me;
Christ behind me, Christ within me;
Christ beneath me, Christ above me;
Christ to right of me, Christ to left of me;
Christ in my lying, my sitting, my rising

Echoes of this aspect of the Breastplate are clearly heard in the *Carmina*, particularly in the poem, 'Dia Liom (*sic*) a Laighe' ('God With Me Lying Down'), which Carmichael took down not this time in the southern isles, but in Harris (in 1866).

God with me lying down,
God with me rising up,
God with me in each ray of light ...

Christ with me sleeping
Christ with me waking,
Christ with me watching
Every day and night.[84]

Yet the source of these ideas lies not in a distinctive Celtic religiosity but in the Hebrew Scriptures, where every conceivable preposition is used to express the closeness of the divine presence. The Lord is *with* us (Ps. 23.4), *underneath* us (Deut. 33.27), *behind* us and *before* us (Ps. 139.5). In St Paul, of course, Christ lives *in* us (Gal. 2.20). What the Breastplate has done (and it is no small achievement) is to bring all the prepositions together in a single stanza. Yet, even so, it has a curious indirectness. 'For

---

83 Hugh Miller, *Scenes and Legends of the North of Scotland*, Edinburgh: Constable, 1857, pp. 166–7.

84 Carmichael, *Carmina*, p. 5.

my shield this day I call' (almost like a court officer calling a witness) clearly lacks the intimacy of 'Our Father, which art in heaven'.

Celtic Hagiography

Another striking feature of early Celtic spirituality is its unabashed hagiography. This appears most clearly in Adomnán, where the whole concern is to glorify the blessed man, 'our patron'. Every detail contributes to creating a picture of someone who scarcely belongs to this world. Columba's name is the same as the prophet Jonah's and points to his dove-like nature. He was of noble lineage, devoted since boyhood to training in the Christian life, and chaste in soul and body. Indeed, 'He was an angel in demeanour, blameless in what he said, godly in what he did, brilliant in intellect and great in counsel.'[85] He prayed and wrote incessantly, performed fasts and vigils almost beyond human endurance, and at the same time was loving to all people.

But it is not on this amazing combination of personal qualities that Adomnán chooses to focus. What fascinates him is the miracles performed by the great man, and he states clearly the order in which he intends to treat them: first, his prophetic revelations; second, his miracles of power; and, third, angelic apparitions.

Some of these miracle stories are strikingly similar to those recounted in the Gospels. In one, Columba turns water into wine. In another, reminiscent of the raising of Jairus's daughter, he brings a young man back to life. Every page is crammed with wonders, but Adomnán still wants to remind us that his account merely skims the surface, and his reminder is couched in language which is a deliberate echo of the conclusion of John's Gospel: 'many things worth recording about the man of blessed memory are left out here for the sake of brevity'[86] (cf. John 21.25).

This hagiographical strain persisted in Celtic spirituality, which long cherished the memory of such saints as Moluag, Maolrubha, Ronan and Bridgit. *Carmina Gadelica* reflects this veneration, many of the invocations being addressed to the saints, or at least including them. But it is interesting to compare this with the hagiography which also appears in later Celtic Protestantism. In some respects, the latter is markedly different. For example, to a significant extent it is a hagiography of the laity. This appears clearly in such a work as Alexander Auld's *Ministers and Men in the Far North*.[87] The period covered is the nineteenth century; the

---

85 Adomnán, *Life*, Second Preface.

86 Adomnán, *Life*, Preface.

87 Alexander Auld, *Ministers and Men in the Far North*, Glasgow: Free Presbyterian Publications, 2000 [1869].

area, mainly Caithness and Sutherland, then largely Gaelic-speaking. Most of the subjects are 'Men': members of the laity who were not ministers, but yet had a recognized spiritual role. They were men of the soil, usually Presbyterian elders, of little education but high intelligence, often gifted with considerable powers of oratory and epigram, revered in life and often legendary in death. Such a culture would have been utterly alien to Adomnán. Once he was so perplexed by being stranded on an island without the benefit of clergy that he invoked Columba to change a contrary wind into a favourable one, arguing, irritably, 'Is it your wish, O saint, that I should stay here among the lay people till tomorrow, and not spend the day of your feast in your own church?'[88] Trivial though Adomnán's plaint may sound, it highlights the fact that in the Columban Church the laity had nothing like the place they enjoyed in later Celtic Protestantism. There were no laymen on Iona.

Another feature of the later Protestant hagiography is the prominence of women. The early Celtic Church had, of course, its Saint Bridgit, but she remains a nebulous figure. Her nineteenth-century Protestant counterparts, by contrast, are colourful personalities: women like Muckle Kate of Lochcarron, a large woman (hence the name) converted from a life of loud profligacy to contrite discipleship; Peggy MacDiarmid, legendary as *Bean a' Chreidimh Mhoir* (the Woman of Great Faith); Catherine Mackay, an irrepressible, carefree jewel of early Lewis evangelicalism; and Catherine's friend, Fionnghal Bheag (Little Fiona), herself a seer. It is remarkable that in a culture so patriarchal women could achieve such status.

Yet there are also striking similarities between the two hagiographies. This is particularly true with regard to what Adomnán called 'prophetic revelations'. Take, for example, his story of Columba's vision of the peril of 'the holy bishop Colman', en route from Ireland to Iona. Miles away in his mother church, Columba suddenly exclaimed: 'Colman mac Beognai has set sail to come here, and is now in great danger in the surging tides of the whirlpool of Corryvreckan!'[89]

In the event, Colman came to no harm: God was merely arousing him to more fervent prayer. But Hugh Miller tells a similar story of Donald Roy of Nigg, a young shinty-player turned into a Protestant lay-religious and described by Miller as belonging to an extraordinary class of men who lived on the extreme edge of the natural world, saw far into the world of spirits and saw, too, into the extreme bounds of both the distant and the future. One day as Donald worked with others stacking corn, he suddenly began alternately raising his hands and clasping them together as if witnessing some terrible scene. Then his companions heard him exclaiming,

---

88 Adomnán, *Life*, II.45.
89 Adomnán, *Life*, I.15.

'Let her drive, let her drive! Dinna haud her side to the sea!' Then he struck his hands together and shouted out, 'She's o'er! She's o'er! Oh, the poor widows o' Dunskaith!'[90] The following morning the wreck of a Dunskaith boat, and the bodies of her crew, were found on a beach.

The same sensitivity to events unseen was attributed to Fionnghal Bheag. One night she had a very strong impression that something was seriously wrong on the island of Rona. The island was normally uninhabited, but two men had recently gone there and as Fionnghal prayed she became convinced that one of them, an acquaintance of her own, was in desperate trouble. At the same time she was gripped by words from Psalm 73, peculiarly appropriate to men clinging precariously to a rock 40 miles out in the Atlantic: 'my steps near slipped, my feet were almost gone'. Sure there had been a tragedy, she sent word to the local doctor, Dr Ross (whose daughter, Annabella, would become the mother of Tory politician, Iain Macleod), informing him that there had been a death on Rona and that he should send someone to investigate. Such was the respect for Fionnghal that Dr Ross instantly complied. There had been tragedy surely enough. They found the two men dead, one outside the bothy and one inside.[91] But the cause of death was never established, either by forensic investigation or by divine revelation.

What is the truth here? Is it that the Celtic temperament instinctively creates such legends? Or that the Celtic soul, being God-intoxicated and connected to the unseen world, is peculiarly susceptible to such experiences? The truth is, there is nothing distinctively Celtic about it at all; and even at its worst it never descends to the levels of silliness which we find in, for example, Athanasius's *Life of Antony*.

Monasticism

Third, the spirituality of the Celtic Church was monastic, and this may have had a far greater influence in defining its character than had its Celtic ethnicity. All the signs are that the original Iona community consisted entirely of monks. Hospitality might be given to passing strangers, and refuge to asylum seekers, but there were no permanent lay residents.[92] It is almost certain, too, that women were banned from the island. The wider Celtic Church may have had married clergy, but the monks were celibate, and if we can take at face value one of the sayings attributed to Columba he was an unreconstructed male chauvinist. According to Bulloch, he

---

90 Miller, *Scenes*, pp. 146–7.

91 Iain Macleod, *Am Measg nan Lili*, Inverness: Highland News, 1948, p. xviii.

92 Dauvit Broun and Thomas Owen Clancy, eds, *Spes Scotorum: Hope of Scots*, Edinburgh: T&T Clark, 1999, p. 122. Cf. Adomnán, *Vita*, 1.32.

allowed no cows on Iona (milk must have come from Mull) and gave as his reason, 'Where there is a cow there is a woman; and where there is a woman there is trouble.'[93] If Adomnán knew that story he had more sense than to repeat it.

Columban monasticism was rigorously ascetic. The saint himself slept on bare rock, with only a stone for a pillow. The food was meagre and plain, and wine was forbidden. Such arrangements reflected the will of Columba himself, who as abbot ruled both Iona and its daughter houses as a total autocrat.

What is not instantly clear is the extent to which Iona was isolated, functioning merely as a retreat for those who wished to practise a pure spirituality without the pressures of the world and the distractions of luxury. There were, as Bulloch reminds us, two kinds of monasticism. One, the Benedictine, followed the example set by Egypt's desert fathers and enjoined withdrawal from the world. The other followed the example of Martin of Tours (c.335–c.400) and viewed the monastic foundation as a base for evangelism. Bulloch believes that this was the model followed by Columba and that Iona was founded to evangelize Dalriata and Pictland. This would seem to be supported by Bede's account (III.4) of the reasons for Columba's mission: 'A priest and abbot named Columba, distinguished by his monastic habit and life, came from Ireland to Britain to preach the word of God in the provinces of the northern Picts.' Further support for the idea of Iona as an outgoing missionary centre can be found in the distribution of Celtic churches, from Lindisfarne in Northumbria to the Butt of Lewis, and from Tiree in the west to Deer in Morayshire. To this we must add the dissemination of the Columba legend itself. If Iona was isolated and its abbot himself seldom seen far from base it is hard to understand why nineteenth-century Hebrideans were still celebrating *Latha Chaluim-Chille* (St Columba's Day) and praying that,

> The tongue of Columba (be) in my head,
> The eloquence of Columba in my speech[94]

But if the Columban Church was a dynamic missionary body, this has clear implications for our whole notion of Celtic spirituality. For example, it is hard to reconcile with the perception that this was an easy-going, theologically eclectic community, tolerant of the faith of others. No one who had come from Ireland to convert the Picts was going to join in an interfaith service with the druids. Instead, Columba is at war with the wizards, beating them in wind-changing competitions, undoing their curses

---

93 James Bulloch, *The Life of the Celtic Church*, Edinburgh: St Andrew Press, 1963, p. 178.

94 Carmichael, *Carmina*, p. 57.

and drowning out their protests in a voice 'like some terrible thunder'.[95] It seems unlikely that such a man would have been much given to the blending of paganism and Christianity. Even less would he have regarded the different faiths as merely the iridescent colours of the one rainbow, as suggested by Carmichael.[96]

Yet, occasionally, the sentiments expressed in Celtic spirituality do seem to verge on the pagan. The fourth stanza of St Patrick's 'Breastplate', for example, seems almost animistic in its invocation of nature:[97]

For my shield this day I call:
  Heaven's might
  Sun's brightness
  Moon's whiteness
  Fire's glory
  Lightning's swiftness
  Wind's wildness
  Ocean's depth
  Earth's solidity
  Rock's immobility.

But these sentiments can well bear a Christian interpretation, particularly in the light of Jesus' declaration that not a sparrow falls to the ground apart from the will of our heavenly Father (Matt. 10.29). In line with this, the very non-Celtic *Heidelberg Catechism* lays down that God, 'still upholds heaven and earth, and so governs them that herbs and grass, rain and drought, fruitful and barren years, meat and drink, health and sickness, riches and poverty, yea, all things, come not by chance, but by his fatherly hand' (Answer 27). It is no hard matter to believe that the movements of sun, moon and stars, the operations of gravity and electromagnetism, and even the indeterminable behaviour of subatomic particles are also regulated by the same paternal benevolence.

Other instances of alleged assimilation to pagan religion seem to be no more than survivals of ancient superstitions. If a staunch Presbyterian elder is horrified when I take out a salmon lure aboard his seagoing fishing-boat, he is not thereby blending Christianity and paganism. Neither were the people of north Lewis when they made an annual offering to Seonaidh, the god of the sea, a practice which persisted into the nineteenth century. As Carmichael acknowledges, this shows 'the tenacity of popular belief' as much as it does 'the tolerance of the Columban church'.[98] A similar

---

95 Adomnán, *Life*, I.37.
96 Carmichael, *Carmina*, p. xxxix.
97 See further, O'Donaghue in Mackey, *Introduction to Celtic Spirituality*, pp. 54–6.
98 Carmichael, *Carmina*, p. 163.

tenacity of belief appears in the fact that among Gaelic-speaking Presbyterians to the present day it is still common to say, *Cha robh e'n dàn*. This is instantly understood to mean, 'It wasn't meant to happen. It wasn't ordained.' But the literal translation would be, 'It wasn't in the (druids') chant (*dàn*).' Etymology, clearly, is no clue to one's theology.

This is not the place to discuss the relation between Christianity and other religions. There are, of course, values which are common to all the great world faiths, and doctrines which are common to all 'religions of the Book'. But in the realm of fact, Christianity makes a claim which, if correct, authenticates it as the unique revelation of God; and if false completely invalidates it. That fact is that in Jesus Christ, and in him alone, God became incarnate. There is not the least evidence that Patrick, Columba or the wider Celtic Church would ever have compromised on this claim. It was what gave impetus to their whole missionary endeavour.

Yet it is by no means certain that Iona was in the vanguard of this missionary advance. The most significant missionaries were Moluag and Maolrubha, along with their lesser associates, Catan and Blaan, and their roots were not in Iona, but in the great monastic centre at Bangor in Ulster, described by W. Douglas Simpson as, 'a hive that sent forth swarms of missionaries whose influence was felt all over western Europe'.[99] It is highly likely, contra Bulloch, that Iona worked to a very different ethos, the monks living in isolation from the world and devoting their time to the offices of the cloisters.

The evidence for this is well marshalled by Gilbert Márkus in a fascinating analysis of 'the regions of the mind' reflected in Adomnán's *Life*.[100] One of these regions is Iona itself, and within this region the monastery provided total care and pastoral support. The second region is the surrounding kingdom of Dalriata, but there is no evidence that the monastery either provided pastoral care or engaged in evangelistic activity in this area. The inhabitants, the Scots, were almost certainly Christians before they left Ireland in the first place; and, though this is nowhere highlighted, they probably had their own priests and bishops to provide all the spiritual ministries they needed.

There remains the third region, the Pictish kingdom of King Bridei and his successors, separated from Dalriata by the great mountain chain of Drumalbane (literally, 'the backbone of Scotland'), running from Ben Lomond near Glasgow to Ben Hope near Cape Wrath. Iona seems a strange choice as the base for a mission across the mountains. The capital of the Pictish kingdom was Inverness, and probably the only Columba story any modern Scot knows is the one about the gates of the defiant

---

99 W. Douglas Simpson, *The Celtic Church in Scotland*, Aberdeen: University Press, 1935, p. 78.

100 Gilbert Márkus, 'Iona: monks, pastors and missionaries', in Mackey, *Introduction to Celtic Christianity*, pp. 115–38.

king opening miraculously to admit the saint.[101] Adomnán refers to this as Columba's 'first' visit, but there is no record of any others. Nor is there a trace of anything resembling evangelistic missions to Pictland; nor of Columba founding a church; nor, apart from one or two instances, of Columba baptizing; nor of evidence that King Bridei was ever converted. The saint, ever diplomat and politician, seems to have been more concerned to live at peace with the king than to convert him, and this was the only recorded outcome of his visit to Inverness: 'From that day forward for as long as he lived, the ruler treated the holy and venerable man with great honour as was fitting.' Bridei, like the rest of Adomnán's characters, exists only to put a stone on Columba's cairn.

It is highly likely, then, that Columban monasticism, if not quite Benedictine, had little sense of obligation to the outside world. Adomnán's frequent references to the manual labour of the monks must be seen in this context. The synthesis between the manual and the spiritual is, of course, wholly admirable, but whether it was ever a deliberate component of Columban spirituality is highly debatable. The monks of Iona certainly worked. They cultivated the fields, they erected buildings, they laboured in the granary, they built boats, and they sailed the seas. But none of this took them into the secular world as it did, for example, France's worker-priests. They toiled only within the monastery, alongside their fellow monks, and purely and solely for the benefit of the monastery itself. Their labour was indeed incessant, but it was no more noble in their case than in that of the rest of toiling humanity. They sweated in order to eat bread (Gen. 3.17).

Religion and Art

What of that other much lauded synthesis in the spirituality of the Celtic Church: the synthesis between religion and art, the main examples being the Celtic crosses and the illuminated manuscripts such as the Book of Kells. Neither genre originated in Celtic Britain, and the craftsmen and artists involved had to work within European-wide conventions, but in both instances they showed astonishing flair and inventiveness. This is particularly true of the manuscripts, which are breathtaking in their detail and in the range and shadings of their colours. They reflect both a boundless reverence for Scripture and a passion for the unity of truth and beauty. It is easy to imagine God peering over the artist's shoulder and pronouncing the same verdict as he pronounced on his own finished creation: 'It is very good!'

---

101 Adomnán, *Life*, II.35.

48

Yet it was the art *of* the monastery, and art *for* the monastery. It was for the monks' library, not for the parish. Glorious though it was as an affirmation of the value of the Gospels, it was neither intended nor fitted to make them more accessible. It said, in an instant, 'The gospel is great!' But it did not say what the gospel was. When Protestantism would later enlist Celtic art in the service of Christianity it would be the art of the word, not of the picture.

Conclusion

We are left, then, with questions:

The first is suggested by that last observation. Why does conventional wisdom forbid us to include Celtic Protestantism in any assessment of Celtic spirituality? The Calvinism of Gaelic Presbyterianism bears the mark of the Celt as surely as did the monasticism of St Columba. It even bred its own monasticism.

Second, is there any real link between ethnicity and spirituality? Alexandria produced Arius as well as Athanasius; North Africa, Tertullian as well as Augustine; Wales, John Owen as well as Pelagius; and Scotland, David Hume as well as John Knox. Besides, we owe our dour Scottish Calvinism to a Frenchman.

Finally, what really appeals to us in Celtic spirituality? Are we seriously concerned for orthodoxy, scared of banshees, beholden to saints and desperate to sleep on bare stone floors? Do we covet the gift of second-sight, long to be able to perform signs and wonders, and dream of changing the direction of the wind?

Maybe! But,

> For my shield this day I call:
> A mighty power:
> The Holy Trinity!

Further Reading

Donald E. Meek, *The Quest for Celtic Spirituality*, Edinburgh: The Handsel Press, 2000.

This is the outstanding treatment of the subject, but I have refrained from consciously drawing on it in this chapter in the hope (probably vain) of maintaining a semblance of independence.

Domhnall Uilleam Stiubhart, ed., *The Life and Legacy of Alexander Carmichael*, Port-of-Ness, Isle of Lewis: The Islands Book Trust, 2008.

3

'LET US WORSHIP GOD!'

Worship in Scottish Literature from Robert Burns to James Robertson

Alison Jack

Between Robert Burns's 'The Cotter's Saturday Night'[102] and James Robertson's *The Testament of Gideon Mack*[103] there are over two hundred years and a world of change in the practice of and attitude towards worship in Scotland. Burns's father-figure calls his family to worship with a resounding and confident 'Let us worship God!' In contrast, Robertson's doubt-ridden minister Gideon finds some sort of solace in the 'dessicated chaos [and] formal religion gone to pot' of the service he leads in the Monimasket Care Home. This chapter will explore the movement from the one attitude to the other as it is reflected in some of the literature written by Scots from the late 1700s to the present day. Given the constraints of space, discussion of individual texts will be brief, and the choice of texts will be limited, covering Presbyterian worship in mainly English-speaking Scottish fictional communities. However, through the strikingly nostalgia-soaked representations of such worship, a shift away from the centrality of worship in both family and formal congregational settings will be noted, and the struggle to find a new way to express one's spirituality will be demonstrated.

Family Worship in Burns, Galt and Carlyle

Famously, Robert Burns's brother Gilbert claimed that the scene depicting family worship in 'The Cotter's Saturday Night' was based on their own experience as children and that

---

102 Robert Burns, 1785–6, 'The Cotter's Saturday Night', in J. A. Mackay, ed., *Robert Burns: The Complete Poetical Works*, Darvel, Ayrshire: Alloway Publishing Ltd, 1993, p. 149.
103 James Robertson, *The Testament of Gideon Mack*, London: Penguin, 2006, p. 71.

Robert had frequently remarked to me, that he thought that there was something peculiarly venerable in the phrase, 'Let us worship God', used by a decent sober head of a family introducing family worship. To this sentiment ... the world is indebted for 'The Cotter's Saturday Night'.[104]

In the poem the father is likened to a 'priest', mediating God to his people in his reading of Scripture and leading in prayer, all expressed in perfect English rather than the Scots of earlier in the poem. Criticized now for its heavy sentimentality and sanitized nostalgia, the poem was nonetheless a huge success in its day, praised for the way it expressed the simple virtues of the lives of Scots peasants, from the pen of one who came from such a background but was able to present the picture with a degree of distance. Notable for our purposes is the comparison the poem goes on to make between the homely scene and formal congregational worship. Such acts of worship, Burns suggests, are marked by their artifice, pomposity and concern for show:

> Compar'd with this, how poor Religion's pride,
> In all the pomp of method, and of art;
> When men display to congregations wide
> Devotion's ev'ry grace, except the heart!
> The Power, incens'd, the pageant will desert,
> The pompous strain, the sacerdotal stole:
> But haply, in some cottage far apart,
> May hear, well-pleas'd, the language of the soul,
> And in His Book of Life the inmates poor enroll.[105]

Simple family worship, Burns argues, is characterized by its heartfeltness: ministers lack this integrity, and in their concern for artfulness run the risk of alienating God himself, who is portrayed as preferring the worship of the emotionally engaged poor.

Several similarly nostalgic and sympathetic pictures of worship in the home are offered in the literature of the nineteenth century. John Galt's narrator, the Reverend Micah Balwhidder, writing from the vantage point of 1810, notes in his entry for 1764 that a public house had been set up in the parish, which does not meet with his approval, although its proprietor was

a respectable man, and no house could be better ordered than his change. At a stated hour he made family worship, for he brought up his

---

104 Quoted in J. Walter McGinty, *Robert Burns and Religion*, Aldershot: Ashgate, 2003, p. 214.

105 Burns, 'The Cotter's Saturday Night', p. 150.

children in the fear of God and the Christian religion; and although the house was full, he would go into the customers, and ask them if they would want any thing for half an hour, for that he was going to make exercise with his family; and many a wayfaring traveller has joined in the prayer. There is no such thing, I fear, no-a-days, of publicans entertaining travellers in this manner.[106]

Family worship is once again highlighted as a refreshingly positive and wholesome activity, central to the lives of working folk. Writing later in the century, although also referring to an incident in the past, Thomas Carlyle paints a moving scene of domestic worship:

It was ten p.m. ... when I arrived at my Father's door; heard him making worship, and stood meditative, gratefully, lovingly, till he had ended; thinking to myself, how good and innocently beautiful and manful on the earth, is all this: and it was the last time I was ever to hear it. I must have been there twice or oftener in my Father's time; but the sound of his pious *Coleshill* (that was always his tune), pious Psalm and Prayer, I never heard again. With a noble politeness, very noble when I consider, they kept all that in a fine kind of remoteness from us, knowing (and somehow *forgiving* us completely) that we did not think of it quite as they.[107]

All of these examples present those who lead family worship as men of huge integrity and inspiration, but all point, somewhat sadly, to their place as being firmly in the past. Carlyle himself regrets their passing, but is unable to follow their example. There is a sense that the world has moved on.

Worship in Hogg's *Confessions of a Justified Sinner*

Equally looking to the past, but with a very different perspective on the wholesomeness of family worship, James Hogg offers a contrasting view in his novel of 1824. While there is clear evidence to suggest that Hogg had participated in daily family worship as a child, and continued this custom in his own family, recommending the practice to others and regretting its demise,[108] in his *The Private Memoirs and Confessions of a Justified*

---

106 John Galt, *Annals of the Parish*, World's Classics, Oxford: Oxford University Press, 1986 [1821], p. 30.
107 Thomas Carlyle, *Reminiscences*, World's Classics, Oxford: Oxford University Press, 2000 [1881], p. 82.
108 See P. D. Garside's Introduction to James Hogg, *The Private Memoirs and Confessions*

Sinner, there are few positive and uncritical examples of the practice. In the Editor's Narrative, an episode is described which aligns the editor with a position of sense and religious moderation, and the woman who will become Robert Wringhim's mother with religious extremism. The new Lady Dalcastle insists on praying with her husband on their wedding night, to which he retorts:

> It strikes me, my dear, that religious devotion would be somewhat out of place tonight ... Allowing that it is ever so beautiful, and ever so beneficial, were we to ride on the rigging of it at all times, would we not be constantly making a farce of it: It would be like reading the Bible and the jest-book, verse about, and would render the life of man a medley of absurdity and confusion.[109]

In the comic scene which follows, she prays with increasing fervour, while he falls asleep, snoring loudly. An echo of this critical attitude towards inappropriate and extreme religiosity is to be found embedded in Robert's Confessions, in his servant Penpunt's Auchtermuchty Tale. In this, 'the people o' the town o' Auchtermuchty grew so rigidly righteous ... There was nought to be heard, neither night nor day, but preaching, praying, argumentation, an' catechizing in a' the famous town';[110] the Bible is quoted in unexpected situations, and the 'deils' are greatly alarmed. Only Robin Ruthven, naturally 'cunning', and used to the company of fairies, who overhears the devils scheming, is able to see through the preaching of the devil in disguise as a minister. The message the devil chooses to bring is that his hearers are in the bonds of iniquity, and as the narrator comments, 'Nothing in the world delights a truly religious people so much, as consigning them to eternal damnation.'[111] Once the preacher's cloven feet have been revealed, 'frae that day to this is it a hard matter to gar an Auchtermuchty man listen to a sermon at a', an' harder ane still to gar him applaud one, for he thinks that he sees the cloven foot peeping out frae aneath ilka sentence'.[112] This example takes us away from our focus on family worship, but highlights that in both sections of Hogg's *Confessions* the dangers of taking religious discourse beyond that which is reasonable are explored. Here warm nostalgia for the past is less important than a moderate, post-Enlightenment critique of worship deemed inappropriately fervent and unreflective.

---

of a Justified Sinner, Stirling/South Carolina, Edinburgh: Edinburgh University Press, 2002 [1824], p. xvi.

109 Hogg, *Confessions*, p. 5.
110 Hogg, *Confessions*, pp. 136–7.
111 Hogg, *Confessions*, p. 139.
112 Hogg, *Confessions*, p. 140.

In passing, we should note that the Auchtermuchty Tale unites the texts from the beginning and the end of the time frame I have imposed on my discussion. As Peter Garside suggests in his Notes to Hogg's *Confessions*,[113] the Tale closely echoes the language and sentiments of Burns's 'Address to the Unco Guid, or the Rigidly Righteous' from 1784. The epitaph to the poem includes the lines 'The Rigid righteous is a fool,/ The Rigid Wise anither', and the text for the epitaph is Ecclesiastes 7.6, 'Be not righteous over much; neither make thyself over wise; why shouldest thou destroy thyself?' The devil's visit to the self-destructive, rigidly righteous folk of Auchtermuchty is also referred to in James Robertson's *The Testament of Gideon Mack*, a book which abounds with intertextual links with Hogg's novel. Gideon reports that during his time in the depths of the river, the devil-figure tells him:

> I preached at Auchtermuchty another time, disguised as one of your lot, a minister, but the folk there found me out. Fifers, thrawn buggers, they were too sharp. But I do like Scotland ... And I like the way you deal with religion. One century you're up to your lugs in it, the next you're trading the whole apparatus in for Sunday superstores.[114]

With typical clear-sightedness, the devil-figure charts the sweep of the place of religion, as expressed in worship not just in Scotland but also in Scottish fiction over the past two hundred and more years. The lack of reference to family worship in a surprising range of texts from the latter part of the nineteenth century and the beginning of the twentieth highlights this move.

Family Worship in late Nineteenth-Century Literature: Mrs Oliphant and Robert Louis Stevenson

Margaret Oliphant's novel *Kirsteen,* published in 1888, but presenting a picture of Scotland 70 years before, and Robert Louis Stevenson's *The Master of Ballantrae*, published in 1889 but set firmly in the eighteenth century, make no mention of families coming together either daily or even weekly to worship together. The act of going to church is mentioned in *Kirsteen*, both while Kirsteen is briefly in Glasgow with her sister and while she is working in London, but nowhere described. Both novels, however, offer emotionally charged scenes where characters are driven to pray. On her deathbed, Kirsteen's mother begs Kirsteen's father to pray God's blessing on all of their children: he says nothing, silenced by his

---

113 In Hogg, *Confessions*, p. 242, note 136(d).
114 Robertson, *Gideon Mack*, p. 283.

rejection of Kirsteen and her older sister Anne; instead she prays for them, but declares he said the prayer for, as she says, 'the man's the priest and king in his own house ... I just said the Amen'.[115] The father fails to live up to the traditional role, although the mother protects his position in the family. The prayer reveals the destructive cruelty at the centre of this family, in which worship has no meaningful place.

A similarly distorted picture of prayer is offered in *The Master of Ballantrae*, again with no counterbalancing description of family or congregational worship. On one occasion, while walking through the shrubbery area in which the duel between himself and his brother James had taken place, Henry tells his son, in the presence of Mackellar, his servant and the narrator of the story, that he had seen the devil here, and tried to kill him. Horrified, Mackellar, ever concerned to protect the boy from the excesses of his family, recommends they 'remember a bit prayer here', and Henry begins

'O Lord ... I thank Thee, and my son thanks Thee, for Thy manifold great mercies. Let us have peace for a little; defend us from the evil man. Smite him, O Lord, upon the lying mouth!' ...

'think you have forgot a word, my lord,' said I [Mackellar]. 'Forgive us our trespasses, as we forgive them that trespass against us.'[116]

Mackellar's intervention is meaningless, however, when both he and Henry later admit they are unable to forgive James for the way they perceive he has treated them. Further on in the novel, another example of Mackellar at prayer is given, in very different circumstances. He and James are on board the ship the *Nonesuch*, sailing towards Henry and his family in America, and he admits to the reader that 'my religious duties (I grieve to say it) [were] always and even to this day extremely neglected'.[117] During a storm, he is driven to his knees to ask God to take both him and James:

'Thou madest me a coward from my mother's womb ... But lo! Here is Thy servant ready, his mortal weakness laid aside. Let me give my life

---

115 Margaret Oliphant, *Kirsteen*, Everyman, London: Dent, 1984 [1888], p. 265. In her biography of Mrs Oliphant, Elisabeth Jay explores Oliphant's own struggle with the role of priest in her family, once her husband has died: 'she attributed the absence of a sense of familial religious community to the problem of gender-defined roles: it was a general nineteenth century assumption that although the moral and religious upbringing was the mother's special responsibility, the priestly function of leading formal worship, even at family prayers, fell to the male. Yet, even as she acknowledged her collusion with this prejudice, she was clearly puzzled as to how her boys could have imbibed it, given their reliance upon her guiding hand in every other aspect of their lives', Elisabeth Jay, *Mrs Oliphant: A Fiction to Herself*, Oxford: Oxford University Press, 1995, p. 152.

116 Robert Louis Stevenson, *The Master of Ballantrae*, London: Penguin, 1996 [1889], p. 123.

117 Stevenson, *Master*, p. 156.

for this creature's; take the two of them, Lord! ... and have mercy on the innocent!'[118]

This, perhaps the most selfless act in the novel, an offer of the sacrifice of self in order to save others, nevertheless involves a prayer asking for another to be killed. In the novel, relationships with God, expressed in such acts of worship, are portrayed as being as distorted, damaged and damaging as the relationships between the brothers, their father, and the women and children in their lives. The distortion is highlighted by the reaction of the ship's crew, who credit Mackellar's devotions with saving the ship from the storm, and by the way that Secundra Dass, James's servant, is able to use what he has overheard of the prayer to enlighten his master to James's advantage. In *The Master*, as in *Kirsteen*, such acts of family or personal worship are looked back upon with scepticism rather than nostalgic sentimentalism.

Alternative Views of Worship: 'Kailyard' and O. Douglas

The subset of Scottish fiction known as 'kailyard',[119] from around the time of *The Master* and *Kirsteen* and just after, offers a very different understanding of the role of family worship in Scottish homes (and indeed of public worship). The scene in J. M. Barrie's *A Window in Thrums* in which the family gathers in worship before their son Jamie returns to London is even more sentimental than Burns's 'The Cotter's Saturday Night':

> I have always thought that Hendry's reading of the Bible was the most solemn and impressive I have ever heard. He exulted in the fourteenth of John, pouring it forth like one whom it intoxicated while he read. He emphasised every other word; it was so real and grand to him ... He brought us near to the throne of grace ... You may take a final glance at the little family; you will never see them together again.[120]

From a slightly later date (after World War One) but from a similar genre, O. Douglas (the pseudonym of Anna Buchan) also presents a very romantic view of expressions of faith, often centred on reflections about religious places. The churchyard where the faithful servant Betsy is brought to be

---

118 Stevenson, *Master*, p. 158.

119 'Kailyard', a small patch of ground next to a cottage where cabbages were grown, is the name given to the movement in late nineteenth-century Scottish fiction characterized by a sentimental idealization of life in rural villages.

120 J. M. Barrie, *A Window in Thrums*, London: Hodder and Stoughton, 1938 [1889], pp. 201–2.

buried is described as 'beautiful beyond words that March day when Betsy came home'.[121] When the family visit Iona on holiday, although they are deeply disappointed by the bustle of the place, they are also 'much impressed by its dignified simplicity and beauty', and Lady Jane describes it as 'fairyland', a place to be left to dream, where 'nothing could be too wonderful to happen'.[122] Even in this rarified context, some acceptance of the changes that have taken place are noted: the dying Betsy tells Lady Jane to find the money she has saved for her funeral in her Bible, as 'it's a fine place tae hide onything, for folk dinna fash the Bible muckle thae days'.[123]

Such fiction, nostalgic, with an underlying confidence in traditional expressions of religion, regretful of the changes that have led people away from the old ways, was tremendously popular at the time it was written. However, its popularity has waned, and it has been the subject of some critical disdain. Novels such as these offer an interesting contrast to the more sceptical and less optimistic fiction of the end of the nineteenth and beginning of the twentieth centuries, although their message is not the dominant one of their time in terms of their continuing resonance.

Public Worship in Burns and Galt

If the Scottish literature of the late nineteenth century broadly moves away from an idealized view of family worship in the past, with some notable exceptions, the literature of the turn of the century and beyond turns its attention, where it discusses worship at all, to public worship, the practice of family prayers now a distant memory. Of course, earlier writers also portray public worship, and before moving on to more recent literature, I shall offer some brief examples from Burns and Galt.

I have already noted the distinction Burns draws, in 'The Cotter's Saturday Night', between the heartfelt worship of the peasant family and the 'pageant' which public worship is prone to becoming. In other poems, however, a very different picture of public worship is offered. In 'The Holy Fair' from 1785/6, there is certainly an exploration and condemnation of the double standards of the Church at this most complex and curious time of festival, the annual Communion. But there is also a link forged between worship and, as Walter McGinty describes, 'an enjoyment of life in a physical and sensual way'. Burns 'dares to speak of "*faith* an' *hope* an' *love* an' *drink*" in the same breath, and not see any

121 O. Douglas (Anna Buchan), *The Day of Small Things*, London: Nelsons & Sons Ltd, 1933, p. 202.

122 Douglas, *Small Things*, p. 246.

123 Douglas, *Small Things*, p. 199.

incongruity'.[124] In passing, the various theologies and preaching styles of local ministers are described and critiqued with impressive brevity and insight. The poem presupposes a considerable amount of shared knowledge about such matters.

By the end of the time-span covered by John Galt's *Annals of the Parish*, such interest in church affairs has waned. Balwhidder looks back on his induction to the parish, and the uproar it caused, but notes that 'during the time of the psalm and the sermon' members of the congregation 'behaved themselves', only making a 'clamour' at the point of the induction.[125] A respect for the act of worship prevails. However, industrialization brings many changes to the parish, and the young, many brought in to work in the mill, if they engage with him at all, confound his 'arguments, which were the old and orthodox proven opinions of the Divinity Hall, as if they had been the light sayings of a vain man'.[126] By 1809, Balwhidder accepts the help of another minister, but is still asked to officiate at baptisms and weddings, the people believing, he comments, 'there is something good in the blessing of an aged gospel minister'.[127]

The *Annals of the Parish* is a deceptively subtle account of changing attitudes towards the Church in Scotland. In the first half of the novel, Balwhidder responds to the old, settled world ruled by the landed gentry by preaching on the evils of smuggling ('I preached sixteen times from the text, Render to Caesar the things that are Caesar's'[128]), the plight of elderly women in the parish,[129] the need for repentance, the horror of war and the sinfulness of extra-marital sex. In the second half of the novel, he is driven to preach of the 'evil and vanity of riches', sermons which are misunderstood as promoting 'levelling doctrines',[130] and 'religious and political exhortation on the present posture of public affairs'.[131] As numbers at worship fall away, Balwhidder understands his mission as trying 'to prevent Christian charity from being forgotten in the phraseology of utility and philanthropy'.[132] As Balwhidder is forced to confront the political realities of the day, he and the worship he leads are shown to become less and less relevant to his parishioners. When he is placed in a wider context, and preaches in 1779 to a congregation at the General Assembly which includes the Commissioner, the King's representative, taking 2 Samuel 19.35 as his text, 'Wherefore, then, should thy servant be yet a burden

124 McGinty, *Burns and Religion*, p. 212.
125 Galt, *Annals*, p. 6.
126 Galt, *Annals*, p. 129.
127 Galt, *Annals*, p. 205.
128 Galt, *Annals*, p. 11.
129 Galt, *Annals*, p. 44.
130 Galt, *Annals*, p. 137.
131 Galt, *Annals*, p. 180.
132 Galt, *Annals*, p. 147.

to the King', he asserts boldly that the Church has 'no need of the King's authority, however bound we were in temporal things to respect it'. While the Commissioner compliments him on his 'apostolic earnestness', his patron Lord Eglesham tells him he had 'gone beyond the bounds of modern moderation'.[133] Galt presents the shift in the perception of the Church through the preaching of his narrator, which tries to react to the upheaval of society around him, but which is shown to be increasingly open to misunderstanding and out of touch with the spirit of the age.

Worship in the Twentieth Century: J. MacDougall Hay and Lewis Grassic Gibbon

A similar, even more marked shift can be traced in the preaching and presence of ministers in Scottish novels from the early part of the twentieth century. While there is no mention of any acts of worship in George Douglas Brown's iconic novel *The House with the Green Shutters*,[134] church worship plays a more significant role in *Gillespie*, by J. MacDougall Hay, a Church of Scotland minister, although it is presented in a deeply ambivalent way. Churchgoing is both an opportunity for the advancement of business and a disappointment to a central character in the novel. Janet, Gillespie's servant is entranced by an engraving of Jesus blessing the children: 'She loved Christ for His love of little children; and often as she held the babe in her arms [Gillespie's son] she would gaze up at His face in awe.'[135] She declares she wishes to go to church, and

> Gillespie acquiesced and suggested the Parish Church, because he was a deacon in the Free Church. It would do his trade no harm if one of his household were connected with the other church. She went for two Sundays, and was vastly disappointed in Mr Stuart, who spoke too quickly. There was no stirring of angels in the heavens, no singing in the skies, and she returned famished to Jesus and the little children and her own babe.[136]

Mr Campion, the teacher, declares that 'the last place in Scotland where you will find the Cross so much as mentioned is in the Divinity Hall', and finds worship 'dull, insipid, futile'.[137] In contrast, Mrs Galbraith, Gillespie's

---

133 Galt, *Annals*, pp. 98–100.
134 George Douglas Brown, *The House with the Green Shutters*, London: Penguin, 1985 [1901], p. 172.
135 J. MacDougall Hay, *Gillespie*, Edinburgh: Canongate, 1983 [1914], p. 130.
136 MacDougall Hay, *Gillespie*, p. 131.
137 MacDougall Hay, *Gillespie*, p. 169.

nemesis, experiences in the harvest at the farm she had once owned with her husband 'a sense of pardon and peace, and a deep desire for revenge'.[138] She tells her friend Morag that the land is 'so beautiful and full of God'.[139] This sense of the land as the source and inspiration of a spiritual life is reiterated at the end of the novel, after the deaths of Mrs Gillespie and her son Eoghan, and Gillespie himself: 'The ploughman on Muirhead Farm went on ploughing the lea, ministering to the faith that is imperishable in the breast of man.'[140] The eternal aspect of such an expression of faith is contrasted with the transitory effect of formal congregational worship. Eoghan is taken to church with Mr Kennedy to hear the charismatic Mr Maurice, whose preaching on the story of the fallen woman anointing Jesus' feet deeply moves him: 'The wings of the cherubim were adrift in the church ... [he felt he was] in the hollow of God's hand ... God is here!'[141] However, when he tries to bring a sense of this experience to his alcoholic mother, she rejects it in favour of more whisky. Similarly, he shares an intense moment of worship with his grandfather, as they pray for the safety of Iain, his older brother at sea. Singing Psalm 20,[142] it seemed they were 'in communion with the Almighty ... as if [the old man] were summoning legions of angels from the throne of Heaven'.[143] The narrator comments ironically that as they were committing Iain into the 'care of the Great, All-Seeing father ... water lifted Iain away into the vast darkness and the desired haven where there is quiet'.[144] In this novel, traditional, formal religion in all its guises is shown to be powerfully affecting but ultimately no match for the realities of life or the forces of nature.

The later set of novels, *A Scots Quair*, suggests that even this power of organized religious worship in Scotland to affect its participants, however momentarily, is fading. In *Sunset Song*, Chris asserts what the novels will go on to reveal: 'I don't believe they were ever religious, the Scots folk ... They've never BELIEVED. It's just been a place to collect and argue, the kirk, and criticize God.'[145] The form this criticism of God takes is constant criticism of and comment about the ministers who lead their worship and live among them. Chris's description of the third of the three candidates

---

138 MacDougall Hay, *Gillespie*, p. 159.

139 MacDougall Hay, *Gillespie*, p. 160.

140 MacDougall Hay, *Gillespie*, p. 446.

141 MacDougall Hay, *Gillespie*, p. 295.

142 The role of the metrical psalms in descriptions of worship in Scottish literature cannot be underestimated. These psalms, whether sung or said, form the backbone of worship from the beginning to the end of the period under discussion. They are almost always presented in a positive way, although Revd Wringhim's use of Psalm 109 while leading worship in his lodgings in Edinburgh, to condemn George and his father, is striking (Hogg, *Confessions*, p. 24).

143 MacDougall Hay, *Gillespie*, p. 305.

144 MacDougall Hay, *Gillespie*, p. 306.

145 Grassic Gibbon, *Sunset Song*, London: Penguin, 1986, p. 213.

who preach for the Kinraddie pulpit before World War One offers a revealing picture of the expectations of worship at the time:

> Stuart Gibbon said the Lord's Prayer in a way that pleased gentry and simple. For though he begged to be forgiven his sins as he forgive those that sinned against him – instead, as was more genteel, crying to be forgiven his trespasses as he forgave those that trespassed against him – still he did it with a fine solemnity that made everybody that heard right douce and grave-like; and one or two joined in near the end of the prayer, and that's a thing gey seldom done in an Auld Kirk kirk.[146]

His sermon on the Song of Solomon opens up to the surprised congregation that the text has more than one meaning, and may be read as 'Christ's description of the beauty and fine comeliness of the Auld Kirk of Scotland'.[147] Chris's reflective response, with its sensitivity to class distinctions in the community, will be in real contrast to the responses of others to the preaching they are exposed to after the War. By then, Robert Colquohoun is the new minister of Kinraddie, with a very different approach; his preaching deemed 'rank sedition', making folk 'fair uncomfortable'.[148] The loss of a connection between preaching and the experience of those attending the service may be traced in the service Colquohoun leads at the newly erected war memorial. His sermon is misunderstood and rejected for being 'just sheer politics', and instead it is the piper's playing which 'vexed and tore' at their hearts.[149] When he decides to preach a forceful sermon when preaching for the church at Segget, it is judged as 'meaty and strong and preached with some fire',[150] but as Chris notes, 'they [the congregation] hadn't a notion what the sermon meant', that it was condemning rather than affirming them. As the tragic events of the second novel unfold, and Colquohoun suffers some sort of breakdown, his sermons become calls for an individual, internalized faith ('blether[ing] away in the clouds'[151]), and as the narrator notes, 'They heeded as little the whine of his Christ as the angry threat of his Struggling God.'[152] The reader senses in Chris's benediction, pronounced over the body of her husband who has died in the pulpit, that the novel is charting an inexorable movement towards a loss of connection between traditional worship and Scottish life: 'It is finished.'[153]

---

146 Grassic Gibbon, *Sunset Song*, p. 54.
147 Grassic Gibbon, *Sunset Song*, p. 54.
148 Grassic Gibbon, *Sunset Song*, p. 249.
149 Grassic Gibbon, *Sunset Song*, p. 253.
150 Grassic Gibbon, *Cloud Howe*, London: Penguin, 1986, p. 25.
151 Grassic Gibbon, *Cloud Howe*, p. 182.
152 Grassic Gibbon, *Cloud Howe*, p. 189.
153 Grassic Gibbon, *Cloud Howe*, p. 222.

This is emphasized in the third novel, *Grey Granite*, in which one of the only points of contact with organized religion is the Revd MacShilluck, a ridiculous, hypocritical and reactionary figure with no moral authority. As in *Gillespie*, the strong suggestion is made that it is through connection with the land ('enduring, encompassing'[154]) that Scots find a sense of their spirituality.

Worship in the Work of Fionn MacColla and James Robertson

The final two novels in our survey of the portrayal of public worship in Scottish literature come from a later period, but reflect similar concerns and alternatives. Both offer the perspective of ministers, those who lead worship, with less emphasis on the experience of members of the congregation. In Fionn MacColla's *The Ministers*, published in 1979 after the author's death, no examples of congregational worship are offered. Instead, in the debates and interior monologues of the very different ministers portrayed, oppositions between words and silence, works and contemplation, the physical and the spiritual are explored. The novel is interesting in the context of this chapter for its focus on the experience of one of the ministers, Ewen MacRury. His exploration of meditative worship is beautifully described, as is the suspicion with which this approach is viewed by his peers. MacRury comes to realize:

> In spite of the dust raised by the multitudinous trivial scuffling in the dead-level plains, all that was of real and ultimate moment was taking place invisibly 'in the high places', in the heights of *being*.[155]

Later, he tries to describe the content of such experiences to his sceptical and suspicious colleagues:

> It is an experience of love, poured out in, and drawn forth from, simply, the Object of Love … Love looking at the Object of Love, and unable to see anything else, and not wanting to see anything else ever.[156]

Their response is to recommend he goes to another parish, to keep this revelation and experience unspoken, and although MacRury agrees to leave, the reader is left with a sense that he is leaving the edifice of the Church for something that is very 'Different', a 'little moment in the light'.[157]

---

154 Grassic Gibbon, *Grey Granite*, London: Penguin, 1986, p. 219.
155 Fionn MacColla, *The Ministers*, London: Souvenir Press, 1979, p. 108.
156 MacColla, *Ministers*, p. 196.
157 MacColla, *Ministers*, pp. 251–2.

The alternative offered in *The Ministers*, communion with a Higher Power motivated by love, is very different from the alternative to the Church presented in James Robertson's *The Testament of Gideon Mack*, although both share the sense that the worship of the Church is no longer adequate. Gideon describes how he follows his father in his approach to preaching, tending to 'abandon the prepared structure and let the words take [him] wherever they were going', although, as he admits, he puts his trust 'in language rather than in God'.[158] The tension between Gideon and his kirk session centres on the appropriateness of language for worship: he wants 'poetry ... mystery ... beauty ... splendour', while 'they want the Word of God in a language they can understand'.[159] Successfully preached words for Gideon are 'words firing out of me and hitting a few targets', although he concedes 'whether they had any effect on the listeners was another matter all together'.[160] In preaching for Monimaskit, he compares himself to Robert Colquhoun in *Cloud Howe*, who risks tackling a contentious and contemporary issue, while admitting that Colquhoun 'was a man of far greater moral courage' than he, as his topic, nuclear weapons, had been condemned by many motions at General Assembly. His sermon still provokes 'an audible insucking of breath', however, and he is called to the parish.[161] Two further instances of public worship are worth noting here. The first is led by Lorna Sprott, after Gideon has had his experience in the cave. She preaches a message of hope out of the experience, which he believes is a misreading of his story, although she asserts, 'Today I felt inspired.'[162] The second is Catherine Craigie's funeral, in which, Gideon comments, the music she had chosen, La Cucaracha, 'sounded totally exotic in the Old Kirk, and totally joyous'.[163] In this novel, worship and words are uneasy, unreliable companions, subjective and with an uncertain effect. The reference to music, and to Catherine Craigie who, although 'she rejected the Church, she also understood its significance'[164] offers the slightest glimpse of an alternative to well-worn words in worship and a rejection of the Church outright. In the funeral there is something of the 'chaos' Gideon notes in the worship in the care home, but here it is not 'desiccated' but vital and real, of significance.[165]

Of course the novel has much to say about much more than public worship. What it offers on this topic, however, is very much in the developing

---

158 Robertson, *Gideon Mack*, p. 68.
159 Robertson, *Gideon Mack*, p. 69.
160 Robertson, *Gideon Mack*, pp. 70–1.
161 Robertson, *Gideon Mack*, p. 136.
162 Robertson, *Gideon Mack*, pp. 326–8.
163 Robertson, *Gideon Mack*, p. 336.
164 Robertson, *Gideon Mack*, p. 333.
165 Robertson, *Gideon Mack*, p. 71.

tradition of earlier Scottish fiction. In both family and formal congregational worship, the connection between participants' experiences and the worship offered is gradually lost. The Bible becomes less understood, applied or even known, the language of worship becomes less relevant, and its ambivalence is highlighted, although surprising alternatives to traditional language may be hinted at. The portrayal of ministers also becomes less genial and more pointed, when they are given any role at all in Scottish fictional societies.

Conclusion

The picture that has been offered here is a bleak one on the whole, although it would be wrong to finish this chapter on an entirely negative note. In 'The Offering', Liz Lochhead may express a dominant view of worship in Scottish literature in the late twentieth and early twenty-first centuries, that 'Never in a month of them [Sundays]/ should you go back./ Fond hope./ You'll still find you do not measure up ... / You'll still not understand/ the singing, the action or the word.' [166] However, more tentative and quieter voices were to be and may still be heard, perhaps best exemplified in some of Edwin Muir's poetry. In his poem 'The Incarnate One', 'The Word made flesh is here made word again', a statement of faith inspired by the sight of 'Calvin's kirk crowning the barren brae', although even here 'King Calvin with his iron pen' is compared unfavourably to the 'better Gospel in man's natural tongue'.[167] In common with much of the literature we have considered here, Muir's search for meaningful worship takes him beyond the confines of the Church into the realm of the 'natural'.

---

166 Liz Lochhead, 1984, 'The Offering', in Meg Bateman, Robert Crawford and James McGonigal, eds, *Scottish Religious Poetry: An Anthology*, Edinburgh: Saint Andrew Press, 2000, p. 288.

167 Edwin Muir, 1956, 'The Incarnate One', in *Collected Poems*, London: Faber & Faber, 1984, p. 228.

Part Two

THEOLOGIES OF WORSHIP

4

THE THEOLOGY OF WORSHIP

A Reformed Perspective

David Fergusson

The theology and practice of worship have received significantly more attention in recent years. In the work of Geoffrey Wainwright there has been
even an attempt to construct an entire systematics from the perspective of
worship.[168] There are several reasons for this resurgence in interest in the
subject and by inspecting these under four headings – history, philosophy,
ethics and ecumenism – some initial insight into the theology of worship can
be gained. From there, we shall proceed to outline Reformed approaches
by examining the two characteristic notes or marks of the Church.

The Study of Doctrine in the Context of Worship

History

The study of the history of doctrine reveals the way in which doxological
practices preceded and shaped the formation of dogma. Without asserting
an absolute priority of doxology over dogma, one can acknowledge the
importance of worship in shaping Christian belief. This is already true of
Hebrew religion where, in the Psalms, the celebration of salvation history,
law, divine rule and wisdom all contribute to the shaping of Israel's faith.
Similarly the elaborate sacrificial system and holiness code reveal long-
standing practices which, for example, condition faith and belief in atonement for sin. New Testament scholarship has also made us aware of those
credal fragments in the letters of Paul and elsewhere which reflect liturgical
usage in early Christian worship, for example the Christ-hymn in Philippians 2.[169] Theology was decisively shaped by a range of practices such as
praying to Jesus, baptism in the threefold name, and the celebration of the

---

168 Geoffrey Wainwright, *Doxology: A Systematic Theology*, London: Epworth, 1980.
169 For discussion of the significance of worship in the New Testament see Larry Hurtado,
At the Origins of Christian Worship, Carlisle: Paternoster, 1999.

Lord's Supper as recorded in 1 Corinthians 11. In the patristic period, the development of dogma was also influenced by established practice.[170] Thus in the Arian controversy, Athanasius could appeal to the widespread practice of addressing prayer to Jesus. Against Pelagius, Augustine could cite the practice of baptizing infants for remission of sin. Anselm's theory of the atonement invoked the categories of the Church's penitential system, while eucharistic controversies in the Middle Ages were determined by the language of the liturgy. One would also have to view Mariology and the subsequent dogmatic definition of the immaculate conception and bodily assumption of Mary in light of long-standing practices of devotion that first emerge in the patristic period. In all this, however, it is not merely a matter of doctrine tracking widespread practice. Critical doctrinal reflection can act as a corrective upon our doxological habits.

Philosophy

The work of the later Wittgenstein has been interpreted and deployed by theologians in a range of ways, not all of which are consistent. But one widely recognized contribution of Wittgenstein is the stress on practice and forms of life in the acquisition of meaning. When a builder shouts 'slab' to his colleague he is not engaging in a simple act of naming, as earlier theories of meaning suggested.[171] Instead he is issuing an instruction about how and when to deliver the next slab to his colleague who is laying them in a particular order. The salient point of this illustration is that meanings are only acquired through initiation into the practice and forms of life that shape the world of the building site. Words are not learned by looking out at the world and receiving examples of how to label the objects of experience. Learning takes place through action, exchange and participation in a complex set of rule-governed practices. Instead of a detached visual recognition, meaning is grasped through touch and sound in complex, communal activity.

These observations about meaning are significant for an account of theological knowledge. We know God not so much by attaching labels to experiences, events or phenomena but through participation in a range of rule-governed practices and forms of life. An alternative way of expressing this is to say that we can only speak of a knowledge of God in terms of exposure to and immersion in the life of the community. This will typically require catechesis, baptism, regular participation in worship, and the disciplined practice of loving God and one's neighbour.

170 This is shown repeatedly in Jaroslav Pelikan, *The Emergence of the Catholic Tradition* (100–600), Chicago: University of Chicago Press, 1971.

171 This example is drawn from Ludwig Wittgenstein, *Philosophical Investigations*, Oxford: Blackwell, 1953, pp. 8–10.

On this account of meaning, we now become better placed to appreciate the integral connection of worship to a practical knowledge of God. The worship of the community informs our knowledge of God. We are initiated into ways of seeing the world, ourselves and other people that are theologically significant. Without the regular patterns of worship, the language of faith and its modes of perception will make little or no sense to us. This is a central theme of George Lindbeck's *The Nature of Doctrine*, one of the most influential texts of the last twenty years.[172] We learn faith in a way analogous to a child learning its first language. Experience and belief, too long abstracted from worship in theology, are now perceived to repose upon the practices of the worshipping community.

Ethics

Recent return to Aristotelian virtue ethics in both philosophy and theology has brought a renewed stress upon the importance of habit in the moral life. We act well typically through the development of good habits. These require formation through acknowledgement of the texts, authorities, traditions and practices of the Christian community. The most important single voice here is that of Stanley Hauerwas. Training in the Christian life, he argues, requires induction into the practices of worship, familiarity with the examples and stories of the saints, and the reorientation of one's life by the claims of Christ and his Church. This is stressed in a counter-cultural spirit. The distinctiveness of Christian living requires attention to the ways in which the worship, fellowship, belief and moral witness of the Church reshape our lives.

It has been sometimes pointed out that there is a Catholic moment in the ethics of Hauerwas. The attention given to the authority of the Church, the lives of the saints and the Aristotelian–Thomist tradition positions this style of Christian ethics much closer to Roman Catholicism than the neo-liberal Protestant views it typically criticizes. On the other hand, the writings of Hauerwas need also to be seen in the context of Reformed emphases upon personal holiness, the Christian life, the discipline of the Church community and the transformation of society. The influence of John Howard Yoder and the radical Reformation are also apparent and enable him to describe himself as a high church Methodist with Mennonite leanings. Many of Hauerwas's recent essays are published sermons. These reflect a commitment to the power of the preached Word to change the lives of its hearers. It is through the regular practice of communal worship that we are trained to live as God's people in the world. 'Our Sunday worship has a way of reminding us, in the most explicit and ecclesial of

---

172 George Lindbeck, *The Nature of Doctrine*, London: SPCK, 1985.

ways, of the source of our power, the peculiar nature of our solutions to what ails the world.'[173]

The work of Hauerwas should be seen in the same post-liberal paradigm as Lindbeck. It is developed by others from a range of perspectives. In a discussion of pastoral care, Willimon points to the importance of worship in consoling, healing and renewing us amid the crises of life. He appeals to worship as central to what distinguishes Christian pastoral care from secular forms of counselling and therapy.[174] Miroslav Volf, in a recent collection of essays, speaks of belief-shaped practices and practice-shaping beliefs to describe the integrity of doing and believing in the Christian life. 'Christian practices have what we may call an "as-so" structure: *as* God has received us in Christ, *so* we too are to receive our fellow human beings.'[175]

Ecumenism

The ecumenical movement has also made a contribution to the renewed sense of the importance of worship for Christian doctrine. Through study of shared practices a greater sense of ecumenical convergence has been achieved, even where there this has not yielded structural unity. This has been fostered by biblical scholarship and historical study of Church traditions.

The process leading to the formulation of *Baptism, Eucharist and Ministry*, the Lima document of 1982, is instructive in this context. In particular, the section on the Eucharist makes significant ecumenical progress by shifting attention away from rival theories of the real presence by focusing on the wider context of eucharistic worship. This was achieved in part through the liturgical reform movement and the creation of an ecumenical liturgy for sacramental celebration. The Eucharist is set within the context of divine worship broadly considered. It contains most, if not all, of the following elements: praise; confession of sin; declaration of pardon; proclamation of the Word; confession of the faith; intercession for Church and world; words of institution; anamnesis; epiklesis; commemoration of the faithful departed; prayer for the coming of the kingdom; the Lord's Prayer; the sign of peace; praise; blessing and sending. The stress on the ecumenical sharing of these aspects of eucharistic worship has contributed

---

173 Stanley Hauerwas and William H. Willimon, *Resident Aliens*, Nashville: Abingdon, 1993, p. 171. In similar vein, Sam Wells has sought to describe the range of ways in which worship is ethically formative. 'How Common Worship Forms Local Character', *Studies in Christian Ethics*, 15 (2002), pp. 66–74.

174 William Willimon, *Worship as Pastoral Care*, Nashville: Abingdon, 1979.

175 Miroslav Volf, 'Theology for a Way of Life', in Miroslav Volf and Dorothy C. Bass, eds, *Practicing Theology*, Grand Rapids, Eerdmans, 2002, p. 250.

to a process in which historical differences are minimized, though not overcome.

Theological Description of the Forms of Worship

Attempts to define worship as if it were one single thing or activity, and then to organize everything else around this, are liable to cause distortion. This is a mistaken 'essentialist' strategy, which will tend to miss vital elements. Instead, the task is better conceived as offering a description of worship that is informed both by its centrality for Christian belief and practice, and also by the central credal affirmations of the faith. We should think in this context of 'description' rather than 'definition'.

Attention to linguistic study of the various terms for 'worship' in its biblical and post-canonical usage is necessary but not sufficient for the construction of a theology of worship. The Hebrew verb *chawah* is most commonly used to describe the activity of divine worship. It refers to the act of bowing down or rendering obeisance to whom it is due. In the Greek New Testament, the verb *proskuneo* is used in many places with much the same sense of bowing down. *Latreuo* is also employed several times for public worship, and denotes the idea of offering service. Church worship is thus described as service; we still refer to the church service in English or the *Gottesdienst* in German. The English term 'worship' itself derives from an Anglo-Saxon word for 'honour' (*weorthscipe*) suggesting again that worship is an action of honouring one who is worthy. It can be used of persons other than God in different contexts. Thus, using archaic English, we might address 'the Worshipful the Mayor'. A better-known example is found in the order for the solemnization of matrimony in the Book of Common Prayer (1662): 'With this I ring I thee wed, with my body I thee worship, and with all my worldly goods I thee endow.'

In much confessional writing, the biblical sense of honouring the divine majesty is prominent. The description of God in the Westminster Confession of Faith is characterized in the following terms: 'To (God) is due from angels and men, and every other creature, whatsoever worship, service, or obedience he is pleased to require of them' (III.2). In the Reformation criticism of idolatry in the Church, the honouring of God alone is frequently stressed in the exposition of the first table of the Decalogue. So the Shorter Catechism informs us that 'The First Commandment forbiddeth the denying, or not worshipping and glorifying, the true God as God, and our God; and the giving of that worship and glory to any other which is due to him alone' (Answer 47). All this must find a place in a theology of worship, yet the honouring of God is neither a necessary nor a sufficient condition for an adequate description of worship. There are several reasons for this. We can honour and acknowledge God in ways that extend beyond worship, for example in our daily work, in the life of the household, in political and social activity. It is the particular form that this honouring takes which requires articulation in a theology of worship. Worship, moreover, involves a wide range of activities not all of which are entirely captured by the notion of acknowledging or honouring God. The range of forms cited in the New Testament recalls us to this diversity, as does the practice of the synagogue. Indeed the Psalms already attest the variety of functions fulfilled by public worship; these include praise, thanksgiving, celebration, recounting, proclamation, confession, petition, instruction and lament. While Christian practice has sometimes found difficulty in accommodating lament and complaint, all these other themes are generally present in the worship of the Church.

Worship as an Action in which God is both Subject and Object

As an event in which God is not merely a passive recipient of our praise, worship creates an exchange between the divine and the creaturely in which God is the subject as well as the object of worship. The dramatic character of worship has often been portrayed by the Protestant account of preaching and by the Catholic description of the Eucharist. The preaching of the Word is an event in which not only the preacher speaks but God addresses the people. It is this that bestows upon worship both its gravity and its joyfulness. In the medieval and Tridentine doctrine of transubstantiation and its accompanying account of ordination, we can recognize that in its description of the fraction at the altar there is an acute sense of the continual action of God in the regular worship of the Church across space and time. Christ is re-presented to his people each time the sacrament of his body and blood is celebrated. In this same context, note should be made of the action of the Spirit in public worship in recent charismatic traditions. The criticism of mainstream Western theology that it was too binitarian is not without force at this point. A fuller account of the person and work of the Spirit should enhance the sense that the Spirit is active in prompting, guiding and enabling worship in all its dimensions. The churches of the global south, in particular, attest a keen sense of spiritual power often articulated by reference to the continual action of the third person.

Worship might be described as a performative action in which both the Church and God participate. It is not merely a human acknowledgement of who God is or what Christ has done. Worship is an event by which God is known and Christ communicated; it is not of our own making for it is dependent upon the grace of God. In this regard, the act of worship is not merely a human recollection or bearing witness although it includes these. It is also an event in which God's grace works for us in repeated, regular and dependable ways, albeit in a manner that refers us to the once for all action of Christ. Appeal can be made in this context to the priestly theology of the Hebrews and the claim that the ascended Christ is seated at the right hand of the Father. Though difficult to formulate conceptually, this language implies that Christ continues through the Spirit to intercede on our behalf. He continues to pray for and with us, even as we pray through him and in him. Worship here becomes the coincidence of divine and human action together.[176]

This can be a powerful and liberating insight, particularly at those moments when faith falters and prayer becomes fitful. Simon Peter is told that though his faith will fail, Christ has prayed for him. So also the ascended Christ continues through the Spirit to intercede for us. The awareness of Christ as the one who perpetually prays for us and also of the company of the faithful who surround us is a source of pastoral encouragement and liturgical strength. In reflecting upon the theology of Holy Saturday in the midst of his own terminal illness, Alan Lewis has written these moving words.

> We face suffering, distress, and death with courage, faith and trust, not by maintaining serenity of psyche or buoyancy of soul within, but precisely by casting ourselves in all the times of emptiness, aridity, and wordlessness – as well as those still more spiritually dangerous times of optimism or elation – upon the gift of grace outside us and around us. God promises to do what we cannot do, and go where we need not go, to enter the dark valley ahead of us and defeat on our behalf the frightening foe. And the Spirit undertakes to pray for us, and stirs others to intercede on our behalf, just when we feel awful, overwrought in body or in spirit, when faith eludes intellect or consciousness and our tongues have lost all utterance.[177]

In stressing the ongoing action of the Spirit in relation to the priestly office of the ascended Christ, we can understand worship as God's action in our midst without compromising the once-for-all character of the work of Christ. In pressing this point, however, we should not overstate it so as to present worship as something that we do not do. Worship is not an intra-trinitarian transaction that takes place over our heads, unrelated to the practices of the visible, empirical congregations to which we belong. An

---

176 This is developed by James B. Torrance, *Worship, Community and the Triune God of Grace*, Carlisle: Paternoster, 1996.

177 Alan E. Lewis, *Between Cross & Resurrection: A Theology of Holy Saturday*, Grand Rapids: Eerdmans, 2001, pp. 430–1.

overstretched Christomonism will lead to the enervating and implausible conclusion that in worship there is nothing much left for us to do.

To illustrate the performative character of worship, we should consider further the Psalms. It is generally assumed that these were memorized and recited in worship before being committed to their present literary form.[178] In celebrating the kingly rule of God, the Psalms not only attest that rule but also contribute to it and participate in it. In part, it is through the praise of Israel that God's rule over creation is exercised. Through a covenant partnership, expressed in the forms of worship, God wills to be known and obeyed. Thus in Psalm 24, though the ark of the covenant is no longer present, the enthronement of God in the praise of the post-exilic people is enacted. Here we see why worship must have a public character. Israel and the Church are called into covenant partnership with God not as an aggregate of disconnected individuals, but as a people which, in its corporate, social existence, worships together. This does not exclude private acts of worship and devotion, but it seems to demand the centrality of the regular, public diet of worship on the Lord's Day in fulfilment of the fourth commandment. This public event has a dramatic quality by virtue of its character as both a divine and a human action. In his Aberdeen Gifford lectures, Karl Barth once insisted, that 'the church service is the most important, momentous and majestic thing which can possibly take place on earth, because its primary content is not the work of man but the work of the Holy Spirit and consequently the work of faith'.[179]

Reformed Exposition of Worship under the Rubrics of Word and Sacrament

In much Reformed writing, the topic of worship is dealt with by reference to the two 'notes' of Word and sacrament. What takes place in worship is expounded by reference to the reading and preaching of God's Word and the right administration of the sacraments.

Set out in confessions, catechisms and theological textbooks, much of the exposition is located within an initial context of sixteenth-century polemics. The need to reform the life of the Church according to the Word of God entailed a good deal of attention to the range of activities that took place in worship. Thus Bullinger's *Second Helvetic Confession* engages in a patient description of the tasks of the minister, the sacramental relation,

---

178 For example, Claus Westermann, *The Living Psalms*, Edinburgh: T&T Clark, 1989, p. 4.

179 Karl Barth, *The Knowledge of God and the Service of God*, London: Hodder & Stoughton, 1938, p. 198.

baptism and the Lord's Supper, religious meetings, church architecture, the language of prayer, singing, canonical hours, holy days, fasts, catechizing, pastoral care of the sick, burial of the dead, ceremonies, rites and adiaphora – the things of indifference. In the *Second Helvetic Confession*, we have something akin to a comprehensive description of worship.

> Although it is permitted all men to read the Holy Scriptures privately at home, and by instruction to edify one another in the true religion, yet in order that the Word of God may be properly preached to the people, and prayers and supplication publicly made, also that the sacraments may be rightly administered, and that collections may be made for the poor and to pay the cost of all the Church's expenses, and in order to maintain social intercourse, it is most necessary that religious or Church gatherings be held. For it is certain that in the apostolic and primitive Church, there were such assemblies frequented by all the godly.[180]

Although this is a rather low-key and urbane account of worship, it is to be commended for its attention to detail and its strong sense of the local, empirical and visible congregation. It is broader in its scope than most Reformed accounts of worship which focus more exclusively on Word and sacrament. These require some comment.

The attention to the preaching of the Word reflects several features of Lutheran and Reformed worship. These include the return to Scripture alone over against tradition as the supreme rule of faith and life; the importance of a right understanding of the faith, reflected also in the translation of the Bible and the liturgy into the vernacular; the commitment to education shared with Renaissance humanism; and also a polemic against the medieval notion of the sacraments as effective *ex opere operato* (by the sheer performance of the act) without reference to the faith of the recipient. In the response to all these concerns, the regular preaching and hearing of the Word became of paramount importance. In much Reformation theology, the preaching of the Word is characterized in sacramental language. For Luther, the Word of God could be described as present in, with and under the words of the preacher. Within the Reformed tradition, the relationship is not described in terms of a consubstantiation but in terms of the capacity of the Spirit to speak through human words that have been properly applied to the proclamation of the Scriptures. Here there is an indirect identity of human and divine speech in a manner that again recalls sacramental language.[181] By contrast, the Roman Catholic

---

180 *Second Helvetic Confession* (1566), Chapter 22.

181 See, for example, R. S. Wallace, *Calvin's Doctrine of the Word and Sacrament*, Edinburgh: Oliver & Boyd, 1953.

tradition has tended to construe the sermon more as a homily, a piece of instruction, subsidiary to the celebration of the Mass.[182]

While Lutheran and Reformed accounts of preaching often drew upon images of sacramental grace to describe its significance and efficacy, there was simultaneously a move in the opposite direction that further reinforced the centrality of the preached Word.[183] The sacraments themselves became annexed to the proclamation of the Word so that their efficacy was derivative from and subordinate to the latter and its proclamation. Here attention was given to Augustine's notion of a *visibile verbum* whereby the sacraments were described in terms of their representation to the other senses of what was heard through the reading and preaching of the Word. This supra-sacramental account of preaching resulted in the widespread Protestant practice of centralizing the sermon in the weekly diet of worship. It finds its roots in the ministry of the prophets and Jesus, and in the New Testament imperative to declare the gospel, an action that itself could simply be described as 'the word of God'. Hence Bullinger's famous dictum that 'the preaching of the Word of God *is* the Word of God'. This was a marginal note added to the text of the *Second Helvetic Confession* – *praedicato verbi Dei est verbum Dei* – reflecting Bullinger's belief in the power of the proclaimed message, even when announced by unworthy ministers.[184] This message, however, always has a derivative and dependent status in relation to Scripture. It does not merely proclaim the message of the Bible but interprets it for a given time and place, so that it becomes again the Word of God.

Expounded in Bullinger's *Decades*, this became something like the standard Reformed view. It establishes the centrality of proclamation in the life of the Church while also insisting upon its subordination to the written Word.[185] At the same time, however, it is recognized that Scripture requires to be interpreted and applied to the situation of the congregation.

---

182 More recently, post-Vatican II pneumatology has stressed the importance of preaching and the need publicly to invoke the Spirit at its outset.

183 This is explored by Alan Lewis, '*Ecclesia ex Auditu*: A Reformed View of the Church as the Community of the Word of God', *Scottish Journal of Theology*, 35 (1982), pp. 13–31.

184 Here I am following the interpretation of Bullinger in E. A. Dowey, 'The Word of God as Scripture and Preaching', in W. Fred Graham, ed., *Later Calvinism: International Perspectives*, Kirksville, MO: Northeast Missouri State University, 1994, pp. 5–18. The alleged differences between Calvin and Bullinger perceived by T. H. L. Parker, in *Calvin's Preaching*, Edinburgh: T&T Clark, 1992, p. 22, seem to me largely overdrawn. With their claims for the centrality of preaching in the Church yet as subordinate to Scripture, there is an important consensus between the two Reformers.

185 In the Lutheran tradition, by contrast, there tends to be an assimilation of the promise of the gospel announced in Scripture with its repetition in the declaration of the preacher. One recent commentator remarks that 'preaching in a sacramental fashion is doing to the hearers what the text authorizes you to do to them'. Gerhard Forde, *The Preached God: proclamation in Word and Sacrament*, Grand Rapids: Eerdmans, 2007, p. 91.

This assigns to preaching, then, not only a singular character in terms of its initial announcement of the gospel. Instead, it has an ongoing, repeatable and regular function within the community of faith by virtue of its capacity to interpret and present Scripture as the living Word of God. Preaching is not a monotonous action that simply repeats in timeless fashion a single message. It might be likened to the different performances of a single musical score, or variations on a theme. Always there is a return to what has been composed; this continues to control what is said. Yet the performance will vary according to the needs, capacities and situation of the hearers. Hence, the preaching of God's Word is facilitated by Scripture and the ongoing action of the Spirit. We find this position elegantly stated in the *Larger Catechism*.

> They that are called to labour in the ministry of the word, are to preach sound doctrine, diligently, in season and out of season; plainly, not in the enticing words of man's wisdom, but in demonstration of the Spirit, and of power; faithfully, making known the whole counsel of God; wisely, applying themselves to the necessities and capacities of the hearers; zealously, with fervent love to God and the souls of his people; sincerely, aiming at his glory, and their conversion, edification, and salvation.[186]

This account of the Word contributed greatly to the dramatic and performative character of worship. Where the preacher speaks, there God too will address us. This attaches to preaching, together with the training and preparation invested in it, the highest seriousness.

One can find scriptural support for preaching in the prophets, in the ministry of Jesus himself and in his command to preach the gospel. Yet the isolation of the sermon from other forms of oral communication has arguably become problematic in Reformed worship. In particular, the relative loss of both instruction and discussion has caused an undue constriction of worship, and an isolation of the preaching of the Word that does it no service.[187] From the beginning of its history, instruction in the faith was important for new converts. The risen Christ bids his disciples not only to preach but to teach all that he commands. Jesus himself had been called a teacher, a rabbi, by those around him. And this didactic task was taken seriously by the early Church in instruction about the foundational events of the faith and the catechizing of candidates for baptism. Instruction never assumed sacramental status, yet it is as prominent in the New Testament

---

186 *The Larger Westminster Catechism*, p. 159.

187 Here I am indebted to Hendrikus Berkhof, *Christian Faith*, Grand Rapids: Eerdmans, 1979, pp. 352ff.

as either baptism or the Lord's Supper. Whether it takes place in or alongside the weekly diet of worship, it is clear that it is closely associated with the upbuilding of the community. Similar remarks can be made with respect to discussion. Conversation is a means of grace in the ministry of Jesus. One thinks of his private exchanges with the disciples, Nicodemus and the Samaritan woman. Moreover, empirical research suggests that many more people come to faith through personal conversation, discussion and exchange than through listening to sermons.[188] In this respect, we should not discount the role of para-church organizations where the faith was actively discussed. These complemented and enriched the preaching of sermons. Their decline in some quarters must be viewed with some concern, particularly at a time when we have become conscious of the counter-cultural significance of Christian formation. The ministry of the Word is not to be constricted, but should be set within wider patterns of communication in the Church.

The necessity and nature of preaching can also be elucidated by parallels with the interpretation of the Hebrew Bible in rabbinic Judaism. With the closing of the canon, there could be no new or additional works that became part of the Tanakh. On the other hand, it was believed that God could speak in new and relevant ways through the canon of Scripture. This required an interpretative act by the teacher within the synagogue. The very nature of a completed canon thus had as its necessary accompaniment in the community of faith a procedure for its interpretation and application to the lives of contemporary readers and hearers. Michael Fishbane speaks about the singularity of Scripture residing in 'the depth of possibilities for true teaching, the legal and theological experience, latent in the text'. He quotes the words of one midrashic commentary. 'When the Holy One, blessed be He, gave the Torah to Israel, He only gave it as wheat from which to extract flour, and as flax wherewith to weave a garment.'[189] It is as if the critical and creative discernment of the interpreter is a corollary of there being a sacred text at all. This work, moreover, takes place within a community of practice. So key passages of the Hebrew Scriptures are used as lectionaries for Sabbaths, as recitations for festivals and fasts, as the focus of public expositions and sermons, and in the reading and praying of the Psalms. These activities all regulate the use and function of Scripture in the synagogue.

Similarly for the Christian minister, a central act of weekly worship is the interpretation of Scripture, not as mere repetition or explanation but as an appropriation and unfolding of its meaning for a particular context.

---

188 For example, John Finney, *Finding Faith*, Swindon: British and Foreign Bible Society, 1992.

189 Michael Fishbane, *The Garments of Torah*, Bloomington: Indiana University Press, 1989, pp. 37–8.

Given the character of the Scriptures of the Old and New Testaments with their reference to Christ in the form of promise and fulfilment, this act of interpretation also has the character of witness. It is an ongoing attestation of the presence and significance of Christ for the Church. Yet, we have argued above, this is not a single, monotonous message – it takes many forms including celebration, upbuilding, teaching, challenging, rebuking, comforting, fortifying and inciting to good works. Understood in this way, we can assign to preaching an abiding importance, but one that belongs to the wider and varied contexts of the Church in the world. This must also include a close relationship to the sacraments, as the Reformers' switching of terms from one to the other suggests. The relationship of Word to sacrament, however, remains problematic in practice, if not in theory, for the Reformed churches.

In the traditional exposition of the sacraments, we often find a generic definition of a sacrament followed by exposition of baptism and the Lord's Supper. This is true both of confessions and catechisms. These begin by defining what a sacrament is, before expounding the different senses in which both baptism and the Lord's Supper are sacramental. Despite their lucidity and precision, these statements also have their drawbacks. The generic account of a sacrament tended to emerge from eucharistic controversies about the nature of the real presence. The effect was somewhat Procrustean when baptism was presented as another species of the genus. Here, despite disclaimers, the effect of baptism was too tightly tied to the action of immersion or sprinkling in the threefold name. Thus the act of initiation became too easily detached from the context and subsequent activities which also mediated divine grace and without which the language of baptism made little sense.

In the case of the Lord's Supper, attention to and disputes over the sacramental nexus also contributed to a loss of the wider ethical significance of the sacrament, the 'as-so' connection described above. The regular reception of God's hospitality in the supper is closely linked in the New Testament to the hospitality that we are called to display towards others. Thus the link between eucharistic celebration and *diakonia* was arguably obscured in formal accounts of worship, but is robustly present in works such as Wolterstorff's *Until Justice and Peace Embrace*. This narrowing of sacramental focus may have been compounded by the tendency to infrequent celebration of the Lord's Supper, the arguments of Calvin and others notwithstanding. In the modern day Church of Scotland, though not perhaps in other traditions, we have a situation in which we can celebrate baptism too often and the Lord's Supper with insufficient frequency. This has led arguably to a situation of sermonic isolation where the preached Word remains as the focal point of the service but often without its prescribed link to the sacraments and remote from other forms of education and instruction. Since at least the late nineteenth century, a body of scholarship has urged the need for more frequent celebration of the Lord's Supper both in faithfulness to the convictions of Calvin and, even more importantly, to the wider ecumenical traditions of the Church catholic. The inertia of the Church of Scotland in relation to this theological consensus requires some explanation. In the early twenty-first century, this remains unfinished business.[190]

---

190 An earlier and somewhat different version of this chapter appeared as 'The Theology of Worship within the Reformed Tradition', in Michael Welker and Cynthia A. Jarvis, eds, *Loving God with our Minds: Festschrift for Wallace Alston*, Grand Rapids: Eerdmans, 2004, pp. 367–80.

5

WORD AND SACRAMENT IN REFORMED THEOLOGIES OF WORSHIP

A Free Church Perspective

Donald Macleod

Dr James Stewart prefaced his 1946 Warrack Lectures with the declaration that preaching had 'a basic and essential place at the very heart of Christian worship'.[191] This reflected Dr Stewart's own Reformed tradition, but its roots lay in the New Testament. As Rudolf Bultmann pointed out, in early Christian worship 'there is neither sacrifice nor priest, nor is it bound to holy places or times'. The 'word' dominated the service.[192] Jesus was primarily a preacher, his commission to the apostles placed a premium on proclamation (Matt. 28.19) and the greatest of them could even dare to say, 'Christ sent me not to baptize, but to preach the gospel' (1 Cor. 1.17). Not all of this preaching, of course, took place in a liturgical setting. Much of it was missionary preaching, often in public spaces and often opportunistic. But preaching was also clearly central when believers assembled together. The primary duty of presbyters was not to serve as priests at a sacramental altar, nor to serve as modern worship leaders, but to labour in preaching and teaching (1 Tim. 5.17).

The concern to ensure appropriate preaching dominated all the arrangements of the Reformed churches. Preaching was indeed a charismatic, Spirit-dependent activity, to be engaged in only by those with a divine call, but it also required natural gifts of intellect and communication. What was needed in the ministry was not primarily liturgical skill, but ability to explain the word of truth (2 Tim. 2.15). This was the impulse behind Calvin's Academy in Geneva, John Knox's vision of a school in every

---

191 James S. Stewart, *Heralds of God*, London: Hodder and Stoughton, 1946, p. 5.
192 Rudolf Bultmann, *Theology of the New Testament*, London, SCM Press, 1952, Vol. I, p. 121.

parish and the numerous Reformed theological seminaries, which sprang up in both the Old World and the New.

In Scotland, this traditional emphasis on the centrality of preaching came under severe pressure in the second half of the nineteenth century. One reason for this was the movement for liturgical reform stimulated by Dr Robert Lee and the Church Service Society. This provided an invaluable service in heightening liturgical awareness, but at the same time it prodded the Church in the direction of ritual, ceremonial and sacramentalism at the expense of preaching; and it did so under little theological control, taking its bearings from historic liturgical forms rather than from the New Testament.

But other factors were also at work to marginalize preaching. In the eyes of many, it was outmoded. Moderns had short concentration spans, they preferred pictures to words, they were profoundly suspicious of anything that smacked of rhetoric, and they wanted dialogue, not monologue. More fundamentally still, churchgoers themselves came to assume that a religious act must of necessity be one in which we speak to God, not one in which we listen to him speaking to us (an alternative liturgy which rests on the terrifying premise that what is being listened to actually *is* the Word of God). Sermons, if they had to be endured at all, must be short, snappy, topical and, ideally, funny.

Except, perhaps, in the smaller Presbyterian churches, located mainly in the Highlands. There, the sermon is still didactic, still central and still long (at least half an hour), and the moment a visitor enters the church the architecture tells her that here is a church committed to a liturgy of listening. The building is first and foremost an auditorium, and the pulpit absolutely dominant. The pews and the galleries are totally focused on it, and it is usually high: sometimes extremely so. There have even been occasions when preachers afflicted with vertigo have had to decline to use it. It also tends to be wide. Presbyterian preachers were not expected to be static. The gospel was to be preached with passion, and the messenger could not be confined to some tiny (and marginalized) crow's nest.

The other remarkable feature is less obvious. There is no communion table. Not only is there nothing resembling the modern communion table, reminiscent of an altar and hinting that the sacrament is really a sacrifice. There is no table at all: at least, not as a permanent feature. One will be produced for the occasion on Communion Sunday, but it will not be an item of standard furniture.

Yet it would be a mistake to imagine that the table doesn't matter. On the contrary it is central to Presbyterians' administration of the sacrament, and this reflected their understanding of the essential nature of the sacrament. It was not a sacrifice, but a supper. This puts the Presbyterian understanding at the furthest possible remove from the so-called Zwinglian. A meal feeds, and the Lord's Supper feeds. It is 'a means of grace' where Christ provides his people with spiritual nourishment.

But a meal or supper requires a table, and from the beginning this, and not an altar, was central to the Presbyterian order. Knox's Liturgy had the communicants sit at a table, the minister himself sitting with them, each communicant receiving from her neighbour the common loaf and the common cup, and then passing them on to her neighbour. The liturgical effect was an acted public *koinonia*: a mutuality of giving and receiving.

The centrality of the table continued long into the history of Presbyterianism. In fact, an Act of the General Assembly of 1645 making it obligatory to administer the sacrament around a table has never been rescinded. This is reflected in Presbyterian nomenclature, where 'the Lord's Table' became a standard designation of the sacrament and 'going to the Table' a standard phrase for taking Communion.

Such a liturgy did, however, create practical difficulties. Even large tables, or multiple tables arranged in the aisles, could seat only a limited number of people, with the result that in congregations of any size there had to be multiple sittings and, by implication, multiple comings and goings; and since each of the sittings had to be accompanied by preaching, the services could become wearisomely long. Many ministers must have found the arrangement irksome, but not till Thomas Chalmers (1780–1847) was anything done about it. In 1823, the last year of his ministry in St John's parish, Glasgow, Chalmers arranged for several rows of pews at the front of the church to be designated 'the Table', and demarcated with white linen. There the communicants sat; and though the innovation was controversial at the time, it prevailed, and this is still the pattern in the conservative Presbyterian congregations.

The use of a table inevitably had further liturgical implications. It is not unusual for the table (the linen-covered pews) to be empty at the beginning of the service, until, just before the distribution of the elements the minister invites the communicants to 'come forward'. This invitation usually includes a reminder that the table is not the preserve of any particular church or denomination. It is the Lord's Table, and all members of any branch of the Christian Church are welcome. From this point of view Presbyterian congregations have long practised the 'mutual Eucharistic hospitality' dreamed of in the 1977 Dialogue between the World Alliance of Reformed Churches and the Secretariat for Promoting Christian Unity.[193]

In terms of dramatic impact, this moment when communicants respond to the invitation to come forward can be one of the most impressive in

---

193 From the *Final Report of the Dialogue between the World Alliance of Reformed Churches and the Secretariat for Promoting Christian Unity*, 1977 (see Meyer and Vischer, eds, *Growth in Agreement*, Geneva: World Council of Churches, 1984, p. 456).

the Presbyterian service. While a psalm is sung, men and women (and children) rise from all over the church and come forward quietly and reverently to the table. In some respects it is the mirror image of the ancient *Missa est*, when catechumens were instructed to leave the service so that believers could celebrate the Eucharist in private. In this Presbyterian practice (never actually prescribed) the non-communicants remain seated. It is the communicants who rise, in a body, often leaving behind husband or wife, brother, sister or friend, and thereby declaring their spiritual marriage to another spouse and their kinship with another, heavenly family. The practice also explains why it is still common in the smaller Presbyterian churches to describe taking communion as 'going forward'. In this context, it is a very public act.

Throughout the service the link between Word and sacrament is clearly underlined. This is why the privilege of administering the sacrament is strictly reserved to ordained ministers of the Word. Yet this is not without its anomalies. For the last 200 years, the Presbyterian churches, reluctantly but of necessity, have made extensive use of lay preachers. Yet these men or women (they have mostly been men) are not permitted to administer the sacraments: a restriction which leaves these churches open to the charge of contradicting their own emphasis on the priority of the Word. How can someone who is deemed fit to perform the greater task (preaching the Word) be deemed unfit to perform the lesser task (administering the sacrament)?

The answer probably lies in the universal tendency to mystify the sacrament, a tendency which owes much to the Vulgate's fateful mistranslation of the Greek *mysterion* by the Latin *sacramentum* (Eph. 5.32). But it is also linked to another issue, little addressed: what exactly do we mean by 'administering' the sacrament? Ministers are not priests, representing Christ at an altar. Nor are they gifted with special powers such that their words can change the substance of the bread and wine and charge them with new virtue. Nor, in the Presbyterian order, is it their prerogative to distribute the elements. The communicants serve each other and the minister sits with them as a communicant.

What then? Their special position in relation to the sacrament derives entirely from the fact that they bring to the service the ministry of the Word. They lead the congregation in prayer. They read the Scriptures. And they preach.

The prayer is first and foremost a prayer of thanksgiving for the body of Christ, for which, at the Last Supper, he gave thanks, knowing it was soon to be broken. But it must also be Trinitarian, offering our thanks to the Spirit, through whom he offered himself, and to the Father, who gave him and who suffered his loss.

The term *epiclesis* is probably not one with which most ministers in the conservative Presbyterian churches are familiar; nor did the idea itself figure in such early Reformed liturgies as Knox's *Book of Common Order* or the 1662 Book of Common Prayer. Yet by the time of the Westminster Assembly an *epiclesis* seems to have been a well-established usage among Scottish Presbyterians and much favoured by English Puritans.[194] In accordance with this, the Westminster Confession (29.3) lays down that the minister is to 'bless the elements of bread and wine, and thereby to set them apart from a common to an holy use'. The *Directory for Public Worship* speaks to the same effect. The minister is earnestly to pray to God 'to vouchsafe his gracious presence, and the effectual working of his Spirit in us; and so to sanctify these elements both of bread and wine, and to bless his own ordinance, that we may receive by faith the body and blood of Christ'.

These references to 'setting apart from a common to a holy use' and 'blessing the elements of bread and wine' never came to be *de rigeur* in the Presbyterian liturgy, but they certainly did become widely prevalent. The danger is that the *epiclesis* may focus on the elements themselves and come to be seen as invoking (and indeed effecting) a change in the bread and wine. Behind this lurks a degree of impatience with the element of mystery in the sacrament. Presbyterians, no less than Roman Catholics, believe in the real presence of Christ in the Supper; and no less emphatically in the real efficacy of the sacrament. At the table, to adapt the language of Melanchthon, we receive Christ 'in his benefits'. The temptation we face is to explain both the presence and the efficacy in terms of a change in the elements, whether by the Roman Catholic idea of transubstantiation, Luther's concept of consubstantiation or some vague notion of a specific presence of Christ in the bread and wine.

The true *epiclesis* is one that calls down the Holy Spirit not on the elements, but on the sacrament: the sacrament as a whole. To some extent this is reflected in the *Directory for Public Worship*, which includes in its *epiclesis* a prayer for God's gracious presence and the working of his Spirit within us, as well as for the sanctifying of the bread and wine. The sacrament is always more than the elements, because the presence of the Father, the Son and the Holy Spirit is communicated to us not by the bread and wine in isolation, but by the communion service as a whole.

In the traditional Presbyterian order, one of the Scripture readings will be a version of the passion narrative, usually from the Gospels, but sometimes from such an Old Testament passage as the song of the suffering servant (Isaiah 52.12–53, reinforced, probably, by singing a portion of Psalm 22). This complies exactly with the directive given by St Paul: we

---

194 William D. Maxwell, *The Liturgical Portions of the Genevan Service Book*, London: Oliver and Boyd, 1931, p. 135.

are to 'proclaim' the Lord's death until he comes (1 Cor. 11.26). The verb *katangellein* is a strong one and it is unlikely that Paul intended to say only that the bread and wine symbolically set forth the death of Christ. It is more likely that from the beginning it had been the practice to include in the Supper an account of the events leading up to the crucifixion: first, no doubt, an oral account but, later, one or other of those 'orderly accounts' to which Luke refers in the preface to his Gospel (Luke 1.2) This accords with the oft-repeated observation that the Gospels are 'passion narratives with extended introductions'; and it is in the context of that narrative, with both its historical and its eschatological dimensions ('until he comes') that the Eucharist is celebrated.

The other indispensable reading is the narrative of institution. In the traditional Presbyterian order this is the *warrant* for the Lord's Supper (bearing in mind the Protestant concern that a sacrament must be of divine institution: a sentiment which led to Communion being designated *an t-ordugh* [the Ordinance] in the Gaelic community). It is this warrant that constitutes the bread and wine signs and seals of the body and blood of Christ. 'Take away the word,' said Augustine, referring to baptism, 'and the water is neither more nor less than water. The word is added to the element, and there results the Sacrament, as if itself also a kind of visible word.'[195] This is no less true of the Lord's Supper. Apart from the Word, the bread is mere bread, the wine mere wine, but by warrant of the words of institution, they cease to be 'common'. The bread becomes *this* bread, the cup *this* cup (1 Cor. 11.26). This does not mean that either is changed into something else, but that both are charged with new significance; and not with a *mere* significance, but with a *potent* significance, so that by the blessing of the divine Spirit (already invoked in the *epiclesis*) they impart and convey the grace that they signify.

Yet it is not enough that the Word be read. It must be preached, so that, as Calvin insists, the people can celebrate 'with true intelligence', understanding what the visible sign means. 'The sacraments,' he writes, 'take their virtue from the Word, when it is preached intelligibly';[196] and again, 'You see how the sacrament requires preaching to beget faith.'[197] This insistence that instruction (and hence understanding) must accompany the sacrament was equally clear in the *First Book of Discipline*, which laid down that the sacrament is rightly administered only when 'the people, before the administration of the same, are plainly instructed and put in mind of God's free grace and mercie, offered unto the penitent in Christ

---

195 *Homilies on the Gospel of John*, Tractate 80.3 (*Nicene and Post-Nicene Fathers*, first series, reprinted 1991, Edinburgh: T&T Clark, Vol. 7, p. 344).

196 J. K. S. Reid, ed., *Calvin: Tracts and Treatises*, London: SCM Press, 1954, p. 161.

197 Calvin, *Institutes of the Christian Religion*, trans. Ford Lewis Battles, ed. John T. McNeill, Philadelphia: Westminster Press, 1960, IV.14.

Jesus'.[198] This, as Maxwell points out,[199] was once carried to such lengths in Scotland that in some congregations the doors were locked prior to the sacrament to ensure that no one who had not heard the sermon would come to the table. Things were never carried to such an extreme within the conservative Presbyterian churches, but within living memory it was certainly very much frowned on for someone to come to the table without attending the preparatory services.

Yet this link between the sacrament and preaching is no peculiarity of Presbyterianism. It goes back, ultimately, to the importance of 'discerning' (*diakrinon*) the body, as laid down by St Paul (1 Cor. 11.29), but it was also highlighted in the ecumenical dialogues of the twentieth century, which made plain 'a common concern for the integration of word and sacrament in the liturgy'.[200] The key factor here is that the Word and the sacrament are not two distinct services, but one. As was pointed out in the Lima (1982) Report, *Baptism, Eucharist and Ministry*, the Eucharist 'always includes both word and sacrament'. The same Report continued: 'Since the *anamnesis* of Christ is the very content of the preached Word as it is of the Eucharistic meal, each reinforces the other. The celebration of the Eucharist properly includes the proclamation of the Word.'[201] It follows, therefore, that 'there should be no celebration of the Eucharist that does not include the Ministry of the Word'.[202]

This is strong language, but the degree of ecumenical convergence on this link between word and sacrament is remarkable. The 1965 Faith and Order study from which the last quotation is taken was conducted by representatives from the Anglican, Lutheran, Methodist, Orthodox, Reformed and United Churches, with three Roman Catholic consultants. This is an interesting reminder that the Order for the Lord's Supper followed by the smaller Presbyterian churches is neither sectarian nor antiquated. It lies clearly and firmly within the age-old, and still vibrant, liturgical tradition of Western Christianity; and precisely because it does so, it cherishes the link between the sacrament and the Word. Indeed, the Presbyterian Supper includes a feast of preaching: the Action Sermon, the fencing of the table and short pre- and post-Communion addresses.

The sermon preached on a Communion Sunday has its own specific designation: 'the Action Sermon'. The reason for this is not that it is

---

198 James K. Cameron, ed., *The First Book of Discipline*, Edinburgh: St Andrew Press, 1972, p. 90.

199 Maxwell, *Liturgical Portions of Genevan Service Book*, p. 143.

200 C. B. Naylor, 'Eucharistic Theology Today', in R. E. Clements, ed., *Eucharistic Theology Then and Now*, London: SPCK, 1968, p. 114.

201 See Meyer and Vischer, *Growth in Agreement*, pp. 476–7.

202 Naylor, 'Eucharistic Theology Today', p. 114, quoting 'A Faith and Order study on the Eucharist conducted in 1965'.

preparatory to some human action (such as distributing the elements). It is rooted in ancient Latin usage, and particularly in the phrase *gratiarum actio,* 'thanksgiving', which in turn goes back to the narrative of institution as recorded in the Vulgate, where the Greek *eucharistesas* (1 Cor. 11.24) is rendered, naturally enough, *gratiis actis*. The Action Sermon is quite simply, then, the eucharistic sermon. As such, it is itself part of the act of Thanksgiving. This gives an interesting sequence: the preaching perpetuates remembrance and the remembrance evokes thanksgiving.

This is why in the Presbyterian communion service the Action Sermon was (and still is) expected to focus on the incarnation and death of Christ. It is deliberately didactic, and sometimes profoundly so, setting forth not only the facts of the cross, but also the doctrine (*logos,* 1 Cor. 1.18) which explains those facts. It proclaims the priestly work of Christ as the divine Son who offered himself as an expiatory and propitiatory sacrifice; and who did so as the One who, in Barth's terms, became the Judge judged in our place, suffering not merely *with* us, but *for* us.[203] The primary movement of this priestly act is God-ward, Christ offering himself without blemish to God (Heb. 9.14), but the Scottish Action Sermon remembered that there was also a priesthood of God the Father. Preached as an expression of *his* love, the cross has a powerful human-ward impact: a 'moral influence' which explains the 'meltings' which were so often a feature of the great Communion gatherings.

The Action Sermon is followed by the preacher's fencing of the table. On the first hearing, this is horrific. What right do we have to put a fence around a divine ordinance? The word 'fencing', however, was used in seventeenth-century Scotland as a technical term for 'constituting' a court, and occurs in this sense several times in, for example, Rutherford's *Letters*. Sometimes he uses it metaphorically, of his own soul-searching, and writes, 'I know not if this court kept within my soul be fenced in Christ's name.' But on other occasions the reference is a court of formal human jurisdiction, probably the Court of High Commission: 'When the Devil fenceth a bastard-court in my Lord's ground, and giveth me forged summons, it will be my shame to disbelieve'.[204]

Taken in this light, the fencing may have meant 'constituting' the Lord's Table. Everything was made ready for the communicants and everything was in place for the Lord to come and preside. This might even be extended to suggest that the Supper is the place where the Lord holds court. One can easily imagine a man like Rutherford viewing the sacrament as the royal court of King Jesus.

---

203 Karl Barth, *Church Dogmatics*, vol. IV.1, Edinburgh: T&T Clark, 1956, pp. 211–83.

204 Andrew Bonar, ed., *Letters of Samuel Rutherford*, Edinburgh: Banner of Truth Trust, 1984, pp. 163, 228.

In truth, however, Rutherford does not seem to have applied the word 'fence' to the Lord's Supper, and, whatever its origin, the term came to refer to the point in the service where the scandalous and profane were warned against coming to the table lest they eat and drink judgement to themselves. This was decidedly the case in the Highlands, where the phrase, 'fencing the table' became in Gaelic, *A' cur gàradh mu'n a bhòrd:* literally, 'putting a fence around the table'.

But even here there was nothing distinctive in Presbyterianism. Exhortations to self-examination, along with warnings against profaning the sacrament, have been standard features of the order for Communion from the beginning. The exhortation prescribed in the Book of Common Prayer is typical:

> For as the benefit is great, if with a true penitent heart and lively faith we receive that holy Sacrament ... so is the danger great if we receive the same unworthily. For then we are guilty of the Body and Blood of Christ our Saviour; we eat and drink our own damnation, not considering the Lord's Body; we kindle God's wrath against us; we provoke him to plague us with divers diseases, and sundry kinds of death.

This is as fearsome as any Presbyterian fencing.

The legendary paucity of communicants in the Highlands probably had little to do with the fencings, though it would be vain to argue that they were never too severe and never discouraging. Yet the word 'fencing' was inherently misleading, and in any case the last thing a Scottish communion table needed was a fence. The exhortation had to move, therefore, from warning the profane to encouraging the saints, and from warning of the danger of coming unworthily to warning of the even greater danger of not coming at all. The duty of self-examination remains, of course. It is, after all, an apostolic directive. But what is crucially important is that we are to examine ourselves in the light of the purpose for which the sacrament was instituted: to provide an appointed place of feasting, remembrance and thanksgiving. As such it is for all who are spiritually hungry, for all to whom the memory of Christ is dear and for all whose hearts resonate to the simple words,

Thank you, O my Father
for giving us your Son[205]

Pre- and post-communion addresses have a long pedigree, going back to the days of Robert Bruce (1554–1631) and Alexander Henderson (1583–

---

205 Words from the modern hymn *There is a Redeemer* by Melody Green, © 1982 Birdwing Music/Cherry Lane Music/Alliance Media/CopyCare Ltd.

1646), and are still part of the normal order in the conservative Presby-
terian churches. Usually brief, the pre-communion address continues the
Passion theme, while the address after communion focuses either on some
Christian duty or on some aspect of the Christian hope.

But while the elements are being distributed there is silence. Maxwell
refers to this as an unhelpful modern innovation unknown to the old
Catholic and Reformed rites,[206] and it is indeed true that the norm in these
rites was for Scripture to be read or a psalm sung while the communicants
were partaking of the elements. We must bear in mind, however, that in
the Presbyterian order there has already been a good deal of reading, singing and preaching: sometimes, indeed, a surfeit of the human voice. The
moment of *anamnesis* is surely an appropriate one for silent meditation. A
great congregation hushed in thanksgiving is a fitting climax to a liturgy
of palpable reverence.

The intimate link between the Eucharist and preaching has a direct
bearing on two urgent practical questions.

First, taking the sacrament to the sick and the housebound. Here, everything depends on what is meant by 'taking'. If it means simply bringing
the elements to the sickbed after they have been consecrated in church, this
carries us far beyond the Reformed understanding of the Supper. It implies
that some change has occurred in the bread and wine, and that as a result
they possess in themselves some quasi-magical properties. Nothing short
of a full-blown doctrine of transubstantiation can justify such an assumption. So long as the bread remains bread and the wine remains wine, there
is no point in merely carrying the elements from one place to another.

But the practice also puts pressure on the link between the sacrament
and preaching. Of course, the preaching need not be elaborate. It may
even, in the circumstances, be brief and minimal (the words of institution,
plus a few words of explanation). But some Word there must be, since the
elements themselves do not constitute a sacrament.

Yet this is no reason to keep the sacrament from the sick and the housebound. It is merely to say that it must be done decently and in order, and
the best way to ensure this is to have the church publicly celebrate Communion in the home of the sick person. What this might mean is illustrated in a *Manual of Forms* drafted by the nineteenth-century American
Presbyterian theologian, Archibald Hodge. The *Manual* takes for granted
that, 'the Lord's Supper is not to be received by any one alone', but it
continues:

Yet in cases of protracted sickness or approaching death, when the
desire is strongly urged by a member of the church to enjoy the admin-

---

206 Maxwell, *Liturgical Portions of Genevan Service Book*, p. 139.

istration of the Lord's Supper, a pastor, with one or more of his session and such communicants as may appropriately be admitted, may proceed to administer the sacrament.[207]

There remain, however, certain clear parameters. The minister must be accompanied by representatives of the eldership, the service must be publicly intimated and open, and the distribution of the elements must be accompanied by appropriate preaching. The bread and wine are brought, fresh, for the purpose (thus relieving the minister of the slightly comic problem of having to get the sacrament to the sick before the 'consecrated' bread turns stale); and the prayer of thanksgiving and *epiclesis* is offered on the understanding that this is a completely new service, and not merely an extension of one previously held in church.

The link between the sacrament and preaching is also relevant to the widely canvassed aspiration to 'put the sacrament at the heart of parish life'. This aspiration, too, is subject to several constraints. The sacrament can be put at the centre of parish life only if, first of all, it is 'rightly administered'. We are not authorized to invent new ways of making the sacrament interesting; and we certainly cannot proceed on the basis that some novelties may double the attendance. To move from its prescribed form is to destroy its power as *anamnesis*.

But even more important is the consideration that before we put the sacrament at the centre of parish life we must put the Word at the centre of parish life. The sacrament is not a converting ordinance. It is for believers. This is not to say that it never converts. An earthquake may convert (Acts 16.26), but that is not its purpose. The canonical order is clear in Acts 2.42. The 3,000 converted at Pentecost devoted themselves to the breaking of bread, but only because, first of all, they had welcomed the apostolic message and been baptized. Mission must begin with the evangel, not with the sacrament.

Yet, by the same token preaching must lead to the sacraments. The goal of Christian mission is not simply to make disciples, but to baptize them (Matthew 28.19); and, by a natural progression, the baptized proceed to the Lord's Table. Irritating though it may be to modern Western individualism, outside the Church (and, by implication, outside the Table), there is no salvation. We are a community united in giving and receiving. But we are also a community united in celebration, feasting upon the one great sacrifice. In both respects, the Table defines us.

---

207 Alexander A. Hodge, *Manual of Forms Conformed to the Practice and Discipline of the Presbyterian Church*, Philadelphia: Presbyterian Board of Publication, 1882, pp. 41–2.

6

BAPTISMAL THEOLOGY AND PRACTICE IN THE CHURCH OF SCOTLAND

Paul Nimmo

Introduction

The history of baptismal theology and practice in the Church of Scotland has for long periods been a rather uneventful one. There were certainly upheavals in sacramental theology at the time of the Reformation, even if baptismal practice itself was not significantly altered, but in the period between the Reformation and the 1950s, the Church's understanding of baptism remained largely unaltered. In recent decades, however, there have been a number of significant developments in the baptismal praxis of the Church of Scotland, with the result that the contemporary baptismal landscape of the Church has a very different appearance.

This chapter surveys the development of the theology and practice of baptism in the Church of Scotland since its inception. The first section of the chapter charts the Reformed beginnings of the Church's view of baptism through an examination of its historical confessions. The second section assesses the landmark work of Thomas F. Torrance and the Church's Special Commission on Baptism in the 1950s, considering in particular the theological relationship between Torrance and Karl Barth in respect of the doctrine. The final section reviews the development of the Church's theology and practice of baptism from the 1950s to the present day.

Baptismal Theology and Practice in the Reformation

At the time of the Reformation in Scotland, the baptismal theology and practice of the Church of Scotland was established and recorded in the

Scots Confession, written in the year of the Church's foundation in 1560. This confession links the sacraments of the new covenant (baptism and communion) to the sacraments of the old covenant (circumcision and the passover), and accords them the following functions:

> to make ane visible difference betwixt his people and they that wes without his league ... to exerce the faith of his Children, and ... to seill in their hearts the assurance of his promise, and of that most blessed conjunction, union and societie, quhilk the elect have with their head *Christ Jesus*.[208]

In respect of baptism in particular, the Scots Confession posits that by it 'we ar ingrafted in *Christ Jesus*, to be made partakers of his justice, be quhilk our sinnes ar covered and remitted' (*Conf. Scot.* xxi). The sacraments, then, are more than 'naked and bair Signes'; it is maintained that while 'wee will nether worship the Signes, in place of that quhilk is signified be them, nether zit doe we dispise, and interpret them as unprofitable and vaine' (*Conf. Scot.* xxi). The Scots Confession thus strikes a certain middle road theologically, between understanding baptism and its elements as merely symbolic and considering the baptismal water in itself to have power.[209]

The baptismal practice of the Scots Confession conforms to its theology, with the concept of 'rycht administratioun' particularly prominent. The sacraments correspondingly had to be 'ministrat be lauchful Ministers ... [and] in sik elements, and in sik sort, as God hes appoynted' (*Conf. Scot.* xxii). The Scots Confession also insisted that 'Baptisme apperteinis asweil to the infants of the faithfull, as unto them that be of age and discretion' (*Conf. Scot.* xxiii). In reality, however, baptism in the Church of Scotland generally pertained *only* to infants, as had been the unquestioned norm in the Western Church as a whole for over a millennium.[210] Indeed, perhaps the most noticeable legislation of baptismal practice stemmed from the

---

208 'Confessio Fidei Scoticana' (1560), in Philip Schaff, ed., *The Creeds of Christendom. With a History and Critical Notes*, Vol. III, *The Evangelical Protestant Creeds*, 6th edn, Grand Rapids, MI: Baker Books, repr. 1998, pp. 437–479, chapter xxi. Further references to the Scots Confession are given in the main text.

209 J. H. S. Burleigh observes in this connection that the language of the Scots Confession becomes 'most fiercely polemical' as it inveighs against both merely symbolic and Roman Catholic understandings of the sacraments, *A Church History of Scotland*, Edinburgh: Hope Trust, 1988, p. 158.

210 Indeed, in 'John Knox's Liturgy' (confirmed by the General Assembly of the Church of Scotland in 1562), the only order of service for baptism given was for an infant: see 'The Book of Common Order', in *The Book of Common Order of the Church of Scotland and The Directory for the Public Worship of God*, Edinburgh and London: William Blackwood and Sons, 1868, chapter XVI, 'The Order of Baptism', pp. 135–49.

insistence in *The Book of Common Order* (1562), in line with the practice of the Reformation churches more generally, that baptism was 'not
ordained of God to be used in private corners ... but left to the Congregation, and necessarily annexed to God's Word'.[211]

The understanding of baptism evidenced in the Scots Confession attests the great influence on John Knox and the Scottish Reformation of
the thinking of John Calvin. In his *Institutes of the Christian Religion* of
1559, Calvin defines a sacrament as

> an outward sign by which the Lord seals on our consciences the prom-
> ises of his good will toward us in order to sustain the weakness of our
> faith; and we in turn attest our piety toward him in the presence of the
> Lord and of his angels and before men.[212]

The key elements of this definition – the promise of God, the faith of the
Christian and the visible testimony – correspond exactly to the definition
in the Scots Confession cited above, and Calvin also anticipates the Scots
Confession in stressing the unity of the covenant, and particularly the con-
nection between the sacraments of the old and new covenants (IV.14.23).
Moreover, when Calvin turns to baptism in particular, we find the same
key scriptural imagery of 'engrafting into Christ' as is attested in the Scots
Confession:

> Baptism is the sign of the initiation by which we are received into the
> society of the church, in order that, engrafted in Christ, we may be reck-
> oned among God's children. Now baptism was given to us by God for
> these ends ... first, to serve our faith before him; secondly, to serve our
> confession before men. (IV.15.1)

Calvin continues from this opening definition to outline three ways in
which baptism is conducive to Christian faith. First, he writes, 'the Lord
sets out ... that baptism should be a token and proof of our cleansing;
... like a sealed document to confirm to us that all our sins are ... abolished, remitted, and effaced' (IV.15.1). Second, Calvin continues, baptism 'shows us our mortification in Christ, and new life in him' (IV.15.5).
Lastly, Calvin observes, 'our faith receives from baptism the advantage of

---

211 *The Book of Common Order*, p. 135. Despite this, private baptism was a common
practice in the Church of Scotland over the ensuing centuries, even after it was once again
condemned in 1690 by an act of the General Assembly – see Henry Sefton, 'Revolution to
Disruption', in Duncan Forrester and Douglas Murray, eds, *Studies in the History of Worship
in Scotland*, 2nd edn, Edinburgh: T&T Clark, 1996, p. 80.

212 John Calvin, *Institutes of the Christian Religion*, tr. Ford Lewis Battles, Philadelphia:
Westminster Press, 1960, IV.14.1. Further references to the *Institutes* are given in the main
text.

its sure testimony to us that we are not only engrafted into the death and life of Christ, but so united to Christ himself that we become sharers in all his blessings' (IV.15.6). It is therefore clear that, for Calvin, 'all the gifts of God proffered in baptism are found in Christ alone' (IV.15.6).

At this point, however, Calvin's theology reaches a troublesome juncture. Having so stressed the role of Christian faith in the sacraments in general and in baptism in particular, Calvin requires an alternative justification for the baptism of infants for, as David F. Wright notes, Calvin was 'utterly determined ... that infant baptism be not only preserved but also administered as universally as possible'.[213] Calvin therefore invokes a parallel between Christian baptism and Jewish circumcision: while the outward ceremony in each case is very different, nevertheless the promise, the thing represented, the foundation, and the inner mystery are the same (IV.16.4).[214] The underlying reason for this correspondence is the unity and continuity of the covenant, for the promise of God is not only to the parent, but also to the child, 'even to the thousandth generation' (IV.16.9). Children – that is, the 'children of believers' (IV.15.22) – are therefore to be baptized 'into future repentance and faith, and even though these have not yet been formed in them, the seed of both lies hidden within them by the secret working of the Spirit' (IV.16.20).[215]

In the much later 1646 Westminster Confession of Faith, which remains a subordinate standard of faith for the Church of Scotland, Calvin's theology of the sacraments is followed closely.[216] That noted, Thomas F. Torrance contends that there were certain differences of emphasis between the Westminster Confession on the one hand and the work of Calvin and the older Scottish tradition on the other at this point. He argues that, for the Westminster Confession, the sacraments 'are not seals of the Word of the Gospel, but seals of faith in the Gospel', and that while the sacraments are therefore 'seals of the covenant of grace ... the evangelical character and range of that covenant are restricted'.[217] In particular, suggests Torrance, this particular emphasis on the covenant, in accordance with the prevailing

---

213 David F. Wright, *Infant Baptism in Historical Perspective: Collected Studies*, Milton Keynes: Paternoster, 2007, p. xxxi.

214 In this point, Calvin was directly followed not only by the Scots Confession, as noted above, but also by John Knox himself (see Thomas F. Torrance, *Scottish Theology: From John Knox to John McLeod Campbell*, Edinburgh: T&T Clark, 1996, p. 36) and by Craig's Catechism of 1581, in Thomas F. Torrance, ed., *The School of Faith: The Catechisms of the Reformed Church*, London: James Clarke, 1959, p. 153.

215 This concept of 'the seed of faith' is not unproblematic theologically, and it becomes even more problematic in view of Calvin's doctrine of predestination: after all, if an infant is one of the elect anyway, then baptism will not affect her election in any way; whereas if an infant is reprobate at the outset, then no amount of baptismal immersion will help.

216 John W. Riggs, *Baptism in the Reformed Tradition: An Historical and Practical Theology*, Louisville and London: Westminster John Knox Press, 2002, pp. 84–5.

217 Torrance, *Scottish Theology*, p. 146.

federal theology, leads the sacrament of baptism 'to be regarded as a con-tractual union demanding a contractual response'.[218] One small but per-haps significant material change occurs in respect of the theology of infant baptism. While advocating infant baptism along similar covenantal lines to Calvin, the Westminster Confession eschews Calvin's concept of 'a seed of faith', and links the efficacy of the sacrament of baptism directly with election. It thereby explains the efficacy of infant baptism by recourse to the divine will: 'grace promised is not only offered, but really exhibited and conferred by the Holy Ghost, to such (whether of age or infants) as that grace belongeth unto, according to the counsel of God's own will, in his appointed time'.[219]

Such, then, are the Reformation and post-Reformation documents that most influenced the theology and practice of baptism in the Church of Scotland in the following centuries.

The Special Commission on Baptism

In the eighteenth and nineteenth centuries, as previously, the normal bap-tismal practice in the Church of Scotland was infant baptism, founded on a covenant theology and involving the parents taking baptismal vows on behalf of their children. Eligibility for baptism was governed by a General Assembly Act of 1712, which stated that 'Children born, within the Verge of the visible Church, of Parents one or both professing the Christian Religion, have a Right to Baptism.'[220] Provision was made for exceptional cases: but the Act stipulated that baptism was explicitly the 'Right' of the child of a Christian parent.

The Act of 1712 remained unaltered for over 200 years, but was then progressively clarified and supplemented in a series of further Acts. In 1933, an Act of the General Assembly required that one or both of the parents who 'profess the Christian religion' had themselves to be bap-tized, or, if the parents were unknown or absent, that the child was 'under Christian care and guardianship'.[221] And in 1951, a further Act specified that one or both parents had to be Church members, who 'earnestly desire that their child may be baptized, and undertake the Christian upbringing

---

218 Torrance, *Scottish Theology*, p. 148. In passing, one might argue that Torrance was opposing something of a caricature of federal theology at this point, cf. his brief outline of the matter in *Scottish Theology*, pp. x–xi. I am grateful to John Scott for his insights in this connection.

219 *The Westminster Confession of Faith* (1646), Edinburgh: T&T Clark, 1881, xxviii.6 (p. 152). The question of whether this recourse to an eternal and inscrutable divine will represents an advance over Calvin in the area of baptismal theology will not be addressed here.

220 Quoted in *Reports to the General Assembly* (hereafter *RGA*) (2002), p. 13/16.

221 *The Acts of the General Assembly* (hereafter *AGA*) (1933), p. 38.

of the child'.[222] If these demands were satisfied, then the baptism of the infant remained a 'right'.

This progressive shift in baptismal legislation, while not indicating a great shift in baptismal theology, evidenced that the Church of Scotland was facing both a growing diversity of baptismal practice in its parishes and a correspondingly growing frustration with the failure of successive Acts of the General Assembly to address it. There was an underlying fear, explicitly expressed in an overture to the General Assembly in 1953, that this diversity marked 'a diversity of belief as to the meaning of Baptism'.[223] The same overture called for the General Assembly to 'appoint a Special Commission to carry out a fresh examination of the Doctrine of Baptism, and ... to stimulate and guide such thought and study throughout the Church as may lead to theological agreement and uniform practice'.[224]

To this end, the General Assembly in 1953 set up a Special Commission on Baptism, convened by Thomas F. Torrance. Over the following years, it produced a landmark series of comprehensive reports on baptismal theology and practice in the New Testament and in the history of the Church, ultimately offering up a contemporary statement of the doctrine of baptism for the Church of Scotland.[225] It was produced in 1962, but was ultimately accepted by the General Assembly of 1963 as a 'valid statement' of the doctrine rather than, as the Panel and many others had desired, as its 'authoritative interpretation'.[226]

The Commission Report echoes both the Scots Confession and Calvin in a number of ways. It is strongly centred on Christ and his benefits, positing that the 'meaning' of baptism 'lies in Christ himself' and that baptism 'directs us and our children to the saving act of God's love which he has already fulfilled for us in Jesus Christ' (SCR, p. 224). Moreover, it emphasizes the baptismal image of the ingrafting of the Christian into Christ and of the union with Christ that baptism thereby effects (SCR, p. 226). Furthermore, the three ways in which Calvin found baptism to be conducive to faith are all prominent: it sets forth 'what God in Christ has done, is doing, and will do for us' (SCR, p. 224); it allows us to 'share in his life and in all that he has done for us', including his death, resurrection, and ascension (SCR, p. 226); and it 'makes the individual share in the fruit of Christ's finished work' (SCR, p. 226).

---

222 AGA (1951), p. 31.

223 Quoted in RGA (1962), p. 709.

224 Quoted in RGA (1962), p. 709.

225 The Report of the Special Commission on Baptism appeared in RGA (1962), pp. 709–23; its final version was published in 1966 (as The Doctrine of Baptism, Edinburgh: Saint Andrew Press, 1966), and reappeared – this time in more inclusive language – in RGA (1991), pp. 224–30. It is the latter version which is cited in this chapter; further references to the Special Commission Report (SCR) are given in the main text.

226 RGA (2002), p. 13/15.

However, the Commission Report seems to move into fresh theological terrain for the Church of Scotland in its contention that 'There is thus *One Baptism* ... Christ and the Church participate in the One Baptism in different ways – Christ actively and vicariously as Redeemer, the Church passively and receptively as the redeemed community' (*SCR*, p. 224).[227] In this way, as Bryan D. Spinks notes, 'the doctrine of Baptism was given a firm Christological basis, and the one baptism of Christ and its salvific implications were ... the hermeneutical key to unlock subsequent discussion'.[228] 'In Baptism,' the Report observes, 'it is Christ himself who acts, uniting the baptised to himself, who once and for all united himself to humanity in his incarnation' (*SCR*, p. 226). At the same time, the Report subsequently continues, '[T]hrough sharing in his Spirit we are made members of his Body and are admitted into the visible fellowship of his Church' (*SCR*, p. 226). Baptism is therefore not so much about what the individual does or even what the church does, but about what God has done in Christ and continues to do through the Spirit (*SCR*, p. 226). There is thus a fundamental human passivity in the event of baptism: 'our part is only to receive [baptism], for we cannot add to Christ's finished work' (*SCR*, p. 226).

This is not to ignore the context of baptism, however. The Commission Report reiterates that both the act and the relationship as a whole take place within the fellowship of the Church, that corporate fellowship of the baptized faithful (*SCR*, p. 228). Baptism is only to be administered where there is 'provision, promise, and assurance that the baptised will be brought up in the family of God and instructed in the Christian faith' (*SCR*, p. 230).

Given the passivity of baptism emphasized in the Commission Report, and its reference to the biblical accounts of Jesus receiving and blessing little children and of the apostles teaching that children also belong to

---

227 Indeed, the 1955 (interim) Report quoted J. A. T. Robinson to the effect that 'In the New Testament the Sacrament of Baptism and the Vicarious Baptism of Christ are spoken of so indivisibly that it is impossible to distinguish what has been done for us by the Cross and resurrection and what by the Sacrament of that Baptism,' *RGA* (1955), p. 618, which particular report was later published separately as *The Biblical Doctrine of Baptism*, Edinburgh: St Andrew Press, 1958. This exegesis has not been uncontroversial: see, for example, the criticism by Wright in *Infant Baptism in Historical Perspective*, pp. 270, 293 and 305, the disagreement of James D. G. Dunn in *Baptism in the Holy Spirit*, Louisville: Westminster / John Knox Press, 1977, p. 6, and the observation in response by Iain R. Torrance in 'Fear of being left out and confidence in being included: The liturgical celebration of ecclesial boundaries', in Bryan Spinks and Iain Torrance, eds, *To Glorify God*, Edinburgh: T&T Clark, 1999, pp. 161–2, especially footnote 3.

228 Bryan D. Spinks, '"Freely by His Grace": Baptismal Doctrine and the Reform of the Baptismal Liturgy in the Church of Scotland, 1953–1994', in Nathan Mitchell and John F. Baldovin, eds, *Rule of Prayer, Rule of Faith*, Collegeville, Minnesota: Liturgical Press, 1996, p. 221.

the household of faith, it is no surprise that the Commission proceeds to endorse infant baptism. It argues that little children are to be baptized, 'in reliance upon the promise that belongs to them as well as to us, and in expectation that [Jesus] will bless them now as he did then' (SCR, p. 226). This baptismal direction for infants is, however, limited to the community of faith: children are only to be baptized when their 'parents or guardians are within the life and discipline of the Church' (SCR, p. 230). While there is an explicit acknowledgement that 'Baptism and faith belong inseparably together,' this is followed by the qualification that 'it is not upon our faith or our own faithfulness that we rely, but upon Christ alone and upon his faithfulness' (SCR, p. 228). It is therefore through grace alone that baptism 'covenants us to a life of faith and obedience to the Father in Jesus Christ, and calls us to faith and obedience as long as we live' (SCR p. 228). The parallel between baptism and circumcision, while mentioned by the Commission Report (SCR, p. 227), plays no explicit role in the justification of infant baptism. This in turn means that, in contrast to Calvin, the theology which governs infant baptism is not different from the theology that governs adult baptism: there is only one baptismal theology presented.[229]

Theologically, then, the Commission Report seems to shift the balance of emphasis from the covenant with Christ to the person of Christ: from the promises made by those undergoing baptism (or, more normally, their parents) to the promises fulfilled by Jesus Christ. It thus seems to attempt to banish any trace of legalism in its understanding of the covenant, in an effort to locate the true meaning of baptism in grace alone.[230]

Although the Commission Report did not become the authoritative interpretation of the sacrament, it was nevertheless accompanied by a new Act of the General Assembly which replaced the previous Acts on baptism.[231] This Act attempted to put an end to the foregoing diversity of baptismal practice in the Church of Scotland. The Act read:

> Baptism may be administered to a child – (1) whose parents, one or both, have themselves been baptized, are in full communion with the Church, and undertake the Christian upbringing of the child ... (3) whose parents, one or both, have themselves been baptized, profess the

---

229 The Special Commission does allow for the baptism of adult converts, albeit 'not ... as a seal of the believer's decision of faith, but only as a seal of the promises of Christ' (SCR, p. 228). Explicit legal provision for the baptism of 'an unbaptized adult upon personal profession of faith', however, was only finally made by the Church of Scotland in 2000, cf. RGA (2002), pp. 13/19 and 13/20.

230 Once again, it may be that the Commission Report's apparent desire to remove all traces of federal theology rested on a very particular understanding of federal theology itself.

231 Wright, Infant Baptism in Historical Perspective, p. 305.

Christian faith, undertake to ensure that such child grows up in the life and worship of the Church and express the desire to seek admission to full membership in the Church.[232]

The most important amendment in this Act is that the language of the 'right' of a child to baptism has been removed – it may, after all, seem difficult to speak of a child's 'rights' in face of the grace of God. Instead, the qualifications for baptism are on the part of the parents, namely that they both be 'in full communion' with the Church of Scotland.

While the Commission Report demands that baptism be 'administered in a form which accords with its biblical institution and meaning' (*SCR*, p. 229), it also demands that, whether it is received as a child or as an adult, baptism be 'administered with the same doctrine and in the same essential form' (*SCR*, p. 230). No mention of this is made in the Act, however, and no provision is made for the baptism of adults: infant baptism retained its normative status. Indeed Spinks considers that the Act did little more than to reiterate the previous Acts, and did not reflect the new emphases of the Commission report.[233]

It is interesting at this juncture to consider briefly the relationship between the theology of the Special Commission Report and the theology of Karl Barth, the most significant Reformed theologian of the twentieth century and a theologian with whom Thomas F. Torrance had significant interactions and engagements.

There are many correspondences between the doctrine of baptism in Barth's *Church Dogmatics* and the baptismal theology of the Commission Report. First, Barth similarly believes that 'Jesus Christ is the origin, theme and content of Christian baptism as of Christian faith'.[234] Second, Barth also strongly emphasizes in his doctrine of baptism the prevenience of divine grace in the Christian life, noting that 'The Christian life begins

---

232 Quoted in *RGA* (1991), p. 231. In case (3), a District Elder would be appointed by the Kirk Session 'to shepherd them into full communion and to exercise pastoral care of the child concerned', quoted in *RGA* (1991), p. 231. Cases (2) and (4) cover the situations of adherents and of orphans respectively.

233 Spinks, '"Freely by His Grace"', p. 229. Moreover, Spinks contends, the new baptismal rites drawn up in 1968 in light of the Report embodied on the part of the Kirk 'a loss of nerve': 'There remained a sharp divide between the *Lex credendi* of the reports and the *Lex orandi* of the revised liturgy,' '"Freely by His Grace"', p. 232. Moreover, Spinks posits, the later 1979 liturgy retreated from the few textual gains made in 1968 (p. 233); it was only with the 1986 liturgy that the pre-Special Commission federal theology was removed and the unilateral covenant of grace was emphasized (pp. 236–7); and it was in the 1994 liturgy that the grace freely given through the vicarious work of Jesus Christ (and thus the theology of the Special Commission) was fully reflected in the baptismal liturgy of the Church of Scotland (p. 241).

234 Karl Barth, *Church Dogmatics*, Vol. IV, Part 4 (IV/4), tr. Geoffrey W. Bromiley, Edinburgh: T&T Clark, 1969, p. 88. Further references to this volume are given in the main text.

with a change which cannot be understood or described radically enough, which God has the possibility of effecting in a man's life in a way which is decisive and basic for his whole being and action' (IV/4, p. 9). Third, Barth highlights in his baptismal theology the vicariousness of the life and work of Jesus Christ:

> [Jesus Christ] was elected and ordained from all eternity to partake of the sin of all in His own person, to bear its shame and curse in the place of all, to be the man responsible for all, and as such, wholly theirs, to live and act and suffer. (IV/4, p. 59)

Indeed, Barth writes that it is revealed to the Christian that 'his own history took place along with the history of Jesus Christ' (IV/4, p. 13). In all these ways, the baptismal theology of Barth and the doctrine of baptism of the Commission Report exhibit a strong relation.

Where the great difference lies is in the understanding of baptism itself, and, in particular, in the understanding of the relationship between baptism with the Spirit and baptism with water. For the Commission Report, there is in baptism both an act of Christ and an act of the Church; while these are to be distinguished, however, they are not to be separated. Indeed, the Commission Report argues that, 'when [the Church] acts in his Name, baptising people, Christ himself baptises with his Spirit, acknowledging and blessing the action of the Church as his own' (*SCR*, p. 225). This follows from the Commission Report's insistence that there is only one baptism, in which both Christ (originally) and the Church (derivatively) participate. The baptism of the Church therefore *mediates* the baptism of Jesus Christ by the power of the Holy Spirit.

For Barth, however, these two baptismal acts must be kept strictly apart. Hence Barth distinguishes between baptism with the Spirit (a divine action) and baptism with water (a human action). So far, Barth is with the Special Commission. However, the whole point for Barth is that water baptism does not *mediate* Spirit baptism, but rather *responds* to it. There are here, for Barth, two inalienably distinct subjects and actions. Primarily, there is the gracious action of God upon the individual by the power of the Holy Spirit, which is the unequivocal foundation of the Christian life; to this divine action, however, Barth argues that 'there belongs secondarily a work, action and conduct ... for which man is freed, empowered and summoned by the divine change which comes over him' (IV/4, p. 42). Christian baptism with water is, then, 'the first form of the human answer to the divine change which was brought about in [Jesus Christ]' (IV/4, p. 90). Water baptism in the church is not a bearer, means or instrument of grace, nor is it a mystery or a sacrament (IV/4, p. 102). Rather, as a free and responsible act of the Christian in a Christian community, water baptism is an act of obedience and hope, which finds its meaning in the renunciation of the old self and the pledge to a new life in Jesus Christ (IV/4, p. 195). For Barth, this freedom and responsibility, along with the ability to renounce, pledge and hope, belong to adults: there is thus no place in his doctrine of baptism for infant baptism (IV/4, p. 194). Infant baptism may be an ecclesiastical reality, but for Barth it is theologically indefensible.

For all the similarities between the report of the Special Commission and of Barth, then, it can be seen that important differences render their respective understandings of the theology and practice of baptism very different. These differences are rooted in diverging exegeses of the relevant New Testament passages.[235] The Commission Report focuses on the passivity of the believer and even of the Church in the act of baptism, emphasizing the activity of God that is mediated by the Church in the sacrament. Barth highlights instead the need to respond to the gracious activity of God in Jesus Christ with free and responsible human activity and thus not only conceptually but also practically distinguishes baptism with the Spirit and baptism with water. The result is a radically different outcome for the practice of baptism: for the Special Commission, infant baptism is normative; for Barth, infant baptism is abnormal.

Baptismal Theology and Practice since the Special Commission

After 1963, discontent continued in the Church of Scotland. A wide variety of baptismal practice continued, particularly in respect of implementing the 'conditions' of the 1963 Act under which baptism might be allowed. The terms in which the doctrine of baptism were understood gradually came to be challenged, in particular with respect to the impact upon the mission of the Church of consistent application of the Act.[236]

In 1983, the Panel on Doctrine, acting on the instruction of the General Assembly of 1981, reported on baptism, noting explicitly the awareness on the part of the Church of Scotland in its historical background of understanding the sacrament of 'dissent in its midst, surfacing intermittently in special cases'.[237] The Panel report records in some detail the pastoral problems which the 1963 Act bequeathed to the Church of Scotland, particularly in connection with infant baptism. It recognizes that human fail-

---

235 For details, see RGA (1955), pp. 610–62 – which report was subsequently revised and appeared as *The Biblical Doctrine of Baptism*, Edinburgh: Saint Andrew Press, 1958 – and Barth, IV/4, pp. 179–85.

236 John L. McPake, 'Contemporary Developments in Baptismal Theology within the Church of Scotland' (unpublished paper), p. 3. I am grateful to the author for permission to quote from his paper.

237 References to RGA in this paragraph are to RGA (1983), pp. 154, 159, 159, 160–1, and 161.

ings often occur in keeping baptismal vows, and it resolutely condemns *indiscriminate* infant baptism.[238] However, the 1983 statement strongly endorses the theological argumentation and conclusions of the Special Commission Report, similarly approving of infant baptism and endorsing the Christocentric and vicarious nature of baptism.[239] The statement also condemns outright the idea of non-baptismal services of infant dedication, presentation and blessing. It posited that 'For the Church to invent something of the sort ... would be for her to move into an area in which she has no charter to operate ... [and] could only result in increased theological confusion.' It concluded strongly: 'Anything which might tend to perplex Church members or to increase theological confusion by seeming to promote an apparent alternative to, a watered-down version of, or a half-way house towards baptism, is a disservice to Christ and his message.' Infant baptism was to remain normative.

Nevertheless, the 1983 report recognizes a tension between the legal situation – as demanded by the 1963 Act – and the gratuity of the grace of God in baptism, between right discipline and unconditional grace.[240] It observes that 'Sadly, conditions rigidly insisted upon before baptism may seem to obscure or even deny the unconditional character of grace in the eyes of perhaps poorly informed parishioners.' It concludes that such a tension has to be accepted, but contends that 'in the long run, firmer and more imaginative exercise of baptismal discipline should result in fewer confused and ill-considered requests for baptism'.

The perceived legalism of the 1963 Act surfaced again, however, in 1990, when a move was made to restore the old wording from the 1933 Act which referred to the infant's 'right' to baptism.[241] Again, the background was one of 'reports of variation in practice and disregard of the terms of the 1963 Act'. The Panel on Doctrine concluded in 1991 that the

---

238 This was no doubt partly in response to the 1982 *Baptism, Eucharist, and Ministry* document of the World Council of Churches, which states that those who practise infant baptism 'must guard themselves against the practice of apparently indiscriminate baptism and take more seriously their responsibility for the nurture of baptized children to mature commitment to Christ' (B.16).

239 Spinks, '"Freely by His Grace"', p. 233. McPake notes that the General Assembly of 1985 approved a report desiring to: 'Affirm that Baptism constitutes a basic unity among Christians which is fundamental; agree with "Baptism, Eucharist and Ministry" that Infant and Believers' Baptism should be "equivalent alternative" forms of administration in any reunion between paedo-baptist churches and churches which practice only Believers' Baptism; and recognize that the historical reason for the division of the Church at this point would thus be removed' (*RGA*, 1985, p. 28), thus unwittingly overthrowing the prevailing 'consensus' paradigm inaugurated by the Special Commission Report, 'Contemporary Developments', pp. 4–5.

240 All references to *RGA* in this paragraph are to *RGA* (1983), p. 160.

241 References to *RGA* in this paragraph are to *RGA* (1991), p. 222 and *RGA* (1992), p. 186.

1963 Act was indeed 'unduly restrictive' and did not reflect the theology of the 1963 Special Commission Report. The Panel's efforts to amend the 1963 Act floundered, however, when a large degree of resistance to further amendment was encountered – ironically, 'from quite different (and largely self-cancelling) perspectives'. In view of these mutually contradictory responses, and given that the difficulties being encountered were pastoral rather theological, the Panel could only conclude the following year that 'it is difficult to see how this matter can usefully be resolved by legislation'.

In 1999, a report on how the Special Commission Report and the 1963 Act had impacted the work of the Church concluded that the experience of the Church had been broadly positive.[242] However, it registered both the disapproval of those who were against infant baptism and the (diametrically opposed) disapproval of those who objected to the requirement of parental faith. It also noted the pastoral difficulty involved in implementing the Act, and the way in which feelings of rejection had been caused when requests for baptism were refused and evangelical opportunities had consequently been lost. It also recorded that there remained 'widespread dissatisfaction at the inconsistent way in which policy is implemented at a local level', and mentioned the particular difficulties faced in frontier mission situations such as inner cities and chaplaincies. The report recommended that no changes should be made to the Act, but that Services of Thanksgiving should be formally recognized by the Church (contra the policy of the 1983 report) and that the case for infant baptism should continue to be made.

The Panel on Doctrine reported back in 2002 and 2003 on the 1999 text, having also reflected further on some of the more recent developments in baptismal theology in the Reformed tradition in particular and in the Church universal.[243] These reports set forth something of a paradigmatic change in the baptismal doctrine of the Church of Scotland and a parallel reshaping of the law of the Church in relation to baptism. As McPake notes, the 2003 Report identifies with the sense of the 1999 Report that 'the "consensus" paradigm embodied in the Special Commission on Baptism and Act XVII (1963) [had] broken down'.[244] Alongside the legislated practices of the Church of Scotland, a small but significant

---

242 All references to *RGA* in this paragraph are to *RGA* (1999), pp. 20/68–9 and 20/73–5.

243 *RGA* (2003), p. 13/5: such developments included the placing of baptism in the wider context of Christian initiation, the possibility of a dual-practice model of baptism, the trend towards endorsing the decision of parents to allow their children to decide in later years in respect of their own baptism, the ongoing research on the place of infant baptism in the early Church, and the trend towards viewing adult baptism as normative.

244 McPake, 'Contemporary Developments', p. 4.

(and growing) number of ministers were practising infant dedication as opposed to infant baptism and were openly in favour of instituting believers' baptism. Moreover, the 2003 Report notes that baptism had a 'low profile ... in much of our church life' and that the proportion of children being baptized nationally was falling rapidly.[245]

Much of the theology of the 2003 report is in line with that of the earlier Special Commission.[246] It remains strongly Christocentric, finding the meaning of and call to baptism rooted in the life and command of Jesus Christ. It finds the promise of baptism in the gift of the Holy Spirit at Pentecost and observed that baptism, as the beginning of the Christian life, incorporates the individual into both the local and the universal community of the Church. Ultimately, baptism represents a seal upon the gift of grace and the response of faith.

However, there has been noticeable movement in a number of ways as well. In terms of its purpose, the 2003 report highlights the need for any reworking of the doctrine of baptism 'to back up calls for unity ... to overcome divisions ... [and] to demonstrate that in Christ all human differences are transcended'.[247] This ecumenical focus, echoing the call to unity found in the *Baptism, Eucharist, and Ministry* document is prominent throughout the report. Materially, there have also been a number of perceptible developments. First, the report writes of the need 'to correct false exaggeration of the freedom of grace', a statement which might be considered to go against the tendency of the original Special Commission Report to highlight the active grace of God and the passivity of the person being baptized. Second, exegetically, it is no longer claimed that the one baptism of Jesus Christ and the baptism of the Christian are inseparable. References to baptism as interpreting Jesus' own life, death and resurrection are treated under the heading 'The Imagery of Baptism in the Gospels', and it is noted that his imagery may reflect 'Jesus' understanding of the event of baptism'. The event of Christian baptism itself, however, is firmly rooted in the Great Commission of Matthew 28.19. Third, and perhaps correspondingly, the role of the response of faith is assigned a greater prominence, with baptism as, 'at one and the same time, a seal upon th [e] gift of grace and our response to it'. In baptism, the love of God is met by the response of faith, which response is itself conceived as a gift of God.

Perhaps the greatest movement, however, is to be found in the fact that in the 2003 report baptism upon profession of faith is considered to be the *primary* model of baptismal practice, with child baptism as a *complementary* model.[248] This is a new development for the Church of Scotland, but

---

245 *RGA* (2003), pp. 13/3 and 13/7.
246 All references to *RGA* in this paragraph are to *RGA* (2003), p. 13/8.
247 References to *RGA* in this paragraph are to *RGA* (2003), pp. 13/3, 13/10–11, 13/15.
248 References to *RGA* in this paragraph are to *RGA* (2003), pp. 13/8, 13/4 and 13/13.

is in line with the Panel's views that baptism on profession of faith is the primary image of baptism in Scripture and that the 1963 Special Commission had 'presented a maximalist case for infant baptism'.[249] While infant baptism does find scriptural justification in the report – on the grounds of the baptism of households (and thus neither through the concept of the covenant nor through the parallel with Jewish circumcision) – it is no longer regarded as the primary form of baptism.

The main practical implication of this development was that the Church of Scotland approved of and instructed the preparation of services for the thanksgiving and dedication of a new child.[250] Such services were to be seen, not as 'an alternative to the celebration of Baptism, but in recognition of the need to provide a flexible response to the situation of primary mission which is the Scotland of today'. The Church also amended its existing Acts to reflect its new understanding of baptismal theology and practice, thereby allowing for: another family member to act *in loco parentis*; the baptism of adults with learning difficulties; emergency baptism by the non-ordained; and the carrying out of conditional baptism.

Conclusion

From the above survey, it can be seen that, after centuries in which it evidenced little evolution, the recent past has seen significant developments in the understanding of baptism in the Church of Scotland. There have been a number of reasons for the sudden change of theological pace: fresh insights into the meaning of Scripture; new understandings of baptismal praxis in the early Church; significant developments in pastoral contexts and needs; and all these in a radically and rapidly changing world. As the Church of Scotland pursues its mission in the present day, its witness will continue to depend on this ability to continue to reform its theology and practice – of baptism and beyond – in obedience to the Word of God, in dialogue with the tradition, and in service of the world.

---

249 In this connection, Wright describes the Special Commission Report's claim that 'if the New Testament had meant to exclude infants from Christ's Baptism, it would have used language ... to make this quite clear' as being 'quite untenable', *Infant Baptism in Historical Perspective*, p. 5 n. 6.

250 References in this paragraph to *RGA* are to *RGA* (2003), p. 13/6, *RGA* (Minutes of the Proceedings) (2003), p. 20, and *RGA* (2003) p. 13/16–17. The new services were subsequently published by the Church of Scotland Office for Worship & Doctrine as *A Welcome to a Child*, Edinburgh: Church of Scotland, 2006.

7

TONE-DEAF TO MYSTERY

Worship, Preaching and Pastoral Care

David Lyall

This chapter argues that there is a close and natural relationship between worship (which in a Scottish context will inevitably include preaching) and pastoral care. That said, there is evidence of long-standing misunderstanding, if not mutual antipathy, between those whose main interest is in liturgy and those whose main interest lies in pastoral care. The criticism which each group makes of the other perhaps lies in the realm of caricature – but of course most caricatures usually contain an element of truth.

In her book *Ritual and Pastoral Care* Elaine Ramshaw summarizes the mutual accusations which have divided pastoral carers (especially counsellors) from the so-called 'specialist ritualists'. The counsellors too often feel that ritual lacks warmth and empathy; that its fixed forms are too insensitive to 'where the patient is'; that it staunches the flow of feelings; that it 'generalizes' the client's feelings; that it tends to reduce pastoral ministry to the magical. In return, the ritualists have attacked counselling as an anaesthetic or palliative which attempts to treat symptoms in isolation from the total situation, sidestepping confrontation with the deeper issues raised by personal crisis. The counsellor isolates the individual from community support and cuts him or her off from the stabilizing anchor of ritual. Ramshaw summarizes the arguments as follows:

> We all know too well the truths that give rise to these counter-accusations. Ritual can indeed be formalist, distancing, insensitive to the specificity or pace of the individual's needs, intent on enforcing a procrustean pattern. Equally sadly, even 'pastoral' counselling can be privatised, narrowly focussed on the needs of the moment, insufficiently grounded in the depths of the tradition, tone-deaf to mystery.[251]

---

251 Elaine Ramshaw, *Ritual and Pastoral Care*, Philadelphia: Augsburg Fortress, 1987, p. 14.

So there is the contrast in its starkest expression. On the one hand there are the liturgists whose interest is mainly archaeological, trying to un-cover and recreate worship as it once was allegedly with little concern for pastoral relevance; on the other hand, there are the counsellors, suppos-edly value-free, trying hard not to impose their own beliefs, yet sometimes taking on quite uncritically the philosophical presuppositions as well as the techniques of the secular therapies, and unwilling to countenance any contribution to psychic or spiritual health to be found through participa-tion in the worship of the Church.

But it need not be like this. Walter Brueggemann is an internationally famous Old Testament scholar who has also contributed significantly to a biblical theology of pastoral care. In an essay on 'The Transformative Power of the Pastoral Office', he argues that 'pastoral care is essentially a liturgical enterprise'.[252] How does he arrive at this conclusion?

Brueggemann argues that pastoral care informed by biblical faith, in comparison with counselling, is committed to a very different understand-ing of what it means to be human. If the aim of counselling is adjustment, fitting comfortably into society, that of pastoral care is transformation. The task of pastoral care is to feed the imagination in such a way that people see life and its possibilities differently. He argues:

> Not only is the substance of this imagination crucial, but so is where and in what ways it is practiced and made available among us. This al-ternative imagination is shaped, mediated and made available primarily through the practice of liturgy.[253]

It is for this reason, therefore, that he argues that 'pastoral care is essen-tially a liturgical enterprise' and that 'it should be possible to set as a requirement for personal or individual conversation, disciplined participa-tion in a liturgical activity of the pastoral care community'.

He is arguing that worship itself is – or should be – a source of pastoral care, that worship provides a new way of understanding reality, that wor-ship provides a new set of symbols around which people can reorganize their lives. Would that it were so! At any rate he presents us with a very different understanding of the relationship between worship and pastoral care, not one of conflict but one in which worship and pastoral care are complementary with the pastoral relationship finding its context in a litur-gical context which challenges accepted conventional values and makes possible new ways of seeing things.

---

252 Walter Brueggemann, *Interpretation and Obedience: From Faithful Reading to Faithful Living*, Minneapolis: Fortress Press, 1991, p. 176.

253 Brueggemann, *Interpretation and Obedience*, p. 176.

Preaching the Word as Pastoral Care

Can preaching be pastoral? Is it possible for sermons to be constructed primarily to bring healing to broken hearts and peace to troubled minds? To those who preach, it might seem strange that these questions are even being asked. Yet to those who seldom hear sermons, and to those who regularly 'sit under' preachers of a certain style, the questions may not seem out of place. The words 'sermon' and 'preaching' do not have positive connotations in popular parlance!

What is the relationship between pastoral care and the proclamation of the gospel? One view is that of Eduard Thurneysen for whom pastoral care is essentially a proclamation of the Word of God to the individual.[254] The individual is a sinner under judgement and grace and the Word is primarily one of forgiveness. For Thurneysen, then, pastoral care is a form of preaching. But is the opposite true? Can preaching become a vehicle of pastoral care?

I do not wish to argue that pastoral care is the sole function of preaching. The history of the Church's proclamation is far too rich and diverse to make such a claim and a stress upon the need for preaching to have a pastoral dimension must not lead to a silencing of the Church's prophetic voice. With these qualifications how may a pastoral dimension be expressed in preaching?

The pastoral dimension may be expressed through preaching which embodies *acceptance and availability*. It is not difficult to identify ways in which preaching might be a barrier to pastoral care. Pastoral relationships are not readily established by preachers who through their words and their demeanour in the pulpit come across as cold and judgemental. On the other hand, preachers who demonstrate a pastoral heart, both in their handling of the biblical material and in their attitude to contemporary social issues, come across as human beings who are compassionate towards the frailty of others as well as being in touch with their own vulnerability. By their words and demeanour in the pulpit they create the conditions which encourage others to approach them with their sometimes unspeakable burdens. It is when preaching itself communicates the 'core conditions' necessary for therapy, that is acceptance, empathy and integrity that preachers make themselves available pastorally.

Preaching may create opportunities for pastoral care *accidentally* as we observe in the following story from a colleague in ministry:

It was a terrible sermon. One of these efforts which was 'untimely born', and better not to have been born at all. Poor structure. Lack of focus.

---

254 Eduard Thurneysen, *A Theology of Pastoral Care*, Richmond, VA: John Knox Press, 1962.

Theologically ragged. And the preacher was tired. The congregation was in single figures and made up of complete strangers to me. It had the feeling of being a waste of everybody's time!

Somewhere in the middle of this sermon was the story of a man who had left church in a fury during the reading of the parable of the Prodigal Son. It was his fortieth birthday. All his life he had been upstaged by a brother who had left home and wasted his life. The whole family lived in a state of constant anxiety over the waster, while the decent 'stay at home' brother was taken for granted. Arriving in church on his birthday to hear the Prodigal Son being celebrated was just too much to hear. He left in a rage but it was the beginning of a new honesty.

At the end of the service, a lady asked to speak to me. From beginning to end the sermon had described her life, especially the man's reaction to the Prodigal Son. The outcome was a long discussion about sibling rivalries, family tensions and the recovery of faith in God. A poor sermon strangely used by God to help a woman reshape her life.

In this incident, the 'normal' preaching of the Word of God on central themes of the gospel triggered recognition and response. The preacher was unknown to the individuals, but the preaching carried over into personal conversation that proved pastorally healing. This story illustrates well the recurring mystery of preaching where people ask 'how did you know?' There are few preachers who will not be able to identify with this experience. Carefully crafted sermons, begun early in the week based upon careful exegesis and sound theology 'fall flat'. Other efforts thrown together on a Saturday night amid the fag ends of the week's time and energy ring bells for people. Of course we must not carry this to extremes! In the long run careful preparation on a regular basis brings its own dividends in those weeks when it is not possible.

Preaching may attempt to have a pastoral dimension *intentionally*. I suspect, though, that when we set out to preach pastoral sermons in a vacuum, when we set out to preach *about* pastoral issues, the sermons fail to achieve all that we might have hoped for. We may communicate information, we may convey something of our attitudes and our availability (valuable though these may be) but we fail to move people. Perhaps good pastoral sermons are those preached in direct response to a given situation. One of the best, theologically and pastorally, was that preached in Lockerbie Parish Church by Professor James Whyte, then Moderator of the General Assembly of the Church of Scotland, just days after the air disaster. In that sermon, he recognized the need for justice but not for retaliation. He identified the suffering of the innocent at the hands of evil human beings and in conclusion he asked:

Where was God in all of that? Can anyone doubt that he was right there in the midst of it? If here in the midst of evil we find goodness, if here in the midst of darkness we find light, if here in the midst of desolation we find ourselves strangely comforted, can we doubt that our lives are touched by the God of all comfort, the God whose consolation never fails?

It is the experience of humankind, that when we walk through the valley of the shadow, we are not helped by smooth words spoken from a safe distance, but by those who have known the darkness and are prepared to share it with us, and hold us till we see the light. This is the way the comfort of God touches us and holds us. For it is as we share the suffering that we share the comfort. 'Our hope for you is unshaken,' says Paul, 'for we know that if you share in our sufferings, you will also share in our comfort.[255]

In the days that followed, I met no one who did not find that sermon anything other than 'right' and deeply moving.

One of the most sensitive arenas in which to preach is the hospital chapel. Imagine a typical Sunday morning congregation of 10–15 people who have opted to attend Sunday morning worship. Some will have come because they always go to church on Sunday; some will have come to escape the boredom of the ward; some will not know why they have come, but came anyway. In a typical hospital congregation there might be people having radiotherapy or chemotherapy, a young mother giving thanks for the birth of a new baby, some elderly people recovering from illness but wondering whether they would ever be able to return to independent life in their own homes, people facing tests to discover the cause of worrying symptoms. In such a congregation normal human feelings of hope and fear, of joy and sorrow, of anxieties about life and death exist at an abnormally high level. Some of that little congregation I would have met while visiting on the wards, others were total strangers. What does one say? Whatever is said cannot take more than five minutes and it has to be spoken directly, not read from a script or even from notes. There are two dangers in preaching in such situations. One is to keep to generalities, being careful to say nothing which people might take the wrong way, leaving people untouched (apart from those who always take things the wrong way!). The other is to speak too directly, almost rubbing peoples' noses in the realities of their situation. In the course of time I began to develop a different kind of approach, what I call *parabolic preaching*.

---

255 James A. Whyte, *Laughter and Tears: Thoughts on Faith in the Face of Suffering*, Edinburgh: St Andrew Press, 1993, p. 95.

Consider the story at the end of Mark 4. The disciples are in a boat with Jesus on the Sea of Galilee. Suddenly there is a storm and the disciples are scared for their lives. And Jesus? – well he is fast asleep in the stern. So they wake him up with the plaintive cry 'Master, do you not care if we perish?' Jesus wakes up, rebukes the wind and calms the waves with the words 'Peace, be still.' By parabolic preaching I mean retelling that story with little embellishment, retelling it as a story which happened to the disciples, certainly not applying it to the situation of the patients in front of me but knowing that those who have ears to hear will identify with that cry 'Master, do you not care if we perish?' and knowing that they may also hear the words 'Peace, be still', perhaps pointing out that while on that occasion he calmed the storm which raged around the disciples, he also spoke a word of calm to the storm which raged inside them. The point of parabolic preaching is not to make connections, not to spell out applications in detail but to let those who are able make their own connections and to trust the Word to speak to their hearts.

My experience of preaching in these difficult situations (where issues of life and death and hope and despair were never far from the surface) was that, when the Bible story was told *as a Bible story* but with an emphasis upon the people involved, then some people heard it as no more than a Bible story, but that there were others, those able to hear, who made connections with their own story, and did indeed hear a word which spoke to them. The technique – if it is indeed a technique – is to preach in such a way that the imagination is evoked so that the good news explicit or implicit in the Bible story becomes (existentially as it were) gospel in the heart of the hearer.

It is important to ask of every sermon we preach where the gospel can be found in it. And if we can agree that gospel is good news and not good advice, then every sermon will be an example of pastoral preaching.

Eucharistic Worship as Pastoral Care

Within the Reformed tradition, very little has been written about the pastoral dimension of the sacraments with the notable exception of Ralph Underwood's *Pastoral Care and the Means of Grace*.[256] There is of course a different emphasis within the Anglican and Roman Catholic traditions. While the Reformed churches regard only baptism and Holy Communion as sacraments instituted by Jesus, churches in the Catholic tradition recognize seven sacraments of which confession and the sacrament of the sick have an obvious and direct pastoral relevance. And while the Eucharist has

---

256 Minneapolis: Fortress Press, 1993.

a central and normative place in Anglican and Catholic worship, in the Reformed and Free churches the ministry of the Word is dominant with less frequent celebrations of Communion. Anglican and Roman Catholic patients expect to be offered Communion by their hospital chaplains, as an aid to recovery; Presbyterians may think they are being offered the last rites!

Despite its relative infrequency of celebration, Reformed churches in the tradition of Calvin and Knox have a 'high' theology of the sacraments. This is in contrast to the Zwinglian emphasis in which the service was no more than a commemoration of the death of Christ. There is, in my view, a correlation between a high view of the Eucharist and its pastoral significance as I think can be demonstrated by an exploration of certain themes central to an understanding of the Eucharist. These are:

- Real presence.
- Eucharistic sacrifice.
- Eschatological hope.

Real presence

This is a phrase the interpretation of which has led to much controversy between (and within) denominations. There is however much that is held in common, not the least of which is an awareness of the *spiritual presence* of Christ in the sacrament. No one can claim that the Westminster Confession of Faith is a document with 'Romanist' leanings, but even that Confession says that those who come to this table in faith 'not carnally but spiritually receive and feed upon Christ crucified and all his benefits'; it also speaks of Christ being 'spiritually present to the faith of believers'.

This has been a consistent theme in Reformed sacramental theology. In the sixteenth century, John Knox's successor as minister of St Giles in Edinburgh was a man called Robert Bruce. In a famous sermon on the Lord's Supper, Bruce posed the question 'What do we get in the sacrament that we do not get in the preaching of the word?' His answer was 'Nothing, but we get a better grasp of it.'[257]

Second, experience teaches that the grace of the real presence of Christ is communicated not only in the arena of public worship. It can also happen in more intimate celebrations. A parish minister recounts the following incident.

---

257 Robert Bruce, *The Mystery of the Lord's Supper: Sermons on the Sacrament preached in the Kirk of Edinburgh by Robert Bruce in AD 1589*, translated and edited by Thomas F. Torrance, London: James Clarke, 1958, p. 84.

I was visiting a home to give communion to a man who was very ill, indeed on the point of death. He had one son, mentally handicapped and the mother said to this son 'Now, Drew, this is not for you.' I asked 'Why not?' The mother said, 'But he has never joined the church!' To which I replied 'He is baptized. He is one of God's children.' 'You mean he can take communion?' 'Of course,' I said, and her eyes filled with tears as that little family gathered round that bedside table of the Lord.

Of course enough questions are raised by this story to occupy the attention of the systematic theologians for long enough. What is the relation between baptism and confirmation? Are only the baptized 'God's children'? How important is 'understanding' to receiving the sacrament? (I suspect this is a very Presbyterian question.) Significantly the minister involved in the above incident later suggested to me that 'something on the changing face of pastoral theology or rather how pastoral concern changes theology might be in order'. Precisely! What this parish minister was articulating was the realization that his own pastoral theology was being forged in the crucible of pastoral experience. While the tradition of the Church is an indispensable factor in formulating our theology, for working ministers their 'owned' theology as opposed to the theology which they learned in college is generated out of the continual interaction between the tradition and their pastoral practice. The interaction, the 'mutually critical correlation', is important. Pastoral practice driven totally by the tradition leads to arid theology and irrelevant practice. Pastoral practice driven entirely by a pragmatic response to the situation leads to the non-engagement of a disembodied theology and an unprincipled practice. For the minister and family involved in the above episode, the real presence of Christ was not just a theological concept. It was the lived experience of 'holy communion' of that family with the Lord.

There is a third way in which the idea of 'real presence' is directly related to the experience of grace and that is through an analogical relationship with pastoral care. On reflection I realize that I have experienced grace most directly in human relationships. It has happened in the normal run of relating to family and friends; and it has happened in more particular relationships of pastoral care and counselling. All of these relationships were characterized by the fact that another person was 'really present' to me, enabling me to hear words spoken that I normally could not hear, words of both confrontation and affirmation, judgement and of grace.

It should not surprise us that we find such strong parallels between this sacrament and pastoral care. In this sacrament, word and sign are intimately related. And in pastoral care? Is there not the same kind of relationship between the words which are spoken and the quality of the relationship in which they are spoken? Is there not a sense in which the caring relationship is itself a sacrament, or a parable of the gospel, pointing beyond itself to the grace of a caring God? Is it not within the context of that relationship that words can be spoken and heard and their deeper personal meaning grasped? Does it not confirm for us that the communication of Christian truth is not propositional but relational? The Word became flesh and dwelt among us full of grace and truth.

Eucharistic sacrifice

I now turn to another two words which in the past have divided Christians in their understanding of the sacrament. But properly interpreted, I believe that these two words illuminate what is going on at the heart of ministry. The words are 'eucharistic sacrifice' or 'eucharistic offering'. Again I want to steer clear of past controversies about the interpretation of these words and simply point out that they are present either explicitly or implicitly in most communion rites.

In most of the contemporary liturgies, however, the emphasis is not upon any sacrifice that a priest makes upon the altar, but upon the sacrifice which we ourselves make as we approach the table. In the Church of England's Alternative Service Book we find the words:

Accept through him, our great high priest
this our sacrifice of thanks and praise

In the most recent Church of Scotland *Book of Common Order*, there is at the heart of the great communion prayer these words:

Most gracious God,
accept this our sacrifice
of praise and thanksgiving
and receive the offering of ourselves
which now we make
our thoughts and words, desires and deeds

But what does it mean to make an 'offering of ourselves'? What content do we, we who are pastoral carers, give to the phrase 'thoughts and words, desires and deeds'? Is it not that along with the whole people of God, we offer all that is best in us as a response to the gospel. Our time, our talents, our skills, our training – all these are offered to God as a response to the gospel. These constitute our eucharistic offering, our thank offering. But we need to be clear that they are a *response* to the gospel, gifts offered in freedom and not out of inner compulsive needs. Those who have studied Frank Lake's dynamic life cycle do not need to be reminded of the dynamics of grace and the dynamics of works. Whether in our own personal counselling, in supervision or in spiritual direction we need to become aware of our own pathology so that the offering of care which we make as part of our reasonable service is truly a free response to the grace which we have already received and not a neurotic attempt to answer our own deepest needs.

All this is true – but there is a truth which is deeper than this. For our eucharistic offering consists of more than our gifts and skills. In our pastoral care, as in our worship, our eucharistic offering must consist also in the offering of our weakness and vulnerability. I suspect that for most people who find themselves in pastoral ministry, ordained or lay, there is an element of surprise. Many people come into pastoral ministry not because of their strengths but from a point of weakness. Having gone through a difficult time in their own lives, they have found themselves accompanied through the valley of shadows and cared for, and in being cared for themselves, they have experienced healing, grown in self-awareness and to their own surprise found themselves accompanying others on their journey. For many carers, the transition from being wounded to becoming healer is part of the journey.

Brokenness and vulnerability are part of our eucharistic offering. This should not surprise us. 'This is my body,' said Jesus, 'broken for you.' The mystery of grace is that healing flows from the cross. Some of the most moving services that I have had the privilege of leading have been communion services in the hospital chapel. For those who were regular communicants in their own churches, for those who had not been to Communion for a long time and even for those with no prior experience of sacramental worship, the dominical words about a broken body and blood shed 'for them' touched a deep and healing chord within them at that moment of their own physical vulnerability.

Eschatological hope

The early Church was most vividly and intensely aware of living in the time between the times, between the time of the events surrounding Jesus' first coming and the expected time of his second coming. Both the memory of his first coming and the hope of his second coming, the *eschatological hope,* were very real to these first Christians. For them, the sacrament of Holy Communion belonged to the 'time between the times' as both memory and hope; both a remembrance of mighty acts which had already taken place, and a promise, a foretaste of what was yet to be. For us, as the events surrounding the first coming have receded into history, so also has any awareness of a second coming become less central to our beliefs.

What are the implications for pastoral care of these words 'you proclaim the Lord's death until he comes'?

It is easy to forget that when the early Church celebrated the sacrament, it was indeed a celebration. And it was a celebration because it was based on a twofold memory. It was certainly based upon the events which took place 'on the night on which he was betrayed,' events related to betrayal and crucifixion and death. This must not be forgotten though I have to say that I believe my own Presbyterian tradition has overdone this aspect somewhat. But each celebration of the sacrament by the early Church must have been infused with another set of memories ... and these were memories of a breakfast on the beach when the risen Lord stood before them and said 'Come and have breakfast,' and of that other occasion when on the road to Emmaus, the risen Lord made himself known to them in the breaking of bread.

So from the beginning, the celebration of Holy Communion embraced an awareness not only of the death of Christ but also of the experience of resurrection and with that experience, a foretaste of the ultimate triumph of God.

'As often as ye eat this bread and drink the cup, you proclaim the Lord's death until he comes ...' What then can we make of these words? Can I suggest that we interpret these words as an invitation, not certainly as an invitation to predict future events but rather as an invitation to invoke present imagination? When creeds and credal statements are interpreted literally, the result is usually disagreement and frustration; but when creeds and credal statements are interpreted imaginatively, the result can be a fresh awareness of the transforming power of the gospel.

An understanding of what we are about as we approach the table can work a comparable transformation of what we are about in our ministry of pastoral care. For if our understanding of the sacrament is shaped by both memory and hope, if we remember not only the reality of the darkness of the cross but also the reality of the light of the resurrection, then we shall also bring a different perspective to our ministry. It will be a ministry that can give us strength not only to accompany others through the dark places of the human journey but also to bring to bear in our pastoral ministry the transforming light of the gospel.

As we approach the holy table, as we partake of the elements of bread and wine, as we nurture within our hearts the thought that as often as we do this, we proclaim the Lord's death until he comes, as we do these things, is it possible that deep within us there can be stirred such an evocation of the imagination that our pastoral ministry is undergirded by the kind of hope which is central to that care and counselling which we call pastoral?

Of course we must be careful when we use the language of hope in pastoral ministry. There are practitioners, both secular and pastoral, who offer a hope which is too easy, like Bonhoeffer's cheap grace. That is not what I mean, I mean something deeper than that. I want to take seriously what Donald Capps says in his book *Agents of Hope*[258] when he argues that while for other caring professionals, hope is a by-product of their work, for pastoral carers, hope is at the very core of their activity. Hope is central to pastoral ministry because hope is integral to the gospel.

What does this mean in practice? In his *Ethics*,[259] Dietrich Bonhoeffer makes a distinction between things that belong to the Penultimate, and those things that belong to the Ultimate. To the Penultimate belongs all our human activity, all our decision-making, all our successes and all our failures; to the Ultimate belongs only one thing, the justifying, saving Word of God.

Bonhoeffer 1945, an imaginative and moving reconstruction of his last days in prison, was performed at the Edinburgh Festival Fringe in 1996. As the play draws to its conclusion, we hear coming over the loudspeaker system, the infamous words which summoned Bonhoeffer to his execution. 'Pastor Bonhoeffer, come with us.'

But with a profound insight into the thought of Bonhoeffer, the writer does not end the play with these words. The play ends with Bonhoeffer on his knees, praying in the words of Psalm 150:

Praise the Lord
Praise God in his sanctuary
    praise him in his mighty firmament
Praise him for his mighty deeds
    praise him according to his exceeding greatness ...

The final words addressed to Bonhoeffer become the penultimate words of the play. The word of condemnation is only the penultimate word. The final word is the Word of God, the word of grace.

Is there not here a word for our ministry of pastoral care? To the penultimate belongs all our human words, all that we have to offer, our training and our skills, our good intentions and our mixed motives. Yet in pastoral care, we offer that care in another context, the context of the Ultimate. In our pastoral care, with our imagination transformed by words of resurrection and hope, we know that beyond our words – and beyond our silence – there is another word. We offer our pastoral care imaginatively aware of the possibility of new beginnings. We sit with the depressed, believing that

---

258 Philadelphia: Augsburg Fortress, 1995.
259 London: SCM Press, 1955.

there is no human darkness into which a glimmer of light cannot break through, that the last word is not of despair but of hope. We stand by the remorseful in the conviction that there is no human folly which cannot be forgiven, that the final word is not of judgement but of grace. We support the bereaved, believing that there is no human grief which cannot in some measure be consoled, that the last word is not of death but of life.

Part Three

THE LIVING PAST

8

DISCIPLINE AND THE MAKING OF PROTESTANT SCOTLAND[260]

Jane Dawson

During the early modern period 'discipline' in Scotland became what Humpty Dumpty called a portmanteau word, 'You see it's like a portmanteau – there are two meanings packed up into the one word.' As Alice realized even in a Looking-Glass world this could create overloading but Humpty Dumpty had the answer, 'When I make a word do a lot of work like that … I always pay it extra.' Having been neglected, the place of discipline within worship needs to be paid extra attention and the general role discipline played in the making of Protestant Scotland also needs to be examined.[261]

This portmanteau word packed up two meanings: it described both the specific process of ecclesiastical censure and the entire polity and governance of the Scottish Kirk. In its broad sense the word discipline featured in the titles of the founding manifestos, the *First Book of Discipline* written in 1560 and the *Second Book of Discipline* set forth in 1579.[262] In its narrower definition, it coined the phrase 'to underlie discipline', when an individual accepted censure from the Kirk's courts. The portmanteau of discipline held two intimately related facets of the Church which belonged together. Polity and censure were equally essential to the existence of the Church and this was acknowledged by making ecclesiastical discipline the third mark by which a 'true Church' could be recognized. As

260 I am grateful to Nikki Macdonald for discussions about the 'performance' of penance in sixteenth-century Scotland. It is hoped she will be undertaking a fuller study of this topic in the near future.

261 The shining recent exception to that neglect can be found in Margo Todd's chapter 'Performing Repentance', in her *The Culture of Protestantism in Early Modern Scotland*, New Haven: Yale University Press, 2002.

262 *The First Book of Discipline*, ed. J. K. Cameron, Edinburgh: St Andrew Press, 1972; *The Second Book of Discipline*, ed. J. Kirk, Edinburgh: St Andrew Press, 1980.

the Scottish *Confession of Faith* proclaimed in 1560, the preaching of the Word and the right administration of the sacraments were the first two marks of the Church accompanied by 'Ecclesiastical discipline uprightlie ministred, as Goddis Worde prescribes, whereby vice is repressed, and vertew nurished.'[263]

For the Scottish Reformers discipline lay at the heart of what the Church was and did. Combined with preaching and the sacraments the three marks gave the Church a public face. The integrity of the national Kirk depended upon these marks being displayed and recognizable within the parishes of Scotland. At this local level the proper functioning of ecclesiastical censure underpinned and guaranteed the presence of preaching and the sacraments. At the national level the existence of the hierarchy of ecclesiastical courts, the kirk sessions, presbyteries and General Assembly, gave the Kirk its organization and polity. By clearly displaying the three marks, the Scottish Kirk could substantiate its claim to be a 'true' Church and could boast of being one of the 'best reformed' in Europe.[264]

Being an outward sign of the building up or 'edification' of the Church described in the Pauline Epistles, the strict enforcement of discipline offered the best indication of a Church's healthy growth. Expanding Calvin's metaphor of discipline as the sinews holding together the body of the Church, the Scottish Reformers extended the unifying property of discipline to encompass the kingdom of Scotland. Unlike their Huguenot and Dutch brethren, the Scots claimed and subsequently achieved a comprehensive, national Church. As a corollary, the Kirk's disciplinary regime was assumed to embrace the entire population of the kingdom, irrespective of rank. As the *First Book of Discipline* expressed it, 'To discipline must all the estates within this Realme be subject, as well the Rulers, as they that are ruled.'[265] In this context ecclesiastical censure was the main instrument for upholding the laws of God throughout the realm which formed an essential obligation for the covenanted nation Scotland was assumed to be. Acting as the sinews binding the ecclesiastical and political bodies of Scotland, discipline was essential to their well-being; without it there would be no Church and no covenanted people. In 1590 James Melville summed up the vital importance of discipline,

that discipline was maist necessar in the Kirk, seeing without the saming, Chrysts Kingdome could nocht stand. For unless the Word and

---

263 *The Scots Confession*, 1560, ed. G. D. Henderson, Edinburgh: St Andrew Press, 1960, Art. xviii, p. 44.

264 *'The Booke of the Universall Kirk of Scotland': Acts and proceedings of the General Assemblies of the Kirk of Scotland*, ed. T. Thomson, 3 vols, Edinburgh: Bannatyne Club, 81, 1839–45, Vol. 1, p. 246.

265 *The First Book of Discipline*, p. 173.

Sacaraments war kiepit in sinceritie, and rightlie usit and practesit be direction of the discipline, they wald soone be corrupted. And therefor certean it was, that without sum discipline na kirk, without trew discipline, na rightlie reformed kirk; and without the right and perfyt discipline, na right and perfyt kirk.[266]

Discipline's central role in erecting and maintaining the visible Church found dramatic expression within Protestant worship. While all three dimensions of ecclesiastical censure were present within congregational worship, the themes of restoration and purity dominated. The penitential drama was enacted during Sunday worship and repentance provided the motive for a new service, the General Fast. Discipline also played a significant role in the administration of the Lord's Supper and in certain circumstances affected the sacrament of baptism. The routine operation of judicial censure was deliberately removed from worship and located instead within the new Kirk's courts which ranged from the kirk session at parish level, through the presbytery for the district and the General Assembly for the kingdom. The enforcement and compliance levels achieved by these ecclesiastical courts were impressive compared to their civil counterparts. As a consequence of their success, they brought a new standard of religious and moral uniformity to Scotland and they were instrumental in helping to produce a strong confessional identity among the Scots. The constant pressure of ecclesiastical censure helped alter aspects of sexual behaviour and accelerated the decline of the blood feud in Scotland. Equally important was the progressive internalization of discipline by succeeding generations of Scots which produced a lasting impression upon the Scottish mentality. This produced some unexpected consequences with the rise of personal diaries and autobiographies growing from the seed-bed of self-examination required by a penitent. Through the experience of worship and via its other channels the external and internal discipline introduced by the Reformers helped mould the character of modern Scotland.

Repentance

After the Reformation the enactment of the penitential cycle took centre stage and became an important section of the weekly Sunday morning service. The drama which unfolded before the congregation's eyes made it one of the easiest sections of the service to understand and probably one of the most interesting as one's neighbours were on view 'making their repentance'. Some parishioners even slipped out of the building during

266 J. Melville *The autobiography and diary of Mr James Melville*, ed. R. Pitcairn, Edinburgh: Wodrow Society, 1842, p. 280.

the preaching of the Word, the central focus of Sunday worship, and returned to church for the penitents' confessions which followed the sermon. Watching the humiliation of fellow members of the community and
hearing the precise details of sins being confessed might have appealed to
some individuals' baser feelings but the congregation was also witnessing
a ritual conveying the core of the Protestant message. As the sermon was
intended to convey in words, the penitential drama proclaimed through
action, 'the forgiveness of sins in Christ' which lay at the heart of the
'Evangel'.

The weekly drama gave vivid expression to central truths about divine
and human justice, mercy, repentance, forgiveness, amendment of life and
eternal salvation. The actions and words transported the audience along
the path of salvation that every Christian needed to follow; moving from
the awareness of sin and of divine judgement, to true repentance and the
seeking of forgiveness and, through divine grace, to reconciliation and
amendment of life. By employing ritualized action the three dimensions
involved in discipline, the judicial, purifying and the restorative could be
expressed at different dramatic points and yet held together as a unit. The
drama emphasized the positive restorative message of the recovery of a
sinner from the 'bondage of Satan' and the sterner judicial and purifying
theme of separation of the sons of light from those of darkness.[267]

Early modern Scotland was a non-literate society where drama and gesture were more powerful communicators than words alone. By themselves
the dramatic props, processions, special locations, actions and gestures
narrated most of the story of this penitential cycle to the congregation.
They demonstrated the separation, suspension and reconciliation of one
who had transgressed the accepted norms of the community. Having broken the rules and been placed outside that community, voluntary participation in this penitential drama was the route by which a transgressor
could accomplish his or her return to the community. Much of the accompanying paraphernalia was deeply familiar to the congregational audience
because the sackcloth, props and public confession had formed part of
late medieval Catholic practice. After 1560 elements of the actions and
key gestures had also continued in use within non-ecclesiastical contexts,
such as the formal blood-feud reconciliations or as part of burgh court
business where antisocial behaviour such as defamation was punished.

Different layers of meaning were accommodated in early modern culture by combining the dramatic performance of set actions with a more

---

267 The text of 'The Forme of Publique Repentance' was part of the 'The Order of Excommunication', which was finalized by John Knox, authorized by the General Assembly and
printed in 1569, text in J. Knox, *The Works of John Knox*, ed. D. Laing, 6 vols, Edinburgh:
Bannatyne Club, 1846–64, Vol. 6, pp. 449–70. For key prayers within 'The Forme of Publique
Repentance', Knox, *Works* Vol. 6, pp. 458–60.

complex explanation carried by the spoken or written word, for example, the transfer of land or sasine still required the physical transfer of a divot of earth from one party to the other in the presence of witnesses in addition to a written document. In civic pageantry, such as a royal entry, long explanatory verses, often in Latin, were declaimed alongside set-piece tableaux. The imagery and meaning of such spectacles were widely understood, while the elaboration given by the words was aimed at a smaller audience. Men and women in sixteenth-century Scotland were adept at reading non-verbal signals and they expected the core message of a spectacle to be conveyed by sight rather than sound alone. Such audience expectations demanded the central message of the penitential drama be performed in front of them during the Sunday morning service. As a response to audience pressure this penitential drama was spontaneously developed, formalized and ritualized during the opening decades of the new Kirk's life. Though the 'script' was written by the clergy, the 'screen-play' was devised by the lay audience.[268]

The main actors in the drama were the penitents whose role began at home early on Sunday morning.[269] They had to appear bareheaded and barefoot and dressed in special attire with a linen shift, or even more degrading and uncomfortable, one made of hairy sackcloth. A penitent's humiliating garb was unmistakeable and could neither be disguised nor hidden, it constituted enough covering to be decent but without the normal clothes or accessories associated with dignity and status. To add to the spectacle of their journey to church, some penitents were ordered to process from their house carrying a prop, a non-verbal label classifying the sin. In the case of violent crime the 'offensive weapon' was carried, such as a murderer instructed to bring a 'bloody knife' or a wife the shears with which she had hit her husband. Other penitents wore a paper hat or a paper around the neck on which was written their name and offence. All penitents had to leave early for church and be in their assigned position at the church door from the time of the second bell calling the parish to worship, there to await the congregation's arrival for Sunday morning worship.

Standing at the entrance to the building placed penitents at the threshold of the church, outside the fellowship of the congregation and unable to enter the building until escorted into it. Penitents were often instructed to draw further attention to themselves by requesting the congregation's

---

268 The 'script' was sketched in the seventh Head of the *First Book of Discipline* and elaborated in Knox's 'Order of Excommunication', *Works*, Vol. 6, pp. 449–70. The 'screenplay' of the penitential drama has been reconstructed from the kirk session records thoroughly researched by Professor Todd.

269 The following description of the penitential drama is heavily indebted to Todd's chapter on 'Performing Repentance'.

prayers as its members passed on their way into church. Physically and spiritually, penitents were placed outside the community as a warning and a potential danger to the health and purity of the congregation. Flanked by elders who thereby 'protected' the congregation from being contaminated or infected, the penitents were processed from the church door. Before the sermon began they were escorted to a specially demarcated area close to or beneath the pulpit. A new item of ecclesiastical furniture was created to accommodate penitents during worship: the 'stool' or 'pillar of repentance' was a bench or stools set aside for that purpose and placed in its special location, often having the word 'Repentance' carved on the wood. Once installed on the stool penitents had to stand or sit facing and in full view of the congregation. Since penitents were only sentenced to the stool if their sin or subsequent disobedience had caused 'scandal' to the congregation and was therefore a 'public' offence, repentance and restitution also had to be public. Being on prominent display was essential for such public humiliation and penitence. Penitents' ingenious attempts to cover their faces, with women pulling their plaids over their heads and men wearing extra large bonnets and the large sums paid to avoid or reduce the Sundays sitting on the stool demonstrated that this was a very effective method of humiliation.

When the sermon had finished the full spotlight was directed upon the penitents. Directed by the minister, the main acts of the drama were now performed with every penitent playing 'the contrite sinner' and watched critically by their congregational audience. Each penitent in turn named themselves and their offence and then on their knees gave a full confession requesting the forgiveness of God, of the church and of any person directly injured or offended by their action. This followed a monologue form punctuated by appropriate gestures or in some cases became a catechetical-like dialogue with the minister who supplied substantial prompting or assistance. Penitents would conclude their confession with the promise that, with God's grace, they would not re-offend.

Since the confession was intended to reflect the penitent's inner feelings it needed to sound heartfelt and contain specific personal declarations delivered with a measure of spontaneity or at least verisimilitude. Not surprisingly, confessions tended to follow a similar pattern and frequently contained set phrases and stylized gestures of self-condemnation; for slander the tongue might be held accompanied by the ritual phrase 'Tongue, you lied.'[270] The spoken word accompanied by symbolic gestures created a very powerful statement in a society where the oral and aural tradition

---

270 The same gesture was used in non-ecclesiastical contexts see E. Ewan, 'Tongue you lied: The Role of the Tongue in Rituals of Public Penance in Late Medieval Scotland', in Edwin D. Craun, ed., *The Hands of the Tongue: Essays on Deviant Speech*, Kalamazoo, MI: Medieval Institute Publications, 2007, pp. 115–36.

continued to carry great weight. For witnesses to see and hear a person commit him- or herself to a specified course of action created a contract in Scottish legal thinking and more generally such a commitment became a matter of honour. Without the recognition and honouring of such obligations early modern Scottish society could not have functioned because it had no police or other modern methods of law enforcement. In this context declarations of repentance made in public could not be lightly made.

The commonest sign of repentance, and one which increasingly came to be expected, was the shedding of tears. It was important for the penitent to look and sound the part and appear as convincingly contrite as possible. The Reformers' attempt to gauge inner feeling by judging external countenance, gesture and speech had the opposite effect: more attention inevitably became focused upon these externals and there emerged an unspoken pressure upon penitents to give a 'good show'. In some churches this even extended to a 'dress rehearsal' for penitents the day before to ensure they had learned their parts.

A parallel procession at the end of the service to the church door escorted the penitents who had further Sundays to serve on the stool of repentance to stand on the threshold once more while the congregation departed. Those penitents who had reached their final Sunday were able to perform the last act in their particular drama. Following the full confession, the minister would ask the congregation if they judged the penitent to be properly repentant and to have given the congregation full satisfaction for their offence. Having received an affirmative answer, he would then absolve the penitent, receiving them back into the body of Christ.[271] In token of this reconciliation, the elders, minister and individuals directly offended or just those seated nearest the stool, would shake the hand or embrace and kiss the 'received'. By walking from the stool of repentance to take a seat among the congregation, the former penitent crossed the invisible boundary to rejoin the Church and would be at liberty to leave with everyone else at the end of the service.

For those witnessing the penitential drama in the decades following the Reformation an unspoken contrast with late medieval penitential practice always remained in the background. Penance had ceased to be a sacrament

---

271 For the absolution the minister switched from 'We' (used in the prayers) to 'I'. 'If thou unfainedly repentis thy former iniquity, and beleves in the Lord Jesus, then I, in his Name, pronunce and affirme that thy sinnes ar forgevin, not only on earth, but also in heaven, according to the promises annexed with the preaching of his Word, and to the power put in the Ministerie of his Church', Knox, *Works*, Vol. 6, p. 460. There was little reference in the service to the power of the keys and there seems a slight ecclesiological fuzziness on the subject since the minister excommunicated in the name of the congregation but reconciled a penitent by the authority annexed to the preaching of the Word and held by the 'ministrie' (i.e. in early modern Scots the kirk session as a corporate body and so the chosen representatives of the congregation).

where the penitent confessed his or her sins privately to a priest.[272] Instead the congregation and its representatives, the 'ministrie' or kirk session, received public confessions, though there continued to be an important role for 'private admonition' following the procedure laid down in Matthew 18.15–16.[273] Interestingly, the hierarchy of sins which had been an important constituent of medieval confessional practice was silently retained. In their judicial role kirk sessions had no qualms about imposing a hierarchy of 'tarrifs' for different sins. One fundamental distinction now lay between those sins which were by their nature 'public' and always required a public penance and those which might only need 'private' discipline, provided repentance was forthcoming.[274] To demonstrate the contrast to the 'quick fix' allegedly used by the medieval ecclesiastical courts, the Reformed Kirk felt an almost oppressive need to demonstrate that excommunication was a last resort. This generated a protracted process with warnings and final warnings over a minimum of three Sundays before a sentence of excommunication could be pronounced the following week.[275]

The Protestant Reformers were determined that the particular theological meanings they attached to the penitential drama should be properly understood by the congregation. Following their general approach to worship, the spoken word was given pride of place and symbolic actions and gestures were downgraded which produced a ponderous framework with the penitential drama being constantly interrupted by explanations provided by the minister. This running commentary was set down in the 'Order of Excommunication' which provided the forms of service for excommunication, for the reception of an excommunicated person and for public repentance which gave specific prayers and admonitions which the minister addressed to the penitent and to the congregation.

The heavily didactic prayers and admonitions hammered home the soteriological message of bringing a sinner to repentance and, whenever possible, to restoration to the fellowship of the congregation. The peni-

---

272 Since the confessional box was a Counter-Reformation invention, a medieval confession was 'private' rather than anonymous. Public penance was also well established for major sins or crimes.

273 Matthew 18.15–18 was the biblical warrant for the whole process of ecclesiastical censure. The widespread use of private admonition has been underestimated since it usually failed to be recorded. However, the discovery of a draft minute-book for the South Leith kirk session alongside the 'top copy' demonstrates that private admonition was extensively used. I am grateful to Linda Dunbar for this point and look forward to the publication of her edition of the South Leith records by the Scottish Record Society.

274 Public offences were defined in *The First Book of Discipline*, pp. 165–7 and 171 and the 'Order for Excommunication', Knox, *Works*, Vol. 6, pp. 449–51.

275 In St Andrews during 1564 the 'last chances' offered John Biccarton elongated the process of excommunication to cover three months. D. Hay Fleming, ed., *Register of the minister, elders and deacons of the christian congregation of St Andrews, 1559–1600* 2 vols, Edinburgh: Scottish History Society, 1st ser. 4 & 7, 1889–90, Vol. 1, pp. 194–206.

tent's visible progression through the stages of public repentance mirrored the spiritual journey undertaken by every Christian on their own path to salvation and served as a powerful reminder that everyone was a sinner. The message that all were in need of divine mercy and each person might in future need to perform public repentance if they publicly offended provided an important counterpoint to the careful exclusion of those infected by sin. When the penitent was presented to the congregation, the minister stressed the congregation's solidarity with the sinner and the need for communal contrition as the church accepted its corporate responsibility for the offences committed in its midst. Everyone was urged to examine their hearts, accuse themselves before God and ask for mercy. Collectively, they offered to the penitent to 'join our sins with your sin and repute your fall our own ... [also] join our prayers with yours' and together petition God to restore the body of Christ.[276]

Other meanings of the penitential drama cut across this central theme of forgiveness. The language of disease prevention through amputating infected limbs emphasized the importance of separation and exclusion as did the imagery of purity and freedom from the thrall of Satan.[277] Also present was a strong undercurrent underlining justice and punishment which connected the drama during worship with the judicial function of the kirk session when it sat as a court and passed sentence. The Reformers' theological need to refute the view that penitential suffering contributed towards the forgiveness of sin led to a less than convincing insistence that the sole aim of the penitent's humiliation was to produce genuine contrition. The continued employment of forms of punishment such as imprisonment, being placed in the jougs or branks (iron collars and manacles or a scold's bridle) or being placed on bread and water further undermined this stance. Punishment did fulfil discipline's judicial aspect and the community's demand that justice should be seen to be done for restoration to be possible.

Discipline and the Sacraments

The major sanction which the Church could wield to uphold its discipline was 'excommunication' whereby an individual was excluded from the ecclesiastical community in general and the sacraments in particular.[278]

---

276 'Order of Excommunication', Knox, *Works*, Vol. 6, p. 458.

277 The amputation imagery was drawn directly from Matthew 18.8–9. The images of the Church as the spotless bride of Christ and of the fight against sin and Satan drew upon a wealth of biblical allusions.

278 The Reformation did not alter the meaning of excommunication and the Reformed Kirk still claimed the power of the keys (Matt. 18.17–18). A different ecclesiology removed the emphasis upon St Peter and his papal successors and grounded the power in the Church collectively which was represented by the local 'ministrie' or kirk session.

The Reformers only recognized two sacraments, baptism and the Lord's Supper, and both were to be administered 'in the face of the congregation'. In a similar manner to the Sunday morning service, the exercise of discipline directly affected the sacraments.

The exercise of discipline had a significant effect upon the administration of the Lord's Supper and the 'fencing of the tables' carried great dramatic power. It was axiomatic that those who had been excommunicated from the Church were denied access to the Lord's Supper, though a statute from an early Synod of Fife forbidding any excommunicated person from becoming an elder suggested it took a while for everyone to understand fully the Reformed polity and the implications of excommunication.[279] Those under the formal ban of excommunication formed a small percentage of the total excluded from Communion. It was a significant part of their penalty that those currently under discipline were not permitted to receive communion. The exclusion of unreconciled penitents was the equivalent of the pre-Reformation 'lesser excommunication' and demonstrated discipline's judicial dimension as the kirk session policed breaches of the moral code thereby keeping the body of Christ free from contamination by 'manifest sinners'. The seriousness with which this was taken caused parishes to go to considerable lengths to ensure penitents completed their sentences on the stool and were reconciled in time to share communion.

A third category excluded from the Lord's Table were those who had failed the pre-communion examination. This test undertaken by the kirk session of the level of moral behaviour and doctrinal knowledge to be found among the members of the congregation was a proactive implementation of discipline. It was designed to prevent those who through ignorance or sin could not approach the table in faith and to preserve the purity and health of the eucharistic body of Christ. All potential communicants were expected to furnish proof of their belief; at the minimum an individual needed to be able to recite the Lord's Prayer, Ten Commandments and the Creed, and increasingly knowledge of the Catechism was also required. Provided their moral behaviour was also deemed acceptable, a prospective communicant received a small metal token from the examining elder or minister. Since they were such a significant and visible 'prop' for the Communion Sunday drama, communion tokens rapidly developed into a new indicator of social and moral respectability.

Every member of the parish was expected to attend church on a Communion Sunday and to be absent without good reason was to become liable to discipline. From the point of arrival at the church, those with tokens

---

279 L. Dunbar, 'Synods and Superintendence: John Winram and Fife, 1565–1572', *Records of the Scottish Church History Society* 27 (1997), pp. 217–38.

were distinguished from those without them; in Perth different doors were used by the two groups and they sat separately. To be denied a communion token brought a public shame witnessed by the entire community. Elders would be stationed to supervise entry and collect the tokens either at the door or as communicants approached the tables. Though all listened to the sermon, those who were excluded from Communion were either sent from the church or kept strictly apart from the tables and the elements. The holy space where the holy meal was celebrated was 'fenced' protecting the purity of the visible body of Christ. This stark separation of those deemed worthy from their unworthy neighbours could not have been more dramatically displayed. In a parallel fashion to the penitential drama of Sunday morning worship, the fencing of the tables drew a very public boundary line. The visible separation on Communion Sunday was believed to reflect, however imperfectly, the division between saved and damned at the Last Judgement. The 'fence' protecting the communion tables was sometimes a physical barrier, reminding the congregation of the medieval wall or rail previously separating the sanctuary and altar from the nave of the church. That sacred space had been reserved for those in holy orders, a material boundary dividing clergy from laity. By contrast in the Reformed Kirk access to the sacramental space was open to all those with the appropriate level of doctrinal knowledge and moral behaviour.

In the other sacrament the exercise of discipline created considerable defensiveness among the Reformers when they sought to justify the prevention of an excommunicated person presenting his or her child for baptism. The reasons given drew heavily upon the concept of the 'people of God' with parallels between Old Testament Israel and sixteenth-century Scotland. Despite explaining that the sins of parents, in best biblical fashion, should be visited upon their offspring, a major concession was made to remove the impression that the baby was being victimized. If the father had been excommunicated, the mother or concerned friends were permitted to present the child for baptism but only with the proviso that they publicly repudiated the obstinacy of the excommunicated father.[280] Such a reversal of the normal pattern whereby the father presented his child gave a stark signal of exclusion: neither the excommunicated person nor their posterity were to be counted as members of the people of God. The fear that their child would be deprived of baptism proved an important incentive for couples found guilty of sexual sins not to defy the kirk session and speedily to 'make their repentance'. The pre-Reformation belief that at death unbaptized children went to limbo rather than heaven created great pressure upon parents to conform and proved very hard for the Protestants to eradicate.

---

280 *The First Book of Discipline*, p. 170.

The cleanliness, health and purity of the sacraments were dependent upon a lively regime of ecclesiastical censure. Discipline held the visible Church together and, as James Melville explained, the three marks of the Church could not be separated without grave danger and the only way to achieve a 'right and perfyt kirk' was to have 'right and perfyt discipline'.

General Fast

In the eyes of the Reformers public repentance was not confined to individuals but could and should sometimes be a corporate activity. Unique among European Reformed churches, the Scottish Kirk devised a special order of service to express such communal penitence. The 'Order of the General Fast' was first published in 1566 and was used at national, regional and local level during the early modern period.[281] A Fast was employed as a corporate action to combat a specific crisis, most commonly a disaster such as the arrival of plague, a bad harvest or serious storms which were assumed to indicate the wrath of God. Fasts could also be used to face political disasters, becoming a method of lawful political protest against a government policy or the international situation.[282] This kind of response fitted 'naturally' into early modern Scots' view of the operation of the world which rested upon providentialist explanations for events and assumed God's intervention at all levels of life from the personal up to the international. Participating in a Fast provided a limited replacement for the assorted methods used by the medieval Church to help people cope with events over which they had no control.

The theological language and context of the Order of the General Fast was derived from the close parallels drawn between the experience of Old Testament Israel and of Reformed Scotland. Both were in a covenant relationship with God and a communally experienced disaster was interpreted as a sign of God's judgement at the people's failure to fulfil their covenant promise. Consequently, repentance was the obvious and most efficacious response. The language of the Old Testament prophets furnished the descriptions of the communal sins which were being punished and frequently this incorporated biblical calls for social justice. Running alongside the view of the Scots as a new people of God was an alternative Old Testament image of the 'faithful remnant'. It provided a framework enabling a Fast to be also presented as a propitiatory action by the religiously committed on behalf of their irreligious countrymen and

---

281 For the full text see, Knox, *Works*, Vol. 6, pp. 391–426. It is fully discussed in W. Ian P. Hazlett, 'Playing God's Card: Knox and Fasting, 1565–6', in R. Mason, ed., *John Knox and the British Reformations*, Aldershot: Ashgate, 1998, pp. 176–98.

282 Hazlett, 'Playing God's Card', p. 176.

as a witness by the 'faithful' to their neighbours. Fasts were proclaimed by the civil authorities as well as the Kirk when localities were afflicted by plague or similar calamities. In such circumstances propitiatory action by the community allowed its members to face the terrifying events which frequently threatened their existence.

Running over eight days and incorporating two Sundays, a Fast provided a forum for the open display of communal humiliation and repentance. The complete abstinence from food lasted from the first Saturday at 8 p.m. to the first Sunday at 5 p.m. and for the remainder of the week only bread and drink were to be consumed. There were generous concessions for the sick or elderly because the public observation of the Fast was deemed more important than actual abstinence. Dress was also employed to demonstrate corporate humiliation, with 'no gorgeous apparel' to be worn during a Fast.[283] The normal pattern of Sunday worship was extended to three hours for the morning service and two for the afternoon devotions. A reading from the Law (Deut. 27 and 28) and a different confession of sins were specified and the preacher was to explain in his sermon the Law, the punishments and blessings it brought, Christ as the end and perfection of the Law and the need for all to repent, have a steadfast faith and demonstrate amendment of life.[284] The Reformers stressed that the power of corporate prayer from humble hearts was the most potent weapon available to alter the course of events: God would listen and intervene.

The new theological message which the Reformers were seeking to teach the Scots was that there was nothing mechanical or mechanistic about penance and contrition must be heartfelt. Great stress was placed upon penitents, whether as individuals or communities, demonstrating both an affective and an informed response. This was expressed in the way early modern society understood best, by action as well as words, thereby allowing some medieval rituals to be recycled. Such continuity eased the kingdom's transition from a Catholic to a Protestant country but brought its own dangers. The greater the stress upon the internal emotions and the need to give them expression the more likely it was that the performance became an end in itself. The gulf created at the Reformation by destroying the security offered by the medieval sacramental system was partially filled in Scotland by placing acts of individual and corporate repentance within the context of corporate worship.

In 1517, Luther's protest and the movement now recognized as the Protestant Reformation began as an attack upon the medieval penitential system. The mighty Lutheran doctrine of justification by faith alone became

---

283 Knox, *Works*, Vol. 6, p. 416.
284 Knox, *Works*, Vol. 6, p. 420.

one of the theological bedrocks for the Scottish Reformed Kirk. There is a historical irony that penance, despite losing its status as a sacrament of the Church, came to occupy a more central role in Scottish ecclesiastical life following the Reformation than it had within the medieval system.

9

PATTERNS OF WORSHIP IN REFORMATION SCOTLAND

Jane Dawson

It was no coincidence that the Scottish Reformation Crisis started during Sunday morning worship with a crash. On 11 May 1559 in St John's parish church in Perth John Knox's sermon on the cleansing of the Temple provoked an iconoclastic riot, which rapidly spread to the rest of the burgh and provoked the Wars of the Congregation, 1559–60. The settlement of those wars brought the formal establishment of the Reformed Kirk throughout the kingdom in the summer of 1560. Since it was never reversed, this marked the creation of a Protestant Scotland. In addition to being the first link in that momentous chain of events, the transformation of worship lay at the heart of the change to Protestantism: the new theology was experienced and understood by most Scots through the medium of worship. Within early modern Scotland those new patterns of worship created a new Protestant culture.[285]

That first round of smashing led to many others as the Protestants seized the opportunity to 'cleanse' the churches of Scotland. This campaign of destruction had specific targets, especially the physical apparatus associated with the Mass and the cult of the saints: altars and statues were broken or defaced, wall paintings were whitewashed, saints' relics and communion vessels were removed. With the exception of the friaries, the external structures of church buildings were left intact because they

---

285 The new patterns of worship are described by G. Donaldson, 'From Reformation to Covenant', in D. Forrester & D. Murray, eds, *Studies in the History of Worship in Scotland*, Edinburgh: T&T Clark, 1984; W. Maxwell, *A History of Worship in the Church of Scotland*, London: Oxford University Press, 1951, ch. 3; W. McMillan, *The Worship of the Scottish Reformed Church, 1560–1638*, London: James Clarke, 1931. The new Protestant culture is discussed by M. Todd, *The Culture of Protestantism in Early Modern Scotland*, New Haven: Yale University Press, 2002, and the general historical background in J. Dawson, *Scotland Re-formed, 1488–1587*, Edinburgh: Edinburgh University Press, 2007.

were to continue to serve as places of parish worship.[286] Those ecclesiastical buildings deemed surplus to parish requirements were abandoned or converted to secular use. The loss of the regular orders, the downgrading of the cathedrals to parish churches and the decommissioning of many chapels removed the liturgical variety present in the medieval Church.

For most communities this led to a dramatic and thorough reordering of the interior of their parish church and in places such as St Andrews the change sometimes took place between one day and the next.[287] The church looked and felt different for the parishioners because its internal space was no longer divided into the nave and the sanctuary and consequently no physical boundary, such as a rood screen, separated the clergy from laity. With all side altars removed, the church interior now comprised a single space which served as one large stage and auditorium where all the action could be seen and heard and the audience was itself part of the drama. The east end where the high altar had stood ceased to be the focal point for worship and that function was now occupied by the pulpit, usually placed against the south wall. Since all churches had been built along an east–west axis such a switch in the building's orientation did not automatically make good architectural sense. Even where it proved less convenient, the new arrangements continued as a fundamental reminder to the congregation that the sacrifice of the Mass had been totally repudiated and the preaching of the Word now formed the heart of public worship.

Using time rather than space, there was a similar conscious attempt to eliminate the climax of the Eucharist provided by the words of consecration. Medieval practice had achieved a moment of great intensity when all sensory attention was focused upon one location where the priest raised the host, a bell was rung and those present dropped to their knees. To remove all these associations with the doctrine of transubstantiation, the Reformers carefully altered the rhythms as well as the wording of the Lord's Supper, flattening the crescendos and ensuring no single focal point was highlighted. In geometric terms they aimed to replace the sharp point of attention fixed at the priestly apex of a triangle by a smooth congregational circle of attentive experience.

With blank or white walls and the disappearance of images, candles and incense, no visual or sensory 'distractions' remained within Protest-

---

286 For the ingenious solutions devised to cope with the very large parishes found in the Highlands and Islands and the inconvenient sites of many parish churches, see J. Dawson, 'Calvinism in the Gaidhealtachd', in A. Duke, G. Lewis and A. Pettegree, eds, *Calvinism in Europe, 1540–1620*, Cambridge: Cambridge University Press, 1994, pp. 231–53.

287 J. Dawson, '"The Face of Ane Perfyt Reformed Kyrk": St Andrews and the early Scottish Reformation', in J. Kirk, ed., *Studies in Church History Subsidia 8: Humanism and Reform: The Church in Europe, England and Scotland, 1400–1643*, Oxford: Oxford University Press, 1991, pp. 412–36.

ant churches. The Reformers had produced the equivalent of a bare stage that directed the gaze and the ear upon the words and actions of the minister and congregation making it essential that the words be audible and comprehensible and everything be performed in full view. The rejection of Latin, which had acquired a special patina of holiness as the language of worship, in favour of the vernacular, underlined the massive didactic thrust of Protestant worship. However, because Scotland had several vernaculars, Gaelic and Norn in addition to Scots, and with the Bible and liturgy printed in English this was not without its problems.[288]

The removal of the separation between nave and sanctuary also changed the experience of worship for the laity by eliminating those individual lay devotional worlds which had coexisted alongside the clerical celebration of the Mass.[289] After the Reformation, all public worship was communal and even during silent prayer members of the congregation would be praying together on the same subject. Being denied a visual prompt inside the church or when passing external statues or wayside crosses, individual devotion increasingly became confined within the home. Other external gestures, such as crossing oneself or saying rosary beads were roundly condemned as 'popish' practices and became the subjects of censure. Carrying a Bible or psalm book under one's armpit rapidly emerged as a signal of Protestant identity, though it functioned as a passive badge rather than a devotional action.[290]

Destruction being easier than construction, the campaign to dismantle the complicated and colourful structure and appendages of medieval religious practice was comparatively straightforward. From the standpoint of future generations it was a cultural disaster as the glories of medieval art, music and, to a lesser extent, architecture were cast aside, broken or ritually burned: this was the sharp end of a revolution in the worship and beliefs of the Scottish people. The iconoclasm was normally supervised to prevent too much looting and to emphasize the religious purpose of the exercise, though at times the violence created its own intimidating momentum. The campaign successfully achieved its destructive objective and after 1560

---

288 C. Jones, ed., *The Edinburgh History of the Scots Language*, Edinburgh: Edinburgh University Press, 1997, and, for the Reformation and Gaelic, see D. Meek, 'The Reformation and Gaelic culture' in J. Kirk, ed., *The Church in the Highlands*, Edinburgh: Scottish Church History Society, 1998, pp. 37–62; The Gaelic translation by John Carswell of the *Book of Common Order* was the first book ever printed in that language, *Foirm na N-Urrnuidheadh: John Carswell's Gaelic translation of the Book of Common Order*, ed. R. L. Thomson, Edinburgh: Scottish Gaelic Texts Society, 1970.

289 The devout used the equivalent of a parallel liturgy as set out in the *Lay Folk Mass Book*, evocatively described by E. Duffy, *Marking the Hours: English People & their Prayers, 1240–1570*, New Haven CT: Yale University Press, 2006.

290 For an example of the Bible under the armpit as a self-conscious Protestant badge from as early as 1570, Dawson, *Scotland Re-formed*, p. 279.

most Scots were not offered any opportunity to choose between a Roman Catholic and a Protestant form of worship. Whatever their views, Scots had to make the best they could of understanding the new patterns, the theology they conveyed and the new requirements of the Reformed Kirk.

Constructing a permanent replacement for the sophisticated patterns of worship of the medieval Church required the slow building of a new Protestant culture over several generations. Despite the huge emphasis upon removing the past there was a quiet and important stream of continuity easing the transition from old to new.[291] Ritual and drama remained under a different guise and actions 'spoke' loudly alongside the words. The intense pressure exerted by society's expectations brought modifications in the practice of worship which went beyond Reformed theory, especially in the celebration of the rites of passage of birth, marriage and death. Following the forceful iconoclasm the laity faced the shock of adjusting to the radically different manner in which they were expected to participate in worship. Since in the new ecclesiology public worship could not exist without a gathering of the faithful, the presence of a congregation was essential and its members found themselves at the centre of liturgical action. Every time it gathered the congregation lent physical reality to the church as the body of Christ and the phrase 'in the face of the congregation' was frequently on the Reformers' lips; in a profoundly literal sense the visible Church was the parish at worship. The Lord's Supper was always a communal meal and baptism was also normally incorporated into the Sunday service. Sunday worship revolved around the sermon which by definition required listeners and both sacraments were necessarily accompanied by the preaching of the Word.

Though attendance at church was essential, it was not sufficient by itself: each member of the congregation had to be attentive enough and understand sufficiently to be open to the saving grace on offer through Word and sacrament. Active lay participation was compulsory for the first time and the congregation joined in the dramas of the Lord's Supper, baptism and public repentance and had its special role in church music with the communal singing of the metrical psalms. Reformed ecclesiology demanded the fulfilment of a novel set of religious obligations and Scots were forced to make major adjustments to their style of religious observance. Having abolished the regular orders, a single pattern of holiness was not only on offer to everyone but was also expected from all. For the Reformers Scotland's covenant relationship with God underpinned this drive to create a 'holy nation' and in particular to uphold 'pure' worship.

The destruction had stripped away most of a church's interior furnish-

---

291 Todd sees an element of continuity as an essential ingredient in the successful establishment of the new Protestant culture, see *Culture of Protestantism*, Conclusion.

ings leaving a single space emphasizing the largest surviving item, the pulpit, which in many parishes was enlarged to include a reader's desk on the lower tier, occasionally a middle exhorter's tier and the preacher's pulpit at the top. The large stone font that had stood at the church door had been replaced by a small basin, often attached by a metal bracket to the pulpit in a plain but potent reminder of the link between Word and sacrament. In many churches the wooden communion tables which replaced the fixed stone altar were stacked away when not in use, which was both a practical measure and a further distancing from the view that divine power adhered to any of the equipment surrounding the eucharistic celebration. The 'stool of repentance' was the sole new item of furniture and it was located under or close to the pulpit. Fixed seating only gradually encroached upon the church's interior space as the socially prominent paid for the construction of 'lofts', 'seats' or 'desks'. The rest of the congregation sat on small portable stools or the floor, or stood during the service. One unintended consequence of removing spatial and physical boundaries between clergy and laity was to give greater visibility to the social hierarchy of the community: where people sat was determined by their status, age and sometimes gender. Although the medieval laity had performed some religious actions in strict order of rank, such as kissing the pax board during the Mass or the annual Corpus Christi procession, local social structure was given visual solidity and permanence by the construction of pews. Inevitably, this produced disputes about precedence, some of which became heated and led to violence, such as at Peterhead where a rival's pew was hacked apart and burned within the churchyard.[292]

Regular exposure to the Word, preferably expounded by a preacher, was believed by the Reformers to be the main method by which Scotland would be converted to a lively Protestant faith. Having abandoned liturgical variety, the preaching service with a range of additions became the format for all public worship. The most noticeable loss was the former liturgical calendar with its great feasts and fasts which marked the similar rhythms of the religious and agricultural year. While the campaign to eradicate festivities, especially Christmas, had limited success, it did detach such celebrations entirely from Reformed worship. An element of seasonality slipped back via the back door, especially through the retention of an annual, spring Communion, preserving much of the practice of the Lent preparation and Easter Communion. Although some of the language and the customs associated with saints' days survived within post-Reformation Scotland, they did so within an entirely non-ecclesiastical

---

292 In 1621–2 there was a feud between Andrew Fraser, younger of Muchalls in Buchan, and Sir William Keith of Ludquharn, which began over seating in the new kirk at Peterhead. The case ended up in front of the Privy Council.

setting: the boundary between the sacred and the profane had been re-drawn.[293] The 'week' came to dominate perceptions of time and because Sunday was the sole, official, holy day an embryonic weekend emerged, though not one filled with leisure. With the congregation required to be inside their parish church for the start of the service, attending at a set time and place became the norm. Scots developed the habits of 'timekeeping' in the modern sense; a useful skill when industrialization arrived.

The outline of the services which Scots attended after the Reformation was laid down in the *Book of Common Order*. Having originally been compiled for the English-speaking congregation in Geneva in 1556, it was formally adopted as the Kirk's liturgy by the General Assembly in 1562 with extra services such as a General Fast and Order of Excommunication being added in subsequent years.[294] However, the minimalist style of the *Book of Common Order* has masked the rich and complex experience of worship, particularly when viewed from the perspective of Scottish lay men and women. For them the summons to church on Sunday arrived in the familiar guise of the bell, ringing first as a warning to get ready and a signal for penitents to set out for church, a second ring for the call to church and a third to signal the arrival of the minister to begin the preach-ing service. In many parishes the doors were locked after the third bell and some latecomers were forced to lean through the window to hear the sermon and avoid the penalty for non-attendance.[295]

A reader's service occupied the period between the second and third bell, though this would constitute the main Sunday morning service in those parishes which did not have a minister to preach the sermon.[296] Since it did not merit its own section within the *Book of Common Order*, the service's importance has been undervalued. Each week most parishioners heard part or all of this service, if only for the mundane reason of securing a good seat for the sermon. Led by a reader, it followed a simple pattern with readings from the Bible alternating with communal psalm-singing and prayers.[297] In the early years which followed the Reformation crisis,

---

293 See Todd, *Culture of Protestantism*, chs 4 & 7.

294 For the text of the *Book of Common Order* in its 1556 and 1564 editions see J. Knox *The Works of John Knox*, ed. D. Laing, 6 vols, Edinburgh: Bannatyne Club, 1846–64, Vol. 4, pp. 141–214; Vol. 6, pp. 275–380; for the General Fast and Order of Excommunication, Vol. 6, pp. 381–470. For a liturgical discussion see W. Maxwell, *The Liturgical Portions of the Genevan Service Book*, London: Oliver and Boyd, 1931.

295 The astute Robert Gib of Falkirk explained to the kirk session that he had leaned in the church window on Easter Day 1622, 'out of no evil intention' but rather 'for the earnest [desire] he had to hear the word preached', Todd, *Culture of Protestantism*, p. 41.

296 The office of reader was created in 1560 by *The First Book of Discipline*, ed. J. Cam-eron, Edinburgh: St Andrew Press, 1972, pp. 105–7.

297 The prayers included the confession of sins, which was also found in the main Sun-day morning service so probably only formed part of the reader's service when there was no sermon.

listening to the Bible in the vernacular would have been a great novelty: there would have been many new stories and an opportunity to hear the actual scriptural words describing more familiar ones. Hearing the text spoken was their chance for direct access to the Bible for the majority of Scots who were non-literate.

The high level of memorizing skill present in early modern Scotland would also have helped immeasurably with the metrical psalm-singing: another novel experience for the laity. With its easier verse format and simple musical style, it was not uncommon for people to have learned by heart the whole of the metrical psalter. This great songbook of the Christian Church down the ages, expressing much of human experience and interaction with God, became the best-known section of the Scriptures within Reformed Scotland. The Reformers' intense logocentricity ensured that hearing and understanding the words was given priority with the music explicitly subordinated to this process. In church, the use of a precentor, or in some burgh churches a choir, to lead the singing helped the laity to learn this new congregational skill.[298]

Singing the psalms gave the laity their own voice in worship and during the reader's service they were used as the congregation's direct response to the biblical readings. As the words themselves were biblical and unchanging, the psalm texts were doctrinally 'safe'. Communal psalm-singing provided a vital element of interactivity and in many liturgical contexts represented the congregation leading themselves in prayer. The metrical psalms were the most noticeable constituent of Protestant worship to move outside the church and become part of daily life. In a military context they became the 'battle-hymns of the Lord', sung by soldiers before battle and in other confrontations. They were employed as a political statement in 1561 when on Mary, Queen of Scots' first night back in Scotland John Knox and a group of fellow Protestants sang psalms underneath the Queen's window at Holyrood Palace. Similarly, the hundreds who processed through the streets of Edinburgh in 1583, singing Psalm 124 in four-part harmony to welcome back their exiled Presbyterian ministers, were making a forceful point to the hostile Arran regime.[299]

The abrupt opening of the preaching service in the *Book of Common Order* without even an introductory sentence indicates it followed directly

---

298 I am grateful to Timothy Duguid, my PhD student, for discussion concerning the music and the Scottish psalter during this period. Thomas Wode's beautifully illustrated part-books for the Scottish psalter demonstrate that some musical elaboration was available and might have developed into a more sophisticated musical tradition if circumstances had been different, see I. Woods Preece *Our awin Scottis use: Music in the Scottish Church up to 1603*, Glasgow: Universities of Glasgow and Aberdeen, 2000; D. James Ross, *Musick Fyne*, Edinburgh: Mercat Press, 1993.

299 Dawson, *Scotland Re-formed*, pp. 227–311.

from the reader's service. The ringing of the third bell and the formal arrival of the minister signalled a new phase of worship reminiscent of former processions inside the church. The minister's garments, ordinary lay dress with an academic-style gown, emphasized his learning but visually denied any priestly function. However, because he was the preacher of the Word and the mouthpiece of the congregation when addressing God, the special status of the minister was constantly signalled during public worship. A regular sermon was a novel experience for the congregation and for some of its listeners would have provided a welcome religious and intellectual challenge. If a preacher stopped before the hour his audience felt short-changed, though outstanding preachers, such as Robert Blair who developed 'fan-clubs' were encouraged to extend their sermons to two hours. Sixteenth-century Scots had well-developed aural skills and were used to listening and absorbing the messages conveyed by what they heard. Some who were literate and enthusiastic also took notes. The surviving notebooks give an impression of the style and coverage encountered by parishioners though like the few printed sermons they recorded sermons for special occasions, such as communions or fasts.[300]

In their sermons ministers sought to provoke an emotional response from their listeners as well as teach them the new doctrines. In common with general Reformed practice, a Scottish sermon series followed a single biblical book, starting from the beginning and slowly working through to the end. The initial section of the sermon dealt in detail with the biblical text and then moved into its exegesis. The final part provided the text's 'application', relating its message to contemporary life often in specific ways. Common teaching devices, such as clear numbered points and repetition, were used to make the key ideas memorable and imprint them in the congregation's minds. The use of vivid word imagery helped raise the emotional temperature.[301] Questions, now read as rhetorical, were probably intended to elicit a verbal response or affirmation from the congregation.[302] Sighs, weeping and the raising of hands in the air were not uncommon congregational reactions to a sermon or prayers. Not everyone remained engaged, and sleeping was sufficiently common for elders to employ a stick to prod people awake: those who lay face down on the church floor during the sermon were obviously taking the day of rest too literally.

---

300 I am grateful to Professor Ian Green, who is currently undertaking a study of sermon literature in early modern Britain, for discussions about sermons.

301 In Gaelic sermons early modern preachers carried over some of the former bardic conventions and some of the classical common Gaelic vocabulary to create a tradition of vivid imagery and word pictures which has survived to this day; D. Meek, 'The pulpit and the pen: clergy, orality and print in the Scottish Gaelic world', in A. Fox and D. Woolf, eds, *The Spoken Word: Oral Culture in Britain, 1500–1850*, Manchester: Manchester University Press, 2002, pp. 84–118.

302 Todd, *Culture of Protestantism*, pp. 53–4.

One major incentive to remain attentive was the need to 'rehearse' the key points of the day's sermon to the head of the household that evening or to understand sufficient Reformed doctrine to pass the next pre-communion examination. The enforced learning of new ideas was probably a considerable burden for many parishioners. However, in an age without compulsory schooling, Protestant worship might have offered an interesting challenge for some and it certainly provided a significant incentive to learn to read and thereby gain unmediated access to the Scriptures.

The attention to the sermon paid by the penitents sitting on the stool of repentance could easily be monitored because they were in full view of the rest of the congregation. The penitential drama formed an important part of the Sunday morning service and one which offered a more visual message acted out in front of the congregation. It brought processional movement through the church interior when the penitents were led to and from their place on the stool before and after the sermon and their public confession to the congregation introduced a different and probably highly interesting spectacle.[303] Witnessing those who were temporarily 'excluded' from the body of the church reinforced the sense of the inclusion among the members of the congregation and underlined the importance of their communal actions.

Sunday worship filled most of the day because following the morning service there was a session for catechizing, which involved adults as well as children. This explicitly turned worship into a lesson, where both question and answer had to be learned by heart and doctrinal knowledge was the goal. In the afternoon, a shorter service repeated the morning pattern, with readings this time taken from the New rather than the Old Testament. Time not spent in church on a Sunday was not free for normal leisure activities: no games and certainly no drinking were permitted. The church courts strove to impose a strict Sabbatarianism, punishing any Sunday work and emphasizing church attendance and quiet religious pursuits as the only acceptable Sabbath activities.

This weekly cycle was interrupted by the celebration of the Lord's Supper. The hope expressed by the General Assembly in 1562 that urban parishes would hold communion four times a year and landward parishes twice a year proved too optimistic.[304] Once a year during the spring

---

303 For a full description see my chapter on 'Discipline and the Making of Protestant Scotland' in this book.

304 'The Booke of the Universall Kirk of Scotland': Acts and proceedings of the General Assemblies of the Kirk of Scotland, ed. T. Thomson, 3 vols, Edinburgh: Bannatyne Club, 81, 1839–45, Vol. 1, pp. 30–58. The First Book of Discipline discussed the doctrine and practice of the sacraments (pp. 90–3) and set down a quarterly celebration (p. 183). For a discussion of practice, see G. Burnet, The Holy Communion in the Church of Scotland, Edinburgh: Oliver and Boyd, 1960.

became the most common Scottish pattern; an unacknowledged continuation of the medieval practice of celebrating a parish Communion at Easter. The Lord's Supper developed into a major event which spanned at least two Sundays and involved substantial preparation by the entire parish so that the whole process sometimes spread over a couple of months. Every prospective communicant needed to be examined by the minister or elders as to their faith and life and only if they passed this test would they receive their communion token.[305] This time-consuming process was taken very seriously by the kirk session and by most parishioners, since exclusion from the Lord's Table brought social and religious shame. Gaining one's token was a considerable incentive to remain alert during the weekly catechizing and sermons.

Fasting remained closely associated with the period before receiving communion: a further link with the past and the officially discarded Lent. Preparation peaked during the Saturday service preceding Communion Sunday, which concentrated upon the themes of repentance and divine justice as preachers warned about sin and hypocrisy. With all eligible parishioners expected to communicate, multiple sittings were needed during the Communion Sunday to accommodate everyone, giving a strong sense of a communal gathering involving the entire community. On the following Monday a service of thanksgiving was held to round off the weekend of worship with the normal Sunday restrictions on work covering all three days of the communion. A second or even third Sunday was needed in many parishes to cope with the numbers of communicants. By the early seventeenth century this pattern of holding Communion foreshadowed the later 'communion seasons' with their emotional intensity, communal jollity and the appendages of a 'holy fair'.[306]

At the centre of this celebration was the communal meal of the Lord's Supper carefully choreographed to convey a new understanding of the Eucharist. The Reformers' general rejection of Latin as the language of worship and insistence that everything must be seen and heard was most noticeable in this service: comprehensibility and audibility were essential. Having emphatically rejected the doctrine of transubstantiation and being highly suspicious of any suggestion of mystery and priestly sacrifice, the Reformed service was self-consciously unadorned and overtly congregational. Everyday tableware was employed for the communion vessels made of wood, pewter and only later of silver. Designs such as a mazer cup used for communal drinking and especially for hospitality or kin reconciliation were copied to dispel associations with the elaborate chalices of medieval

---

305 See chapter on 'Discipline and the Making of Protestant Scotland'.

306 L. E. Schmidt, *Holy Fairs: Scottish Communions and American Revivals in the early modern period*, Princeton: Princeton University Press, 1989.

usage. At the tables the communicants sat on benches and handed the bread and the wine to each other as in a family meal. Receiving both elements was new to the laity and ordinary bread was rather different from the small, unleavened wafers previously placed on the tongue by a priest. Judging by the quantities consumed the wine was drunk rather than sipped politely in modern fashion.

Every attempt was made to remove the association of sacred or magical power adhering to the elements themselves. Even the words of institution were not pronounced at the table but occurred within the earlier reading from 1 Corinthians 11, which provided the biblical warrant.[307] In their sermons and the short 'exhortation' given to each sitting, the preachers laid immense emphasis upon the spiritual presence of Christ to be experienced within the believer's heart during this re-enactment of the Last Supper. This could generate an intense emotional atmosphere and produced ecstatic experiences among some communicants as they participated in the meal. The reverent ceremony of the occasion was heightened by the slow procession of communicants moving to and from the tables carefully marshalled by the elders. It highlighted the division between those excluded from communion and those included; a pre-figuring of the Day of Judgement.[308] Once seated all communicants possessed an equal status and might compare themselves to the apostles sitting eating with Jesus. Within the hierarchical society of early modern Scotland this dramatic expression of the doctrine of 'the priesthood of all believers' could generate a sense of religious and social liberation.[309] Sitting at a communal board rapidly established itself as a much-valued part of the Scottish Communion service. The attempt in the early seventeenth century to introduce kneeling to receive communion was greeted with outrage since it appeared to undermine the entire ethos of existing Scottish practice.[310]

Baptism, the only other sacrament recognized by the Reformers, was also demystified and simplified. Although the water was retained, now held in a small basin, the holy oil, salt, wax and spittle were not and

---

307 Maxwell, *Liturgical Portions*, p. 121. No words of delivery were given in the form of service but there is evidence that some were used. See Maxwell, *Liturgical Portions*, pp. 126–7; 138–40.

308 See chapter on 'Discipline and the Making of Protestant Scotland'.

309 Much of the medieval imagery of purgatory and the dance of death had conveyed a similar sense of equality.

310 Posture to receive communion varied within the European Reformed tradition, for comparisons, see P. Benedict *Christ's Churches Purely Reformed: A Social History of Calvinism*, New Haven, CT: Yale University Press, 2002, ch 15. Although kneeling was used during prayer and for public repentance, in Scotland kneeling to receive was strongly associated with the adoration of the elements and so with the doctrine of transubstantiation. The kneeling article was the most contentious of the Five Articles of Perth (1617–18) and of the liturgical changes introduced by King Charles I during the 1630s. For a discussion of Scottish views, see D. Mullan, *Scottish Puritanism, 1590–1638*, Oxford: Oxford University Press, 2000.

along with the cross on the forehead were dismissed as 'inventions devised by men' and abandoned.[311] A child was normally brought to the Sunday morning service by its father and the baptism was conducted 'in the face of the congregation' after the sermon. This placement brought the practical advancement of minimum disruption from a baby's cries to the preaching and the doctrinal point that the sacrament was a reception into the 'body of the faithful' and conclusively anchored to the preaching of the Word. In response to strong lay feelings if a child were sickly a form of emergency baptism might be undertaken by the minister usually accompanied by a few elders or 'godly' to form a minimal congregation. This considerable concession accommodated the deeply rooted fear that an unbaptized child could not enter heaven if they died, even though such an assumption had no place within Reformed theology. The medieval practice of permitting midwives or any Christian to baptize a baby *in extremis* was firmly rejected: those caught were treated as Roman Catholics.

Since the bond of 'gossipry', as the relationship between godparent and the baby's kin was called, played an important part in Scottish social networks, the Kirk's second and largely silent concession to society's expectations permitted the continued use of godparents, often renamed witnesses.[312] Rather than directly tackling godparenting, kirk sessions concentrated upon keeping numbers down and ensuring the baptismal celebrations did not create too much disruption to worship or the Sabbath. Women suffered most from the new attitude to baptism because their role as 'gossips' was downplayed and the specifically female celebration of 'churching', when the mother completed her 40 days of confinement and returned to normal society, was abandoned. Compared to its medieval predecessor, the Reformed Kirk drew a more restrictive line between public worship and private celebration and pushed the latter firmly into the non-religious sphere. Where previously a blurred continuum had linked the sacred and the profane, a chasm was opened.[313]

Although no longer a sacrament, marriage was designated by the Reformers as an 'ordinance of God' and they generated a major effort to bring the ceremony more firmly under ecclesiastical control. To be valid and regular a marriage was deliberately placed within that most public

---

311 *First Book of Discipline*, p. 91.

312 J. Dawson, '"There is nothing like a good gossip": Godparenting, baptism and alliance in early modern Scotland', in M. Mackay and C. Kay, eds, *Perspectives on the Older Scottish Tongue*, Edinburgh: Edinburgh University Press, 2005, pp. 38–47. In Scotland, unlike England, 'gossip' was used to describe a male godparent. Female godparents did continue but the male responsibility of presenting the child emphasized a more patriarchal approach.

313 The increased stress upon 'order' and 'decency' in worship and specifically within church was found across the confessional divide and was also a feature of Counter-Reformation Catholicism as well as Protestantism; for a comparative perspective see D. MacCulloch, *Reformation: Europe's House Divided, 1490–1700*, London: Allen Lane, 2003, Pt III.

of arenas, 'the face of the congregation', being celebrated during Sunday morning service. Underscoring marriage's public nature the reading of the banns on the three Sundays preceding the wedding also had its place within public worship. As with baptismal parties, a comparatively light regulatory touch was extended to cover the celebrations which followed on the Sabbath. A much sterner disciplinary view was taken of cases of sexual misbehaviour, before and within marriage, which occupied much of the time of the kirk sessions and other church courts.

The greatest change concerning rites of passage and probably the most difficult for the laity to accept was the absence of a formal service for the dead. Since belief in purgatory had been abandoned and any suggestion of praying for the dead was unacceptable, the Reformers did not include a burial service in the *Book of Common Order*. Within a very short time, however, funeral sermons were being preached in the church following an internment; Knox himself preached the sermon after Regent Moray's assassination in 1570 and reduced the congregation of 3,000 to tears. Grand funeral processions for society's elite filled with heraldic pageantry and including the traditional giving of alms became even more elaborate after the Reformation. For all ranks the feasting of the wake and its accompanying customs continued in an entirely non-ecclesiastical context. What did remain inside the church, in spite of acts of the General Assembly forbidding the practice, were the graves of the social elite. Following a period of artistic uncertainty as to what might be acceptable in a Reformed society, the late sixteenth and early seventeenth century witnessed an upsurge in elaborate, aristocratic tombs within the Lowlands: in the Western Highlands the magnificent tradition of funerary carving was permanently lost to be replaced in the seventeenth century by inferior imitations.[314]

The overpowering sense of continuity between the living and the dead that had marked late medieval piety was given new expression in the 'burial aisles' located in parish churches. These were often Protestantized versions of the side chapels founded by ancestors of the local elite to accommodate the prayers for their dead. Retaining their hallowed location and their link with past generations, these aisles frequently doubled as the lower storey of the family's 'loft' or seats for Sunday worship: a laird might almost literally be standing on the shoulders of his forebears.[315] For the lower levels of society, burial within the churchyard remained of crucial importance and

---

314 For the glories of late medieval sculpture, see K. Steer & J. Bannerman, *Late Medieval Monumental Sculpture in the West Highlands*, Edinburgh: RCAHMS, 1977.

315 A. Spicer, '"Defyle not Christ's kirk with your carrion": burial and the development of burial aisles in post-Reformation Scotland', in B. Gordon and P. Marshall, eds, *The Place of the Dead: Death and Remembrance in late medieval and early modern Europe*, Cambridge: Cambridge University Press, 2000, pp. 149–69.

an extremely strong awareness of consecrated or sacred ground persisted, even though it fitted uneasily within Reformed theology. With minimal assistance from the rituals of public worship, early modern Scots coped with the high levels of mortality they had to face. The Protestant deathbed retained the traditional communal and reconciling characteristics of its medieval forerunner and replaced extreme unction by a public confession of faith, Bible readings and psalm-singing.[316]

The other two rejected Catholic sacraments of confirmation and ordination also reappeared in Protestant clothes. Following their public examination in the catechism the admission of teenagers to their first communion was signified by the public reception of the communion token which marked their passage into adulthood. In the presence of the collegial authority of fellow ministers or the presbytery and with much dignified ceremony, a new minister was inducted to his charge through the ritual presentation of a Bible and the keys to the pulpit. This conveyed the same powerful and visible message of the separation of clergy from laity as had ordination by a bishop. Underlying such superficial differences, there was a strong element of continuity to ease the transition from the Catholic past to the Protestant future. From the medieval sacramental cycle, Protestant versions of the Eucharist, baptism, marriage, penance, confirmation and ordination were embedded within Reformed church worship and, as before, the consolation of the dying took place at the deathbed.

The colour and liturgical complexity of previous worship was succeeded by a solid diet of the Word and a single pattern of communal parish worship replaced the variety and fragmentation of much of medieval devotional life. The laity had lost some aspects of devotional life they had previously controlled themselves, such as religious guilds or the private cycle of prayers they said during Mass. In their place they had gained a new centrality within worship as the congregation filled the liturgical stage, though the role of the minister as the director of the service increasingly dominated proceedings. While Protestant worship was heavily logocentric and strongly emphasized its doctrinal and didactic aspects, it also produced an emotional atmosphere which sought to generate an affective response from the members of the congregation.

Through the medium of weekly worship the Reformers slowly built new patterns of religious belief and behaviour and by the end of the sixteenth century a new Protestant culture and identity had emerged. In 1559, a battle over worship lay at the heart of a revolution that had established Protestantism within the kingdom of Scotland. In 1638, a second revo-

---

316 A. Spicer, '"The rest of their bones", fear of death and Reformed burial practices', in W. Naphy and P. Roberts, eds, *Fear in Early Modern Society*, Manchester: Manchester University Press, 1997, pp. 167–83.

lution erupted when the received pattern of Reformed worship in Scotland was under threat. The National Covenant, signed in part to uphold 'true religion', had momentous consequences for the entire British Isles with Scotland's rebellion leading to the all-embracing Wars of the Three Kingdoms, 1638–60. In the century between the two revolutions, the new Reformed patterns of worship took such strong root in the kingdom that they became an integral part of Scottish national identity. As King Charles I found to his cost, Scots were prepared to die for the right to conduct their Sunday worship in the manner to which they had become accustomed.

10

THE SCOTO-CATHOLIC MOVEMENT IN PRESBYTERIAN WORSHIP *c.1850–c.1920*

Stewart J. Brown

Between the 1850s and the 1920s, Presbyterian worship in Scotland underwent profound changes, which taken together formed a sweeping movement of renewal or revival, known as the Scoto-Catholic movement. These changes included the introduction of written prayers, set liturgies, shorter sermons, benedictions, robed choirs, organs, anthems, more frequent Communions, the celebration of private Communions for the sick, funeral services and the more elaborate decoration of church interiors, including the increased use of stained glass windows. For some, the changes were little short of revolutionary. 'If worshippers of a past generation', observed a Church of Scotland General Assembly report in 1890, 'were to enter some of our churches, they would find little to remind them of the traditional forms with which they and their fathers were familiar.'[317] The changes began in the established Church of Scotland, and the promoters of change were broad church liberals and high church ritualists.

The renewal of worship in Scottish Presbyterianism was a gradual process, and the changes were often vigorously opposed by more traditionally minded ministers, elders and lay members. There were two main phases to the renewal movement. The first phase, between roughly the later 1850s and early 1890s, was characterized by innovations aimed at making Scottish Presbyterian church services more attractive, decorous and reverent, and closer to historic patterns, including those of the pre-Reformation and Continental churches. The innovators were largely concerned with asserting the position of the established Church of Scotland as a national

---

317 Quoted in A. K. Robertson, 'The Revival of Church Worship in the Church of Scotland', unpublished PhD thesis, University of Edinburgh, 1956, p. 215.

Church, and with developing forms of worship that would have a broad appeal to the Scottish people, especially the educated urban middle and upper classes. This phase was associated with the figure of Robert Lee, broad church minister of Greyfriars Church, Edinburgh, and with the work of the Church Service Society, formed in 1865. The second phase of the movement, from the early 1890s into the 1920s, was characterized by an increased emphasis on doctrinal issues in worship, and particularly on the Church as the spiritual body of Christ. The reformers of this second phase were concerned less with national religion, and more with asserting the identity of the Church of Scotland as a true branch of the one universal Church. This phase was associated with the vision of James Cooper, high church minister and professor, and with the work of the Scottish Church Society, formed in 1892. While the reformers of the renewal movement were never more than a minority within the Church of Scotland, their influence upon public worship was profound and lasting.

The First Phase

The movement for the renewal of Scottish Presbyterian worship began as part of the general recovery of the Church of Scotland in the 1850s. The established Church had been dealt a heavy blow at the Disruption of 1843, when over a third of its ministers and perhaps half its lay members had left the Church, in protest over what they perceived as efforts by the state to undermine the Church's spiritual independence. The outgoing ministers had included many of the Church's most effective and dedicated preachers and pastors, and the prospects for the 'remnant' established Church for a time appeared bleak. According to the census of religious worship in 1851, only about 32 per cent of the Scottish churchgoing population attended the established Church. Adding to the difficulties, many members of the educated upper social orders – landowners, urban professionals, merchants and manufacturers – were being drawn to the Episcopal Church. Some had been attracted to Episcopal worship while attending public school or university in England, others while living abroad, whether through military or imperial civil service or through commerce.

During the early 1850s, the Church of Scotland began to recover from the Disruption. There was renewed pastoral commitment and effectiveness in preaching, exemplified by an able group of broad church, or liberal Presbyterian ministers, among them Norman MacLeod, John Caird, John Tulloch and R. H. Story. The established Church grew in confidence and recovered a sense of itself as the expression of the national religion of the Scottish people. One of these broad church reformers was Robert Lee (1804–68), minister of the historic Old Greyfriars Church in Edinburgh from 1843 and professor of biblical criticism at the University of Edinburgh from 1847. Lee had grown profoundly unhappy with what he viewed as the uninspired, ill-organized, unattractive and tedious forms of worship that were prevalent in most Presbyterian churches of Scotland. He believed that Presbyterian worship placed far too much emphasis on the sermon, which often lasted an hour or more, and was frequently dry, repetitious and boring. He was also concerned over the long extempore prayers given by most ministers, prayers that could ramble on for 20 to 40 minutes, and were often ill-digested repetitions of tired phrases, biblical quotations, theological jargon and pious instructions, which had little meaning as addresses to God and which were largely ignored by the dozing congregations. He objected also to the droning of psalms by congregations without instrumental accompaniment. His other concerns included infrequent Communions (celebrated once or twice a year in most congregations) and the lack of a funeral service. The dreary conduct of worship in most Presbyterian churches, he believed, was not only driving many of the educated classes to the more attractive services of the Episcopal Church, but was also discouraging the attendance of the working classes.[318] It was, in short, a serious obstacle to any recovery of the Church of Scotland's national influence.

In 1845, Greyfriars Church was destroyed by fire. When the church was eventually rebuilt and reopened in 1857, Lee took advantage of the new beginning to introduce a series of innovations. The rebuilt church was equipped with stained-glass windows. He composed and printed his own liturgy, including prayers which he read at services and set congregational responses. He introduced regular Bible readings into his services, opened each service with a solemn call to worship (instead of the customary psalm) and closed the service with a benediction. While the traditional practice was for congregations to sit while singing the psalms and to stand to pray, Lee had his congregation stand to sing and kneel to pray. He also worked to improve the quality of music, making increased use of hymns and introducing, in 1864, an organ into the church. This was the first organ to appear in an established church since 1807, when the Church courts had ruled organs to be contrary to the law of the Church of Scotland. In all these innovations, Lee had the support of his largely middle-class and educated Greyfriars congregation.

Much of the Church of Scotland, however, was outraged by the innovations. The Presbytery of Edinburgh condemned Lee's order of service in 1859. Lee responded by appealing to the General Assembly. Over the next several years, his innovations were the subject of intense debate in the

---

318 R. Lee, *The Reform of the Church of Scotland in Worship, Government, and Doctrine*. Part 1, 2nd edn, Edinburgh: Edmonston and Douglas, 1866, pp. 1–83.

Church courts. For his opponents, Lee's innovations were contrary to the law of the Church of Scotland, and were aimed at Anglicanizing, or even Romanizing the Church. They would drive away sincere Presbyterians and further weaken the established Church. For Lee, however, his innovations contradicted no Church law and were aimed at restoring a proper decorum and reverence to worship. He observed that Calvin, Knox and the Reformers had used set liturgies, and he argued that prayers carefully composed in advance were a more reverent means of addressing God than the rambling extempore prayers of the majority of ministers. Although Lee received support from the broad church group, his opponents carried the day. In 1865, at the instigation of Dr W. R. Pirie, professor of church history at the University of Aberdeen, the General Assembly passed the so-called Pirie act, aimed at halting innovation in worship. By the Pirie act, presbyteries were given the power to review any changes in worship, and to suppress them if they were viewed as contrary to Church law and usage, regardless of the wishes of the congregation.[319]

Lee, meanwhile, was unrepentant and continued with his innovations. In December 1865, he conducted a marriage ceremony in Greyfriars, which included read prayers, sung Amens and a *Te Deum* sung to a Gregorian chant.[320] New charges were brought against him. At its meeting in May 1866, the General Assembly was to decide on the legality of Lee's prayer book, and there was every expectation that this and other innovations would be suppressed. Before the Assembly met, however, Lee suffered a stroke, which left him incapacitated. He died in 1868, with no decision taken on his innovations.

Lee's reforms in worship were by now gaining a number of supporters. They included ministers, such as John Tulloch and Norman MacLeod, who had travelled abroad and were familiar with worship on the Continent. They also included ministers, among them George W. Sprott, who had served as ministers in colonial churches and gained a more global perspective on worship. In January 1865, while Lee's reforms were being fought over in the Church courts, several of these ministers formed the Church Service Society. Its purpose was 'the study of liturgies – ancient and modern – of the Christian Church, with a view to the preparation and publication of forms of Prayer for Public Worship'. The Church Service Society sought to draw upon the whole tradition of the universal Church, including the pre-Reformation Latin Church and the Greek Orthodox traditions. As one member, A. K. H. Boyd, observed at a public meeting in June 1866, 'most educated people in Scotland' were now of the opinion

319 R. H. Story, *Life and Remains of Robert Lee*, 2 vols, London: Hurst and Blackett, 1870, Vol. 2, pp. 54–107, 212–94.

320 D. Murray, 'Disruption to Union', in D. Forrester and D. Murray, eds, *Studies in the History of Worship in Scotland*, 2nd edn, Edinburgh: T. & T. Clark, 1996, p. 93.

'that by the natural reaction, that by the natural swing of the pendulum at the Reformation, we went perhaps just a little too far in stripping our service of those circumstances of dignity which might have been allowed to surround them'.[321] In 1867, the Society published a volume, *Euchologion*, containing various forms of service for baptism, Communion, marriage and funerals. This proved highly influential, and went through seven editions in the next 30 years, with subsequent editions adding different forms of worship for Sunday services and other special services. The Society also collected an archive of liturgical works to promote further study.[322] The aim was not to develop a single liturgy for the Church of Scotland, but rather to offer various forms of prayer and worship, drawn from a variety of traditions, which congregations might use in their Presbyterian services.

The Church Service Society stirred considerable interest. In 1870, its membership included 150 ministers.[323] By 1900, about a third of the clergy of the Church of Scotland were members and some 10,000 copies of the various editions of the *Euchologion* had been published.[324] Increasingly, ministers used the forms of service from the *Euchologion* in their regular public worship, and in the celebration of marriages and in funerals, adapting the forms to their tastes and those of their congregations. Beginning about 1900, the Society began publishing a series of 'Liturgies and Orders of Divine Service used or prepared for use in the Church of Scotland since the Reformation'. These included scholarly editions, with introductions and notes, of the Second Prayer Book of Edward VI and Knox's *Book of Common Order*.[325] One aim was to show that the early Reformed Church of Scotland had used set liturgies and that it was legitimate for congregations now to draw upon these, and other liturgical traditions, to enrich their worship.

The liturgical work of the Church Service Society also encouraged improvements in the provision of praise in public worship. Following the introduction of the organ in Greyfriars Church, other Church of Scotland churches began adding organs. The process was initially very slow, because of the opposition of traditionalists and the fear of censure by presbyteries. Then in 1873–4, the Scottish revivalist campaign of two American evangelists, Dwight L. Moody and Ira D. Sankey, greatly popularized organ music in religious services. The movement for organs now quickened. Along with organ music, more and more congregations began

---

321 Quoted in Robertson, 'Revival of Church Worship in the Church of Scotland', p. 140.

322 J. Kerr, *The Renascence of Worship*, Edinburgh: J. Gardner Hitt, 1909, pp. 65–71.

323 Story, *Robert Lee*, Vol. 1, p. 136.

324 Murray, 'Disruption to Union', p. 97.

325 J. Clark Saunders, 'George Sprott and the Revival of Worship in Scotland, Part II', *Liturgical Review*, 8 (1978), p. 12.

establishing choirs, which received musical training, to enhance further the quality of praise in regular services. There was also, from the 1860s, a greater use of hymns to supplement the congregational singing of psalms. In 1870, the General Assembly authorized a *Scottish Hymnal*, including some 200 hymns, for use in church services; this was followed, in 1898, with a new hymnal, the *Church Hymnary*. In 1904, a committee of the General Assembly of the Church of Scotland conducted a survey of praise in its congregations. Out of a total of 1,414 congregations, 1,249 congregations responded to the survey. Of these, 1,096, or 88 per cent of the responding congregations, had an organ or harmonium, 1,050, or 84 per cent of the responding congregations, had a choir, while nearly all congregations used a published hymnal.[326]

The Church Service Society was successful in its reform activities in part because it avoided doctrinal discussions and concentrated on practical improvements in worship. This enabled it to gain broad support. The work of the reformers was also assisted by the Pirie act of 1865. That act, it will be recalled, had been intended to suppress innovations, by giving presbyteries the power to suppress changes in worship, regardless of the wishes of congregations. But the effect of the act was very different. Presbyteries proved reluctant to interfere in arrangements for worship agreed to by congregations, and as a result the reformers were left alone, unless there was significant division within a congregation over the innovations.[327]

Some individual ministers adopted very 'high' sacerdotal forms of worship. One of these was John Macleod (1840–98), who in 1862 became minister of Duns in the Scottish borders. Macleod was one of the initial members of the Church Service Society and a man of luminous spirituality. At Duns, he placed an altar cloth over the communion table and introduced the practice of monthly Communion. He held services on the commemorative days of the Christian year, including Christmas and Easter. He was also influenced by the writings of the Scottish evangelical Edward Irving (1792–1833), who had proclaimed the imminent return of Christ in glory. Macleod joined the Catholic Apostolic Church, which had been formed by Irving and his followers to draw the Christian world together in preparation for Christ's return and which developed an elaborate liturgy drawn from a number of ecclesiastical traditions. But Macleod also retained his ministry in the Church of Scotland. In 1875, he was translated to Govan, where he combined a high sacerdotal worship with a social commitment. In 1888–9, he presented a series of sermons on Holy Communion, which would have immense influence on Scottish worship. The sacrament, he insisted, was not simply a commemoration of Christ's passion and death

---

326 Robertson, 'Revival of Church Worship', pp. 212–14.
327 Murray, 'Disruption to Union', p. 93.

on the cross; it was also a living celebration of Christ's continuing priesthood, 'which He is now fulfilling in the Upper Sanctuary in the heavenly
world'.[328] A compelling personality and powerful preacher, Macleod held
the intense loyalty of his congregations both at Duns and Govan.[329]

Another influential innovator was J. Cameron Lees, minister of St Giles
Church, Edinburgh. One of the original founders of the Church Service
Society, Lees served as minister of Paisley Abbey (1859–77), and then of
St Giles in Edinburgh (1877–1909). He took a leading role in restoration
work, aimed at reviving late medieval grandeur, in both these historic
churches. The work at St Giles included the removal of unsightly partitions, the introduction of regimental battle flags over the nave, and the
restoration of medieval religious images, including St Giles and a large
brass cross. Shortly after his arrival, he produced a prayer book, drawing
materials from Latin, Greek, Anglican and Reformed traditions. In 1884,
he reintroduced daily services in St Giles for the first time since 1650.
Lees had his opponents, including the indefatigable anti-Catholic agita-
tor, Jacob Primmer. But Lees was effective in his defence, while he also
benefited from his close friendship with the Queen.[330] In time, he managed
to popularize Scoto-Catholic reforms in worship, winning for them, in the
words of one historian, 'an established place at the centre of the life of the
National Church'.[331]

Societies for promoting liturgical reforms, meanwhile, began appearing in other Presbyterian denominations. Within the United Presbyterian
Church, a Devotional Service Association was formed in 1882. It published a service book, *Presbyterian Forms of Service*, in 1891. In the Free
Church, a Public Worship Association was founded in 1891 by liberal
evangelicals, including Professor W. G. Blackie of New College, Edinburgh, and Professor A. B. Bruce of the Free Church College in Glasgow.
It produced a new *Directory of Public Worship* and an *Anthology of
Prayers*, drawn from various traditions. With the union of the United
Presbyterian Church and the Free Church in 1900, the church service
societies of the two Churches joined to form the Church Worship Associ-
ation of the United Free Church, and it produced a service book, the
Directory and Forms for Public Worship in 1909.[332] Organs, meanwhile,

---

328 J. Macleod, *The Gospel in the Institution of the Lord's Supper*, Glasgow: James Mac-
Lehose, 1907, p. 102.

329 A. Wallace Williamson, *Dr John Macleod: His Work and Teaching*, Edinburgh: William Blackwood and Sons, 1901; D. M. Murray, 'John Macleod of Govan: A Distinctive High
Churchman', *Liturgical Review*, 8 (1978), pp. 27–32.

330 Norman Maclean, *The Life of James Cameron Lees*, Glasgow: Maclehose, Jackson and
Co.,1922, pp. 207–29, 452–3.

331 Robertson, 'Revival of Church Worship', p. 185.

332 Murray, 'Disruption to Union', pp. 97–8; J. R. Fleming, *A History of the Church in
Scotland 1875–1929*, Edinburgh: T. & T. Clark, 1933, pp. 196–7.

were permitted in the United Free Church from 1872 and in the Free Church (following an intense struggle) from 1883; the organ movement was assisted by grants for organ purchases from the Scottish-American steel magnate, Andrew Carnegie.[333] The reform movement in these Presbyterian denominations was by no means universal, and many churches, especially in the Highlands and Islands, clung to the old ways in worship, rejecting organs and hymns, and continuing extempore prayers and sermons, and bi-annual Communions. However, by the end of the century, the reform movement and the adoption of more 'catholic' forms of worship, with set orders of service, read prayers, hymns and organ music, and the celebration of the Christian festivals, had spread widely, not only in the Church of Scotland, but in the other main Presbyterian denominations as well.

The Second Phase

As the renewal of public worship became more and more widely accepted, even respectable, some individual reformers believed that the movement was not going far enough. They suspected that too many were embracing the innovations largely for aesthetic reasons – because they liked the beauty, decorum and poetry that the innovations brought to public worship – and that there was not enough attention to the spiritual reality behind the forms. The Church Service Society, dominated by broad church liberals, discouraged doctrinal discussions of the meaning of worship, believing these would be divisive and threaten the unity of the reform movement. But for a group of high church reformers, to avoid discussing the doctrine behind the forms of worship was to miss the whole point of the movement.

For these high church reformers, doctrine was vital. When they spoke of reviving 'catholic' worship within the Church of Scotland, it was to recover its identity and authority as a true branch of the Holy Catholic and Apostolic Church. The high church reformers included William Milligan, professor of biblical criticism at the University of Aberdeen, John Macleod, Thomas Leishman, George W. Sprott, and the brothers H. J. and A. W. Wotherspoon. They were influenced in part by the political campaign to disestablish the Church of Scotland and seize its endowments and properties; this campaign began in the mid 1870s and was waged with fervour through the 1880s and 1890s. For the high church reformers, the disestablishment campaign was not simply an assault on Scotland's national Church: it was an assault on Christ's Church. For them,

---

333 J. R. Fleming, *A History of the Church in Scotland 1843–1874*, Edinburgh: T. & T. Clark, 1927, pp. 209–10; Fleming, *History of the Church in Scotland 1875–1929*, pp. 204–5.

the Church of Scotland was not simply the Church by law established – the 'state Church', as its opponents claimed. No, it was something much greater, a true branch of the spiritual body founded by Jesus Christ, preserved through the centuries by the Holy Spirit, and possessing, in its liturgies, holy days, music, poetry, symbolism, church architecture, a sacred inheritance. 'We must learn to feel more deeply than we yet do,' proclaimed Milligan in his closing address as moderator of the General Assembly of 1882, 'that *we* are an integral part of Christ's body, and in vital connection with the whole body. We are not a mere fortuitous concourse of religious atoms ... We are a portion of what is called in the creed the "holy Catholic Church", planted in Scotland by the Divine Head of the Church Himself.'[334]

One of the most influential of these high church reformers was James Cooper (1846–1922).[335] Born and raised in Elgin, Cooper had from an early age imbibed a deep respect for the Scottish Episcopal Church. An admirer of E. B. Pusey and the Anglo-Catholic tradition in the Church of England, Cooper introduced a number of high church innovations, in his first charge in Broughty Ferry from 1873 and then at the East Church, Aberdeen, from 1881. These included Christmas services, Holy Week services, the administration of private communion to the sick, and daily services, at which he knelt at a desk, facing eastwards. In 1882, 11 of the 27 elders at the East Church formally complained of his high church practices to the presbytery of Aberdeen. After a lengthy review, the presbytery mildly censured some of Cooper's language, but otherwise found his innovations allowable. It was a significant vindication of high church worship within the Church.[336] Many found Cooper's innovations attractive, and his communion roll rose from 1,535 in 1881 to 2,280 by 1889.[337] Beginning in 1886, he called for a union of the Church of Scotland and the Scottish Episcopal Church on what he termed 'ancient lines', by which he meant the principles and practices of the Church during the first four centuries.[338] He would later expand this call to include union with the Church of England. He claimed, moreover, that the clergy of the Church of Scotland shared in the apostolic succession, carrying Christ's commission to preach and administer the sacraments, in their case through the laying on of hands at ordination by presbyteries rather than bishops.[339]

---

334 Quoted in H. L. Yancey, 'The Development of the Theology of William Milligan', unpublished PhD thesis, University of Edinburgh, 1970, p. 337.

335 H. J. Wotherspoon, *James Cooper: A Memoir*, London: Longmans, Green and Co, 1926.

336 D. M. Murray, 'James Cooper and the East Church Case at Aberdeen, 1882–3', *Records of the Scottish Church History Society*, 19 (1977), pp. 217–33.

337 Wotherspoon, *James Cooper*, p. 135.

338 Wotherspoon, *James Cooper*, pp. 146–7.

339 J. Cooper, *The Revival of Church Principles in the Church of Scotland*, London:

By the later 1880s, there were growing tensions within the Church Service Society between the high church group and the broad church majority.[340] Then in 1892, Cooper, Milligan, Macleod and other members of the high church group founded a new association, the Scottish Church Society. Its stated main purpose was 'to defend and advance Catholic doctrine as set forth in the ancient Creeds and embodied in the Standards of the Church of Scotland'. It promoted further liturgical innovation, but was especially concerned with expressing the doctrines behind the forms of worship, and with asserting that the Church of Scotland was not only a national Church, but also a true branch of the ancient Catholic and Apostolic Church. 'We have to recognise,' insisted Milligan, its first president, in 1893, 'that we are one with all the faithful during the centuries which proceeded the Reformation, as well as during those which followed it, and that we have a common right with the Catholic Church to all of good which she has accumulated.'[341] The Scottish Church Society organized retreats and conferences, and issued publications. It called for more frequent Communion, and a more reverent view of the sacraments. Above all, it decried the sin of schism and emphasized the duty to support the national Church. For the Anglican Cosmo Gordon Lang, vicar of St Mary's, Oxford, and a future archbishop of York and Canterbury, speaking in 1894 in Aberdeen, the Scottish Church Society represented the beginning of a Scottish Tractarian movement for the recovery of catholic worship and church principles.[342]

Combined with the work of the Scottish Church Society was a renewed interest in church architecture and decoration, including the preservation and restoration of older churches. In 1886, the Aberdeen Ecclesiological Society was formed, largely through the efforts of James Cooper, to promote the study of worship and church architecture. A similar Glasgow Ecclesiological Society was formed in 1893, and in 1903, these two societies joined to form the Scottish Ecclesiological Society. There were regular meetings to discuss papers, which were published in the *Transactions*. Under the influence of these societies, work was undertaken to restore cathedrals and churches, and to provide more tasteful arrangements in seating and furnishing. But the aims were not simply antiquarian or aesthetic. 'We think,' observed Cooper, in his presidential address

Mowbray and Co., 1895; J. Cooper, *A United Church for the British Empire*, Forres [no publisher], 1902.

340 D. M. Murray, 'Doctrine and Worship: Controversy in the Church Service Society in the Late Nineteenth Century', *Liturgical Review*, 7 (1977), pp. 25–34.

341 W. Milligan, *The Scottish Church Society*, Edinburgh: J. Gardner Hitt, 1893, p. 12.

342 Cosmo Gordon Lang, *The Future of the Church of Scotland*, Edinburgh: J. Gardner Hitt, 1895, pp. 10–11. See also J. Wordsworth, *The Episcopate of Charles Wordsworth*, London: Longmans, Green and Co., 1899, pp. 277–8.

to the Scottish Ecclesiological Society for the session 1913–14, 'that CHURCHES, whether old or new, are primarily *Houses of God*, Homes of Christian Devotion.' When churches were allowed to fall into ruin, he added, it was 'the desecration of what is holy'.[343] Through the influence of these societies, one historian has noted, Scottish 'churches were beginning to resemble places of worship, rather than mere auditoria. Chancels, stained glass, Holy Tables, robed choirs, even prayer desks appeared.'[344]

In the early years of the twentieth century, the Scoto-Catholic movement began to lose some of its energy and zeal. William Milligan died in 1893 and John Macleod in 1898, and Cooper, now a professor at Glasgow University, lacked their charisma. Many in the reform movement, moreover, were finding the high church principles and ritualism of the Scottish Church Society too extreme. Dissatisfaction with advanced ritual was made clear in the Barnhill case of 1901–04, when Thomas Adamson, a high church disciple of Cooper, was disciplined by his presbytery. Adamson's innovations had included decorating the communion table (which he referred to as an altar) with cross and candlesticks, praying with his back to the congregation, adopting the eastward position when celebrating Communion, mixing water and wine, elevating the cup, and kneeling to receive communion. For many, Adamson was aping high Anglicanism and the presbytery disallowed several of his practices.[345] In 1905, A. Wallace Williamson, high church minister of St Giles, Edinburgh, and along with Cooper the most prominent member of the Scottish Church Society, resigned his membership. The Society, he believed, was becoming too divisive.[346] The beginning of union negotiations between the Church of Scotland and the United Free Church in 1908 put a further brake on innovations in worship. Scoto-Catholic innovations and calls for a broader union with the Episcopal Church now threatened to alienate more traditionalist Presbyterians in the United Free Church and thus to undermine the union movement. The outbreak of World War One, moreover, diverted attention away from further liturgical reforms.

The Scoto-Catholic movement had transformed Presbyterian worship between the 1860s and World War One. To be sure, the reformers were always a minority in Presbyterian Scotland, and in the case of the high church Scottish Church Society, a very small minority. Nonetheless, the

---

343 J. Cooper, 'The Restoration, Repair and Re-use of Ancient Churches in Scotland', *Transactions of the Scottish Ecclesiological Society*, 4 (1913–14), p. 117.

344 Robertson, 'Revival of Church Worship', p. 258.

345 D. M. Murray, 'The Barnhill Case, 1901–1904: The Limits of Ritual in the Kirk', *Records of the Scottish Church History Society*, 22 (1986), pp. 259–76.

346 Lord Sands, *Life of Andrew Wallace Williamson*, Edinburgh: William Blackwood and Sons, 1929, pp. 174–83.

reformers included individuals – Lee, Macleod, Milligan, Cooper and others – of compelling presence, vision and commitment, and the innovators exercised an influence far beyond their numbers. Through the work of the Scoto-Catholic reformers, the worship in most Presbyterian churches became more ordered and elaborate, with set orders of service, calls to worship, benedictions, read prayers, regular Bible readings, hymns, choirs and organs. Church buildings increasingly included stained glass, more attractive furnishings and more colour and light. Sermons grew shorter, averaging 30 minutes or less by the beginning of the twentieth century. There were now services for funerals, marriages and special occasions. The great festivals of the Christian year, especially Christmas and Easter, were increasingly commemorated with services. In 1923, the General Assembly of the Church of Scotland officially 'commended' a set of defined forms for regular worship, the *Prayers for Divine Service in Church and Home*, which included orders of service for the ordination of ministers, licensing of probationers, admission of elders, dedication of churches and other occasions. Perhaps most important, the Scoto-Catholic movement had helped congregations in the Church of Scotland, and other Presbyterian denominations, to recover a sense, through their worship, of their continuity with the ancient Catholic and Apostolic Church, to see themselves as part of a long chain of believers stretching back through the centuries and to realize that they were heirs, not simply of a Scottish Reformation heritage, but of the rich treasury of the Church universal.

SACRED SPACE

Reading Scottish Church Buildings

Nigel Yates

Introduction

From 1560 the established Church in Scotland, to a greater or lesser extent, was part of the family of Calvinist or Reformed churches that stretched across parts of France, the Netherlands, southern Germany, Switzerland and the western fringes of Eastern Europe. The Scottish Reformation was, however, more complicated than that. From 1560 until 1690, when a fully Presbyterian Church was established in Scotland, there was a close relationship with the, rather differently, Reformed Church of England, particularly after James VI of Scotland became James I of England in 1603. Second, unlike the Reformation in England, Scandinavia and parts of Germany, the Reformation in Scotland was a 'bottom up' rather than a 'top down' affair, and this meant that its progress across Scotland was far from even, with Reformed ministers not making much headway in parts of the Western Highlands and Islands, or in the north-east of Scotland, until late in the sixteenth and early in the seventeenth century. These areas remained strongholds of Roman Catholic recusancy, and in Barra and South Uist the majority of the population never became Protestants. It was these same areas, the north-east especially, which after 1690, and the final abolition of episcopacy in Scotland, also became the strongholds of the Scottish Episcopal Church. The established Church itself was also divided by schisms from the late seventeenth century, the most serious of which was the Disruption of 1843 that led to the creation of the Free Church of Scotland. This chapter will look, therefore, at the architectural legacy of the various Presbyterian churches in Scotland together with that of the Roman Catholic and Scottish Episcopal churches. In every case, of course, the design and furnishings of church buildings was determined by the form of worship that individual congregations wished to follow. In that respect the treatment of 'sacred space' in Scotland was no different in principle from that in any other part of the Christian World.[347]

The Impact of the Reformation

The problem that faced the Church of Scotland after 1560 was that, as was the case with most other Protestant churches in Europe, it had inherited the buildings of the pre-Reformation church designed for a very different type of worship. In pre-Reformation churches the focus was on the altar, where the priest offered the holy sacrifice of the Mass for the living and the dead. The priest was the mediator between God and humankind and this was emphasized by the separation of the clergy in the chancel, and the laity in the nave, by a screen on top of which were the figures of Christ, the Blessed Virgin Mary and St John the Evangelist. In Protestant worship the minister was a teacher not a mediator. Though churches differed in their attitudes to the structure of the new services, and therefore the retention or otherwise of pre-Reformation furnishings, the emphasis was always on the pulpit rather than the altar. In liturgical terms the Reformed Church of Scotland was one of the most radical of the Reformed churches so the degree of iconoclasm after 1560 greatly exceeded that in the Lutheran churches of north Germany and Scandinavia, the quasi-Calvinist churches of England, Ireland and Wales, and even the fully Reformed churches of Hungary, the Netherlands and Switzerland.[348] The pattern in Scotland is very clear. All 'superstitious' carvings, woodwork and stained glass were destroyed so that nowadays only the most minimal fragments of such pre-Reformation furnishings survive. Altars were overthrown and screens ripped out. Small churches, which in Scotland generally consisted of a nave and chancel only, often under the same roof, were reordered so that the new pulpit was placed in the middle of the building with seating arranged to face it from three different directions. Galleries or lofts were usually erected across the east and west walls so as to increase the accommodation for worshippers. Redundant chancels were frequently turned into private pews for important people. In the towns the larger churches were divided into two or more separate churches, each arranged so that the pulpit became the primary liturgical focus and with seats on the ground floor and in the galleries

347 This chapter is, to a great extent, a brief synopsis of a much more detailed forthcoming study entitled *Preaching, Word and Sacrament: Scottish Church Interiors 1560–1860*, to be published by T&T Clark in 2009.

348 See especially Bernard Reymond, *L'Architecture Religieuse des Protestants*, Geneva: Labor et Fides, 1996, and Nigel Yates, *Liturgical Space: Christian Worship and Church Buildings in Western Europe 1500–2000*, Aldershot: Ashgate, 2008.

arranged to face it. Division of this sort occurred at St Mungo's Cathedral in Glasgow, at St Nicholas in Aberdeen, St Mary's in Dundee, St Giles in Edinburgh, St John's in Perth and the Church of the Holy Rude in Stirling. Most of the former monastic churches were eventually allowed to fall into ruin and this fate even befell some of the former cathedrals, such as those at Elgin, Fortrose, St Andrews and Whithorn. At other pre-Reformation cathedrals, such as those at Aberdeen, Brechin, Dornoch, Dunblane and Dunkeld, only parts of the building remained in use for worship and the remainder fell into ruin.[349]

Two features of Reformed Scottish worship which made an enormous impact on church buildings were the decision to abandon any form of musical accompaniment to the services and to receive Holy Communion sitting at long tables. The former resulted in the removal of organs from churches and the latter the abandonment of a permanent communion table. A desk for the precentor, who led the unaccompanied singing of the psalms, was usually placed in front of the pulpit. Trestle tables, to be covered with white cloths, were brought into church as required for the fairly infrequent celebrations of Holy Communion. Bernard Reymond has noted that this emphasis on sitting communion, in both Scotland and the Netherlands, and desired by the Puritans in early seventeenth-century England, was the exception rather than the norm among the Reformed churches of Europe. In Calvinist Switzerland, Southern Germany and Eastern Europe a permanent communion table was normally placed in a central position in the church, usually in front of the pulpit.[350] Even in the Netherlands sitting communion seems not to have been adopted at first but congregations walked past the table or tables to receive communion.[351] The purity of Scottish liturgical practice was also emphasized by the abandonment of the traditional font for the baptism of infants. Scottish churches normally had pulpits to which were attached two brackets, one to hold the baptismal bowl and the other to hold the hour-glass by which the minister was able to time the length of his sermon.

New Churches 1560–1690

Although one of the earliest post-Reformation churches in Scotland – St Columba's at Burntisland, built between 1589 and 1596 – was square in shape, by far the most popular form of post-Reformation Scottish

---

349 See Peter Galloway, *The Cathedrals of Scotland*, Edinburgh: Scottish Cultural Press, 2000.

350 Reymond, *L'Architecture Religieuse*, p. 31.

351 J. R. Luth, 'Communion in the Churches of the Dutch Reformation to the Present Day', in Charles Caspers, Gerard Lukken and Gerard Rouwhorst, eds, *Bread of Heaven: Customs and Practices Surrounding Holy Communion*, Kampen: David Brown, 1995, pp. 99–117.

church was the T-plan and there were early examples of such buildings at Anstruther Easter (Fife), Careston (Angus), Dunlop (Ayrshire), Kirkmaiden (Dumfries and Galloway) and Pitsligo (Aberdeenshire). The great advantage of the T-plan church was that it provided the maximum amount of accommodation for worshippers within a reasonable distance of the pulpit and precentor's desk, so that all could see and hear. Contrary to popular opinion, T-plan churches were not peculiar to Scotland. They were built by other Calvinists, by Anglicans, Lutherans and even Roman Catholics in other parts of both the British Isles and mainland Europe.[352] However, there were other churches in Scotland, such as Greyfriars, Edinburgh, built between 1612 and 1620, which like their counterparts in other areas in Calvinist Europe – for example the Westerkerk of 1620–38 in Amsterdam – were still designed like late medieval, aisled hall churches, but with the focus on the pulpit in the middle of one of the long sides. G. D. Henderson has described the average Scottish parish church of the seventeenth century as:

> A bare hall with probably one or two lofts or galleries, the pulpit in the middle ... with a sandglass attached, and a ring for holding the basin of water on baptismal occasions; beneath the pulpit the lectern or reader's desk; somewhere close by the stool of repentance or pillar or pillarie; in some churches also a special seat for the elders; the rest of the church divided into Sections where stood the 'dasks' of the various heritors and their tenants ... When Communion was observed the middle of the church was cleared to make room for the long table round which the members gathered.[353]

Penitential discipline remained strong in the Church of Scotland until the middle years of the nineteenth century. Many churches in the Scottish Borders retain the 'jougs', an iron chain and collar to which penitents were attached before the service began. They were then led into church to sit on the penitent's stool or stand on a platform and be ranted at by the minister. Examples of such penitent's platforms can still be seen in the churches at Bourtie (Aberdeenshire) and Duirinish (Skye), where they date from 1806 and 1832 respectively.

During the first half of the seventeenth century Kings James VI and I and Charles I endeavoured to bring the Church of Scotland into line with the Church of England, and at a time when the latter was moving away from strict Calvinism to adopt a much more high church theology

---

352 See Nigel Yates, *Buildings, Faith and Worship: The Liturgical Arrangement of Anglican Churches 1600–1900*, 2nd edn, Oxford: Oxford University Press, 2000, pp. 93–6.

353 G. D. Henderson, *Religious Life in Seventeenth Century Scotland*, Cambridge: Cambridge University Press, 1937, pp. 154, 193.

and liturgical practice. The Articles of Perth in 1618 attempted to make the Church of Scotland adopt some traditional Anglican practices, such as kneeling at Communion. There is little evidence that the provisions of these Articles were ever enforced and the reception given to the new Scottish Book of Common Prayer in 1637–8 suggests that any attempt to have done so would have been strongly resisted. Little attempt seems to have been made to design quasi-Anglican churches in Scotland in the early seventeenth century apart from the one at Dairsie (Fife), built by Archbishop Spottiswoode of St Andrews in 1621. This had a raised chancel separated from the nave by a screen displaying the Royal Arms, but no plan or illustration of these arrangements has survived. When episcopacy was reintroduced into the Church of Scotland after the restoration of Charles II to the thrones of England and Scotland in 1660, no further attempt was made to introduce Anglican patterns of worship or styles of church building. When the bishops were deprived of their sees in 1690 for continued loyalty to the exiled James VII and II there was little difference between their loyal followers and the, now fully Presbyterian, Church of Scotland in terms of either worship or the design of their buildings.

Church Building and Arrangement 1690–1860

Between 1690 and 1860 all Scottish Presbyterian churches, whether of the Church of Scotland or any of the dissenting Presbyterian groups, fell into one of three categories: the first, and normally the earlier, type of building was a rectangular one with the pulpit on one of the long sides; the second was the T-plan arrangement with seating facing the pulpit from three arms of equal length; the third, and normally the later type of building, was the rectangular one with the pulpit on one of the short walls. Other, less popular types of building – the Greek cross, circular, square, elliptical or octagonal – were essentially variants on the three basic types. There are no surviving examples of Scottish Presbyterian churches before the second half of the eighteenth century. The earliest survival is the splendid St Nicholas West of 1752–5 at Aberdeen. This has the pulpit in the middle of one of the long sides with galleries around all four sides. Seating is provided by box pews throughout. St Peter's at Glenbuchat (Aberdeenshire), refitted in 1792, has the pulpit in the same position but only a single loft, across one of the short walls. The box pews are placed directly on the earthen floor, with some of them having removable partitions so that they can be converted into table pews on Sacrament Sundays. St Blane's at Southend (Argyll and Bute), built in 1773–4, also has the pulpit on one of the long walls, with a U-shaped gallery around three sides of the interior. Here the seating is not in the form of box pews but in that of benches. The

Scottish Presbyterian churches seem to have been among the earliest in Europe to replace box pews with benches. The reasons are far from clear but may have been something to do with the fact that benches were both cheaper to erect than box pews and could accommodate more people. Between 1800 and 1860 there are far more surviving examples of substantially unaltered Presbyterian church interiors in Scotland, though they are largely confined to the most rural areas. That with the highest proportion of surviving pre-1860 interiors is Shetland where no fewer than eight examples survive in a relatively small area.

Of the more experimental churches built in Scotland between 1690 and 1860 none retain their original furnishings intact. Probably the earliest was the church at Hamilton designed by William Adam in 1732, comprising a circle with four projecting arms in the shape of a cross. Later examples include the circular church of 1767–9 at Bowmore (Islay), the octagonal churches of 1773 at Kelso and 1780 at Dreghorn, and the elliptical church of St Andrew at Edinburgh built in 1785–9; even later ones include the octagonal churches of 1807 at Perth (St Paul's) and 1811 at Glenorchy; St Stephen's, Edinburgh, completed in 1828, was externally square but internally octagonal. Every one of these designs had the intention of seating as many people as possible, preferably in excess of 1,500, within a reasonable distance of the pulpit and precentor's desk.[354] Another, and very unusual, experimental church was the one erected at Inveraray between 1795 and 1802. This was a double one with a dividing wall between the English- and Gaelic-speaking congregations. Pulpits and precentor's desks were placed against this internal wall, with a staircase in the wall leading to the spire in the middle of the roof.[355]

By far the most important piece of furniture in any Scottish Presbyterian church was the pulpit. It normally had both a backboard and a tester or canopy, often with a crown or domed top. The backboard incorporated the seat for the minister and the tester assisted the projection of the minister's voice into the church. Scottish testers were small, more like those in Anglican churches in the British Isles, compared with the vast testers that are found, and one still finds, in the Calvinist churches of the Netherlands. In front of the pulpit was the precentor's desk and both pulpit and desk were usually decorated with velvet hangings, as was the case with Anglican pulpits and reading desks of the same period. Occasionally, as at Dyke (Moray), built in 1781, the pulpit had two desks – the counterpart of the Anglican three-decker – with the lower desk occupied by the beadle. Seating in Scottish Presbyterian churches, whether in box

354 George Hay, *The Architecture of Scottish Post-Reformation Churches 1560–1843*, Oxford: Clarendon, 1957, pp. 92–9, 122–7.

355 I. G. Lindsay and M. Cosh, *Inveraray and the Dukes of Argyll*, Edinburgh: Edinburgh University Press, 1973, pp. 165–7, 282–7.

pews or open benches, tended to be allocated by the kirk session, frequently in return for an annual seat rent. This was common practice in other churches in the British Isles, in some of which pew rents were not abolished until well into the twentieth century. Important landed families usually had their own allocated seats in church, frequently in a laird's loft. The earliest surviving of these lofts are the Forbes loft of 1634 at Pitsligo (Aberdeenshire) and the Ker of Cavers loft of 1661 at Bowden (Scottish Borders). Splendid later lofts include the Hopetoun loft of 1700 at Abercorn (West Lothian), the Cranford loft of c.1705 at Kilbirnie (Ayrshire), the Reay loft of 1728–9 at Tongue (Highland) and the Sutherland loft of 1739 at Golspie (Highland). Laird's lofts continued to be erected in Scottish Presbyterian churches until well into the nineteenth century: 1803 at Torphichen (West Lothian), 1825 at Durisdeer (Dumfries and Galloway), 1828 at Glenbuchat (Aberdeenshire), 1830 at Yester (East Lothian), 1848 at Murroes (Angus), c.1860 at Whalsay (Shetland) and 1875 at Luss (Argyll and Bute). Some lofts were provided with heated retiring rooms where the laird and his family could partake of refreshments, provided by his servants, between the morning and afternoon services.

Until the middle of the eighteenth century, Communion in Scottish Presbyterian churches was usually celebrated at long trestle tables brought in for the service, an arrangement which has been retained by a small number of congregations to the present day. Gradually, in most churches, these temporary tables were abandoned and replaced with permanent ones, but still designed for sitting Communion. One of two alternative arrangements was normally adopted. In the first case one or two long tables were placed along the length of the church, either in front of the pulpit in buildings in which it was on one of the long walls, or between the pulpit and the entrance in buildings where the pulpit was placed on the short wall opposite the entrance. Good examples of the first type, with the tables still *in situ*, are Croik (Highland) and Kilmodan (Argyll and Bute). Good examples of the second type, also with the tables *in situ*, are Ardchattan (Argyll and Bute), Howmore (South Uist) and Lochbroom (Highland). At South Ronaldsay (Orkney) there is a square communion table directly in front of the pulpit and long tables between it and the entrance doors on the two short walls. At Rogart (Highland) the long communion table is placed in a pew to one side of the pulpit. The other type of communion arrangement was, as at Glenbuchat, noted above, to create a series of box pews with movable partitions which could convert into long tables when required. Arrangements of this type can still be seen at Ceres (Fife), Durisdeer (Dumfries and Galloway) and Spott (East Lothian). A later variant of this arrangement was for the front pews in churches to have hinged ledges, which could be opened up to form narrow communion tables, an arrangement still to be seen at Halladale Free Church (Highland).

Roman Catholics and Scottish Episcopalians

The fact that both these minority ecclesial bodies in Scotland were restricted in their activities by penal legislation before the last decade of
the eighteenth century meant that they had to worship in secret, usually
in rooms in private houses. The earliest Roman Catholic churches were
in converted domestic premises. An excellent example of such a building, with very simple furnishings, survives at Tynet (Moray). However,
by 1790, a newly built church at nearby Presholme was described as
'the first ... which was recognisably a church building'.[356] It was in the
'Gothick' style then favoured by many Anglicans in England, Ireland and
Wales. Similar buildings were erected at Aberdeen in 1803–04, Paisley in
1808, Dumfries in 1813, Dalbeattie and Edinburgh in 1814, and Glasgow and Greenock in 1816. None of these retain their original furnishings but the surviving plan of the 1824 church at New Abbey (Dumfries
and Galloway) shows a simple rectangle with the altar at one end in
a raised sanctuary and a box pew on either side. The remaining box
pews were placed either side of a central passageway facing the altar.
There was no pulpit so sermons were presumably delivered from the
altar steps.[357]

Scottish Episcopalians had initially worshipped in buildings indistinguishable from Presbyterian ones except for the provision of a fixed communion table, normally placed in front of the pulpit. As with the Roman
Catholics, their earliest permanent churches date from the last quarter of
the eighteenth century, but none have preserved their original furnishings.
A contemporary illustration for the new church of St John the Evangelist
in Edinburgh, built in 1816–18 at the very substantial cost of £18,013,
shows a building with the pulpit and reading desk placed either side of a
vested altar with painted glass in the window behind. Clearly by this date
Anglicans in Scotland had moved out of the restrictions of the penal era
and were building churches similar to those built by their co-religionists
elsewhere in the British Isles. With the Presbyterians still banning the use
of musical accompaniment in their churches, and the Roman Catholic
episcopal leadership in Scotland still opposed to any elaboration of the
very simple services of the penal era, it was the Scottish Episcopalians who
pioneered the reintroduction of organs to Scotland. Ones were noted in
the chapels at Kelso and Peterhead in the 1790s, and by the early years of
the nineteenth century organs were in use in chapels in Aberdeen, Banff,
Dundee, Edinburgh, Glasgow, Leith and Montrose. By contrast it was not
until the 1820s that organs had been introduced in the Roman Catholic

---

356 C. Johnson, *Developments in the Roman Catholic Church in Scotland 1789–1929*,
Edinburgh: John Donald, 1983, p. 153.

357 Dumfries and Galloway Archives, GGD 313/N7/27.

churches at Aberdeen, Banff, Edinburgh, Fochabers, Glasgow, Greenock and Paisley.[358]

A similar division between Scottish Episcopalians and Roman Catholics can be seen in their attitude to the ecclesiological movement in church architecture. Whereas in England both Anglicans and Roman Catholics had been strongly influenced by the 1840s, in Scotland it was only the Episcopalians who jumped on the bandwagon, while the Roman Catholics remained aloof until well after 1860: Scottish Episcopalian examples of early ecclesiological churches, six of which retain their furnishings intact, were generally associated with those members of the church who had also adopted the radical new forms of Anglican high churchmanship promoted by the Oxford Movement of the 1830s. Many were members of aristocratic or landed families. At Jedburgh (1841–4) the impetus came from the Marchioness of Lothian and the architect employed was John Hayward, a committed disciple of both the Tractarian and ecclesiological movements. The new church was provided with a rood screen, a stone altar and a pulpit entered through the wall from the vestry, all features of high church Anglican buildings of this period. The arrangements were similar at Dalkeith (1843–6), built by the Duke of Buccleuch as his private chapel, and at Dalmahoy (1850), financed by Lord and Lady Aberdour. By the 1860s, the ecclesiological interior had become the norm among Scottish Episcopalians. There are good examples at Kelso (Scottish Borders) of 1869, Challoch (Dumfries and Galloway) of 1871–2 and Fort William (Highland) of 1876–80. From 1850, the church also began to build cathedrals for the church's seven dioceses: Perth in 1850, Inverness in 1866 and Edinburgh in 1874. Even when the Roman Catholics eventually began to design buildings in an ecclesiological manner, they tended to be much more modest than Episcopalian ones, an exception being the elaborate chapel of 1896–1911 built for the Marquess of Bute at Mount Stuart, near Rothesay. When a Roman Catholic hierarchy was re-established in Scotland in 1878 all except one diocese established existing parish churches as their cathedrals; the exception was the diocese of Argyll and the Isles, where an impressive new cathedral at Oban, designed by Sir Giles Gilbert Scott, was opened in 1932.

Presbyterian Churches after 1860

There were two liturgical developments in Scottish Presbyterianism in the second half of the nineteenth century that had an important impact on the design of church buildings. One was the gradual abandonment of Com-

---

358 James Inglis, 'The Scottish Churches and the Organ in the Nineteenth Century', Glasgow PhD, 1987, pp. 80–1.

munion sitting at tables for Communion delivered to people in their seats. The other was the introduction of organs and choirs which led to the abandonment and removal of the traditional precentor's desks. A third contributor to architectural change was the Scoto-Catholic movement of the late nineteenth and early twentieth centuries. From the 1870s, except in parts of the Highlands and Islands where traditional patterns of church design continued well into the twentieth century, two new types of Scottish Presbyterian church interior became commonplace. One, and the more common of the two, was the replication of the church interiors favoured by the Free churches in other parts of the British Isles. This was the pulpit platform arrangement in which buildings were arranged with the entrance on one of the short walls with the pulpit platform on the opposite short wall. In addition to the pulpit, the platform housed a communion table, from which the elders delivered the sacrament to the congregation in their pews, and seats for the elders; during the twentieth century lecterns and fonts were usually added. The organ and choir tended to be placed in a gallery behind the pulpit. The congregation was, normally, provided with three blocks of seating in the body of the church, with the seating in the side blocks angled towards the pulpit, and seating in galleries across the entrance and long walls. It was comparatively easy to adapt those churches that already had the short-wall pulpit arrangement to the new pulpit platform one. Other churches, with the long-wall pulpit or T-plan arrangement, could be similarly adapted, in the former case by 'turning' the interior to create the new arrangement. The Scoto-Catholic movement resulted in the creation of neo-medievalist Presbyterian churches, quasi-Anglican in character, in which the choir was placed in the chancel with a communion table and seats for the minister and elders against the end wall, and the pulpit, lectern and font placed at the entrance to the chancel, but permitting the congregation in the nave a clear view of both choir and communion table. Some of the most important surviving medieval churches in Scotland, such as those at Haddington and Linlithgow, were reordered in the manner favoured by the Scoto-Catholics. This was also the case at Glasgow Cathedral and Paisley Abbey.

Among the new buildings built by Presbyterian congregations, many, especially within the Free Church of Scotland, preferred the pulpit platform arrangement as being completely free from 'popish' influences, although even churches of this type were prepared to insert stained glass windows. Some of the early twentieth-century stained glass in Scotland, especially that designed by Douglas Strachan, is among the highest quality stained glass anywhere in the British Isles. Scoto-Catholic buildings were, however, erected by a significant number of parishes in the Church of Scotland. One of the earliest was Govan Old Church in Glasgow in 1888. The principal designers of Scoto-Catholic churches were the architects R. R.

Anderson, P. M. Chalmers and Sir Robert Lorimer. Between them they were responsible for such buildings as Dunblane Cathedral, fully restored and largely rebuilt between 1889 and 1914, Holy Trinity at St Andrews, remodelled in 1907–09, and a larger clutch of new churches in the Scottish lowlands, such as Ardwell and Colvend in Dumfries and Galloway. A few of the non-Presbyterian Protestant churches in Scotland also adopted ecclesiological designs, the most magnificent example being the Thomas Coats Memorial Baptist Church in Paisley, designed by Hippolyte Blanc at a cost of £110,000 and opened in 1894.[359]

Modern Church Architecture

The Scoto-Catholic movement and the Gothic revival continued to have an enormous impact on church building in Scotland until after World War Two. One of the earliest experiments in radical reordering was that carried out at the Canongate Church in Edinburgh in 1947–50. Here two architects with a deep reverence for both the Scottish architectural tradition and the historical development of liturgy, George Hay and Ian Lindsay, re-created a late seventeenth-century type of Anglican interior to complement its late seventeenth-century Dutch-style fabric. The previous session house was converted into a new apsidal sanctuary with canopied clergy desks and a 'Laudian drape' covering for the communion table. A canopied pulpit was placed on one side of the chancel arch and a lectern on the other. The side galleries were removed so that all the seating was on one level.[360] However, the reordering of the Canongate Church was essentially a recapturing of an ideal church from the past. Whereas in mainland Europe, and even some other parts of the British Isles, some genuinely modern church buildings had been designed as early as the inter-war period and began to mushroom in the 1950s, in Scotland there has been little in the way of truly contemporary church design. The pioneer was St Columba's, Glenrothes, a new building for the Church of Scotland, opened in 1962, centrally planned with a pulpit, font, lectern and communion table in the middle, seating for the congregation on three sides, and for the choir, located with the organ, on the fourth. This was followed by similar designs at St Mungo's, Cumbernauld, in 1966 and Craigsbank Church in Edinburgh in 1964–7, the latter 'intended to evoke the atmosphere of ... a Covenanting service held in the open air, in a natural amphitheatre'. A number of Roman Catholic

---

359 Clyde Binfield, 'A Working Memorial? The Encasing of Paisley's Baptists', in W. M. Jacob and Nigel Yates, eds, *Crown and Mitre: Religion and Society in Northern Europe since the Reformation*, Woodbridge: Boydell Press, 1993, pp. 185–202.

360 R. S. Wright, *The Kirk in Canongate*, Edinburgh: Oliver and Boyd, 1956, pp. 141–3, plates 16 and 17.

churches, inspired by the liturgical reforms of the Second Vatican Council, which laid much more emphasis on the corporate nature of worship, were also designed in a thoroughly modern style: St Bride's, East Kilbride (1963–4); St Patrick's, Kilsyth (1965); Our Lady of Sorrows, South Uist (1965); St Mary Magdalene's, Edinburgh (1966); and St Andrew's, Livingstone (1970).[361] The Scottish Episcopal Church, despite the lead it took among the Anglican churches of the British Isles in respect of liturgical revision, has preferred to retain a more traditional approach to the treatment of its buildings apart from one or two experiments in charismatic churches in Edinburgh and Glasgow.

---

361 John Hume, *Scotland's Best Churches*, Edinburgh: Edinburgh University Press, 2005, pp. 134–40.

12

HOLY COMMUNION IN THE CHURCH OF SCOTLAND

Patterns and Prospects

Peter Donald

The celebration of the sacrament of the Lord's Supper in the Church of Scotland is marked by its variety in style and form in these opening years of the twenty-first century. The degree of freedom in regard to forms of worship, a noteworthy aspect of the Reformed tradition since its early days, has spawned a range of responses on the part of ministers of Word and sacrament who preside in these matters. The precise implications of the ordination vow to 'uphold' the worship and doctrine of the Church of Scotland are clearly open to interpretation.

The Church of Scotland maintains as liturgical and doctrinal standards seventeenth-century texts. In the first flush of the Reformation in the sixteenth century, the shunning of the perceived idolatry of the Mass and the desire for Holy Communion to be a regular and communal action had prompted a flurry of liturgical and theological publications, picking up on everything from the preparation of the communicants to their posture when the bread and wine were shared. An order in English prepared by John Knox for exiles in Geneva, and a matching order in Gaelic prepared by John Carswell, gave full and sound direction on the rule of prayer; [362] the Scots Confession gave the authoritative interpretation of what was to be believed and what not. [363] And while it was clear that prayers were not absolutely to follow the same wording at every time and in every place, there was a sense of 'common order', the holding together of strands both

---

362 *Coena Domini*, ed. I. Pahl, Freiburg Universitätsverlag Freiburg, 1983, pp. 471–80; G. Donaldson, 'Reformation to Covenant', in D. Forrester and D. Murray, eds, *Studies in the History of Worship in Scotland*, Edinburgh: T&T Clark, 1996, pp. 39–48; D. Meek, 'The Reformation and Gaelic Culture: Perspectives on Patronage, Language and Literature in John Carswell's Translation of "The Book of Common Order"', in J. Kirk, ed., *The Church in the Highlands*, Edinburgh: Scottish Church History Society, 1998, pp. 37–62.

363 See chapters 18 and 21 of the Scots Confession.

theological and liturgical. This was somewhat diluted in the seventeenth century when the Westminster standards current still to this day were prepared: there was a degree more of distancing from attachment to set forms. Nevertheless, it would be reasonable to conclude that while there was variation in practice, it was for centuries variation on a theme – fairly minor, one might say, up into the nineteenth century. Since then, however, a wide variety of new patterns have come into play. Scottish church worship changed through the explosion of hymn writing and the liturgical movements, also through the debates and divisions which led to the secessions and the Disruption, and not least on account of intellectual shifts on the back of the Enlightenment. In the twentieth century there were three successive books of 'Common Order' published by the Church of Scotland, and at the same time a growing disposition to shape the tradition according to local preference.

In 2005, a Working Group was established following a report by the Panel on Worship to the General Assembly to reflect on the place and practice of Holy Communion in the Church of Scotland. It comprised a range of voices attentive to current practice and thinking both within and beyond the Church. It sought to take on board the very many resources of thought on the sacrament, both doctrinal and liturgical, but discovered that in more recent times, when there has been a blossoming in the publication of set forms and also undoubtedly an increase in informal experimentation and innovation in local practice, there has been remarkably little pause for drawing threads together. Because there are some tensions over modes of practice, one of the opportunities for the Working Group therefore was to look at these disparate threads and at the same time to encourage the Church at large to be likewise engaged; this work is still in progress. It was in connection with sacramental practice that in the fifth century Prosper of Aquitaine coined his pregnant thought about the so-called *lex orandi*: 'look at the sacred witness of the public priestly prayers which, handed down by the apostles, are celebrated in the same way in all the world and in every catholic church, so that the rule of praying should establish the rule of believing'.[364] Theology draws its life from worship and then there is a reciprocal task, in so far as liturgical[365] resources and practices have been developed, to align how we pray with what we think and believe.

While Communion has been of huge significance since the days of the early Church, through the scriptural witness and from the earliest writings

---

364 Quoted in G. Lathrop, 'Knowing something a little: on the role of the *lex orandi* in the search for Christian unity', in T. F. Best and D. Heller, eds, *So We Believe, So We Pray*, Geneva: World Council of Churches Publications, 1995, p.38.

365 Liturgy/liturgical refers not merely to set *forms* of worship but, first, simply to the 'work' of praising God, by forms and extempore.

outside the Canon, equally differences of opinion and order have also been surfacing since those earliest days. And in among the rich diversity of rites both in East and West, and a continuing flow of reflection and creativity, there have been also some fairly serious arguments. Certainly no position that held communion practice and understanding to be unchangeable could bear critical scrutiny, but there are questions about the limits of diversity. The Reformation threw up many such questions, though neither for the first nor the last time. However, there was a sense in which the floodgates opened when the Western Church became so fissured through the sixteenth and seventeenth centuries. Both the scope of theological reflection and the ordering of worship have produced something like a new world in which, for all the apparent points of overlap between one worshipping congregation and another, the variety has become very considerable indeed. The pertinent question follows as to whether this is problematic or pregnant with possibilities.

The unity of the Church, focused in gatherings for the Lord's Supper (cf. 1 Cor. 11), is not necessarily under threat from the variety of practice, and yet it may be. The significance of the communion meal is more than incidental to the good news we proclaim. As a sign and seal of the gospel, it bears witness to Jesus the Christ who lived among us, who died and rose again, and who will come again in glory. The metaphor of the body of Christ, with its ready applicability (following the teaching of Paul to the Corinthians) both to the Church and to the bread which we break at the Lord's Supper, affirms the centrality of the meal to the community who would be known as Christians. There arises then the challenge about accountability – both in the sense of how we may best be faithful to God and one another within the Christian fold, and how effectively our Communion practice anchors our mission as Church.

As we seek to understand patterns and prospects for celebrations of the sacrament, where does the variety in the making take us? Clearly there is rich potential in having options for reforming and ever reforming, of modernizing and appealing to contemporary culture, as well as taking account of historic traditions. It is one of the attractions of the Church of Scotland in which the spirit of forebears is honoured, who preached so passionately against the dry reading of forms of worship so that there might be 'edification'. On the other hand, disunity around the Lord's Table, whether between denominations or as people dissatisfied with one sort of practice or another, pushes us to Paul's question to the Corinthians, namely, how well do we handle that which has been handed on from the Lord himself? To be Church, to celebrate the Lord's Supper when we gather together, how do we address ourselves to the problem of not being united? The unity we seek is that fullest experience of a shared faith and hope and love in Christ and we would wish to believe that our sacramental gatherings are a foretaste of the heavenly banquet, at which all may sit down together. There is therefore a need for dialogue, for a deep encounter with one another – fellow-Christians within our own church establishment, and fellow-Christians wherever we find them, in time and space. It matters again and again to consider how both our worship and doctrine in the Lord's Supper builds our anticipation of Christ's coming again, and in the meantime sends us out to be the body of Christ in the world. The familiar motto of our sort of Church, *reformata sed semper reformanda*, speaks precisely of that, in that our *need* to be reformed is as Christ our Lord needs to take hold of us.

Where will the common threads be found in the patterns of celebration? The necessary place to start is with the pairing of Word and sacrament. The gospel to be proclaimed both in Word and sacrament is one and the same. Both draw centrally on the life, death and resurrection of Jesus Christ and, in dependence on the Holy Spirit, anticipate his return. The sacraments recognized in the Church of Scotland are those recognized to have been instituted by Jesus himself, namely baptism and the Lord's Supper.

Furthermore, with Christ's ministry being continued on earth, the ordering of the Church is focused around Word and sacrament. The tradition, Reformed and catholic, would not allow a minister of Word and sacrament to be in any sense alone in guiding celebrations of Holy Communion, but neither would it support – as yet in the Church of Scotland – a celebration being held without one being present. The presidency is conferred on the one who has been recognized to be called and ordained. This said, however, for all that the minister is thus a key shaper of worship, it matters also to see minister and people as joined together in a common work. The Word must be heard as well as preached, the meal shared as well as presided over; and each and every Church member, whether ordained or not, has a servant calling outside assembling for worship.

The pairing of Word and sacrament asks for consideration of the simple questions of who is to be trusted, namely Christ himself (the question of faith), and of how there may be a common belonging among those who so trust (the question of order). However, we are more than able to complicate these questions! The estimation of Jesus as the King and Head of the Church has been the pillar, yet at the same time the ground of much debate. For Holy Communion, the most ancient debate which of course very much surfaced also in the Reformation period is around the question of how the bread and wine are the body and blood, and what exactly happens on the back of the words, 'Take, eat, this is my body', etc. It would take more space than we have to unpack even the Westminster standards, but we might note that there is both a clear line against transubstantiation and an affirmation of Christ being 'really' and 'spiritually present to the faith of believers' in the sacrament. It was always insisted that the text in 1 Corinthians 11.23–27 should be read when the sacrament was celebrated.[366] Yet it has to be said that in more recent times the language of symbol has become freely used in a somewhat reductionist way that some certainly would regret;[367] and as far as the Corinthians text goes, it is not always used and sometimes deliberately, so as to allow other patterns of meaning to be woven in. None of this is to prejudge a conclusion on the matter, but room for debate there certainly is, as on the closely related matter of the so-called *epiclesis*, the prayer for the Holy Spirit to come upon both communicants and bread and wine, which for some is exceedingly important and for others apparently not necessarily thought of.[368] Or to take another point of focus, the ancient inspiration of an anaphora, an offering of thanksgiving (eucharistic prayers) in and through Christ, with a hallowed tradition of solemnity, focus and full participation, is sometimes observed, sometimes not. At play here may be the desire for accessibility and a relevance in (post-)modern idiom, as also a sensitivity to differing contexts of celebration; on the other hand, there is a yearning somehow to express catholicity and holiness, a communion of the saints across both time and place. Ultimately the question returns of who Jesus Christ is, risen and ascended or very much present in the face of the other, and perhaps there are no simple lines to be drawn. But it is notable that for all that the Church is keen to be open to innovative forms and able to communicate to generations not raised on the Catechisms and the Creed and Commandments which underpinned them, the lingering questions which have exercised generations past do not go away. How Holy Communion, like the Word, comes from Christ and is offered by the Church, demands most careful reflection at the same time as we would maintain it to be gift and promise, a holy mystery that is by definition never entirely within our grasp.

There is also a degree of restlessness around matters of order. There have been conspicuous shifts, in some places at least, in thinking about who may participate and in what roles. The presidency of the minister of Word and sacrament is for the most part unchallenged, but some will search the Scriptures and also reflect long and hard on the realities of their

---

366 See the Westminster Confession of Faith, ch. xxix and the Westminster Directory of Worship.

367 'Symbol' of course has an ancient pedigree as a theological term: all the more reason to use it with care. Cf. A. Schmemann, *The Eucharist*, New York: St Vladimir's Seminary Press, 2003, pp. 27–48.

368 There is also the view, taken by Donald Macleod and building on the silences of Western liturgies Catholic and Reformed, that the *epiclesis* is not helpful: 'Calvin into Hippolytus', in B. D. Spinks and I. R. Torrance, eds, *To Glorify God: Essays on Modern Reformed Liturgy*, Grand Rapids: Eerdmans, 1999, pp. 263–7.

local situation where perhaps a minister is not readily available, or it might be thought advantageous for someone else to preside on the grounds of many having gifts. This question will only be asked more in time to come. The role of ordained elders then comes up for scrutiny, since the historical background of the kirk session being responsible for discipline and admission of communicants to the Lord's Table readily translated into the elders helping to serve the bread and wine. The effects of changing church architecture and design become relevant here, and will be returned to; however, at this point it might merely be observed that in the worship service itself, well-established traditions of the elders occupying special seats and uniquely holding certain roles have altered, and in some places very much. And in the area of preparation for Holy Communion, where again an established Church of Scotland tradition was for elders not just to visit members in their homes but also to examine and to assist in the 'fencing' of the table by the granting of admission tokens, this has all but died out. Eldership is a flourishing office of the Church but elders' participation in matters of ecclesiastical discipline is a shadow of former times. In parallel with this, the exhortation text so explicitly upheld in John Knox's sixteenth-century *Book of Common Order* got short shrift in its twentieth-century counterparts. It would always have been expected that those who attended to hear the Word would remain throughout the Communion celebration, but there was a time when many present might not have communicated; that is still the case, especially in some Highland situations. However, in many worship gatherings nowadays, almost all present will fully participate, including children and others who have not been formally admitted (by the kirk session still!) to formal membership of the Church. The debate over children's participation in 1991[369] produced official guidelines on how this should be enabled, but the situation on the ground is mixed. In some places, children are hardly offered the opportunity and therefore given a diet only of the Word; elsewhere, some might take the opinion that there is great laxity, with perhaps even the strong links between baptism and the Lord's Supper being to an extent overlooked. On a different tack, ecumenically the Church of Scotland would welcome professing members of other churches fully to participate in the sacrament, but there are blocks on this being reciprocal, most notably in the Scottish situation with the also large Roman Catholic Church. On the Roman Catholic side, the questions of order are significant. The 'bonds of communion', episcopally guaranteed and ultimately with the bishop of Rome, have been broken. Presbyterianism in the *ecclesia Scoticana* does not convince.

---

369 See the Board of Education report, 'Too young to matter', *Reports to the General Assembly of the Church of Scotland*, Edinburgh: printed for the Church of Scotland, 1991.

As well as the recurring questions of faith and order, the other obvious threads to pick up briefly are those of time and place. The sacrament has been most usually celebrated in the Sunday congregation and in the church sanctuary. In the Highlands there is still in a number of situations a Communion season, a succession of services before and after the one in which bread and wine are served. And yet across Scotland Communion is also celebrated often in smaller gatherings, around the meeting of a kirk session or on a midweek evening, sometimes in the homes of people who are housebound, or in hospitals and residential care situations. However, while there would be few if any locales in which there were no regular communion services (not always the case in Church of Scotland history), there are also very few places in which there is Communion weekly as a main Sunday service. Generally speaking, and even though some church members will attend almost only for communion services, the church is built more around the preaching of the Word than the celebration of the sacrament.

Altogether this sends something of a mixed message. How important is it that the people of God should gather around the table? How do we order the interiors of our churches? Is Holy Communion an occasional add-on or is it constitutive of the Church's very being? If we might search again for commonalities, it may be to say that our faith is nourished by action as well as by word, and that eating and drinking connects us not only to the moment of our redemption (the Last Supper so powerfully focusing that) but to the creation as a whole (represented in the bread and wine) and the last things (the anticipation of the heavenly banquet). And the Lord's Supper is both a gathering of the faithful and a dispersing or sending out, with heavy implications for how life is to be lived between the times. Jesus feeds us not so that we might know ourselves to be religiously observant but that we might continue his work. So far perhaps a clear pattern is not so obviously emerging out of such threads, and thereby hangs the challenge. Those who have attempted to convert the Church to weekly celebrations and to bring the sacrament to be at the heart of our corporate life have met with resistance. The 1979 *Book of Common Order* gave perhaps the clearest attempt to instil such a thought, but it did not catch on. In the ordering of buildings, there may be as much confusion as clarity. The large majority of buildings will have a prominent, sometimes all but immovable communion table placed altar-wise, and yet for most of the time this will be bare – except to be used as a place on which to lay offerings of money! Still, as there begin to be now a few indications of doing away with the table as a permanent fixture just as parties might also do away with a pulpit, voices are raised in protest perhaps more at the loss of table than at the loss of pulpit. There may be widespread keenness for a down-to-earth Word, but thankfully people still yearn (at least on occasion!) to anticipate taking their seats in the heavenly places.

It would be unfair, however, to dwell only on matters unresolved. The Lord's Supper is celebrated on the Lord's Day and there is something immensely important about that. There are varying admixtures of solemnity and joy in these celebrations, but there is no doubting of the significance of the occasions. There is a desire for participation and meaningfulness which only grows as people both reflect on and experience what is offered by the Church; without any scientific means of measuring it, it does *seem* that there are more and more opportunities for sacramental intimacy, and that this is warmly welcomed. And the notes which have always been strongly sounded within the Reformed tradition, of both delighting in the creation through the ordinariness of bread and wine, and of being serious in our anticipation of heavenly judgement and joy, reverberate long after the liturgies finish. The informal fellowship of eating and drinking when worship is over (services of the Word included) is a treasured aspect in very many congregations. Christian discipleship (very much including mutual love) and sacrificial witness are markers of the lives of many Church members through all the times they are not in the church sanctuary.

The place of the Lord's Supper is that it is infinitely more than a religious ritual. It focuses an intimate belonging both to Christ and to one another. There is implied both preparation and follow-on as well as the event itself. Regularly, preparation is about more than the work of a few in preparing the space and the food and the vessels; for all concerned, the word, and silence, of encounter with God makes us ready. And for the event and follow-on, there is the example of the crucified Christ, service even through suffering, which stands over and against tendencies to bullishness and the desire to dominate; there is a sacred sharing which is at odds with otherwise so personalised grasping for the secret of life; and in the context of poverty, war and all sorts of other struggles, there is a sowing of visions, a building of courage, a path on which to follow until death is no more. Fed by our Lord and Saviour, we should have everything to give, as we have had so much given to us.[370]

Changing days bring changes of experience. A measure of debate and difference may be a healthy sign of the high value of the sacrament of the Lord's Supper, but the reality of scandalous divisions across the churches, and concerns about the range of diversity within the Church of Scotland itself, call us equally to appreciate what we hold in common, and what beckons as a shared inheritance and hope. To have a uniform pattern of celebrating Holy Communion would be a sign of the impoverishment of

---

370 Some of the earliest Church tradition (e.g. Justin Martyr) as well as regular contemporary practice support special collections for the poor whenever there is Communion, as well as action beyond the sanctuary.

the imagination. But then we also would wish to affirm the integral link between Word and sacrament; the need for a regularity of celebrations; the dependence upon the active work of Jesus Christ and the Holy Spirit as well as the significance of the work of the people who so depend; and the placing of the sacrament in the context where it focuses not on an ancient ritual but God's salvation of the world.

Part Four

COMMUNITIES AT WORSHIP TODAY

13

SCOTLAND'S ROMAN CATHOLIC PEOPLE AT WORSHIP

Owen Dudley Edwards

> That the Scot at prayer is something of an awkward figure is well known, the attainment of grace a matter of grudging negotiation rather than any sweet surrender to the light. Just how well his faith of Presbyterianism accommodates his needs is eloquently confirmed by this excellent book.

Thus the London *Daily Telegraph* hailed Dr Callum Brown's 1987 volume *The Social History of Religion in Scotland since 1730*. Ignorance clothed in racialist snobbery was what many of the *Daily Telegraph*'s habitual readers expected for their money, and any other eyes resting on it could shrug it off with the knowledge that grunts are what you expect from pigs. Ten years later, the London publishers, Methuen, relinquished the book, which its author then revised, and Edinburgh University Press reissued it under the new title *Religion and Society in Scotland since 1707* (1997). The back of the now paperbacked book flew the above review extract as its blurb's sole critical evidence of quality. For a Scottish university press to assume that its Scottish prospective purchasers would disinter their bawbees in response to stupidity and offensiveness on this scale, reminds us that we have dismissed Bigotry from our watchtowers only to enthrone Mammon warmly clad in pig-ignorance.

The unknown reviewer would no doubt congratulate himself on having simultaneously insulted women, Presbyterians and all other Scottish worshippers, being one of that breed of academic hacks whose ignorance counts its bliss in the number of its libels. The late Hugh Trevor-Roper thus rose from the stepping-stones of his dead selves to more lucrative (if more ludicrous) things. The dismissal of the entire female gender to invisible insignificance, the reduction of all religious faiths to one, the

187

stereotyping of a people to a collective noun manipulated for derisive effect – all were, and in some hack-nests still are, the stock-in-trade of the mischief-making ignoramus. Even more loathsome, if possible, is the readiness to pronounce on prayerful conduct.

Prayer at its utmost is private prayer, whether mentally articulated to one's God amid acts of public worship, or uttered alone aloud or silently. In the case of almost all human beings, their prayer is their secret. Whatever their outward label, their inner prayers, if any, are unknown save to God. Aged Catholics saying a rosary, consisting of one Our Father, ten Hail Marys and one Glory Be to the Father, Son and Holy Spirit, the whole recited five times over, might seem to the outsider to be trapped in unthinking repetition: in fact it may work for the prayerful as a setting in which to converse more intimately with God, as an orchestra's music contextualizes a song. A Presbyterian pastor articulating a prayer extempore seeks to speak for all hearers while implicitly inviting them to agree or constructively disagree in their minds with what he or she says. But common prayer strengthens itself by the simultaneous action of the people whether in common singing of a hymn or psalm, or in a Quaker meeting where all are sitting in silence. Communal silent meditation asserts its own prayer by the act of fellowship at worship, as well as the internal actions of individuals. A congregation all looking at a single sacred picture pray in the unity of their action and in every separate variety of reaction. Scottish Catholics often light a candle to accompany private prayer for some cause: they may do so in church, when a service is not taking place, and then their candle becomes one of an array lighting up a dark corner individually and collectively. Such unity exists across time as people read or hear a text worshipping in silent response to their eyes or ears, be it the first chapter of John's Gospel, or commentaries in the Talmud, or instructions in the Qur'an, or Buddhist epigrams. But we cannot read the prayerful mind of anyone else.

The *Daily Telegraph*'s insult to Scottish Catholics is thus but one among its many. This particular insult is of unintentional value, in that it throws into relief the chief crisis in Scottish Catholic identity, the denial of Catholicism's Scottishness. That denial is dying or dead today, and its killers were mostly not Catholics. The heroic welcome given to Pope John Paul II in Scotland in 1982, a greeting essentially from the people rather than, as in England, primarily from an elite, resulted from the work of Church of Scotland clergy in public and in private, going back to 1961 when the then Moderator of the General Assembly of the Church of Scotland, the Revd Archie Craig, supported by the Church's three relevant committees, determined to visit Pope John XXIII, who took him in his arms.[371]

---

371 Elizabeth Templeton, *God's February: A Life of Archie Craig 1888–1985*, London: BCC/CCBI, 1991, pp. 102–05.

This followed (and ended) 400 years of bitter conflict between Protestant and Catholic churches. But the sentiment of the dead or dying denial is one we can easily trace down the centuries, from pagan druids denouncing Christian incursions, through Iona-trained monks maintaining the superiority of their dating of Easter to the Roman usage, to the General Assembly led by many of its Moderators declaring from 1923 to 1951 and beyond that Scotland's Catholics were an alien race whose further entry should be prohibited and whose present numbers should be returned to Ireland.[372] Many an Irish-born or Irish-descended Catholic may have told themselves that their religion was truly Irish, and that they would shortly leave this Scotland, so lacking in true Catholicism. Ironically but inevitably Scotland's Catholics of Irish origin had to stop thinking of themselves as other than Scots at the very date when Presbyterian denial of Catholicism's Scottishness became an official Church of Scotland priority: 1923. But was Catholicism alien to Scotland? Throughout the twentieth century Scottish Catholics increased and documented insistence that it was not. They would do so first through amateur, and then through professional medieval historians, the latter led by Dr Leslie Macfarlane of the University of Aberdeen, whose biography of its founder, the fifteenth-century Bishop Elphinstone,[373] drove all medieval and Renaissance Scottish history into its European social, diplomatic and European contexts, above all by Macfarlane becoming one of the world's greatest authorities on the Vatican Archives. It was also Leslie Macfarlane who questioned the crude Western historiographical fallacy that nationalism began with the French Revolution by showing how remarkably nationalist, in any serious meaning of the term, Scottish publicists showed themselves not only in the Declaration of Arbroath in 1320 but thence up to the Reformation. Well-meaning if faintly absurd hymns took up the same assertion of Scottish Catholicism's medieval credentials, as in

Come back, come back to Scotland
Our Lady of Aberdeen!

---

372 See Stewart J. Brown, '"Outside the Covenant": the Scottish Presbyterian Churches and Irish Immigration, 1922–1938', *Innes Review*, 42 (Spring 1991), pp. 19–45, and 'Presbyterians and Catholics in Twentieth-Century Scotland', in Stewart J. Brown and George Newlands, eds, *Scottish Christianity in the Modern World*, Edinburgh: T&T Clark, 2000, pp. 255–81, also Harry Reid, *Outside Verdict – an Old Kirk in a New Scotland*, Edinburgh: St Andrew Press, pp. 104–36.

373 Leslie J. Macfarlane, *William Elphinstone and the Kingdom of Scotland – the Struggle for Order*, Aberdeen: Aberdeen University Press, 1995 [1985]. Among other innumerable services to scholarship, his was the chief hand in the great exhibition on 'Scotland and the Papacy' (City Art Gallery, Edinburgh, 1982), which provided the historical dimension to Pope John Paul II's visit that year.

What Church of Scotland claims of Scottish Catholicism's alien status had actually meant was that Scottish Catholicism was alien to the Church of Scotland. But was even this true? Doctrinally, there was far less dividing the churches than either of them would admit then, although today it is not so much that the gap is narrowing, rather that we can now see how narrow it is. Common ground against soul-destroying greed and government intoxication with war and nuclear weapons provides admirable bases for mutual respect and appreciation of similarities, as Keith Patrick Cardinal O'Brien and several Moderators have shown. Sociologically, Catholicism and Presbyterianism are populist in contrast to the firm Erastian basis of the Church of England. The Presbyterian Church of Scotland won its status as state Church in 1689, suffered some eroding of its populism by the United Kingdom's attempts to enforce local magnates' power of appointment of ministers, won back half of its populist credentials through the Disruption of 1843, and in reunion in 1929 came more and more to cherish its place as a peoples' church. Roman Catholicism had been the religion of the medieval people, but also of the medieval potentate unless or until the potentate found greater profitability in Protestantism. Scottish Protestantism was distinguished in Europe by establishing itself against the wishes of its own rulers (unlike, say, the Dutch revolt against Philip II of Spain). But Irish Roman Catholicism had survived in opposition to an alien ruling elite, and Ireland's one really successful mass incursion by plantation had been Scots populist Protestants in Ulster. Ulster and the west of Scotland have in fact been profoundly and perpetually interconnected down the centuries. Map-readers see them as separate countries, but Macdonalds or Macdonnells – the Clan Donald – would historically have seen the North Channel as their own private lake. Many of the inhabitants migrated from one to the other, some seasonally. Protestants no less than Catholics were subject to alien influences, all the more when the alien element seemed purely geographical. Accordingly, what was true of Catholics in urban or urbanizing Ulster would hold true for Catholics in comparable Scottish environments. Up to the meeting of Archie Craig and John XXIII many Catholics and Presbyterians in Ulster and Scotland saw one another as damned, and avoided one another's society where possible, partly because they saw danger in dealing with those destined for the devil. But this actually made them more like one another. However much divided, they eyed one another continually and noted one another's conduct, partly to find evidence of turpidity, partly to ensure the enemy did not hold moral high ground at one's expense. In terms of worship, it seems to have increased the Sabbatarianism of all parties. It also increased both parties' anxiety to show themselves more respectable, and it became a kind of worship. Calvinists needed to show themselves worthy of spiritual leadership and saved by predestination, and thus sought to display what Catholics would call the outward sign of inward grace. Catholics might be less ready to rely on predestination, but the effects were much the same. The fanaticism with which Protestant and Catholic middle-class ladies insisted on either themselves or their servants/children polishing the brasses on the front door bell, post-box and knocker, was a form of worship, displaying obvious virtue, shaming the slovenly especially of the other religion, and remotely echoing the instructions to the Israelites in Egypt to mark their doors so that the Angel of Death would pass by on his errand to slaughter the firstborn sons of the Egyptians. Turning to the bell-polishers' polar opposite, the drunken louts supporting Glasgow Celtic and Glasgow Rangers expectorated their foul rhetoric in epithet and chant with sentiments almost as indistinguishable as their vehemence. In academic discourse I once had to discourage a charming atheist sociologist whose classification of varieties of Scottish Catholicism included being a supporter of Glasgow Celtic. There were many Celtic supporters of Protestant or atheist persuasion, although many of them tempered their habitual indifference to Roman Catholic doctrines with a vague sense of the Pope as a mascot. But my sociologist friend was right in one respect. Football has a very serious element of worship within it and the insistence on superiority over one's rival made the similarities between the Ranger and Celtic supporters all the more urgent. The origins of both teams lay in clergy trying to keep their youthful votaries away from street-corner brawls, public-house dissipation and evil company (if male) leading to crime or (if female) worse. So far as I can gather, they worked in mutual support and respect until after World War One when job competition in the post-war slump, disillusionment with the broken promises of the leaders who urged them into war, savage awareness of the 1919–21 civil conflicts in Ireland, and xenophobic rejection of internationalism, led them to turn on one another as the nearest means of coping with frustration, all the more gratifying in apparently having divine sanction in war against the devil's brood.

The history of modern Scottish Catholicism periodizes itself into 1878–1918/23; 1918/23–1961/65; 1961/65–82; 1982–? In other words, from the restoration of the Scottish Catholic hierarchy to the placing of Catholic schools in the state system in 1918 and the signing of the 'Anglo-Irish' Treaty of 1921–2; from the Church of Scotland call for Irish (Catholic) repatriation in 1923 to Pope John XXIII (1959–63) and the Second Vatican Council; from Vatican II to Pope John Paul II's visit to Scotland; from the papal visit to the present. These are crucial turning-points in mentality: the state's acceptance of its duty to further Catholic education and the removal of most of what was Catholic Ireland beyond United Kingdom boundaries gave Scottish Catholics a real stake in Scotland, moving from a missionary culture to a sense of citizenship; the Pope's visit, with the sudden realization that Scottish Protestants were proud to rejoice with their Catholic neighbours was the defining moment when Scottish Catholics no longer needed to think of themselves as second-class citizens. Naturally a church which regards itself as missionary, that is, an outsider church and a church primarily for outsiders, will share much of the same worship as its successors, and a church calling itself Catholic should be least dominated by considerations of its relationship to the state and/or nation in which its worshippers find themselves, but of course it made a vast difference. To make a specifically Catholic point, I am a member of St Columba's parish, Newington, Edinburgh, now well into its second century. When it was founded, a majority of the congregation probably thought of St Columba primarily as an Irish saint in missionary exile; today the majority of the congregation probably thinks of St Columba primarily as a Scottish saint establishing his country as Christian. Many of them would pray to St Columba as someone who would particularly understand their own situation, and they might make the very same prayer asking his inspiration and his assistance in what troubles them. But the change in how they see themselves transforms their vision of St Columba (who may have seen no distinction in being Irish or Scots). Similarly the new goodwill among Scottish Christians after the Pope's visit has made wonderful changes in Scottish Catholics' consciousness of being part of a larger Christianity. Our prayers, we have some reason to hope, will sound less like the Pharisee scorning the publican when we think of our Protestant fellow-Christians, and the same for them. The matter was best summed up by Professor Duncan Forrester:

> a Pope who constantly moves to and fro over the face of the earth admonishing and applying the brakes ... in Scotland urged the Roman Catholic Church to join hands with other Christians in pilgrimage, and to launch confidently into the mainstream of Scottish national life ... to get a move on in making a distinctive and constructive Christian and Catholic contribution to the future of Scotland.[374]

The Pope of course knew, what his audiences did not, that nowhere on earth had Protestant leaders worked so hard and gone so far in urging him to come to their country. But Catholics and Protestants could see and ponder the effects. In particular the Pope singled out Scottish Protestant 'veneration in which you hold the Sacred Scriptures, accepting them for what they are, the word of God, and not of men'. He evidently realized that a cardinal point (pun intended) in Scottish Protestant anti-Catholicism was

---

374 Forrester, 'Introduction', in Gerard Hand and Andrew Morton, eds, *Catholicism and the Future of Scotland*, Edinburgh: CTPI, 1997, pp. 10–11.

a traditional anger against Roman pretension, and met them half-way: 'for there is no eternal city for us in this time but we look for one in the life to come' (citing Hebrews 13.15). He prayed very much in the tradition of the extempore prayer so beautifully realized by countless Scots Presbyterians: 'Lord, let Scotland flourish through the preaching of Thy word and the praising of Thy name!' And he followed that by calling on his new friends to join their Catholic fellow-Scots in praying for an end to the Falklands/Malvinas war then raging:

> In the joy of our concelebration today we cannot permit ourselves to forget the victims of the war, both the dead and the wounded as well as the broken hearts of many families. Let us beseech the God of mercy to give us peace in this our day, the peace of Christ our Lord.[375]

In so doing, he recruited all of Scottish Christianity in the cause of peace, with momentous effects for years to come. He and his successor kept up the crusade for peace against the most powerful politicians in the world. Neither Scottish nor any other Catholics are elbow-jerk papalists, waiting for papal animation like Punch and Judy between performances. The Pope advises; the Catholic is responsible for his or her own actions. We have no Eichmann-like excuses to evade our spiritual responsibilities. But papal leadership lifts many questions otherwise left in public apathy, and in their hatred of war successive popes have given a new force to Christian worship. Successive cardinals, Thomas Winning of Glasgow and Keith Patrick O'Brien of Edinburgh, have kept the issue before Catholic eyes so that praying for peace individually and collectively is vital to our worship in itself and urgent in its implications for our action. O'Brien has been outstanding in making the peace crusade the basis for pan-Christian protest, in full harmony with great Moderators such as the Revd Alan Macdonald. The successive UK governments since the papal visit have given all too much cause for such protest, and Scottish Catholic masses abound with public prayers denouncing wars and weapons of mass destruction. In passing we should notice the Pope's use of 'concelebration', usually meaning two or more priests jointly celebrating Mass, here used to mean common prayer or any other activity of worship. He evidently regarded himself as having concelebrated with Protestants present and willing. In

---

375 Pope John Paul II, *The Pope in Britain – Collected Homilies and Speeches*, Slough: St Paul Publications, 1982, pp. 78–9. For the vital role of the Church of Scotland in ensuring the Pope would come to Britain when Falklands/Malvinas war threatened to prevent it, see Thomas J. Winning, recorded by Fraser Elder in *Always Winning – Thomas Joseph Cardinal Winning 1925–2001*, Edinburgh: Mainstream, 2001, pp. 41, 43. As the first non-Italian Pope since Hadrian VI (1522–3), John Paul II seems to have mildly shared the dislike of Scotland's Protestants for the identification of urban supremacy with Rome.

this he gave a powerful impetus to future Scottish Catholic common cause with fellow-Christians. His formula was also judicious in allowing for Catholic and Protestant differences respecting the dead. Catholics pray for the dead, believing that God, outside time, may receive prayers for the dead regardless of the length of earthly time between the death and the prayer. Protestants do not, officially. The Pope asked that we remember the dead, which covers the two doctrines.

But however significant 1918–23 and 1982, the greatest change in Scottish Catholicism was surely brought about by the Second Vatican Council. Its impact was not immediately evident. Preparing for this chapter, I asked a devout Scottish Catholic what he thought the most important fact in the history of modern Scottish Catholicism, to which he answered: the failure of the then Scottish hierarchy to provide leadership amid the complexity of reorganization in the wake of the Council. This was not necessarily for deplorable reasons. The Scots Catholics had worked in general on the principle of keeping their heads down and avoiding trouble. There had been distinguished exceptions, apart from those occasioned by football pieties. The Catholic masses made silent transition from Liberal to Labour, partly in revulsion against Liberal prime ministers presiding over excessively brutal repression in Ireland, partly recognizing common class interests, partly because of inspired lay leadership notably from John Wheatley showing that the social gospel of Pope Leo XIII could be best realized through Labour policies. Some hysterical priests saw Red Revolution, but a bogey nearer at hand was Black Starvation. Wheatley in the 1920s in any case had one remarkable advantage. Priests who fulminated against the power of the state were confronted by the fact that the state was providing for Catholic education largely on Catholic terms. But Wheatley's early death meant that Catholics in the Labour party worked with what he had gained from church and state with little sign of looking beyond it. Catholic intellectuals flirted with Scottish nationalism in the later 1920s, and revived a Catholic dimension to creative writing, as shown by such figures as Compton Mackenzie, Moray Maclaren, Fionn MacColla, and (with less formal nationalism) Bruce Marshall and A. J. Cronin, the last of whom provided a gratifying Scots myth for the TV age in *Dr Finlay's Casebook*. But in general Catholics took their victory in education as a recipe for quiescence. The example of Ulster here invited extreme caution. Catholic Ulster boycotted the new state of Northern Ireland and thus lost in 1930 educational concessions, which had been offered in 1923. Constitutional Catholic politicians encouraged the boycott; revolutionary ones in IRA activities gave Unionist politicians the excuse they wanted to maintain an apartheid state on national security grounds. Scottish Catholics kept their heads low and their voices lower when violent anti-Catholic mobs in the mid 1930s stoned buses in Edinburgh's Morningside carrying little children in their First Communion best clothes. This truly showed Catholic leadership as well as good Christian principles, but it made for a culture excessively fearful of visibility. Nor could the anti-Catholic violence be dismissed as the work of an individual demagogue, John Cormack, and his temporarily inflamed followers. It happened in Edinburgh, not in Glasgow where Catholicism and Presbyterianism were much more evenly balanced, leaving the fear that such things might happen in Glasgow and, once started, it might replicate some of the worst religious riots of Belfast. In fact it is now clear that the annual dripping of anti-Catholic venom from the General Assembly of the Church of Scotland in Edinburgh was what gave Edinburgh the nearest Scotland came to Fascist urban warfare.

The first real post-Vatican-II Catholic leadership came from the Catholic chaplain at the University of Edinburgh, Father Anthony Ross, OP, whose awareness of clerical deficiencies he made clear when writing the history of the Scottish Catholic community 1878–1978:

> Many priests were tinged with fideism, anti-intellectual and convinced that all would be well if people would only 'keep the Faith' by which they meant repetition of approved statements of belief and regular attendance at church on prescribed days. As the *Catholic Directory* for 1939 illustrates, there was still an abundance of indulgences available which, although intended to encourage the practice of virtue could, and often seemed to, encourage a very shallow type of religion.[376]

A large Catholic minority amid a populistic Protestant majority could unconsciously adapt what it worshipped to its larger neighbour's excessive concerns with respectability, decorum, dullness, defensiveness, resentment and a vague sense of gloomy predestination, joylessness and lovelessness. But simultaneously Scottish Catholics would emphasize such aspects of worship as particularly drew denunciations from Protestants – cults of the Blessed Virgin Mary and the saints apparently dwarfing the worship due to God, for instance. The Second Vatican Council and the pontificate of John XXIII in particular changed such emphases, above all by putting the worship of God in language intelligible to all at Mass. The Latin Mass was very beautiful, more so than the too hastily assembled translations which took its place, but the vernacular in English and (in appropriate

---

376 Ross, 'The Development of the Scottish Catholic Community 1878–1978' in David McRoberts, ed., *Modern Scottish Catholicism 1878–1978*, Glasgow: J. Burns, 1979, p. 44. See also Ross's unfinished autobiography *The Root of the Matter*, Edinburgh: Mainstream, 1989, also his essay 'Resurrection' in Duncan Glen, ed., *Whither Scotland?* London: Gollancz, 1971, pp. 112–27, and its use by the Presbyterian scholar Revd Professor William Storrar, *Scottish Identity – a Christian Vision*, Edinburgh: Hansel Press, 1990.

Western Isles) Gaelic brought the realities of their religion back to the people. The sudden disappearance of saints now acknowledged as mythological was as effective a way of recalling the faithful to real priorities as any. Snobbery played some part in resentment against these changes. Catholicism had been attractive as the oldest Christian club available in Western civilization, and worshippers who had taken pride in their mastery of Latin resented being part of the English-speaking herd. There was little of such reaction in Scotland. A few cranks cranked, notably among ex-Communists hell-bent on maintaining the sectarianism of their old persuasion as their main contribution to its replacement. Perhaps their most visible characteristic was their desperate anxiety to maintain the ghetto mentalities of the past, and the conviction of Protestant damnation.

Some fell into schism and still spew out pamphlets chiefly denouncing Popes since Pius XII as satanic. Others remain in the church and send hate mail to the Vatican accusing the successive cardinals of heresy of one kind or another. Email has only increased the capacity for such activities, since it lessens the time in which thought gives birth to deed. The Vatican would save itself a lot of time and trouble if it declared that no communications breathing hatred can be received by a Church whose Founder died for love.

One vital factor in Scottish Catholicism's embrace of its fellow-Christian churches lay in the work of Leslie Macfarlane, Anthony Ross and others in the Scottish Catholic Historical Association from 1950, moving into higher gear from the mid 1960s. Scottish Roman Catholicism all too often had either been demonized or written out of the history of Scotland. Ross, Macfarlane and the scholars who gathered around the SCHA and its journal, the *Innes Review*, were resolute in demythologizing anti-Catholic Scottish historiography, but rejected apologetic, aggrieved accusation and instead fought for the principle of Scottish total history. The challenge of Scottish nationalism in the last 40 years lent contemporary interest to professional historical controversies, and the increased appetite for Scottish historical writing from all standpoints meant that the history of religion was open for harvest. Scottish Catholic history was visibly at the heart of Scottish historical identity, once medieval history had ceased to be forbidden fruit. The result is that today we have a wealth of histories of Catholic parishes embodying the best endeavours of first-class Catholic historians in Scottish universities, amid the splendour of achievements in more ambitious fields. The leading one-volume history of Scotland is the work of one Catholic, Professor Michael Lynch,[377] and the leading modern histories of Scotland and of Scotland's empire, are by another, Professor T. M. Devine.[378] The

---

377 *Scotland – a New History*, London: Pimlico, 1992 [1991].

378 *The Scottish Nation 1700–2000*, London: Penguin, 1999; *Scotland's Empire*, London: Allen Lane, 2004.

effect of their work is, among much else, to enable most Scottish Catholics to pray before the altar of God without a constant grievance against their fellow-Scots. A few intellectuals maintain the grievance culture, sounding increasingly like Dr Who caught in a disused time-warp.

The altars and their priests were turned to face the people after Vatican II. It symbolized the rediscovery of the priest as one of the people. Before Vatican II many priests took their vows and did their work with no notice-able vocation save their parents' desire for the improved social status a priest in the family would bring. Numbers of clergy may be fewer today, but the vocations at work are much more likely to be genuinely spiritual instead of mere desires for office in a profession assured of economic secur-ity, extraordinary power and community deference. Similarly marriages may be fewer, but they have more chance of being acts of love rather than, as so often throughout human history, for parental socio-economic rewards. But while the reduction in priests has ensured a far higher quality of priest, it has also turned a dream of Vatican II into much more of a real-ity. We are developing a priesthood of the people. Administration falls far more heavily on the laity than before, and the resultant tasks sort them-selves out into tasks attracting those most competent for them. The priest, as a priest, is sacrosanct when celebrating the Mass, particularly its Canon involving transubstantiation of host and chalice into the body and blood of Christ. (Anthony Ross, disabled by massive strokes, could never finish a sentence, but spoke the Canon perfectly when concelebrating Mass.)

The priest in other respects was formerly the recipient of a great deal of secret anti-clericalism in his days as a despot moderated by remote superiors. Today if the problems of the parish are 'man-made' the priest, in all justice, is less likely to be at fault or to be blamed. Women play a far greater role in spiritual as well as in administrative matters, reading church lessons during Mass, taking Holy Communion to housebound per-sons and to patients in hospitals, joining with men to become ministers of the Eucharist. As one such minister, our tasks also involve taking Com-munion services when a priest cannot celebrate Mass, and in my experi-ence it is the women who are the most successful teachers and moderators of our work. We are commissioned after examination, where possible by the bishop, but the awesome task of leading one's fellow-parishioners in prayer and carrying out most of the priest's work at Mass outside the Canon, needs induction through kindly but vigilant supervisors, and many are the women I have cause to thank. Hospital visits ultimately put us on our own, after initial vetting by state as well as church. But not completely on our own. Apart from the unfailing support and assistance from the overworked staff – and we hospital chaplains heartily confirm the excel-lence of National Health nurses – I know of no task where I am in such frequent prayer, hoping that what I do will comfort those I seek, and help them face their lives and perhaps their deaths. We meet many people who would like to receive Communion but have not been to church for many years. Ministers may not hear their confession, but lead them in an Act of Contrition, that is, the expression of genuine sorrow for former rejection of God in whatever unspecified way. The patients may say that they are unworthy to receive Communion, especially after a long absence: we tell them that we also are unworthy, and so is the Pope, and so is everybody else. (The Pope is a very useful symbol of human equality before God.) The Eucharist is given to us to strengthen us, but the beauty of the gift is not a reward. The patient's hospital status naturally makes that gift all the more appropriate. I doubt if I have ever seen such a joyful transformation on human faces as at a patient's return to friendship with God in receiving the Eucharist. To see that, indeed to see anyone receiving Holy Communion, is one of the most wonderful sights a priest or minister can be given. To look on it is to worship oneself. I have also seen such rapture on Presbyterian faces receiving a Eucharist apparently commemorative only, or on Episcopalian faces where the doctrine is at the communicant's choice.

What lies before us is the fulfilment of Christ's demand to glorify God by the love of him and of our neighbour, and to do our work with gratitude for our time, undertaking with thanks our new responsibilities and rejoicing in the mutual love and common apostleship we share with our fellow-Christians.[379]

379 I am deeply grateful to a number of scholars in the preparation of this chapter, and to many more fellow-Catholics and fellow-Christians. Those who qualify as martyrs in the trouble given to them in its preparation are my wife, Bonnie Dudley Edwards, my editor, the Revd Professor Duncan B. Forrester, and our National Library of Scotland.

14

EPISCOPALIANS AND THE EUCHARIST

Ian Paton

> The Eucharist is at the very heart of Anglican life. It is both source and fulfilment of the koinonia we share as Christians and it flows from the baptismal waters from which we were born anew.
>
> (The Dublin Statement, *Renewing the Anglican Eucharist*)

During the last century and a half the most significant change in the pattern of worship for Scottish Episcopalians has been the restoration of the Eucharist as the principal service on Sundays. Episcopalian liturgical history in this sense is like that of other Anglicans around the world: under the influence of the evangelical and catholic movements in the Anglican Church, a eucharistic sacramental theology of the body of Christ informed more and more of the liturgical self-understanding of the Scottish Episcopal Church. That was a sea-change both liturgically and theologically, and the practical result has been that the service of Holy Communion has become the normal service celebrated by Episcopalians not only on Sundays, but also on a wide variety of other occasions, like the meeting of a synod or the anniversary of a marriage.

Ecumenism

More recently, Episcopalian experience of the Eucharist has been deeply influenced by another factor, the ecumenical movement. By 1980, the results of years of scholarship on early texts had affected the shape and text of revisions of the Eucharist in many denominations, and resulted often in eucharistic services that self-consciously owed more to the early Christian centuries than, say, to the Reformation. Such a process of ecumenically and historically convergent revision produced, for the Scottish Episcopal

Church, the Scottish Liturgy of 1982. The 'Blue Book' (as it was commonly known) eventually succeeded the Scottish Prayer Book in the majority of Scottish Episcopal congregations as the normative eucharistic service.

But the ecumenical movement has also fostered liturgical renewal in another direction, that of Christian initiation. As for the Eucharist, the sacramental revival and the insights of scholarship have influenced the creation of new rites of baptism and confirmation. More radically, however, a new approach to the theology of Christian Initiation has been evident in Scottish Episcopal rites and practice.

Baptism

It was the 1982 World Council of Churches document *Baptism, Eucharist and Ministry*[380] (BEM) which began a further process of re-evaluating the place of baptism in the churches. For Anglicans this meant a re-evaluation both of infant baptism and of confirmation. In this process of re-evaluation, the International Anglican Liturgical Consultation (IALC) has been influential, and its statements have had a direct effect on Christian Initiation as practised in the Scottish Episcopal Church.

IALC is a four-yearly conference of liturgists from around the Anglican Communion. It has no official standing in the structures of the Communion, and its members, who are often academics, come mostly but not entirely from Europe and North America. The Toronto meeting of IALC in 1990 was an attempt to follow up BEM by looking first at baptism in the Anglican Communion. IALC 1990 produced an agreed statement, 'Walk in Newness of Life',[381] which advocated a new look at the theology and practice of baptism and confirmation. Previous IALC meetings had stated that all the baptized, including children, ought to be admitted to Holy Communion. IALC 1990 now went further and affirmed that 'Baptism is complete sacramental initiation, and leads to participation in the Eucharist ... Confirmation and other pastoral rites of affirmation have a continuing role ... but are in no way to be seen as "completing" Baptism.'

A combination of social change and ecumenical convergence had left the traditional Anglican approach to Christian initiation behind, at least in Western developed countries. So, in Scotland clergy were less likely to be happy with 'indiscriminate baptism' and teenagers were less likely to ask for confirmation unless they were active members of the Church. A more

---

380 World Council of Churches, Commission on Faith and Order, *Baptism, Eucharist and Ministry*, Geneva: World Council of Churches, 1982.

381 David Holeton, ed., *Christian Initiation in the Anglican Communion: The Toronto Statement 'Walk in Newness of Life'; The Findings of the Fourth International Anglican Liturgical Consultation, Toronto 1991*, Bramcote, Notts, Grove Books, 1991.

positive side could be seen in the many adults seeking baptism or confirmation after finding faith or becoming committed members of the Church for the first time, and in the congregations where unconfirmed children and unconfirmed adults from other churches were being invited to receive communion (this had official sanction from the 1970s). This proved a fertile ground for reflection on the principles put forward by BEM and IALC.

Changes in practice like these have massive implications for a traditional Anglican self-understanding. Many Episcopalians have grown up with the idea that confirmation represents something unique and substantial in their personal journey of faith and in the life of their church, the gateway to receiving communion and becoming a 'full member' of the Church. Baptism expressed the grace of God given to each person, usually in infancy, and confirmation represented the mature acceptance of this gift and the further gift of the Holy Spirit through the laying-on of the bishop's hands. Baptism was about affirming infants and families, and confirmation provided the occasion for Christian education and youth ministry, and gave young members a sense of significance and belonging. If the Scottish Episcopal Church accepts that 'Baptism is complete sacramental initiation', can confirmation retain anything like its traditional place? Will confirmation disappear altogether, and with it the opportunity for instruction in the faith? Or can confirmation acquire a new emphasis as a sacrament of affirmation, commitment and renewal?

Eucharist

In 1994 IALC met in Dublin, and moved on to the next section of BEM on the Eucharist, but it took place just as Scottish Episcopalians were getting to grips with these questions. The Dublin Statement 'Renewing the Anglican Eucharist'[382] was published as they were moving towards producing and approving through Synods, new forms of liturgy for baptism and confirmation based on the principles of IALC 1990. What the IALC meeting in Dublin revealed was how much the debate about a renewed baptismal theology had focused on confirmation, and how little it had focused on the Eucharist. Many years later, my impression is still that we are not talking about the Eucharist very much in this debate. That is, perhaps, a sign, of how far experience and teaching about baptism and experience and teaching about the Eucharist have drifted apart from each other. It seems important to recognize, theologically as well as practically, that it will be in celebration of the Eucharist that the effects of a renewed theology of baptism will be most clearly felt and seen.

---

382 David Holeton, ed., *Renewing the Anglican Eucharist: Findings of the fifth International Anglican Liturgical Consultation, Dublin, Eire, 1995*, Cambridge: Grove Books, 1996.

In fact these effects can already be seen in the practice of many Episcopalian congregations. There is eucharistic worship in which all age groups participate, and communion is received even by small children. There is the widespread use of a fifth eucharistic prayer, designed to be used when children are present, and testimony to its popularity with some adults for its direct language and simple structure. There are education and nurture programmes that present a baptismal understanding of mission or stewardship, for example, and which are designed to be used in the context of the Eucharist. There are also theologies and training programmes for 'Local Collaborative Ministry' which look towards preparing the ministry of all the baptized, ordained or lay. These approaches, like BEM and IALC 1990, are ultimately inspired by a paradigm of 'baptismal ecclesiology' in which baptism is the sacrament and sign of what the Church is. Liturgically this idea is present in the 1982 Scottish Liturgy, where the Great Thanksgiving says,

> Help us, who are baptized into the fellowship of Christ's Body,
> to live and work to your praise and glory.

This part of the prayer – in which, by custom, all now join – has become part of many Scottish Episcopalians' self-understanding, and is already an articulation of the relationship of baptism and Eucharist.

Contemporary Episcopalian reflection on the theology and practice of the Eucharist and on revised forms of liturgy for it, has therefore taken place in the context of these kinds of questions about the theology and practice of baptism and confirmation. As the IALC Statement from Dublin demonstrates, Anglican thinking about the eucharistic liturgy has needed to take account of theological and practical change in some other areas as well.

Ministry

In the Anglican tradition that Episcopalians affirm, congregations of the baptized need presbyters or priests to preside over their liturgical celebrations. Like other churches in the Western European context, the Scottish Episcopal Church includes many small congregations in remote rural regions. In the past, ordained ministry in these contexts has been shared among many congregations, and in some cases Episcopalians in whole islands and Highland districts have been served by just one Episcopalian priest. Present pastoral realities as well as theological understanding have already resulted in a higher degree of ecumenical cooperation (for example, in mutually recognized ministries in a few Partnerships), and to an expansion of non-stipendiary presbyteral ministry. The pattern of 'Local Collaborative Ministry', mentioned above, includes calling some to this form of service in each community – 'Communities should be encouraged to seek out persons from among them who might be ordained as presbyters'.[383]

But is the ministry of the presbyter the only ministry required, in order that a community may celebrate? In the Scottish Book of Common Prayer of 1929, the rubrics call for the ministry of a deacon at celebrations of the Eucharist. It is doubtful whether many congregations have regularly experienced such a liturgical ministry, outside High Mass in some churches, and the first year of a newly ordained curate in others. This is changing. There has already been an ecumenical process of reflection on different understandings of the diaconate, and the Scottish Episcopal Church itself should really be engaged in a deep and radical process of assessing the need for greater diversity of ordained ministry, and therefore for the ministry of deacons, and others. A liturgical plurality of ministries, in line with the intentions of the 1929 Liturgy and its forerunners, is once again possible and desired: 'Many revisions of prayer books throughout the Anglican Communion reflect the recovery of a plurality of ministries within the celebration of word and sacrament.'[384]

The establishment of the Theological Institute of the Scottish Episcopal Church in 1992, as a resource for the whole Province, provides a diversity of training routes for these ministries. The Institute offers mixed mode training to candidates for a variety of stipendiary and non-stipendiary ministries. Part-time training offers a challenge to those responsible for the formation of ministers. The challenge is to maintain, in a non-residential context, the same high standards of education and formation, including liturgical education and formation that can be expected of a residential college. In addition to teaching about the development and principles of liturgy, this will mean paying careful attention to liturgical experience and reflection, through the planning and leadership of worship, among students who only meet each other once a week, or at residential weekends and summer school. 'The church needs leaders, both lay and ordained, who are able to facilitate and enable renewal, and who understand the nature of renewal in community.'[385]

The Communal Nature of Worship

The Dublin Statement draws particular attention to the servant role of ordained ministers within the liturgical assembly: the priest presides, the

---

383 *Renewing the Anglican Eucharist*, p. 22.
384 *Renewing the Anglican Eucharist*, p. 20.
385 *Renewing the Anglican Eucharist*, p. 42.

deacon serves, the congregation celebrates. The statement also draws attention to the need for the liturgical catechesis of members of the assembly, in order that they might better be enabled to fulfil their role as celebrants. There are ways in which this process might be assisted.

The congregational worship committee is becoming a less unusual part of local church structures. Such groups, prepared to learn about worship, and to participate in its planning in partnership with the priest, will become more important as a structural sign to congregations of their role as celebrant. Resources for them, in the form of training workshops and usable planning materials, will be needed. In Scotland, some of this has already become familiar to some congregations, through the ecumenical work of the Iona Community's Wild Goose workshops and publications, and through a renewed emphasis in the Scottish Episcopal Church as in the wider Communion of the need for liturgical formation. IALC has been influential, again, in promoting this area of creative education.

Books

But if lay worship groups are to be encouraged to participate in planning worship, and congregations are to be encouraged to understand and 'own' their worship, as its celebrants, the Church will need to provide simpler and more accessible resources. After 15 years of liturgical revision and creativity, parishes are left with officially published resources that range from beautifully printed Prayer Books, to ring-bound booklets, to 'wee bookies', to paper pamphlets. Many people are feeling lost in a sea of books and paper that is anything but accessible. The next step for the Scottish Episcopal Church, alongside the provision of web-based materials that can be downloaded and used as needed, is surely the publication of a worship book for the Eucharist which will contain all the authorized material between two covers. A new version of the Scottish Book of Common Prayer could bring together the best of traditional-language liturgies still being used, with the contemporary liturgies created over the last 20 years, and new material still being developed. A book is a symbol as well as a resource, and such a book might be seen as a symbol of common prayer, that is, the communally owned nature of Episcopalians' liturgical traditions as the standard from which local adaptation and creativity begins and to which it must return. It might function as a pattern of structures and texts which gives Episcopalian worship coherency and strength, and help clergy and congregations to be accountable to each other (as well as to God!) for their worship. A book might be a first step towards affirming the conviction of the Dublin IALC that the congregation, as locally representing the whole Church, is itself the celebrant of the Eucharist.

Yet, even holding in mind as concrete a standard as a book of common prayer, it is probably true that a further step for Episcopalians may be to foster an eventual move away from the book-bound liturgical spirituality that insists on having or providing every word of every liturgical text that is said, in order that the people may read it as it is being said. We need minimal, easy-to-use liturgy books or cards for people to follow. We need still other material, much of it seasonal in character, which they can hear and respond to within the congregation. Of course, all the liturgical texts would be available to those who desire them, but I have a feeling that the complexity of optional material, and the sheer difficulty of negotiating it, contributes to the experience that was remarked on in Dublin: 'When we assemble, we don't meet.'

The early history of the Scottish Episcopal Church reveals, of course, a reluctance to be so bound by books. This was largely because in the eighteenth century the only available, affordable, and, after 1746, legal books were English 1662 Prayer Books, rather than the Scottish text of 1637 or 1711. And so the tradition of 'wee bookies' was born. But this is not a good reason for wanting to hang on to 'wee bookies'. A better reason is to make the liturgy, which is surely something *done* rather than *read*, more accessible *as liturgy* rather than *as text* to its celebrants, the people of God.

Culture

Liturgical renewal, if it is to be genuine and not contrived, needs to be rooted in the culture of particular peoples. Liturgy does this both by using culturally formed language and symbolism, and by enabling the gospel to engage with aspects of culture that conflict with it.

In Scotland questions of culture are especially acute within the British and European context. It is by their culture that the Scottish people identify themselves in contrast with their larger southern neighbour. Yet within Scotland there are differences of culture which should not be overlooked, such as those between Highland and Lowland, and between rural, suburban and urban areas. This makes it difficult, for example, to claim 'Celtic spirituality' as the only natural language for a universal Scottish liturgy (see the Church of Scotland's 'Second Order for the Sacrament of the Lord's Supper', *Book of Common Order* 1994,[386] which uses Celtic prayer forms and rhythms throughout; also various liturgies used by the Iona Community). Nevertheless the influence of a revived or reinvented Celtic spirituality, with its emphasis on creation, cannot be overestimated, and will influence the liturgical renewal still further.

---

386 Church of Scotland, Panel on Worship, *Book of Common Order*, Edinburgh: St Andrew Press, 1994.

However the most serious cultural challenge to Scottish Episcopalians comes in the form of a direct question to much of our immediate liturgical and institutional past, a question about their identity as *Anglicans*. As ecumenical convergence continues in Scotland, it is going to become less and less easy to forget that the roots of the Scottish Episcopal tradition lie not in Anglicanism at all, but in the reformed Kirk of Scotland. Episcopalians in Scotland have often had to repudiate the charge of being the 'English Church', the Church of England in Scotland. And while the Scottish Episcopal Church is, as we have seen, as much a child of Thomas Cranmer, the Evangelical Revival and the Oxford Movement, as the churches of England or any other province in the Anglican Communion, yet it seems likely ecumenical dialogue and progress is going to make that way of identifying itself seem old-fashioned. Scottish Episcopalians' common heritage is being found now, not just with fellow-Anglicans in England and around the world, but with Scottish Presbyterians, Scottish Roman Catholics, and others, in the same town and nation. And although not much of the common *heritage* of Scottish Christians is liturgical, we do share a common liturgical *challenge*; to free the people of God, the catholic community of the baptized in this land, to celebrate Eucharist together.

The IALC in Dublin observed that although so much Anglican liturgical revision since 1928 has been concerned with updating and revising the inherited common text of the Book of Common Prayer, the next stage of liturgical renewal will have to find new language and forms in which to celebrate. As we share this task with Christians of other traditions in Scotland as well as across the Anglican Communion, Scottish Episcopalians have good roots from which to draw nourishment for growth.

Eucharist and Spirit

Alongside our Scottish and Anglican roots, there is the tradition, going back to the liturgies of the non-jurors and the first Scottish Liturgies, of liturgical scholarship and creativity that produced Thomas Rattray's masterly translation and re-creation of the Liturgy of St James, first published by him as 'The Ancient Liturgy of the Church of Jerusalem' in 1744. Rattray represents the summit of a school that established quite firmly in the Scottish Episcopalian tradition, a eucharistic theology drawn largely from Orthodox liturgical practice, which understands all sacraments, all the life of the Church, and the life of all Christians, as the work of the Holy Spirit. This is why the Scottish Liturgy, since the end of the eighteenth century, has included in the Great Thanksgiving over the bread and the wine, the portion of the prayer known as the *epiclesis*, or invocation of the Holy Spirit upon both people and upon bread and wine. I think that is a root and a tradition worth cherishing and celebrating. It has borne much fruit in the Church of today. And it may bear much more in the Church of tomorrow.

15

WORSHIP AFTER WAR

The Gulf Service of Remembrance and Thanksgiving
1991

Fiona Douglas and Jeremy Crang

In January–February 1991 a United Nations' coalition – in which British forces played a prominent role – fought a brief war with Iraq in order to liberate Kuwait. Two hundred and fifty coalition military personnel were killed in this conflict as well as an estimated 20,000–30,000 Iraqis. Twenty-four British servicemen were among the war dead.[387] The first reaction of the government after the ceasefire was to announce a victory parade in London to mark the return of the troops – a spectacle that the Bishop of Durham, the Rt Revd Dr David Jenkins, condemned as 'obscene'.[388] Nevertheless, in the same way that a national religious service was held in St Paul's Cathedral in the wake of the Falklands conflict in 1982, a United Kingdom ecumenical service of remembrance and thanksgiving was planned to mark the end of hostilities in the Gulf. On this occasion, the government approached the Very Revd Dr William Morris, the Church of Scotland minister of St Mungo's Cathedral in Glasgow, and Dean of the Chapel Royal designate, with a view to holding such a service in his kirk and he readily agreed to lead the worship.[389]

Various explanations were put forward as to why Scotland was chosen to host the event. The government line was that the high proportion of Scottish units among the British forces deployed in the Gulf made it an obvious location for such a service.[390] Others, more cynically, suspected that it was a means of currying favour north of the border where

---

387 A. Finlan, *The Gulf War 1991*, Oxford: Osprey, 2003, p. 85.

388 J. Robertson, 'Attack on bishops as parade plan is approved', *Scotsman*, 5 March 1991.

389 The Very Revd Dr William Morris, interview with Fiona Douglas, 27 November 1995.

390 Morris, interview with Fiona Douglas; J. Nundy, 'Gulf war dead honoured with dignity', *Independent*, 5 May 1991.

Conservative party fortunes had been in long-term decline.[391] The prime minister at the time, John Major, indicates that it was a means of illustrating to the Scots 'the reality of the United Kingdom as a working partnership'.[392]

The decision to hold the service in Scotland was not without controversy. There had been a good deal of opposition to the war within the Church of Scotland and some thought such an event was inappropriate, especially in view of the suffering of the Iraqi Kurds in the aftermath of the conflict. The Revd John Harvey, leader of the Iona Community, expressed his disappointment over the issue:

> Perhaps it would have been better if the church representatives had said to the state: 'No, we will not share your service of thanksgiving, but will you come and join us in a service of repentance, and of commitment to the struggle for a truly new world order, based on the teachings of Jesus in the Sermon on the Mount?'[393]

Some Scots politicians also voiced their concern. Dr Norman Godman, Labour MP for Greenock and Port Glasgow, believed that 'it will be seen as an event bordering on the triumphal, no matter how diffident those attending the service are, and it is my firm conviction that the event should be postponed or cancelled'.[394]

There was a good deal of wrangling over the planning of the service. The normal procedure for arranging a service of this type would have been for the government to contact the Moderator of the Church of Scotland in the first instance. But there was no consultation with either the Moderator, the Rt Revd Professor Robert Davidson, or his Principal Clerk, the Revd James Weatherhead.[395] Instead, Morris was contacted directly by government officials, no doubt partly because this would avoid having to work through a committee and he was known to be sympathetic to the UN action in the Gulf.[396] This breach of etiquette antagonized Davidson: 'We knew nothing about it until it broke and it was done through the Chaplain Royal in Glasgow, whom I must confess should have known

---

391 'Home news', *The Tablet*, 30 March/6 April 1991, p. 3.

392 J. Major, *John Major: the autobiography*, London: Harper Collins, 1999, pp. 421–2.

393 J. Harvey, letter to the editor, *Scotsman*, 28 March 1991.

394 K. Sinclair, 'Major asked to cancel service', *Glasgow Herald*, 8 April 1991.

395 The Rt Revd Professor Robert Davidson, interview with Fiona Douglas, 27 November 1995.

396 'Home News', *The Tablet*, 30 March/6 April 1991, p. 3; Morris, interview with Fiona Douglas. Dr Morris recalls that the first contact was made by Sir Russell Hillhouse of the Scottish Office. Thereafter, he liaised with the Ministry of Defence.

better.'[397] Moreover, Weatherhead regarded the snub as undermining Church governance:

> I do not think the Church is in any danger of direct attacks on its constitutional position, but that position could be gently eroded by well-meaning misunderstanding. Death by a thousand cuts is one thing, but erosion by a thousand smiles is what I fear![398]

Indeed, he wrote to the Scottish Office to explain that, as the government had bypassed the Moderator, according to the Declaratory Articles of the Church the service should not be regarded as a 'national' service in ecclesiastical terms in Scotland, but rather as a 'state' service, arranged at the invitation of the state by one of the parish ministers.[399]

The actions of Morris also ruffled feathers. The government gave him a free hand to plan the service as he wished – with the proviso that Major wanted it to be a service of remembrance and thanksgiving in that order[400] – and this created tensions. It might have been thought that as the service was being held in Scotland, the Moderator Robert Davidson, or the Roman Catholic Archbishop of Glasgow, the Most Revd Thomas Winning, would have been invited to deliver the sermon. Instead, Morris approached a prominent English Anglican, the Archbishop of York, the Most Revd and Rt Hon. Dr John Habgood, to preach. This, he argued, was a fitting ecumenical gesture:

> It seemed to me important that to have a UK service the other national church should be represented, and if they haven't invited any of our clergy to preach in Westminster Abbey or St Paul's at least we would invite one of them to preach in Glasgow Cathedral.[401]

However, it was also the case that the Archbishop of York – unlike Davidson and Winning – was 'sound' on the conflict: 'It was clear,' recalled Morris, 'that Habgood felt that the Gulf War had to happen ... He wasn't likely to turn it into a political platform.'[402]

Morris's invitation to an Anglican bishop from south of the border to give the sermon was regarded by many as an insult to Scotland's leading churchmen. The Episcopalian Bishop of Edinburgh, the Rt Revd Richard

---

397 Davidson, interview with Fiona Douglas.

398 University of Edinburgh, New College Library, 'Gulf War' folder, letter from Weatherhead to G. A. Hart, Scottish home and health department, 26 March 1991.

399 Weatherhead to Hart, enclosure entitled 'National services of worship in Scotland – general principles'.

400 Morris, interview with Fiona Douglas.

401 R. Duncan, 'Cathedral defends sermon by Habgood', *Glasgow Herald*, 8 April 1991.

402 Morris, interview with Fiona Douglas.

Holloway, dismissed it as 'a very cack-handed piece of work' and castigated officials in London for their complicity in this decision: 'I suspect
that some of the people down there think the Church of Scotland comes
under the Archbishop of York's jurisdiction, so they don't see any problems with this.'[403] Indeed, Davidson was forced to issue a statement on the
matter in order to calm the situation:

> The Moderator holds John Habgood personally in the highest esteem,
> and welcomes the fact that one who has been so active in ecumenical
> matters and is now one of the Presidents of the Council of Churches
> for Britain and Ireland has been invited to preach at a United Kingdom
> service.[404]

Major interpreted this outcry over the sermon as a 'wholly characteristic
and ridiculous row' that was typical of government critics north of the
border who wished to stoke up resentment between the Scots and the
English.[405]

Morris created further antagonism by taking it upon himself to write
the prayers that would be spoken by various church leaders during the
service. Not only did this seem to go against the spirit of these ecumenical
occasions, whereby participants from the different denominations normally composed their own prayers, but also some did not like what they
were required to say. Winning, in particular, took strong exception to a
line in his prayer: 'Turn the hearts of all who have been our enemies to
the truth as you have revealed it in Jesus that they and we may know and
do your will':[406]

> My objection to the wording of the prayer was quite simply that this
> was not the occasion to pray that those of other faiths might come to
> recognize Jesus as their Lord and Saviour – indeed I considered it would
> be an insult to the sincerely held faith of our Muslim brethren.[407]

---

403 J. McAlpine, 'Bishop condemns Gulf service', *Scotsman*, 8 April 1991; R. Duncan,
'Cathedral defends sermon'.

404 Church of Scotland Press Office, 'Gulf service – Glasgow Cathedral', press release,
PR/65/4/91, 5 April 1991.

405 Major, *John Major*, p. 422.

406 'The Gulf service of remembrance and thanksgiving', order of service, 4 May 1991.
This order of service can be found in app. 4, F. C. Douglas, 'Ritual and remembrance: the
Church of Scotland and national services of thanksgiving and remembrance after four wars
in the twentieth century', PhD, University of Edinburgh, 1996. We are grateful to Dr William
Morris for providing a copy of this document.

407 Cardinal Winning, quoted in a letter from the Revd Tom Connelly, Catholic Media Office, to Fiona Douglas, 21 February 1996. Also see V. Belton, *Cardinal Thomas Winning: An
Authorized Biography*, Dublin: The Columba Press, 2000, pp. 160–1.

Morris could not understand the Archbishop's concerns:

> I've never been faced with such a situation myself, never having been invited to take part in a Roman Catholic service, but it seemed to me that there was nothing in the prayers which conflicted with Christian, or Roman Catholic, doctrine for that matter. I didn't think that Roman Catholics would have been opposed to the conversion of Islam to Christianity but maybe there are those who are happier to modify that stance.[408]

Nevertheless, Winning was able to alter the wording. Although there was not time to incorporate the amendments in the printed order of service, he changed the offending passage to 'Transform the hearts of all men and women that we may come to a deeper knowledge of your will and so be living instruments of your love.'[409]

Davidson also modified his prayer. He was asked to read: 'Lord, we pray for the power to be gentle; the strength to be forgiving; the patience to be understanding; and the endurance to accept the consequences of holding to what we believe to be right.'[410] However, he added the lines: 'the courage to admit when we are in the wrong; and the grace to repent and ask for forgiveness'.[411] These alterations too were not included in the order of service, but the Moderator was satisfied that any danger of the liturgy becoming triumphalist had been averted. 'It might have,' he recalled, 'if we hadn't modified it to some extent.'[412]

The 'Gulf service of remembrance and thanksgiving' took place on Saturday 4 May 1991 at St Mungo's in the presence of the Queen and Prince Philip, leading political and civic figures, senior officers from the armed forces, representatives from several UN coalition countries, and bereaved families. On arrival at the cathedral, the royal couple, who had been delayed for 40 minutes due to their train breaking down in Lanarkshire, passed through a small military guard of honour before being received at the west door by the Lord Provost of Glasgow, Mrs Susan Baird. After being presented to Morris, Major, and other prominent VIPs, the royal guests were conducted to their seats in the Choir. The music played immediately before the worship was Beethoven's 'Creation Hymn', Bach's 'Jesu, Joy of Man's Desiring', and Schubert's 'Rosamunde', and the choir

---

408 Stewart Lamont, 'Winning in the Gulf service war of words', *Glasgow Herald*, 4 May 1991, p. 1.

409 S. Lamont, 'Muted trumpets herald uncertain fuss', *Glasgow Herald*, 6 May 1991.

410 'The Gulf service of remembrance and thanksgiving', order of service.

411 Lamont, 'Muted trumpets'; transcript of Gulf service, BBC television broadcast, 4 May 1991. We are grateful to Tom Fleming for providing a copy of this transcript.

412 Davidson, interview with Fiona Douglas.

sang Mendelssohn's 'Above all praise and all Majesty, Lord, Thou reignest evermore'.[413]

The service commenced with the congregation singing the national anthem and Morris's opening prayer. 'Remembrance' was the title of the first section. This started with a lesson from Romans 8.35–39, read by the Moderator of the Free Church Federal Council for Wales, the Revd Dafydd Owen. All then sang Psalm 121, 'I to the hills will lift mine eyes'. After this, the Dean of the Chapel Royal, the Very Revd Professor Robin Barbour, conducted the act of remembrance, which began with the words of Laurence Binyon: 'Age shall not weary them, nor the years condemn. The 'Last Post' was then sounded by buglers from the Royal Marines and 'The Flowers of the Forest' was played by a piper from the Queen's Own Highlanders while a commemorative wreath was brought forward to the Dean by representatives of the three armed services. As the pipes died away, the Royal Marine buglers called out 'Reveille'. Following this bugle call, Barbour led a prayer of commemoration and the congregation sang the hymn 'O blest communion, fellowship divine!'[414]

The second section was termed 'Thanksgiving'. This opened with a lesson from Philippians 4.5–9 read by Flt Lt John Peters of the RAF. Prayers of thanksgiving were then offered by the Archbishop of Canterbury, the Most Revd and Rt Hon. Dr George Carey, and all sang the hymn 'Praise to the Lord, the Almighty, the King of creation'. 'Children of One Father' was the designation of the third section. The Chaplain General, the Revd James Harkness, initiated this with a reading from Luke 6.20–31. Winning then led the prayers of intercession and the congregation sang the hymn 'Be thou my Vision'. The fourth section was 'the Sermon' delivered by Habgood. After he had preached, the choir performed the anthem, 'Ye that have spent the silent night', arranged by George Dyson to words by George Gascoigne.[415]

The fifth and final section was on the theme of 'Reconciliation and Peace'. This featured a procession of children of three faiths into the cathedral. Jewish children entered by the central aisle, Muslim children by

---

413 'The Gulf service of remembrance and thanksgiving', order of service; transcript of Gulf service, BBC television broadcast; W. Paul, 'Nation mourns the innocents', *Scotland on Sunday*, 5 May 1991. It should be noted that the MOD provided Dr Morris with orders of service from previous national remembrance and thanksgiving services and he was influenced, in particular, by the format of the Falkland Islands service. This order of service can be found in app. 3, F. C. Douglas, 'Ritual and remembrance'. It might also be recorded that, while the press reported a 20-minute delay, Tom Fleming, who was the commentator for the BBC's television broadcast, recalls that it was nearer 40 minutes.

414 'The Gulf service of remembrance and thanksgiving', order of service; transcript of Gulf service, BBC television broadcast; J. Dalrymple, 'A nation expresses its muted thanks', *Sunday Times*, 5 May 1991.

415 'The Gulf service of remembrance and thanksgiving', order of service.

the south aisle, and Christian children by the north aisle. They gathered around Davidson and a Jewish child read verses from a Hebrew prophet; a Muslim child read lines from the Qur'an; and a Christian child read the words of Jesus. The children, representing the future and unity of the world, then joined hands while the Moderator led the congregation in prayer. This was followed by the act of dedication during which those assembled promised 'to make the human family a reality'. After this pledge, all sang the hymn, 'Lift up your hearts!', and the Blessing was pronounced. At the end of the service, the Queen and Prince Philip were conducted back to the west door where they were presented to the clergy before departing the cathedral.[416]

Despite the disputes over the planning of the service, most commentators agreed that it was a deeply moving occasion.[417] The relative lack of state pomp, the solemnity of the music and the reflective nature of the liturgy all contributed to the poignancy of the event. The choice of Flt Lt Peters – the Tornado pilot whose battered face and evident distress had been paraded on the nation's television screens after he was shot down and captured by the Iraqis – to read a lesson, and of a piper from the Queen's Own Highlanders – a regiment which had lost three of its young soldiers in the conflict – to play a haunting lament, heightened the sense of sorrow.[418] Even the design of the commemorative wreath, which was made from fresh summer flowers, instead of laurel leaves, and thus seemed to signify the beauty of creation, rather than a sacrifice for an ancient warrior tradition, added to the pathos.[419]

Furthermore, while there were occasional glimpses of what might be construed as triumphalism – in his opening prayer Morris announced that 'we are here to give thanks for all who risked their lives for those values which we believe to be right'[420] – the worship was remarkably conciliatory in tone. Not only was there compassion for the suffering of the 'enemy' – Winning called on God to bless the people of Iraq 'where war and oppression have left their bitter harvest of pain and illness, injury and loss, homelessness and hunger'[421] – and a questioning of war as a means of settling disputes – Davidson prayed for – the vision to see and the faith to believe in a world

---

416 'The Gulf service of remembrance and thanksgiving', order of service; transcript of Gulf service, BBC television broadcast; Davidson, interview with Fiona Douglas. There was some criticism that the children were all male.

417 Transcript of Gulf service, BBC television broadcast; Paul, 'Nation mourns'; J. McAlpine, 'Pomp and private grief as a nation remembers', *Scotsman*, 6 May 1991; D. Macleod, 'A certain awkwardness in giving thanks', *Scotsman*, 6 May 1991; editorial, *Scotsman*, 6 May 1991.

418 S. Lamont, 'Muted trumpets'. We are grateful to Graeme Stevenson for his comments on the music played at the service.

419 We are indebted to Tom Fleming for his observations on the wreath.

420 'The Gulf service of remembrance and thanksgiving', order of service.

421 Lamont, 'Muted trumpets'.

set free from violence[422] – but there was also a strong pastoral dimension. Pursuing the theme of innocent suffering through the story of Abraham's challenge to God over the destruction of Sodom and Gomorrah, Habgood concluded his sermon by anticipating a time when grief is reconciled:

> Faith must not disguise or evade the awfulness of war and the atrocities to which it can give birth. But it can look beyond them, beyond the legitimate pride in a task accomplished, beyond the sad mistakes and the unintended consequences. It can look beyond them to the day when our fallible human judgements will give way before the judgement of God, when death will be swallowed up in Christ's victory over the grave, when there will be no more tears, no more sorrow, and when God will be all in all.[423]

The clergy indicated their broad satisfaction with the service. Davidson recollected that he was 'quite happy at the end of the day'[424] and Barbour considered it to be 'the right kind of thing for the occasion':

> I did speak to a few of the people who were there, including someone who had lost a member of her family. I got the feeling, as I have on other occasions, that a service of this kind can be a real occasion of release from pent-up emotions of sorrow and anger, not just on an individual level but in the frame of what I might call the 'stance of a whole society' on matters of right and wrong, life and death. A public occasion of this kind has a healing function, for society as a whole, if it can bring together different denominations and also different religions, as this one did, in a unified act.[425]

The press concurred: 'No-one cried Rejoice! on Saturday', commented the *Scotsman*. 'But the absence of rejoicing made this a far more powerful national occasion than it might have been.'[426]

And peace even seems to have broken out among the clerics. According to Winning, the 40-minute delay at the start of the service helped to ameliorate any lingering animosity over its planning:

> when the procession of clergy had been lined up ready for the 'off', word came about the delay in the Queen's train. This providentially afforded

---

422 'The Gulf service of remembrance and thanksgiving', order of service.
423 'Sermon by the Archbishop of York, Dr John Habgood, in St Mungo's cathedral, Glasgow on the occasion of the Gulf service of remembrance and thanksgiving on Saturday 4 May 1991'. The full text of the sermon can be found in app. 4, Douglas, 'Ritual and remembrance'.
424 Davidson, interview with Fiona Douglas.
425 The Very Revd Professor Robin Barbour, letter to Fiona Douglas, 13 February 1996.
426 McAlpine, 'Pomp and private grief'.

a number of the clergy [the opportunity] to break ranks and to involve themselves in general chit-chat, enjoying one another's company and exchanging various reflections – no doubt in so doing, any possible tensions which may have been present gently ebbed away.[427]

Never had a broken down train served a nobler purpose.

---

427 Cardinal Winning, quoted in a letter from the Revd Tom Connelly.

Part Five

CHANGING PATTERNS OF WORSHIP

16

THE RECEPTION OF THE LITURGICAL CHANGES OF THE SECOND VATICAN COUNCIL

Michael Regan

The date 4 December 1963 will live in the chronology of the Roman Catholic Church for centuries to come. On that day the Fathers of the Second Vatican Council voted in solemn session for the approbation of the first document to be produced by the Council. With only four votes against and with over two thousand in favour the document *Sacrosanctum Concilium*[428] became the document that would have the most immediate and lasting effect on the daily lives of Catholics throughout the world.

With an eye to history it was exactly 400 years since the Council of Trent had voted to leave liturgical reform in the hands of the Pope and the Roman Curia. This time the bishops of the Church had taken possession of the subject and given the guidelines for the reform that was to come. As with the whole of the Second Vatican Council it was building on what had gone before and sought to take the doctrinal insights and statements for granted and to ensure that the pastoral reality of the Church should be addressed by the Council and that the quality of daily Christian living should be renewed. Such pastoral zeal and a desire for renewal did not, however, arrive unexpectedly but was in fact building on the work of a liturgical movement that had been growing quietly for 130 years and which led to the document on the liturgy.

---

428 *Constitutio de sacra liturgia* in N. P. Tanner, ed., *Decrees of the Ecumenical Councils*, London: Sheed and Ward, 1990, p. 820ff. With translation.

Post-Reformation Liturgical Development in the Roman Catholic Church

In the wake of the Reformation and the attacks on the established practice of the Roman Catholic Church by the Reformers, the Council of Trent had restated certain doctrinal positions concerning the Eucharist and the Mass but had left the reform of the liturgy in the hands of the Pope, as noted above. This saw the production of definitive texts of the Missal for the celebration of Mass and also of texts for all of the other sacramental rites of the Church. These liturgical books enjoyed widespread diffusion but were not universal in their use and regional variations in the way the liturgy was celebrated continued to exist. Rome recognized that any local church that could show 200 years of particular usage would be entitled to continue using its own rite, as was the case in Milan with the Ambrosian Rite, Toledo with the Mozarabic Rite or the variety of Rites associated with particular religious orders. The liturgy of Trent reflected a strong continuity with the past, even as it imported new elements into that liturgy and it fixed a particular style. Emphasis was on correct celebration of the liturgy and those who shared in it were largely regarded as *circumstantes*,[429] bystanders or onlookers rather than actors in the liturgy.

The Liturgical Movement

During the seventeenth and early eighteenth centuries there had been little in the way of liturgical development although the Benedictine tradition of St Maur had encouraged scholarship. The life of the Catholic Church in Europe was subject to great upheaval in the late eighteenth century and early nineteenth century, through the activities of Napoleon Bonaparte and his attacks on religious life, particularly in France. With the arrival of some form of peace there was a marked re-establishment of the religious life and alongside this the liturgical movement came into being. This happened first through the influence of Dom Prosper Guéranger, who had purchased and refounded the Abbey of Solesmes. The Benedictine life that he encouraged, which, in accord with the rule of St Benedict, was to prefer nothing to the work of God, that is, the liturgy, led to a reawakening of liturgical study and to the realization of the centrality of the liturgy to the life of the Christian community. To this end, Guéranger produced several books to enable a greater understanding of the liturgy not just for the monks but also for a wider audience and his work *L'année litur-*

---

429 Cf. *Prex Eucharistica I seu Canon Romanus*, Editio Typica, Rome: Libreria Editrice Vaticana, 1970.

gique,[430] which returned to the roots of liturgical time and the way in which the mystery of Christ unfolds in the liturgical cycle, had a profound influence.

What Guéranger started continued throughout the nineteenth century in continental Europe especially in France and Germany. Initiatives that saw the production for the first time of Missals for the laity with texts both in Latin and the vernacular made their appearance in the 1870s and 1880s. A heightened awareness of the importance of liturgy as opposed to ritual was thus developing and received a strong boost with the election to the papacy of Giuseppe Sarto, the Patriarch of Venice, in 1903. As Pius X, he was to set the stage for a major growth in the understanding of liturgy that was echoed in the document of the Second Vatican Council.

Pius X was responsible for a major liturgical renewal with his *Motu Proprio Tra le sollicitudine* of 22 November 1903.[431] In that document he encouraged a return to the sources of the liturgy, a task facilitated by the growth of liturgical scholarship in the nineteenth century. Equally he called for the full, active and conscious participation of all the faithful in the celebration of the liturgy. This became the motto of the liturgical movement and led to a rethinking of the nature of the liturgy. Pius X's call for a renewal also bore fruit pastorally with its influence on a young, former workers chaplain, who had become a Benedictine monk, Dom Lambert Beaudoin. Combining both pastoral and academic reflection Beaudoin saw in the liturgy a source for the life of the ordinary Catholic and he helped spread the message of the liturgical movement. It was in the wake of the Belgian influence that Scotland first came into contact with this renewal through the work of Father Octave Claeys, a Belgian priest of the Archdiocese of Glasgow, who taught at the seminary in Glasgow.

Equally Pius X was instrumental in progressing this liturgical renewal with the call for frequent reception of Communion. Within the Roman Catholic tradition, largely influenced by Jansenism, the link between reception of the Eucharist and presence at the celebration of the Eucharist had been weakened. Even religious were not in the habit of receiving Communion daily and for the average lay person Communion was a relatively infrequent affair. Added to this, the distribution of the Eucharist was often not an integral part of the celebration of the Eucharist but was distributed before or after Mass, so that the links had been lost. Dom Bernard Botte in his book on the early years of the liturgical movement[432]

---

430 *L'Année liturgique*, Paris, 1841–1901; tr. L. Shepherd, Worcester: Stanbrook Abbey, 1895–1903.

431 http://www.vatican.va/holy_father/pius_x/motu_proprio/documents/hf_p-x_motu-proprio_19031122_sollecitudini_it.html.

432 Bernhard Botte, *From Silence to Participation*, tr. John Sullivan, Oregon Catholic Press 1988.

recounts the advice given to his sister, which was to receive Communion before Mass and then to offer Mass in thanksgiving for Communion. The desire of Pius X was for an integration of presence at and participation in the liturgy and he furthered this also with the lowering of the age at which children received Communion for the first time to the age of seven.

The impetus of the liturgical renewal continued throughout the twentieth century with the growth of scholarship and research, Solesmes in France, Maria Laach in Germany, Klosterneuberg in Austria all produced noted writers on the liturgy. This was paralleled by the growth of awareness of the Christian vocation of all the baptized as participants in the one priesthood of Jesus Christ. The integration of Christian living was seen to lie with a living apostolate, nourished by an active liturgical life. The Catholic Action movement of the 1920s enhanced this union and furthered the realization of the significance of the liturgical life for the work of the apostolate.

This ongoing work of rediscovery of the significance of liturgy and the more immediate preparation for the changes to come is due to the influence of Pope Pius XII (1939–58). As leader of a community which views things *sub specie aeternitatis* Pius XII was publishing documents of ecclesiastical significance throughout World War Two, particularly with reference to biblical scholarship and then in 1948 he issued *Mediator Dei*,[433] which was a sustained reflection on the liturgy. It was Pius XII who reformed the liturgy of Holy Week and showed that aberrations had crept into the liturgy, which needed to be corrected. By altering the way in which the liturgy was celebrated, Pius XII made it clear that nothing was unchangeable and therefore the need to renew and review was deemed to be present. Thus there was a liturgical ferment in the Roman Catholic Church that had prepared the way for subsequent change.

On 25 January 1959, just months after his election to the papacy, Pope John XXIII announced the calling of the Second Vatican Council. An unprecedented period of consultation followed, in which the bishops of the Church and various other groups were invited to submit their suggestions for matters to be treated at the Council. There was strong debate from this earliest stage of the possibility of change and the way in which that change was to be implemented. A more conservative group sought to exclude all change from the life of the community, while a more liberal group felt that many changes would be welcome. Such political opposition marked the whole period of the Council and the reception of all its documents and continues to the present time.

The account of the Liturgical Movement helps to underscore the fact of

---

433 www.vatican.va/holy_father/pius_xii/encyclicals/documents/hf_p-xii_enc_20111947_mediator-dei_en.html

the possibility of movement within the liturgical life of the Roman Catholic Church and shows that the innovation of the Council was rooted in a systematic development. The debates of the Council on liturgy have been well documented in a variety of sources and do not need to be repeated here. The document on the liturgy, *Sacrosanctum Concilium* contains a number of indications for the work of renewal but does not give detailed regulations for change. These were worked out gradually over the years that followed the Council as its effect began to take hold in the life of the Catholic community.

The Second Vatican Council

The debates of the Council and the development of the document on the liturgy are chronicled in many places and do not need to be particularly addressed here.[434] Immediately on the promulgation of the document working groups were set in place to undertake the work of revision and presentation of the texts to the people. This happened in two distinct ways. First of all, there was the Roman influence, where new texts were prepared and old texts reviewed in their original Latin and prepared for translation. This work was carried out by a group called the *Consilium ad exsequendam Constitutionem de sacra Liturgia,* consisting of cardinal and bishop members and theological liturgical advisers. From 1964 onwards they oversaw the work of renewal and drafted the various sacramental rites that formed the normative editions of the Roman Rite. Parallel to the work of the *Consilium* there had been established as early as 1963 a mixed commission, a group representing several English-speaking conferences of bishops, to prepare translations for the English-speaking world, this group was called The International Commission on English in the Liturgy. From the autumn of 1964 onwards certain parts of the Mass were celebrated in English and popular responses were created.

At this first stage, the acceptance of the liturgical change was undertaken in a spirit of obedience. The practical task of receiving texts and learning a new way of praying, which moved from a more private manner of participation into a more communal celebration was undertaken, albeit with regret in some quarters that the hallowed tradition seemed to

---

434 The full documentation and transcript of the Council can be found in *Acta synodalia Sacrosancti Concilii Oecumenici Vaticani II.* This multi-volume work published by the *Typis Polyglottis Vaticanis* contains all the preparatory documentation of the Council, the equivalent of Hansard for the proceedings of the Council and also the definitive texts in Latin of the Conciliar documents. Giuseppe Alberigo has published a history of the Council in five volumes, which has been translated into English, and also a concise version was published in 1997. A more accessible account can be found in the book of Rita Ferrone, *Rediscovering Vatican II Liturgy* Mahwah, NJ: Paulist Press, 2007.

be being rejected. From this earliest stage also there was a certain rejection of change to liturgical practice and some saw the process as dismantling the traditions of centuries. Opposition was led by Archbishop Marcel Lefebvre among others. Also founded at this time was a group called Una Voce to campaign for the retention of Latin as the basic language of worship within the local communities.

A major point in the development came in 1970 with the publication of the *Missale Romanum*, 400 years after the *Missale* of Trent had been published. This represented the culmination of a number of years' work by the *Consilium* and was markedly different from the previous text. Promulgated by Pope Paul VI it became the normative text for the Roman Liturgy. Permission was granted for it to be translated into the local languages in its entirety and also for original texts to be added. For the English-speaking world this text was translated by the International Commission on English in the Liturgy and adapted by local bishops' conferences for their use and recognition was given to the translation by the Holy See. The definitive English version was published in 1973. Thus after a period of instability over several years a definitive text was produced and the external form of the liturgy began to settle into a more defined pattern.

At this point it was deemed by many that the previous text had been abrogated and that only this Missal either in Latin or in English could be used. Those who opposed change petitioned the Holy See and for England and Wales permission was given at the request of Cardinal John Heenan of Westminster for the continued celebration of the Mass of Trent in certain places and at certain times. The Latin Mass Society came into existence at this time to defend the older Rite of Mass and the sacraments. There was a not insignificant opposition to the New Order of Mass but the vast majority of parishes made the transition into a vernacular liturgy with the new ritual that surrounded it.

Such transition went beyond simply learning new responses and adopting new postures and began to influence the whole way of being Church. The move from hymn singing to singing as an integral part of the liturgy was undertaken and while a lot of very poor music was initially used, as time developed more reflected composition took place. One major change was the realization that the individual members of the congregation might have liturgical roles to play, which led to the introduction of lay ministers as readers and subsequently as ministers of Holy Communion. In due course it was clarified that females as well as males could serve at the altar and the sanctuary, which had been an all male preserve (apart from the women who cleaned it), now became the place for members of the baptized to fulfil particular roles. Such a move away from the exclusivity of the sanctuary also led to the physical changes in the Church. Altars were placed facing the people so that they gathered around the table of the Lord and altar rails were removed so that the unity of the worshipping community was underlined.

The changes initiated by the Council required both internal and external alteration and this was undertaken in a rapid movement that has generally won acceptance but which as those who were involved with the development understood, would require alteration in the future to fashion and develop a renewed liturgy. The history of this period has also been well documented and resources are available for further study.[435]

The Scottish Response to the Liturgical Changes

Despite some contact in the early stages with the liturgical movement, Scotland had very little involvement in the process of preparation of the Conciliar documents. Scottish priests were aware of some of the liturgical ferment that was happening prior to and during the period of the Council. Priests had trained in France, Italy and Spain and were exposed to some of the new ideas. Other priests were involved in the activity of the Council itself, whether as advisers to the bishops or as secretaries for some of the sessions. However, Scotland was not at the heart of the liturgical movement.[436] The Scottish bishops had dutifully responded to questionnaires from the Holy See but there were no Scots involved in the committees of preparation nor subsequently. This meant that when the document on the liturgy was promulgated in 1963 the first step of the reception of the changes involved bringing them to the notice of congregations. This was done by the teaching authority of the bishops. One such document was the pastoral letter of Archbishop Gordon Joseph Gray of St Andrews and Edinburgh issued in Lent 1964, some six weeks after the promulgation of the Vatican document.[437] As such an immediate response it bears examination. The letter addresses the more obvious and external changes which will have an immediate impact on the people, the move to the vernacular, Communion from the cup, concelebration by clergy and the reform of the Divine Office, the liturgy of the hours. However, Archbishop Gray stresses that the changes should not be simply external nor change for its own sake, he underlines the importance of the liturgy as an outward

---

435 Annibale Bugnini, *The Reform of the Liturgy 1948-1975*, tr. Matthew O'Connell, Collegeville, Minnesota: Liturgical Press, 1990; Piero Marini, *A Challenging Reform*, Collegeville, Minnesota: Liturgical Press, 2007.

436 It is interesting to note in this regard that the publication to mark the centenary of the restoration of the Roman Catholic hierarchy, David McRoberts, ed., *Modern Scottish Catholicism 1878–1978*, Glasgow: J. Burns, 1979, contains no section dedicated to worship or liturgy.

437 Pastoral Letter of Gordon Joseph Archbishop of St Andrews and Edinburgh, 'The Council and the Liturgy', Lent 1964, Glasgow: John S. Burns and Sons.

expression of an inner reality and that the purpose of the liturgy is to draw people closer to God. Archbishop Gray gives a brief catechesis on the very nature of liturgy, which represents a departure from previous understandings for those in congregations and indeed for the clergy themselves.

Prior to this stage the study of liturgy in seminaries was largely restricted to questions of rubrics and the correct performance of the liturgy, and for the people it was a question of presence at rather than participation in the liturgy of the Church. Archbishop Gray's pastoral letter stresses the liturgy as the public work of the community, sharing in the priestly office of Jesus Christ, which requires a renewed understanding of what the end of liturgy is. An indication of this comes in the following quotation from the letter:

> Though as individual members of the Church we fail all too often in our appreciation of the power of the Liturgy, the Church does not. 'The liturgy is the summit towards which the activity of the Church is directed; at the same time it is the fount from which all her power flows.'[438]

This liturgical transformation was undertaken with greater or lesser degrees of enthusiasm depending on the individuals concerned but the basic pattern was repeated across the world and in the English-speaking countries in particular. Archbishop Gray's comments of 1964 were shown to be true with the two extremes of those who wanted everything to change and those who wanted no change both represented, but the mainstream of the Christian community adapted itself to the new liturgy with a degree of enthusiasm. The texts were produced not simply for the Mass but also for the other sacraments as well during the 1970s and by the end of that decade the entire liturgy was available for celebration in the vernacular.

Over the years the Roman Catholic Church in Scotland responded to the challenge of this new liturgical world in a variety of ways. Priests were formed at the Liturgical Institutes of Paris and Rome and later in the United States. Composers were invited to prepare music for the new liturgy. Archbishop Gray served as chairman of the International Commission on English in the Liturgy for a number of years and priests from Scotland served on the Commission.

A major influence on the adoption of newer ways of celebrating came with the papal visit to Britain in 1982. The liturgies of this visit gave an opportunity to all involved to showcase the liturgy at its best and the large celebrations reflected the way in which liturgy was being conducted in the parishes and also created a legacy, particularly musical, for people to use. In Scotland, it became possible for the Bellahouston Mass to be used in

---

438 Gray, 'The Council and the Liturgy', p. 6.

every parish and so there was a repertoire common to all people for any major gatherings. Throughout the British Isles the papal visit helped to show the new eucharistic liturgy but with the choice of the theme of the sacraments, which was linked to the visit, the renewal of all the rites of the Catholic Church was underlined. People became more familiar with the other sacramental celebrations, which had often been private celebrations but which were now shared by the entire community.

This communitarian dimension of the liturgy was further stressed with the development of the Rite of Christian Initiation of Adults, whereby those becoming members of the Church went through a very public process linked to the practice of the early Church rather than the private instruction and reception that had previously been the case. The stress on baptism, confirmation and Eucharist as the sacraments of initiation also meant a change of Lenten focus from primarily a time of self-denial to a renewal of baptismal commitment on the part of the community. Such a baptismal concentration went in parallel with a decline in religious practice in society generally, whereby membership, even notionally, of a Church could no longer be presumed and therefore was developed at a time where the choice of baptism was of greater significance than in earlier times and where the support of a community of faith became significant as local communities fragmented. Equally the baptismal focus had many ecumenical implications.

Over the period of 40 years from the publication of the Constitution on the Liturgy, the reception of the document became ingrained in the way of life of the Catholic community, the external changes to the buildings occurred, the rituals were renewed and the nature of the Catholic community developed. To assist this process, national and diocesan liturgical commissions were established. Courses of training and instruction were held and various publications were issued, newsletters and planning sheets were provided so that people were able to understand that it was not simply the externals that were changing but the internal disposition also that had to change. From a reluctant start the newer ways were accepted and now they are fully integrated into the life of the community. Equally with the passage of time the memory of the older style has faded for many and the reception of the change has become for many Catholics the result of this being their only style of exposure to the liturgy of the Church.

Such a change of context, from a systematic comparing with the old ways to exploring the liturgy from the perspective of only having known the renewed liturgy has had the advantage of being able to assess more dispassionately the changes. This has led to a realization that the older ways can also have a place of choice within the life of the Church, without implying a rejection of the new ways. Such reflection led to the publication of the *Motu Proprio* of Pope Benedict XVI *Summorum Pontificum* in 2007.[439] The *Motu Proprio* reflects the fact that the liturgy develops and changes and also the need for liturgy to speak to people in their own situation. On this account they have been given the choice of the way in which they celebrate, a recognition of pluriformity within the unity of the Church. This pluriformity reflects the fact that within the Church there are many divergent opinions held concerning the liturgy and that the changes from the Second Vatican Council would be more difficult to impose in the modern world because the obedience which led to their initial acceptance is no longer an automatic part of church life.

The introduction of personal taste as a criterion for judgement in liturgy is an innovation of the twenty-first century but illustrates that the words of Archbishop Gray in 1964 remain true, that there is a wide range of opinion within the Church community on how growth takes place in the liturgy of the Church, a liturgy which has never been stable nor uniform since the beginning of its life. Still today there are those who feel that there should be no change and those who feel that everything should change. However, the ordinary life of the Catholic Church is celebrated according to the liturgical books published by the authority of the Second Vatican Council and the Roman Pontiffs, and the vast majority of the world's Catholics are accepting of and grateful for this.

In 1964 Archbishop Gray wrote of the power of the liturgy and its purpose and in his 1945 book *The Shape of the Liturgy*[440] the Anglican Benedictine Dom Gregory Dix also reminded the Church that the liturgy has been celebrated in different ways and different styles down through the ages but that its central purpose has never altered, namely the creation of the *Plebs Sancta Dei*, the Holy People of God. The Second Vatican Council sought to improve the daily standard of celebration and in Scotland most Roman Catholics have accepted the liturgical changes as being of help in their journey of faith and thus have received willingly these liturgical changes. For those who have not found this to be the case, access to an older style of celebration is available on a regular basis. Given the individuality of people's approach to God, it is certain that discussion and development will not cease in the time ahead.

Further Reading

In addition to those texts mentioned in the footnotes two articles of specific Scottish interest are:

---

439 www.vatican.va/holy_father/benedict_xvi/motu_proprio/documents/hf_ben-xvi_motu-proprio_20070707_summorum-pontificum_lt.html.

440 Gregory Dix, *The Shape of the Liturgy*, new edition, Continuum International Publishing Group, London, 2005.

Mark Dilworth, 'Roman Catholic Worship', in Forrester and Murray, eds, *Studies in the History of Worship in Scotland*, 2nd edition, Edinburgh: T & T Clark, 1997, pp. 127–48.

Christine Johnson, 'Music and Ceremony', chapter 19 in Johnson, *Developments in the Roman Catholic Church in Scotland 1789–1829*, Edinburgh: John Donald, 1983.

17

THE WORSHIP OF THE IONA COMMUNITY AND ITS GLOBAL IMPACT[441]

Norman Shanks

When George MacLeod[442] founded the Iona Community in 1938 few would have predicted that it would still be flourishing 70 years later. It was very much a project of its own time and context, born out of MacLeod's conviction, shaped by his experience in Govan and elsewhere, that new ways needed to be found for the Church to carry out its mission and train its ministers, and that the key lay in building community in an increasingly individualistic and materialistic society. The sobering fact is that today, although the social context has changed significantly and although the Church of course has changed too, MacLeod's vision and analysis remains remarkably relevant. Although the Iona Community itself inevitably has changed over the years in many respects (not least in terms of size, structure, and the range of its work and concerns), its essential purpose is still to 'seek new ways to touch the hearts of all', in a phrase drawn from one of our most familiar Community prayers, which is used in worship when-

---

441 In preparing this chapter I am indebted for their advice, comments and suggestions to John Bell and Graham Maule, to my successor as leader of the Community, Kathy Galloway, to two of my predecessors Graeme Brown and John Harvey, and to Peter Millar and Brian Woodcock, both former wardens of Iona Abbey. I am also grateful to Liz Gibson, a Community member who is at present associate minister at Kilmore and Oban, for letting me read her BD dissertation (1998) on 'The evolution and impact of the worship of the Iona Community, 1938–1998'.

442 George MacLeod (The Very Revd George MacLeod MC DD) was made a life peer in 1967 and took the title of Lord MacLeod of Fuinary. He sat on the crossbenches of the House of Lords, where he memorably said he found he was 'getting crosser and crosser'! Fuinary was the family home in Morvern, in the north-west of Scotland. (See Ron Ferguson, *George MacLeod: Founder of the Iona Community*, new edition, Glasgow: Wild Goose Publications, 2001.)

ever Community members gather and each week in the Thursday morning service in Iona Abbey.

This is not the place to attempt to give a summary of the Community's history, or even of its current activities[443]. Within the Community we often wonder at the Community's continuing existence, when so much has changed – 280 members now and still growing; as many women members now as men (it was not until 1969 that women could become members; and now we have a woman leader[444]); no longer do the majority of members live in Scotland; there are now more non-ordained people than ministers of Word and sacrament among the membership; and an increased proportion belongs to a tradition other than the (Presbyterian) Church of Scotland from which the majority came for many years – although particular denominational loyalties are of little consequence alongside our sense of belonging together around our shared purpose.

In fact many of the Community's original and early pioneering projects and priorities have been absorbed into the mainstream of the churches over the years,[445] and many of its concerns and activities are paralleled in the life and work of other church-related groups, in the United Kingdom, the United States and elsewhere. But what remains distinctive about the Community and seems to appeal to all those who are attracted and interested by its work is above all its attempt to discover new ways to express and explore the Christian faith so as to make it real and relevant to contemporary needs and experience – through worship, through affirming that an ecumenical approach is imperative, through holding spiritual and social concerns inextricably together as part of a single reality. For many it seems that the appeal lies especially in the significance of the Community's fivefold Rule,[446] which members are committed to live by, and for

443 See in particular – T. Ralph Morton, *The Iona Community: Personal Impressions of the Early Years*, Edinburgh: St Andrew Press, 1977; Ron Ferguson, *Chasing the Wild Goose*, revised edition, Glasgow: Wild Goose Publications, 1997; Norman Shanks, *Iona – God's Energy: The Vision and Spirituality of the Iona Community*, London: Hodder and Stoughton, 1999 (shortly to be reprinted in a revised edition by Wild Goose Publications).

444 The Revd Kathy Galloway, a Church of Scotland minister, was elected leader of the Community in 2002. Since George MacLeod's leadership (1938–67), each leader has served for a seven-year term – the Revd Ian Reid, 1967–74; the Revd Graeme Brown, 1974–81; the Revd Ron Ferguson, 1981–8; the Revd John Harvey, 1988–95; the Revd Dr Norman Shanks 1995–2002.

445 For example, industrial chaplaincy, aspects of adult Christian education such as housegroups, commitment to nuclear disarmament.

446 The Rule comprises a fivefold discipline involving – daily prayer and Bible reading; economic witness – giving away 10 per cent of disposable income (to the Community, one's local congregation, and charities etc.); using time in a balanced way; meeting together regularly (local 'Family Group' meetings, usually held monthly, and plenary meetings three or four times a year); and a commitment to action for justice and peace. Thus the Rule is to be seen as an expression of the interconnectedness of the Community's concerns and of its integrated understanding of spirituality. Members renew their commitment annually and account to one another in Family Groups for their keeping of the Rule.

the keeping of which we are mutually accountable. And of course there is also the powerful 'magic' of Iona itself, this rather remote little island off the west coast of Scotland, with its heritage within the Christian Church stretching back to the arrival of St Columba in 563, the Celtic monastery, its medieval Benedictine successor, and the recent story of the rebuilding.

It has been most instructive, for the purposes of providing this contribution, to read again some of the foundational material produced by George MacLeod in the early years of the Community, and to discover once more the importance that MacLeod attached to the practice and theology of worship. For example, together with references to the significance of worship in early editions of *The Coracle*, the Community's magazine, in the first half of his 1944 book *We shall rebuild: the work of the Iona Community on mainland and island*, before MacLeod talks about the Community as such, he explores at length the need for change in the Church in view of 'the grave state of our forms of worship in Scotland today',[447] and, in particular, for the recovery of a way of worshipping relevant to and linked with living out the gospel. Here in essence is reflected what has come in more recent years to be described as the Community's incarnational theology and its engaged, integrated spirituality – affirming both the omnipresence of God, immanent and transcendent, permeating 'every blessed thing', and the wholeness and connectedness of human experience. MacLeod makes it clear that the rebuilding of the Abbey was not just an end in itself, nor simply designed to offer a sign of hope in the dark times of the 1930s, the depths of the Depression with the clouds of war gathering: rather it was to achieve a 'total witness' and 'to set our compass and intensely experience in work and worship the Redeemed Community that we would preach'.[448]

Liturgically MacLeod was a traditionalist rather than an innovator: he makes it clear that the Community's approach to worship was 'not an attempt to reassert Romanist devices, or imitate nineteenth century Anglican ways ... rather to prevent the incursion of the less stable strands from these traditions ... a small assertion of the full intended Catholic recovery of the Reformers, which our Church has largely lost'.[449] His overarching aim was to find new, appropriate ways in which 'the eternal Gospel Word might flow again in all its pristine richness into the hearts of men [sic]'.[450] So, in *Only One Way Left*, he emphasizes the need for an eclectic approach – 'what must be done is, once more, to move fearlessly on an open road, culling from different strands in our past such growth as will

447 George MacLeod, *We Shall Rebuild*, Glasgow: Iona Community, undated (US edition 1944), p. 32.
448 George MacLeod, *We Shall Rebuild*, p. 6.
449 George MacLeod, *We Shall Rebuild*, p. 7.
450 George MacLeod, *We Shall Rebuild*, p. 47.

best adorn our time'[451] – and the need also for a greater degree of 'discipline' (a consistent pattern, with the sacraments central and increased congregational participation). He makes it abundantly clear where the ground and inspiration of the Iona Community's activities lies: 'this great vision (of Christ the High Priest in the midst of all things: the present renewal of spirits, of bodies and of the earth) must control us both in our work, which becomes our worship, and in our worship, which becomes a work';[452] and 'the ultimate worship of God is what we do in the realm of service, of obedience in the market-place'.[453]

Ralph Morton, who was the first warden of Community House in Glasgow and also deputy leader of the Community for a number of years towards the end of George MacLeod's leadership,[454] refers to MacLeod's gifts as a leader of worship, a preacher, and a creator of wonderful, soaring, painstakingly crafted prayers[455] and how he 'made worship a happy activity for many by helping them to see the wonder of God's world and to know that they were committed to possible actions'.[456] He tells of how worship from the beginning, and 'the recovery of a full and vital worship related to daily life',[457] was basic to the life of the Community and illustrates how the location of the chapel at Community House, opening on to the restaurant and kitchen, affirmed 'the idea (novel and shocking at the time!) that work, worship and life are a unity'.[458] Ralph Morton was always swift to emphasize that the worship on Iona was never meant to be the most important part of the Community's purpose: the Iona experience was 'for export', and it was what happened on the mainland that really counted. In the early days the craftsmen and young ministers came to the morning service in their working clothes and went straight from there to start their day's work. Similarly today the Iona morning service ends with closing responses but not a benediction: without sitting down staff and guests go to their allotted 'chores' and the benediction does not come until after the evening service, thus both enclosing the day in prayer and affirming that all that is done during the day is part of our 'worship-offering'.

As the rebuilding of Iona Abbey progressed, more and more people had the opportunity of experiencing worship there. The film *Sermon in*

---

451 George MacLeod, *Only One Way Left*, Glasgow: Iona Community, 1955, p. 101.

452 MacLeod, *Only One Way Left*, p. 106.

453 MacLeod, *Only One Way Left*, p. 73.

454 'Inherited wisdom' within the Community suggests that Morton in effect 'ran' the Community during this time, while George MacLeod 'travelled the world' on the Community's behalf, promoting the Community's concerns and activities.

455 See, for instance, Ron Ferguson, ed., *The Whole Earth Shall Cry Glory: Iona Prayers by Rev George F MacLeod*, Glasgow: Wild Goose Publications, 1985.

456 Morton, *The Iona Community*, p. 23.

457 Article 'Worship and daily life' in *The Coracle*, 1963.

458 Morton, *The Iona Community*, p. 78.

Stone (1967) contains material that gives a good impression of its scale and scope. There were notable 'big occasions' – the visit of the Queen in 1956, the open-air Communion in 1963 to mark the 1400th anniversary of Columba's arrival from Ireland, the service in 1965 to mark the completion of the cloisters; but more significant was the regular rhythm – the daily morning and evening services throughout the summer months, and the thoroughly ecumenical and inclusive approach, so that young people attending the summer camps were encouraged to participate alongside the visitors and increasing number of guests living in the Abbey.

During the years since the rebuilding was completed, there have been several very significant developments relating to the Community's worship. First of all, while George MacLeod's successor, Ian Reid, was leader of the Community, it was decided to form a resident group of staff, who would live on Iona and provide hospitality for the guests living in the restored Abbey, sharing the common life with them, running a programme of discussions and social events week by week, and take responsibility for the leading of worship each morning and evening. This was the point at which 'Iona worship' moved into a new phase, shifted up a gear perhaps. Although almost all the elements were already there, the weekly pattern of services now developed into a form very similar to the present one. There was a Sunday morning Communion service, along fairly traditional lines; a service at 9 a.m. each morning except Sunday, based on a 'fixed liturgy' (close to the morning service George MacLeod had brought to Iona in 1938 from Govan Old Parish Church in Glasgow, where a daily service had been established by his kinsman John MacLeod 50 years previously), with Bible readings, songs and short prayers changing each day. There were also services at 9 p.m. each evening – a service of welcome on Saturday, silence on Sunday, a focus on a justice and peace theme on Monday, prayers for healing on Tuesday, guest-led on Wednesday, commitment on Thursday, Communion on Friday. Since 1999, with the shift to a 'six-day week' (and the guests departing on Friday mornings), the commitment service now takes place on Wednesday and the Communion on Thursday, with a flexible liturgy on Friday. None of these services is exclusive: on each occasion it is 'public worship' that is offered, and invariably, as well as guests and staff, visitors to the island and often some of the local island community attend also. In addition, for many years one of the highlights each week has been the 'Pilgrimage', now held on Tuesdays, a guided walk round Iona, stopping at places of historical/religious significance for a brief act of worship – typically involving a reading, a reflection, a prayer and a song. And each weekday afternoon at 2 p.m. there are brief prayers for peace and justice, provided particularly so that day-visitors may share in the Abbey worship, but usually attended also by some guests and staff.

The worship on Iona falls within the responsibility of the warden, who has always been a member of the Community. To that extent it is the worship of the Community and 'owned' by the Community. In fact it is led by different people each day, usually by members of the resident group, sometimes by some of the volunteers who are working at the centres, and each week, as indicated, guests at the centres have the opportunity to share in the preparing and leading of at least one of the services. (In any one week there may be up to around 90 guests staying at the Abbey and the MacLeod Centre, which opened in 1988 on the site previously occupied by the youth camp.) At this point, for the sake of completeness, mention should also be made of the Community's outdoor adventure centre at Camas, formerly a salmon-fishing station, developed by George MacLeod particularly for 'borstal boys', now catering primarily for groups of young people from disadvantaged backgrounds. Part of daily life at Camas also is morning and evening worship, although the form, content and length of it will largely depend on the group who are there at the time.

People come from all over the world to worship on Iona and for most it is a memorable experience. This is partly due of course to the context, the rich heritage and attractiveness of the building and the likelihood of a sizeable, expectant and enthusiastic congregation. It can also of course be due to the form and content of the services: there are 'given' frameworks for each service which, at least for the evening services, the worship leaders are free to use, adapt or depart from. It can be very powerful to come into the church and see, for example, that the Saturday evening welcome service is to be led by the Abbey cook, responsible for the tasty first meal the guests have just enjoyed. The staff leading worship may or may not have experience in doing so prior to coming to Iona. Part of the annual staff-training before the season starts is devoted to this, a wide range of resource material is made available and support and advice is provided as necessary. Frequently there is innovation and creative use of songs, drama, dialogue and symbolic action, often blending the familiar with the new. Sometimes this works well, sometimes perhaps not so well. What appeals to one person in the congregation may be not so congenial to another. Inevitably there are occasions too when, owing to their experience of using the Community's material elsewhere, people come to Iona with misconceived expectations as to what the form or content of the worship there will be. But the framework and the underlying theology and principles remain constant – indeed much in line with what George MacLeod said in the early days; and perhaps above all it is in these, as well as in the expression of them through a particular liturgy, that the impact and appeal of the Community's worship lies.

The Abbey services have been collected and published in successive editions of *The Iona Abbey Worship Book*. In and through the liturgies and resource material contained in the latest edition, published in 2001,[459] together with what is said in the preface and in a short statement 'concerning worship' (themselves adaptations of similar pieces in the previous editions), what is characteristic and distinctive of the Iona Community's worship can be clearly seen. This is perhaps also the point at which to explain that, contrary to many people's understanding, 'Iona worship' or 'the Iona Community's worship' is not to be regarded as only that which takes place on Iona. A comprehensive understanding of the Community's worship has to cover also the worship that is an essential part of the regular meetings of members' local Family Groups (usually based on an 'office', printed in the members' and associates' 'directories', and closely related to the Iona Abbey morning service), and that which takes place at plenary Community meetings, and at events, workshops and conferences, throughout Britain and elsewhere, in which Community members and staff are involved.[460]

The Community's approach to worship is first of all *contextual*: it is prepared for a specific time and place. To that extent any printed liturgy or form of service is a starting-point, a framework or foundation which needs to be built upon, developed and adapted for a particular purpose and occasion, whether on Iona or elsewhere. This is why, although resources and material produced by the Iona Community are widely used by congregations and at ad hoc events all over the world, 'Iona worship' as such is less transportable than, for instance, 'Taizé worship'. (Many churches throughout Britain, the United States and elsewhere hold 'Taizé services' regularly, a blend of silence, prayers and the wonderful Taizé chants, which are clearly meeting a need that is widely felt. Indeed on Iona, in recent seasons, Taizé singing by candlelight in St Oran's chapel on Tuesday evenings after the prayers for healing in the Abbey has been a regular part of the weekly programme.)

The preface to *The Iona Abbey Worship Book* explains the Community's approach further in indicating that the revision of the book every few years is a reflection of 'the growth and creative changes' in life and

---

459 *The Iona Abbey Worship Book*, Glasgow: Wild Goose Publications, 2001.

460 In addition to the work of the Wild Goose Resource Group (see below), Community members in recent years have been directly involved in preparing and leading worship at major gatherings of the World Council of Churches, the World Alliance of Reformed Churches, and the Conference of European Churches, and many denominational, congregational and church-related events within Britain and overseas. A group of former Abbey musicians (*Oran*), under the leadership of Pat Livingston, a Community member, work together in composing new material and leading worship and liturgical workshops at churches, conferences and other events. More recently *Worship Works*, set up by another Community member, Alison Adam, formerly a member of the Wild Goose Resource Group, with a similar purpose, has arranged a monthly singing event in London and fulfilled commitments throughout Britain and in North America.

worship – 'the culmination of two years of discussion, trial, redrafting and theological debate by members of the resident group, in relationship with the Wild Goose Resource Group and in consultation with the wider membership of the Iona Community'. To that extent it is not only context-ual but also *provisional*, since worship, by its very nature, is 'a dynamic process based on relationship, seeking to find expression for that which words cannot express. These liturgies can never be a finished product ... They must point beyond themselves, opening doors to bring people to-gether and windows to set them free.' So, like all material emanating from within the Community, the book is offered as a resource 'to provide more tools and options, with usefulness and flexibility in mind' for use and ad-aptation not only on Iona but far beyond, indeed worldwide: 'If we have something of value we would not want to confine it to Iona. From the time of St Columba that has never been the intention. It is in the common life, wherever we are that community has to be rebuilt, Christ celebrated and prayer offered, by ordinary people in honest and relevant language. Books like this seem to help and for that we give thanks.'[461] Before the liturgies themselves the book says something about 'what the Iona Community be-lieves about worship', rooted in 'the central Gospel conviction that wor-ship is all that we are and all that we do. Either everything we do is an offering to God, or nothing. We may not pick and choose.' It expresses too our search for wholeness, our longing to become fully human, to be fully present to God, who is fully present to us in every aspect of life. In the structure of our lives, including our worship, we are called by grace to respond to God's love and to be obedient to the vision that God has given us of what wholeness is like, primarily through the life, death and resurrection of Jesus Christ;[462] and the daily rhythm of worship on Iona reflects these beliefs.

In her preface to *The Pattern of Our Days*,[463] a collection of liturgies and resources for worship prepared by Community members and staff, Kathy Galloway identifies some features of the Community's worship that are constant. It is *incarnational*, reflecting the belief 'that there is no part of our life that is beyond the reach of our faith. The word of life is as much for our politics as for our prayers.' It is *historical*, drawing from the priorities and themes of the Celtic and Benedictine traditions, acknow-ledging 'the well of Biblical faith of our Reformed forebears', blending the familiar and the innovative. It is *ecumenical*, because we are an ecumen-ical community and part of the worldwide church, using songs and other material from many sources. The Community has played a significant part

---

461 *Iona Abbey Worship Book*, pp. 7–8.
462 *Iona Abbey Worship Book*, p. 11.
463 Kathy Galloway, ed., *The Pattern of our days*, Glasgow: Wild Goose Publications, 1996.

in the increasing familiarity with and use of songs from Africa, Asia and Latin America across Britain but also in the United States and elsewhere, not in a way that is in any sense patronizing but rather out of mutuality, exchange and 'faith-sharing'. It has been authoritatively suggested that every denominational hymnal that has been produced over the last 15 years or so, anywhere within the English-speaking world, has contained a number of songs originating within the Community or among its members. It is *creaturely*: 'we are whole people, God's creation, and we want to respond through our senses as well as our intellect. In movement and stillness, through touch and sight and sound, through smell and taste, we are gifted with many ways to pray.' And above all it is *inclusive*, so that the experience of worship is welcoming and thoroughly accessible and everyone present is able to participate fully: this has to do with not only physical and visual considerations but also with the familiarity of the songs, the intelligibility of the language, the sharing of preparation and leadership, indeed the whole ethos and culture. It is perhaps a measure of the Iona Community's influence on the wider church that the use of opening and closing responses, reciprocal confessions, and symbolic actions, key and regular features of the Community's worship both on Iona and elsewhere, are increasingly widely found in both ecumenical and denominational worship.[464]

Although in the early years of the Community its worship was largely publicly identified with George MacLeod and his gifts as preacher, broadcaster and compiler of prayers, increasingly the creativity and contributions of other members was making an impact. Among them, for instance, were Tom Colvin, with songs gathered out of his experience working in Central Africa for many years, Ian Cowie, with songs and prayers reflecting especially his pioneering work with the Christian Fellowship of Healing in Edinburgh, and Ian Fraser, first as warden of Scottish Churches House, Dunblane (where he was responsible for 'Dunblane Praise' a key text in the worldwide revival of hymn writing from the 1960s onwards), and later at the WCC in Geneva and Selly Oak Colleges in Birmingham. All of these, along with several other Community members, have songs in the latest edition of the Church of Scotland hymnary ('CH4').[465]

However, it is John Bell, Community member and also member of staff, who is most widely associated with the Community's worship at present and indeed who has been largely responsible, along with his colleagues, both for a good proportion of recent material and for the impact the Community's worship has made on the consciousness and life of churches in

---

464 Some of these aspects are pursued in more detail in the chapter of my own book (*Iona – God's Energy*, London: Hodder & Stoughton, 1999, pp. 119–36) exploring the centrality of worship to the vision and spirituality of the Community.

465 *Church Hymnary, Fourth Edition*, Norwich: Canterbury Press, 2005.

many parts of the world. For some years, perhaps until around the 1980s, so far as the Community was known outside Scotland, it was largely due to the charisma of George MacLeod. Within Scotland many looked at it askance as a radical, left-wing, semi-subversive organization that was more interested in politics than religion; and a significant number of congregations, on that account, would resist the possibility of calling a Community member as a minister. Increasingly since the 1980s, largely owing to the work of John Bell and the Wild Goose Resource Group,[466] such perceptions have changed. In the 1990s in England and North America people tended to think the Community was all about Celtic spirituality and an innovative approach to worship. Today, I think, generally there is a more balanced and accurate understanding of the Community's approach and activities that integrates and embraces worship and a concern for justice and peace.

For many, because of his travels throughout Britain, to north America, Australasia and elsewhere, his gifts and achievements as preacher, lecturer, songwriter and musician, and his profile as a broadcaster (on *Songs of Praise*, Radio 4's *Thought for the Day*, etc.) John Bell is the public face of the Iona Community. After completing his studies and training for ministry, John started work with the Iona Community along with his colleague Graham Maule, initially on a voluntary basis, in the 1980s during the leadership of Ron Ferguson. From the work with which they were involved, mostly among young people, emerged the Wild Goose Worship Group, comprising, when it was at full strength, 16 volunteers. The group contributes to the shaping of new ways to worship through workshops, special services and conferences and monthly events like 'Holy City', currently held in Renfield St Stephen's Church, in Glasgow's city centre, which attracts people of all ages to worship, enjoy fellowship, meditative silence, workshops, Bible studies and discussions on contemporary issues of faith and life. In due course, with some financial support for a few years from the Church of Scotland, John Bell and Graham Maule, along with others, formed the Wild Goose Resource Group, semi-autonomous within the structures of the Community, funded partly by the Community and partly out of publishing royalties and payment for the engagements in which its members are involved all over the world (responding to invitations from the United States and Canada, Malawi, Guatemala, Philippines, Japan, Australia and New Zealand as well as many parts of Europe).

At the same time, and very significantly in relation to the wider impact of the Community's work in the field of worship, the Community's

---

466 Largely through its association with the Iona Community, the Wild Goose has come to be regarded as a symbol of the Holy Spirit, allegedly with Celtic origins. Several attempts to authenticate this have been unsuccessful. It is likely to have been a typically creative and appropriate fabrication of George MacLeod's imagination!

publishing activities were moved up a gear, largely to make the material produced by the Wild Goose Worship Group more generally accessible. Through the period from the late 1980s to the present the output of Wild Goose Publications has been steadily increasing and broadening. Initially much of what was produced was resource material in the field of worship; now there are books and audio-visual products also relating to other aspects and areas of the Community's concerns. The volume and range of material over the years has been remarkable.[467] Much of it is the handiwork of John Bell, frequently in collaboration with Graham Maule, refined through practice and experience, with the benefit also of comments from the members of the Wild Goose Worship Group and others. Many of the books contain original songs, some set to original tunes, others to Scottish folk tunes or familiar hymn tunes, some with a focus on particular seasons (Advent and Christmas, Lent and Easter) or themes;[468] others are collections of songs, either in their original form or adapted, from the world church.[469] There are books of shorter songs and chants, larger collections of liturgical material, including prayers, responses, meditations, scripts for drama or symbolic action,[470] the immensely popular *Wee Worship Book* (fourth edition 1999), with liturgies for different occasions, series of sketches and meditations.[471] Most recently, there have been two books about the whys and hows of congregational singing[472] and a series of liturgical booklets for different specific purposes.[473]

The prefaces and forewords to these publications not only provide rich and helpful insights into the thinking behind this material and how it was

---

467 In addition to those books mentioned, see *Wild Goose songs*, vols 1 (*Heaven Shall Not Wait*, 1987) and 2 (*Enemy of Apathy*, 1988); *Love from Below* (1989); *Innkeepers and Light Sleepers* (songs for Christmas), 1992; *The Courage to Say No* (songs for Lent and Easter), 1996; *The Last Journey*, 1996; *Love and Anger* (songs of lively faith and social justice), 1997; *One is the Body* (songs of unity and diversity), 2002; *I Will Not Sing Alone* (songs for the seasons of love), 2004; *Come all you People*, 1994 and *There is One Among Us*, 1998 (both 'shorter songs for worship'). And for the full list, see Wild Goose Publications catalogue, obtainable from The Iona Community, 4th Floor, Savoy House, 140 Sauchiehall Street, Glasgow G2 3DH, or available through the Community's website – www.iona.org.uk.

468 For example, *Psalms of Patience, Protest and Praise* (1993); *When Grief is Raw* (1997), for times of sorrow and bereavement.

469 For example, *Many and Great*, 1990, and *Sent by the Lord*, 1991.

470 For Advent, Christmas and Epiphany (*Cloth for the Cradle*, 1997), Lent, Holy Week and Easter (*Stages on the Way*, 1998), and relating to the life and ministry of Jesus (*Present on Earth*, 2002).

471 *Wild Goose Prints*, 1985–90; *Eh Jesus, Yes Peter?* 1987–99; *He was in the world*, 1995.

472 *The Singing Thing: A Case for Congregational Song*, 2000, and *The Singing Thing Too: Enabling Congregations to Sing*, 2007.

473 For example, *The Love which Heals*, 2003 – a service of grieving and gratitude for those recently bereaved, *A Road to Roam*, 2006 – a way of celebrating sacred space, *Fencing in God's People*, 2007, reflecting the situation in Israel/Palestine.

produced, but also demonstrate the continuity and consistency of the Community's understanding of the significance of worship in relation to the Christian life and the integrity of witness. While there are certain echoes of what George MacLeod and Ralph Morton said in the earlier years, this is reinforced, and also taken farther in today's situation, through the explanation given of the Community's approach and the emphasis, for example, on discipline (in terms of form and process as well as content – a structured liturgy; the importance of practising unfamiliar songs), the significance of place (the shape, layout and use of the worship space; practical instructions, with a careful attention to detail and often suggestions on the use of colour, light, symbol, symbolic action – the whole sense of the drama of worship), context, accessibility, relevance, flexibility, and participation (through empowering lay people to share in the preparation and leadership of services; through the use of responses in prayers and at the start and end of services, modern affirmations of faith, etc.).

The material, whether the content of the songs, prayers, responses or sketches, is clearly biblically based and grounded in orthodox Trinitarian theology. In both songs and dramatic scripts there is a striving to be more 'realistic', 'true to life' than some of the traditional carols and texts and yet, in the seeking to 'rediscover aspects of the Christian story as speaking both from and to adult experience',[474] the sense of mystery and wonder is not lost. At all times the aim is to engage people's interest and attention, to nourish, challenge and call them to committed action. The introduction to the first collection of 'Wild Goose songs' (*Heaven Shall Not Wait*, 1987) is worth quoting from more fully for what it reveals about the thinking and the process:

> We began singing and writing new songs not primarily because we were fed up with the old ones, but because others were and because we recognise that in every era, Jesus looks for new bottles to hold his new wine ... Not every old hymn is a great hymn ... The church always needs new songs, not because the Gospel changes, but because the world changes and God's purposes in the world have to be reinterpreted to become real for the times. God's praise has to be sung in terms which are relevant rather than respectable but dated; and that which causes God's people to shout for joy or to suffer must be given expression which is contemporary with their experience ... Where are the hymns of protest, the songs which carry the despair of dispossessed people and the anxiety of those who do not want to see the earth polluted and human life obliterated? ... Where are the words and music which might yet allow those on the fringes of the church or those who have rejected the

---

474 *Cloth for the Cradle*, p. 10.

trappings of organised religion to deepen their faith and praise their maker? ... Where are the liturgies which allow the sacred to touch and transform the whole fabric of society rather than just the religious bits? ... Where in our contemporary devotions are there glimpses that God, in the twentieth century, can be expected to surprise, contradict, upset, or rile us in order that the kingdom may come? [475]

The variety of the songs, in terms of content, context and musical style, the range and depth of experience they convey, and the eclectic nature of the collections, is highly impressive. Limitations of space permit only a couple of examples (and making a choice is well-nigh impossible!) but these reflect well the directness and simplicity of the language, the orthodoxy of the theology, the topicality of the theme, the attempt to address situations and reflect emotions too infrequently explored in worship, and the persuasiveness of the tone.

First –

Women and men as God intended
daughters of Adam, sons of Eve;
children of earth, loved by their Maker,
those only heaven could conceive;
yet in our loving we are not one
with heaven's high intent:
we are not as God meant ...

Now sing aloud! Jesus our brother
turns every tide of history,
sharing our flesh, bearing our sorrow,
winning an endless liberty.
Out of the grave, alive in the world,
Christ wills all be made new:
this tested word is true.[476]

And second –

If the war goes on
and the children die of hunger,
and the old men weep
for the young men are no more,
and the women learn

---

475 *Wild Goose Songs*, Vol. 1 (*Heaven Shall Not Wait*), pp. 6–7.

476 Verses 1 and 5 of 'Women and men as God intended', 2002, *One is the Body*, pp. 50–1, set to a traditional Dutch melody.

how to dance without a partner
who will keep the score? ...

If the war goes on
will we close the doors to heaven,
if the war goes on,
will we breach the gates of hell;
if the war goes on,
will we ever be forgiven,
if the war goes on ... and on ... and on ...?[477]

Wild Goose Publications, alongside the material emanating from the Wild Goose Resource Group, and following the model of *The Pattern of Our Days* (1996) have produced an increasing number of books with liturgies, worship resources and reflective material composed by a remarkable range of other members, associate members and staff of the Community.[478] It is notable that among these are many women, whose distinctive voice has in a variety of ways added a significant dimension both to the Community itself and to what in the Community's worship is valued by the wider Church.[479] And, in addition, books with resources

---

477 Verses 1 and 5 of 'If the war goes on', 1999, 2001, 2002, *I Cannot Sing Alone*, pp. 50–2, set to a original tune 'Road to Basra'.

478 In 1998 a collection of prayers and meditations prepared by Ian Reid, successor as leader to George MacLeod, proved very popular. *Praying for the Dawn* (2000) was compiled by Ruth Burgess and Kathy Galloway specifically as a resource book for the ministry of healing. Ruth Burgess has also edited and written collections for the seasons of the Christian year (*Eggs and Ashes (Lent and Holy Week)* – 2004, with Chris Polhill; *Hear my Cry: A Prayer Book for Advent* – 2005; *Candles and Conifers (All Saints and Advent)* – 2005; *Hay and Stardust (Christmas to Candlemas)* – 2005; *Fire and Bread (Easter to Trinity)* – 2006) and books of prayers (*A Book of Blessings* – 2001; *Friends and Enemies* – 2004). Chris Polhill has compiled *A Pilgrim Guide to Iona Abbey* (2006). Neil Paynter has edited several books of daily readings and meditations (*Lent and Easter Readings from Iona* – 2002; *This is the Day* – 2002; *Iona Dawn: Through Holy Week with the Iona Community* – 2006; *Growing Hope: Daily Readings* – 2006; *Gathered and Scattered* – 2007) and, along with Helen Boothroyd, *Holy Ground – A Collection of Liturgies and Resources for an Engaged Spirituality* (2005). Joy Mead's *The One Loaf: An Everyday Celebration* (2001) has been followed by several other collections she has brought together. And several of the recent wardens of Iona have produced collections of reflections, meditations and prayers (*Dandelions and Thistles* – Jan Sutch Pickard, 1999; *Advent Readings from Iona* – Brian Woodcock and Jan Sutch Pickard, 2000; *Our Hearts Still Sing* – Peter Millar, 2004).

479 This has occurred, for example, through liturgies, prayers, etc. compiled by Kate McIllhagga, Ruth Burgess, Kathy Galloway, Jan Sutch Pickard and others; four women – Kathy Galloway and Alison Newell (both job-sharing with their husbands), Joanna Anderson and Jan Sutch Pickard have been wardens of Iona Abbey; and Alison Adam (now with her own *Worship Works*), Mairi Munro and Fiona Squires, all formerly members of the Wild Goose Resource Group, have travelled widely within the UK and abroad leading and facilitating worship at workshops, ecumenical conferences and other events.

for worship by several members of the Community have been published elsewhere.[480]

What is common to the material in all these publications and what accounts generally for the popularity of the Iona Community's worship resources is, above all, that it is not produced in an ivory tower or book-lined study remote or detached from the real world. It is original material, produced through a thoroughly collaborative process, tried and tested collectively and participatively within a specific local context whether on Iona or elsewhere. It is significant that what the Wild Goose Resource Group has produced derives above all from, and is rooted in and intended for, an urban context. All the material is intended to be used flexibly and with adaptation and addition as necessary and appropriate to the particular situation. And it is accessible and relevant – even the 'new' tunes are eminently singable, the words are not esoteric theological abstractions but the plain language of everyday, succinctly expressed, and, in addressing and reflecting on the kinds of issues and situations that people encounter, their minds are engaged, their hearts touched and their lives enriched.

The global impact of the Community's worship is attributable partly to the travels of Community members and staff, partly to the availability of resources through Wild Goose Publications and others, but above all to the intrinsic quality of the material. In many parts of North America, Australia, the Netherlands, Sweden and elsewhere, local services and ecumenical events are advertised as 'Celtic' or 'Iona worship', based on the Wee Worship Book and the Iona Abbey Worship Book, using Community material and often attracting people who otherwise seldom attend church. Publishers abroad (including GIA, the largest Roman Catholic publishing house in the US, the largest Lutheran publishers in Sweden and Norway, publishers in Germany, Japan, China and elsewhere) have sought to publish Wild Goose Resource Group and other material; and, where translation is involved, there is always an insistence, so far as the Wild Goose Resource Group is involved, that the process should be as co-operative as the origination in English was. The range of places and events, far and wide, big and small, where Iona Community worship material and its influence are to be found is both encouraging and surprising – from local church services in Scotland to the Thomas Mass in Helsinki, Finland, from big annual gatherings in Britain like Greenbelt and Spring Harvest to the German Kirchentag, from seminaries in the United States, Singapore, the Philippines and elsewhere to major ecumenical events – the 2007 European Ecumenical Assembly at Sibiu, Romania, the 2006 WCC Assem-

---

480 For example, Peter Millar, Iona – a pilgrim guide, Norwich: Canterbury Press, 1997, and An Iona prayer book, Norwich: Canterbury Press, 1998; and Ruth Harvey, ed., Wrestling and resting, London: CTBI, 1999, and Seasons with the spirit, London: CTBI, 2002.

bly in Porto Alegre, Brazil, the 2004 WARC General Council in Accra, Ghana, and many more.

During a recent visit to the United States I had the opportunity to speak with several people with wide experience in the fields of liturgy and church music about the extent to which the Iona Community's approach to worship and the resource material it produces had made an impact on the lives of the churches there. In the appreciative remarks, there was frequent use of words like 'authenticity', 'integrity' and 'freshness', and the common theme was the appeal of an approach that blends the old and the new, which combines and integrates concerns for justice and the 'spiritual life' and which has an immediacy and depth so that it both challenges and moves people, enlarges our vision, deepens our commitment and helps people to engage in sacred experience in and through words that they can understand.

To those of us within the Iona Community responses like this, and the regard in which the activities and resources of the Community appear to be held in many quarters, make us feel both humble and responsible. We are well aware of our limitations, our flaws and our frailty. But we are also immensely encouraged. At the end of our morning service on Iona we say each day, 'We will not offer God offerings that cost us nothing.' Our worship is all our work, and all our work and concerns are our worship. We offer it to the glory of God in the hope that we and others may be strengthened in commitment to leading lives of compassion, justice and integrity.

18

OPEN-AIR PREACHING

Performing Beyond the Walls

Stuart Blythe

Introduction

In this chapter I discuss open-air preaching. I do so with particular although not exclusive reference to Scottish examples of the practice. In this
way I introduce something of the longevity and variety of the historical
tradition. My purpose, however, is to do more than give a historical survey. It is rather to offer an alternative perspective on open-air preaching
to those which are often primarily negative and based upon limited stereotypes. In turn this perspective will be indicative of the potential for future
forms of open-air preaching.

In order to offer this alternative understanding of open-air preaching
I adopt, adapt and apply some of the insights drawn from performance
theorist Baz Kershaw in his book, *The Radical in Performance: Between
Brecht and Baudrillard*.[481] Insights that derive from his argument that the
future potential of 'the radical', understood as that which seeks change, is
better to be discerned in the 'transgressive' 'excesses' of performances that
take place in the streets, rather than in the dramatic productions that are
staged in buildings with their disciplined systems.

The Glasgow Street Preacher: September 2007

The smartly dressed, street preacher announces: 'We can come as a sinner
to Jesus. He says, "All that the Father giveth me, shall come to me. And
him that comes to me I will in no way cast out." Will you come as a sinner
to Jesus? He will take you just as you are?'

He turns from the direction he has been facing, gathers his thoughts, takes
a drink from his bottle of cola, and begins again to address the street.

---

481 Baz Kershaw, *The Radical in Performance: Between Brecht and Baudrillard*, London:
Routledge, 1999.

We are witnessing another performance in a 20-year history of open-air preaching.

This day, few stopped to listen. A small amplification system, however, meant that many would 'hear'. This was the goal, he explained to me, 'sowing the seed', leaving it to God to use the Word preached to free people from their enslavement. Various expressions from bewilderment to hostility were written on the faces of the passers-by who had unwittingly been made into an audience. Some expressed vocally their negative opinions of the preaching and of the accompanying sandwich board notices announcing 'never-ending torment' for the 'lost' and warnings against various 'false doctrines'. Others took more direct action. There was a slight scuffle with some football fans who tried to take and shout into the microphone. Some mimicked shooting the preacher with a shotgun![482]

Most Saturdays in the spring, summer and autumn months, several and varied open-air preachers, including this one, can be found in the main public pedestrian precincts of Buchanan Street and Sauchiehall Street in Glasgow, Scotland's largest city.

A Sense of Unease

Open-air preaching, such as that described above, frequently evokes a negative response from many Christian people. The practice is considered archaic, unhelpful, problematic, embarrassing. Its theological content, style and communicative impact are all criticized. Such criticisms can of course also be levelled at some, if not much, preaching that takes place in church. Be this as it may, there is something about open-air preaching that seems to invite particular criticism. This may relate to its association with fanaticism and fundamentalism. It may relate to the way in which open-air preachers are seen as forcing their views upon people. It may be that such public preaching invades our sensibilities concerning the private nature of religious belief. Then again, another reason may be that while it is unfortunate to have poor preaching in the church, it is agonizingly embarrassing to hear it in the streets. Perhaps, however, an undergirding source of such reservations is the sense that open-air preaching seems somehow 'out of place'.

The Place for Preaching

The place in which most people in Scotland today experience preaching, if at all, will be in a building among a congregation gathered in worship. This relates to the major historical trajectory of preaching, as identified by

---

482 This account is based upon the observation and recording of events that occurred in Buchanan Street Glasgow, in September 2007 and a subsequent conversation with the preacher.

O. C. Edwards when he writes at the beginning of his *History of Preaching*, 'The overwhelming majority of Christian sermons have been delivered at regular worship services, especially those conducted on Sundays.'[483] In turn, from a historical perspective and writing about the Reformed preaching tradition in Scotland, David Read states, 'The sermon was embedded in the act of public worship.'[484] Consequently this is still the place where people expect if not indeed welcome preaching as a necessary source of 'spiritual uplift, challenge and succour'.[485] Broadening beyond the Reformed tradition this context of a congregation gathered in a building for worshipful assembly is also the place where preaching can be variously understood and developed as Word 'and' worship, Word 'as' worship, Word 'and' sacrament, Word 'as' sacrament and so on. Indeed this context, drawing upon building design, liturgical tradition and ecclesiological commitments offers a rich place for preaching to be understood and developed theologically and practically both with respect to worship and to the congregation as the participating people of God.

From the above it should be apparent that to talk of the usual place of preaching is to discuss more than its physical location in a building. Rather buildings have associated with them certain conventions and in turn these conventions are associated with supporting ideologies. Church buildings have associated with them the conventions of worship and the ideologies of ecclesiology variously understood. Place, therefore, becomes more than a description of physical location but a conceptual framework of the way things are in relation to that physical location. While this creates a rich situation for developing theologies and the practice of preaching, it can also create a limiting context. This happens when the practice of preaching becomes so associated with the context that it becomes difficult to conceptualize it outwith that place. When this happens the practice, almost by definition, becomes captive to a particular location. This captivity of preaching can be discerned in much contemporary homiletical thinking. Frequently without question it is assumed that to talk of preaching is to talk of a practice that takes place in a mutually supporting and conceptually reinforcing framework of building, congregation, and acts of worship. This is the place for preaching. Here, whether it is good or bad, preaching seems at least to be in the 'right' place.

---

483 O. C. Edwards, *A History of Preaching*, Nashville: Abingdon Press, 2004, p. 3.

484 David Read, 'The Scottish Preaching Tradition', in Duncan Forrester and Douglas Murray, eds, *Studies in the History of Worship Scotland*, Edinburgh: T&T Clark, 1984, pp. 149–57.

485 While carrying out an investigation into the state of the Church of Scotland in 2001, Harry Reid attended several church services at which he clearly expected to find a sermon preached and although this was not always the case argued for its continuing necessity, Harry Reid, *Outside Verdict: An Old Kirk in a New Scotland*, Edinburgh: St Andrew Press, 2002, p. 38.

Out of Doors: Out of Place

The problem with working from the unquestioned assumption that preaching properly understood takes place in a building in worshipful assembly is that there are alternative genres of preaching that do not function in this context. One such genre is open-air preaching. This expression of preaching variously takes place beyond the established physical, liturgical and ecclesiological walls associated with the usual place for preaching. As a minority practice, in the face of this dominant location, conventions and ideologies, open-air preaching, whether good or bad, seems out of place.

In much contemporary homiletical literature open-air preaching is frequently (implicitly if not explicitly) negated or minimized as to its significance. This is done at times by completely failing to recognize the existence of the genre. At other times, where alternative forms of preaching are recognized, they are simply subsumed into and under the dominant assumptions about the proper place and nature of preaching. So, for example, while Edwards in his *History* acknowledges the existence of open-air preaching, he claims that it can be included within his given definition that preaching is something that takes place in a service of worship. The justification he gives for this is the argument that most such preaching was accompanied by some form of worship.[486] Notwithstanding the oversimplification and generalization of this argument, the consequences of this strategy of incorporation are twofold. It makes opaque the particular features and nuances of open-air preaching. It prevents alternative expressions of preaching challenging the limits established by the dominant assumptions.

Negated and minimized as to its nature and significance it is not surprising that open-air preaching seems out of place. It is somewhat indicative of the state of the research in the area of open-air preaching that to find a comprehensive historical sketch of the practice, one has to go back to a nineteenth-century lecture by Charles Spurgeon, 'Open Air Preaching – A Sketch of its History'.[487] In an accompanying lecture on 'Remarks' about open-air preaching, Spurgeon states the following,

> I fear that in some of our less enlightened country churches, there are conservative individuals who almost believe that to preach anywhere except in the chapel would be a shocking innovation, a sure token of heretical tendencies, and a mark of zeal without knowledge.[488]

---

486 Edwards, *History*, p. 4.

487 Charles H. Spurgeon, 'Open Air Preaching – A Sketch of its History', in Charles H. Spurgeon, *Second Series of Lectures to My Students: Being Addresses Delivered to the Students of The Pastors College, Metropolitan Tabernacle*, London: Passmore and Alabaster, 1881, pp. 54–75.

488 Charles H. Spurgeon, 'Open Air Preaching – Remarks thereon' in *Second Series*, p. 76.

On the one hand this quote indicates that resistance to the practice of open-air preaching is not something new or simply related to contemporary sensibilities and communicative concerns. On the other hand it suggests, as I am arguing, that such resistance can be related to the notion that such preaching by its practice challenges locational and ideological assumptions about the proper place for preaching.

A Biblical/Theological Perspective

Despite its frequent negation and minimization Christian open-air preaching has a long history going back to the Bible itself. Whether one posits the origins of Christian preaching in the Old Testament, with the practice of Jesus, or in the post-Pentecostal Church, we are immediately confronted with notable examples of preaching in the open air. In advancing the practice of preaching per se, appeal is often made to scriptural example and warrant. It is not surprising, therefore, that advocates for open-air preaching often make a similar appeal.

One lengthy defence of open-air preaching is that made by the father of modern Scottish congregationalism, Greville Ewing, in a sermon delivered at Lady Glenorchy's Chapel Edinburgh, on 24 December 1797 and later published in 1799.[489] In various ways in this sermon he appeals to scriptural basis in his defence of open-air preaching. Central to this defence, with reference to Proverbs 1.20–21, he argues that the nature of the gospel is 'Wisdom' that 'uttereth her voice in the streets'. This he claims is exemplified in the lives of, among others, Isaiah, Amos, Jesus, Peter and Paul. He asserts that he is not dismissing the importance of preaching in church but that there is a gospel mandate to take the gospel to every creature, something which preaching only in the church was not achieving. Reference is made to the parable of the banquet in Luke 14.16–24 and the injunction to 'Go out into the high-ways and hedges'.[490] Such a going out is necessary, he argues, not only because people are not attending churches, and not only because those who are may be receiving false doctrines, but because the nature of sin is to keep people from the truth. It is necessary, therefore, for the gospel to go to them and bring light into their darkness.[491] In terms of the scriptural argument Ewing here demonstrates a strategy that is found in other writings advocating open-air preaching. This involves the combination of scriptural passages that vali-

---

489 Greville Ewing, *A Defence of Itinerant and Field Preaching: A Sermon preached before The Society for Gratis Sabbath Schools, On the 24th of December 1979, In Lady Glenorchy's Chapel, Edinburgh*, Edinburgh: J. Ritchie, 1799.

490 Ewing, *Defence*, pp. 20–1.

491 Ewing, *Defence*, pp. 15–21.

date the nature of preaching out of doors with examples of the scriptural mandate for mission.

In this *Defence* Ewing is concerned not only to show that such preaching is a scriptural and ancient practice but also that it is expedient and necessary in his own day. Of particular interest here are the objections which he feels it necessary to address. One such objection is that, while such preaching may have been suited to earlier and more primitive times, it is

> unsuitable now, when men are accustomed to luxurious accommodations, and seem too fastidious to respect even the most sacred things unless they come recommended by external decoration.[492]

In that such an objection may take a contemporary form today, he makes two interesting responses. The first is to claim that the open-air preaching that he is advocating does not have the 'forbidding rudeness of ancient times' but an 'elegant simplicity'.[493] This signals that later forms of open-air preaching need not be committed in terms of style to the practices of the past. His second response is to appeal to the power of the gospel and the experience of the preacher.

> Never surely can the faithful preacher rise so high in expectation, as when he feels himself divested of every thing extraneous; when he has no authority, but the word of God, and no dependence, but the promised blessing.[494]

This particular response resonates with comments made by the North American theologian Charles L. Campbell, one of the few contemporary writers who engage positively with the subject of open-air preaching from an academic perspective. In his essay 'Street Preaching', he states,

> On the streets, superfluous layers are peeled away, and one is left with the very heart of preaching. Street preachers invite the rest of us back to the challenging and exhilarating essentials of our calling. They hold before us an 'extreme homiletic' ... When everything else is stripped away, these two remain for preachers: absolute trust in the Word of God and faithful stewardship of the human voices.[495]

---

492 Ewing, *Defence*, pp. 28–9.

493 Ewing, *Defence*, p. 29.

494 Ewing *Defence*, p. 30–1.

495 Charles L. Campbell, 'Street Preaching', in Stanley P. Saunders and Charles L. Campbell, *The Word on the Street: Performing the Scriptures in the Urban Context*, Cambridge: Eerdmans, 2000, p. 104.

Perhaps what Campbell and Ewing before him expose is that to preach out of place involves a theology of the Word that does not require the safety of worship and the support of the congregation to validate it. So understood, whether or not one is prepared to preach in the open air becomes a matter of faith in a theological position.

A Transgressive Practice

In addition to offering a biblical/theological rationale for open-air preaching Ewing in his *Defence* contends with other objections to the practice. Among these are a number which can be grouped together. These are objections which demonstrate that resistance was being articulated on the grounds that such preaching was challenging the institution, the practices and the clergy of the established Church as well as the stability of the state. It did so by allowing unlicensed lay persons to function as itinerant preachers among the 'profligate and rude'. Underlying these objections were various concerns about training, control, proper decorum and the legitimacy of who could preach when and where; concerns which were being expressed by those with ecclesiastical power who felt threatened. Indeed in direct response to the activities which Ewing was defending, the General Assembly of the Church of Scotland in 1799 passed a Declaratory Act aimed at stopping itinerant missionaries 'whose proceedings threaten no small disorder'.[496] Various attempts were also made to instigate legal proceedings through the tools of the state. Such objections can be seen against a context in which the Church of Scotland was losing its monopoly on religion and there was post French Revolution anxiety in the state.[497] What these objections signal is that to preach out of doors is a practice that not only transcends the physical limitations of church buildings but that in doing so it also transgresses the associated conventions and ideologies associated with preaching in church. Indeed it is this transgressive nature of open-air preaching, whereby the change of physical location is accompanied implicitly or explicitly by wider critiques of established conventions and ideologies that explain why it is a practice that has often been associated with periods of reform and revival. In this respect it is worth noting that those forbidden to preach by the dominant ecclesiological authorities (such as the untrained, lay people and women) have often found a voice in the practice of open-air preaching. Unfortunately in the case of Ewing his *Defence* did not extend to the rights of women to preach.

---

496 Deryck Lovegrove, '"A set of men whose proceedings threaten no small disorder": The Society for Propagating the Gospel at Home, 1798–1808', *The Scottish Historical Review*, 79 (2000), pp. 61–81.

497 Lovegrove, 'A set', pp. 61–3.

To highlight the transgressive nature of open-air preaching is to suggest that its relationship with the Church is perhaps best understood as somewhat ambiguous. On the one hand, open-air preaching is a practice of the Church and is concerned with its life and concerns and community. On the other hand it is captive to no particular worship tradition or ecclesiological position. Rather than being lamented, however, this situation should be welcomed. It is this ambiguity that allows open-air preaching to function prophetically for and against the Church in the world.

A Historical Resistance to Stereotypes

In his short essay on 'Street Preaching', Campbell starting with biblical examples demonstrates that open-air preaching represents a 'Long and Lively Tradition'.[498] He makes reference to a number of historical examples of open-air preaching beginning with the apostles Peter and Paul and then including Francis of Assisi, the Lollards, George Whitfield, John Wesley, the Salvation Army and the Roman Catholic Vincentian 'motor missions'. Campbell, who draws on the historical sketch by Spurgeon, is aware that these examples could be multiplied many times over.

With reference to Campbell's examples, Scotland has had experience of Lollard, Whitfield, Wesley and Salvation Army open-air preaching. Indeed the Salvation Army was introduced to Scotland by two 'Hallelujah Lassies', Sister Eliza Milner and Sister Prentice who crossed the border on Sunday 23 March 1879 and held a number of meetings including some in the open air.[499]

In giving further Scottish examples of open-air preaching attention can be drawn to the activity of Celtic missionaries such as Ninian, Mungo and Columba, the preaching of Reformers such as George Wishart, the open-air preaching at outdoor Communion services associated with Scottish and Irish revivalism, and the field preaching of the Covenanters. In addition to this there has been the itinerant work of individuals such as James Haldane and John MacDonald and later the evangelists associated with organizations like the Open Air Mission, the Faith Mission and the Open Air Campaigners.[500]

One more recent and interesting example of Scottish open-air preaching is that associated with George F. MacLeod (1895–1991).[501] MacLeod, a

---

498 Campbell, 'Street Preaching', pp. 96–9.

499 Major Director Stephen Grinsted of the 'International Heritage Centre' in an email to the author on 11 December 2006.

500 This is not intended to be an exhaustive list – other examples could be gathered.

501 Here the key text for information has been Ronald Ferguson, *George MacLeod: Founder of the Iona Community*, London: Fount, 1990.

Church of Scotland minister was a loyal churchman, one time moderator of the General Assembly, the author of prayers of liturgical and poetic beauty, and a master of preaching in church. He was also the founder of the Iona Community, a reformer, a controversial figure and outspoken critic of religion that separated spirit and matter and issues of faith from the everyday lives of ordinary people. MacLeod in the 1950s was opposed to making a visit of Dr Billy Graham the centrepiece of the churches' 'Tell Scotland Campaign'. One reason was what he regarded as Graham's fundamentalist understanding of the Bible. His opposition, however, was not because he was against mission. Rather, he wanted to encourage mission that brought together proclamation, service and community. This was something that he felt that Graham's approach did not do and might actually become a distraction from.[502] MacLeod spoke on a wide range of issues at events out of church buildings. He also preached in the open air. During his ministry in Govan this was a regular practice and something which thereafter he continued to engage in as opportunity permitted. On some such occasions he disputed Communism and on others advocated support of the Peace cause and opposition to nuclear weapons. Open-air preaching was also an activity that he encouraged others to engage in as part of their local missions. Following the Clydebank blitz of 1941 he encouraged the churches in their united activities to hold open-air services not only on a Sunday night but also during the week, at the time when workers were having their break, in order to bear witness to the unity of the Church in such difficult times.[503] In a letter sent to MacLeod from one of the Iona members who served in Clydebank after the blitz, dated 14 July 1941, the writer talks of attending one of these open-air services. He regrets that those who were present were mainly church people. His desire accordingly was to find a less 'churchy' approach to such preaching. This he says was already being done by the Episcopalian minister in the area who would preach regularly in the open air on matters of pacifism. Such a strategy was one which he thought they should adopt. He states, however, 'But first I want to be sure that we've something to say to those folk who've come through so much and so gallantly.'[504] This sentiment would have resonated with MacLeod who would go and preach in the open air at Clydebank. For MacLeod open-air preaching was a contemporary expression of the Celtic approach to mission. It was an expression of the Church incarnating itself in human bodily form in the marketplaces of society. Indeed the memory of his preaching, at least for some, is that it was indicative of his identification with the situation of people and their aspirations. MacLeod, therefore,

---

502 National Library of Scotland, MacLeod of Fuinary and Iona Community MS, acc 9084/125, undated 'Address'.

503 NLS, MacLeod MS 'Proposal of Co-operation', acc9084/180.

504 NLS, MacLeod MS, 'Letter dated 14th July, 1941', acc9084/180.

offers a particularly Scottish example of open-air preaching that resists the stereotypes that open-air preaching is only carried out by a particular type of person with a particular type of message.

An Excessive Practice

This historical sketch of open-air preaching indicates that it is a multi-textured practice. Throughout the history of this genre there have indeed been significant differences in the nature of expressions in relation to sponsorship, style, theology, preaching personalities, purposes and precise locations used. In turn these individual variants have combined with diversity. Preaching in the open air has been at times an intentional choice, a practical necessity, an enforced option or a combination of all of these. On occasions it has been sponsored by the dominant church authorities and perhaps more regularly been an act of resistance to them in practice and in doctrine. When the latter has been the case the event of such preaching, let alone the content of the preaching, has taken on explicit political significance. Such is exampled clearly in the open-air preaching of Wishart, the Covenanters and Haldane. The relationship of open-air preaching to accompanying acts of worship has also varied. At times, open-air preaching has occurred without any other accompanying acts of worship. On other occasions it has been accompanied by selected acts of worship functioning as means to attract a crowd. Yet again, at other times it has occurred within the context of open-air worship services. Even when open-air preaching has occurred in the context of worship services, however, such as at the Holy Fairs of Communion, the open-air location has had a direct impact on the nature of the preaching. So it was that preaching at such communion events called for the development of an extempore style of preaching. It may also have encouraged preaching performances that sought to compete with other forms of entertainment and attraction.[505] A long tradition, open-air preaching is also a practice that historically has demonstrated dynamic variety in a whole range of areas.

From the above discussion it should be apparent that while preaching in church is the usual place for preaching there is a long and varied tradition of preaching out of doors. This suggests that to preach beyond the congregation gathered in a building for worshipful assembly is not to preach in the 'wrong' place, but in a 'different' place. The change of place, however, is significant. For the multi-textured nature of open-air preaching indicates a potential excessiveness inherent in the practice. This excessiveness is a freedom, fluidity and responsiveness to the prevailing situation found in

---

505 Leigh Eric Schmidt, *Holy Fairs: Scottish Communions and American Revivals in the Early Modern Period*, Princeton: Princeton University Press, 1989.

and made possible by the transgression of the limiting physical, liturgical and ecclesiological walls associated with preaching in the church.

One possible contemporary trajectory for the excesses of street preaching is through the category of performance. Campbell describes street preaching as an 'extreme homiletic'. By this he means that it involves performing the Word by interpretation and proclamation through reading the street in the light of the Word and the Word in the light of the street. This is a powerful understanding of which he gives good contemporary examples. To preach in the street so understood is to enter the drama of contested places with the counter drama of the gospel. In such understandings we have the excesses of faith in a theology of the Word. This may be enough.

It is possible, however, to push this understanding of the excesses of open-air preaching as performance even further. This means not simply reading open-air preaching through the metaphor of street theatre and street performance as though in retrospect but understanding and practicing it as artistic street performance. This would involve actively drawing upon and incorporating into street preaching the insights from the theatrical dimensions of such performances. Here activism and art would be collapsed into one. The preacher would understand them-self to be a performer or at least 'not not a performer'.[506] Attention would thus be given to the challenges of gaining an audience and negotiating a hearing through the verbal performance of words and the making and subverting of symbols and signs in the open air. It would become part of the excesses of open-air preaching to turn a wall into a pulpit, a shop front into a backdrop, a pavement into a stage, a passer-by into a participant, opposition into possibility and entertainment into efficacy. The potential ideological and political prophetic significance of such preaching would be understood. In turn this would become influential on when and where open-air preachers would place their embodied voicing of the gospel and in terms of what they would say, wear and do in such places and at such times. In this way, the historical excesses of open-air preaching would be turned into a strategy of performing beyond the walls. Yet this is a strategy which would not remove open-air preaching from the vulnerability of performing live in the vagaries of this different place for preaching.

Glasgow Street Preacher: Revisited

This preacher stands in a long historical tradition that can claim scriptural support and missional warrant. This is an example of intentional evan-

---

506 I use this phrase adapted from a discussion on political theatre to indicate my awareness that to describe a preacher as a performer is not unproblematic, R. M. Reynolds, 'Moving Targets: Political Theatre in a Post-Political Age', unpublished doctoral thesis, University of Canterbury, 2006, p. 63.

gelical open-air preaching that takes place without any attendant support from acts of worship or congregation. Whether or not we welcome his interpretation of Scripture he is prepared to expose his theology of the power of the Word of God not simply to the Church but in the street. In this place of many competing ideas and ideologies his voice ensures that the name of Jesus is spoken by one who holds to faith. He is a somewhat liminal character belonging it appears neither to the Church, which struggles with this practice, nor to the world which greets him with scorn and opposition. In this state he functions somewhat prophetically to both Church and world as he transgresses the established conventions of both. On the one hand he challenges the Church as to the presence or otherwise of its human public voice in the streets. On the other hand he challenges the world in its consumerism as to the claims of the Christ.

That said, this preaching in many ways reinforces the stereotype. Its purpose is narrow, its content limited, it lacks sympathetic incarnational identification with the lives of those being addressed, and its style is absent of any creativity that responds to the contemporary location and situation. This preaching is missing the transgressive performing excesses that have been and can be part of the practice of open-air preaching. This critique, however, is not made on the basis that such open-air preaching should not happen, nor that it is out of place, but rather on the grounds that it does not live up to the performative potential of its own long and varied tradition.

Conclusion

The conclusion may be that the answer to bad open-air preaching is no open-air preaching. This is the common contemporary default position. The historical longevity and variety of the practice, however, invites a more reflective response. In this respect Walter Brueggemann comments positively upon the street preaching carried out and written about by his colleagues Saunders and Campbell. Such preaching, he argues, unlike church preaching, cannot help but face the facts that the Word is a contested message and that it requires to be spoken with reference to the material reality of peoples lives. In these matters, he suggests, open-air preaching can inform preaching in church and enable it to better function as public theology.[507]

While the above is valid, the tradition of open-air preaching in Scotland and elsewhere suggests that the practice has potential, in and of itself, as

---

507 Walter Brueggemann, 'Foreword', in Stanley P. Saunders and Charles L. Campbell, *The Word on the Street: Performing the Scriptures in the Urban Context*, Cambridge: Eerdmans, 2000, pp. x–xvii.

an expression of Christian preaching. This potential is directly related to its actual performance in open-air locations. In the contemporary situation this is the potential to allow the Word in reality and not simply in cloistered theory, to be experienced and expressed as what it is, a contested public Word. To preach the Word in public places among the public is to speak among people increasing numbers of whom may never attend a church building to hear a sermon. This is the reality. In addition, the public locations offer alternative, interpretative contexts of transgression and excess for the Word and its expression. In one place, therefore, it will be proclaimed as truth to power. In another it will sound the good news of God's solidarity with the oppressed. Here it may lament with a community's loss. There it may share in expressions of humour and joy. In all such situations it will be embodied, a Word in place, an act of witness to the presence of God beyond sanctuary walls. As preaching it will be public theology interpreted and expressed in the midst of everyday life. Of preachers it will demand at times stomach-churning courage. It will require the very best of their interpretative and communicative skills in order to gain a hearing from those who may not share their convictions. Yet, even when the best have given their best the preachers will be confronted with the vulnerability of their humanity and the foolishness of their activity. Such confrontation has the potential to radicalize not only the skills but just as significantly the humanity and the faith of the performers. In turn, when such preachers preach in church, their preaching will be enlivened by the embodied experience of their performances beyond the walls. This may be to the health of preaching in general, in Scotland and elsewhere.

19

SCOTTISH HYMNODY

An Ecumenical and Personal Perspective

John L. Bell

A Short History of Suspicion

To speak of Scottish hymnody in a twenty-first century context one has to acknowledge a historical background of suspicion of the genre and its protagonists.

Had ties to Northern Europe been stronger and emissaries available, Scotland might have become Lutheran. The musical infrastructure had been set in place as hymn texts circulating in Germany and Scandinavia came into the country, courtesy of merchant ships trading between continental Europe and east coast ports. We find in Dundee in 1578 a collection of songs called *The Gude and Godlie Ballatis,* compiled by the Wedderburn bothers and including Scots and English translations of German texts. Such texts in ballad metre were set to Scottish folk tunes, but had limited longevity. The country, under the influence of John Knox was destined to have the mainstream of its national religious life shaped in a different direction: no bishops, no masses, no iconography, no choirs, no organs and no hymns of purely human artifice.

The people's part in worship was to consist primarily in singing metrical psalms, a form pioneered in Geneva and exported to Reformed churches throughout continental Europe and Great Britain. The texts were *sola scriptura*, with the translation eventually popularized by the Church of Scotland in 1650 showing the genius of Presbyterianism – poetry by committee. For most of the next three centuries, unaccompanied psalm-singing was the dominant form of music making in Presbyterian assemblies for worship.

The difficulty in the psalms being at root Hebrew poems written centuries before the birth of Christ was not regarded as an impediment. In a post-resurrection comment recorded in Luke's Gospel, Jesus identified himself as the one who fulfilled what was written of him in the psalms. This allowed for the immediate association of certain texts with his life and ministry – Psalm 22 with the passion, Psalm 24 with the ascension. A more overt acknowledgement of the need to sing specifically Christian praise was made in 1781 with the publication of a supplementary collection of paraphrases of scriptural passages in the same common metre as the 1650 Psalter.[508]

It may have been a weakening of the Calvinist suspicion of human verbal creativity, or it may have been the seduction of attractive tunes being sung by the 'minority' denominations (Episcopal, Methodist, Congregationalist and Baptist); but by the late nineteenth century Presbyterian Scotland began to acknowledge the need for more comprehensive hymnody.

There were already, particularly in the Free Church, wordsmiths of distinction, principal among whom was Horatius Bonar (1808–89) whose elders disapproved of his verse for public worship, but were permissive of its use for children. His texts, more than those of any other Scottish hymn writer of the era, spread throughout the English-speaking world and his hymns are still widely published and enthusiastically sung. Among the more popular are:

Blessing and honour and glory and power

Glory be to God the Father

Here, O my Lord, I see thee face to face

I heard the voice of Jesus say

But there were other Victorian authors in Scotland whose work gained international repute:

Anne Ross Cousin: The sands of time are sinking

Mary MacDonald: Child in the manger

Norman MacLeod: Courage brother, do not stumble

George Mathieson: O Love that wilt not let me go

James Montgomery: Angels from the realms of glory

Walter Smith: Immortal, Invisible, God only wise

Three Generations of The Church Hymnary

In 1896, the Church Hymnary Trust, which represented several Presbyterian churches in the British Isles, produced a book of hymns entitled *The Church Hymnary*.[509] The musical editor was John Stainer, an English

---

508 A scholarly and entertaining review of the domination of psalm-singing in the Church of Scotland can be found in Millar Patrick's *Four Centuries of Psalmody*, London: Oxford University Press, 1949.

509 London: Oxford University Press, 1896.

academic more commonly associated with his cantata *The Crucifixion*. Reading the first lines of the opening dozen items in the book, one becomes aware of the influence this canon of hymnody still exerts:

1 Holy, holy, holy, Lord God Almighty
2 Father of heaven, whose love profound
3 Holy, holy, holy, Lord God of hosts
4 Thou, Lord, art God alone
5 Round the Lord in Glory seated
6 We praise, we worship thee O God
7 Thee, God we praise, Thee Lord confess
8 Sound aloud Jehovah's praises
9 Sing to the Lord a joyful song
10 Glory be to God the Father
11 Lead us, heavenly Father, lead us
12 O Worship the King all-glorious above

Of these, at least half may fairly be expected to have appeared in most English-language hymnals produced in the first three-quarters of the twentieth century.

The book was published in its second edition (*The Revised Church Hymnary*) in 1927 to hansel the union of the Church of Scotland and the United Free Church. This book had a Welsh composer, David Grant, as its music editor and it enlarged and broadened the scope and contents of its predecessor. It was frequently bound with the split-page psalter preceding the hymnal proper, and affection for it is such that it is still used in a considerable number of Presbyterian congregations 80 years after its publication.

The year 1973 saw the third edition of the *Church Hymnary* (CH3), about whose origins less seems to be known than about its predecessors. It enjoyed mixed criticism from the beginning. On the positive side it included new commissioned tunes by composers living in Scotland, though few of these gained wide acceptance. It also attempted to organize contents according to the shape of the liturgy rather than according to doctrine, as was the case with the 1927 book. On the negative side, it paid scant attention to the social and theological shifts of the twentieth century. It grudgingly included songs of personal devotion and caused offence both by omitting stock favourites such as 'What a friend we have in Jesus' and by changing the tunes to other revered texts. It exhibited no awareness of contemporary developments in religious verse and music happening in the 1960s and 1970s. The Taizé Movement, the songs encouraged by Vatican II, the faith and folk movement whose most prestigious exponent was Sydney Carter – none of these were represented; nor was there yet anything of significance from the global Church whose hymnody was beginning to be shared via international gatherings of the World Council of Churches and related organizations.

Two subsequent supplementary publications, *Songs for the Seventies* and *Songs for a Day*, produced by the Church of Scotland's Panel on Worship made little impact on congregational singing. Nor was there much enthusiasm in Scotland (as distinct from abroad) for what became internationally known and acclaimed as the 'Hymn Explosion' detonated in no small way by the industry of Dr Ian Fraser, then warden of Scottish Churches' House and Dr Eric Routley the leading British hymnodist and Congregational minister. Together they encouraged, through gatherings at Dunblane, the production of new materials in contemporary linguistic and musical styles suitable for congregational use.

Was it that Scotland was innately conservative as regards church music? Was it that there was a virus-like national tendency to deprecate indigenous talent and thus discourage text and tune writers? Was it a slavish loyalty to tradition which feared innovation? Was it that church musicians, if educated at all in church music, were more dedicated to choir and organ than to congregational song? Was it a fear of Romanist influence?

Personal Engagement

It was with these questions in mind that, in the late 1970s, my own involvement with congregational song began. Job-sharing with a former architecture student and black South African youth worker we began a series of events, under the auspices of the Glasgow Presbytery of the Church of Scotland, called Last of the Month. These events attracted up to 400 teenagers and young adults from a wide area. They engaged in a range of seminars and then joined in the sanctuary of Glasgow's Anderson-Kelvingrove Church for worship. But what were they to sing, as young people who found little nourishment in the 1973 hymnal and whose musical tastes were increasingly conditioned by the performance rather than participative mentality of the Top Twenty?

As Ian Fraser had done in Dunblane, we began to gather and to write, to draw on indigenous Scottish melodies and the lively protest songs coming from South Africa, to forsake the organ and improvise with *a cappella* songs and ad hoc instrumental ensembles, to draw on the music of the Taizé Community and songs from Malawi and Zambia as disseminated by the Scottish missionary Tom Colvin; and to seek texts which would extol the life and ministry of the incarnate Jesus in language which was accessible to the offspring of the post-war bulge.

There were the Street Level festivals initiated by the Revd Jock Stein at the Steeple Church of Scotland in Dundee, which gave a platform to Christian rock bands and solo artistes. Events such as these reflected the gradual spread of the music of the charismatic renewal within Scottish churches and allowed the repertoire of proven worship-song writers such as Graham Kendrick to have a profile in Scotland.[510] Our contribution in Glasgow was necessarily of a more participative and home-generated nature.

In 1983, my colleague Graham Maule and I moved from working under the umbrella of the Church of Scotland to that of the Iona Community.[511] We had both led weeks on the island and recognized it as a place of liturgical and musical encouragement, particularly when the Abbey was under the wardenship of Ian and Kathy Galloway. Being occasionally on Iona enabled thinking outside the box of the standard Sunday morning ordering of worship. The change of worship themes in the Abbey services every evening – justice and peace, healing, commitment, communion, etc. – encouraged the writing of texts for specific rather than general purposes. They had to be focused – as was the case for Last of the Month – on this biblical passage or that life theme. They had to be produced for these people with their potentials and limitations in this peculiar place. But writing songs was never our primary concern. Such activity could only happen in the context of engaging with God's Word and God's people.

During the early years of our engagement with the liturgy of the Church in Scotland, five aspects of hymnody became important both in our own writing and in gleaning material from elsewhere.

The first was that while not every hymn can be a paraphrase of Scripture, every hymn should be defensible, as regards its text, with the revelation of God's will as contained in the full gamut of the Scriptures.

For us there were clear gaps in the regular diet of both traditional and contemporary material:

• A virtual neglect of the incarnate ministry of Jesus in contrast to the abundance of sometimes quite unscriptural songs about his birth.

---

510 The Community of Celebration – whose music shaped the hymnals *Sound of Living Waters* and *Fresh Sounds* was also influential upon some Scottish churches through its base on the island of Cumbrae in the years 1975 to 1985.

511 An ecumenical community linked to the Church of Scotland, established in 1938 by the Revd George MacLeod, in association with the restoration of the ruined Abbey on the island of Iona.

- A lack of songs which deal with God's continuously revealed passion for justice, evidenced in the Law and the Prophets and the Psalms, all of which Jesus came to fulfil.
- An avoidance of or aversion to materials which deal with the downside of life as is reflected in a third of the Psalms.

Second, we noticed that there had been a blurring of the edges between the corporate song *of* the Church and performance songs *for* the Church. The distinction is particularly important in a Presbyterian context where one of the fundamental aims of Reformed worship was to engage the voice of all the people; but by the 1980s, the erstwhile domination of the ecclesiastical airwaves by the organ was being challenged by alternative instruments and ensembles. (No bad thing, given that there is more in Scripture to substantiate guitars in worship than organs, pipe or electronic.) However with the change in instrumental accompaniment and the formation of praise bands, the cult of the performer and the performance song was beginning to erode the right and the confidence of congregations to engage in corporate praise.

Third, the use of the language of words as distinct from the language of music was also an issue. It was not simply a matter of inclusivity, resisting the way women became surrogate men in the language of the Church, it was also that many twentieth-century writers of both traditional hymns and modern worship songs employed a vocabulary which owed more to the dominance of Victorian writers than to contemporary language and literary styles. For example, in *Mission Praise*,[512] there is little in many of the items to suggest their twentieth century origin. This applies both to the language of devotional songs and to the range of subject matter deemed worthy of intercession before God.

The twentieth century was the one in which space travel, international debt, the global economy, environmental pollution, child abuse, etc. became terms used in everyday conversation. But there seemed to be few places in which such realities were registered in the compassionate song of the church – a stark contrast to the output of the Victorian era in which high child mortality and the expansion of the empire found plentiful reflection in hymns of faith.

Fourth, we became increasingly aware of the implications of being members of the holy catholic or universal Church. Until the 1980s it seemed that the only musical offerings which had been received from the developing world were Kumbaya and the Caribbean Lord's Prayer. Where, we had to ask, were the signs of international giving and receiving which Mott had encouraged in the song of the church? We had managed to

---

512 A collection published in 1984 by Harper Collins.

assimilate texts and tunes from all over Europe, but little of what the Holy Spirit had inspired had filtered through from the developing world. This needed to be addressed in order that our primary identity as a universal rather than a national church might be celebrated.

Finally, there was the issue of Scottish identity, not in a narrow nationalistic sense, but rather in recognition of the fact that this was a peculiar nation in which we should have cultural artefacts which celebrated the impact of Christ on our lives, and reflected the theological understandings and insights engendered in our native land. It was odd to discover that 'developing nations' such as Zimbabwe and Nicaragua had far more evidence of the products of their native composers and wordsmiths than Scotland had. Was it the case that having given the world the 1650 Psalter and, more recently having irrevocably allied Psalm 23 to the tune Crimond, we felt we had done our bit?

Two Supplementary Collections

I was asked around this time to join the Kirk's Panel on Worship. One of the first discussions to which I was party had to do with a possible replacement to or revision of the 1973 Hymnary. In due course, I prepared a discussion paper suggesting that the time was not right. What would be more appropriate would be the publication of a supplement comprising mainly material of the twentieth century, at least some of which would have proved its worth elsewhere.

In 1988 *Songs of God's People* appeared.[513] It was not, by any standards a radical publication. It included two notable exclusions from *CH3*: 'What a Friend we have in Jesus', and 'By Cool Siloam's Shady Rill'. It let Scottish congregations sings songs they already knew but did not have direct access to: 'Amazing Grace', 'How Great thou Art', 'Lord of the Dance'. It included then popular praise songs from Roman Catholic, Anglican and charismatic stables: 'Abba Father', 'How Lovely on the Mountains', 'Seek ye First', 'Shine, Jesus, Shine'. It had a number of chants from Taizé, and popular songs from South Africa such as 'Thuma Mina' and 'We Are Marching in the Light of God'. It had some songs from writers in the Iona Community and used some Scottish folk melodies. And it was vilified in a letter to the *Glasgow Herald* by leading church organists before its contents had ever been agreed on.

When I was asked to introduce the book to an organists' society, the president suggested in his opening comments that 'Once we have heard Mr Bell speak, we may either go out and buy the book and use it, or – as

---

513 Oxford: Oxford University Press, 1988.

one of our members has suggested – go out and buy the book and give it a ritual burning.' In the ensuing discussion, one 'prestigious' church musician vilified the book on the basis that it employed vulgar folk tunes. Ironically the protester was one of a significant number of like-minded critics, all of whom held a high respect for *The English Hymnal* whose musical editor was that well-known setter of sacred texts to folk tunes he had collected – Ralph Vaughan Williams.

The book sold almost a quarter of a million copies. However, its popularity does not endorse its having any great aesthetic or theological value. The truth is that it was a political publication. I felt convinced that Scotland should resist the seduction of books such as *Mission Praise* (originally produced for the 1984 Mission England campaign) which were primarily commercial publications with little or no cognizance of the peculiarity of Scotland's music or spirituality.

Ten years later, a volume of much better musical and poetic quality was produced, again as a supplement. This time, and perhaps uniquely in Europe, its provenance was ecumenical and the book was enabled and endorsed by the participation of representatives from the Church of Scotland, Roman Catholic Church, Episcopal Church, Salvation Army, Methodist Church, Congregational Church, United Free Church and with the (silent) encouragement of the Quakers. Given this constituency, its natural title was *Common Ground*.[514]

Larger in size than *Songs of God's People*, it was also wider in scope. It incorporated songs from throughout the world, and included many items from contemporary North American writers who had hitherto been overlooked by most British denominations with the exception of the Roman Catholic Church. It included both ancient Gaelic texts and tunes and contemporary offerings from Gaeldom in its Scottish and Irish constituencies. It included songs by Bernadette Farrell, Christopher Walker and other writers associated with the Thomas More Centre of the Roman Catholic Archdiocese of Westminster. There were also contributions from a number of Scottish writers and composers.

The significance of this publication is not so much in its sales. It did not equal *Songs of God's People,* partly because Scottish congregations were not used to having a new hymn supplement every ten years, and also because many congregations were holding out for a new hymnal altogether. Its significance is more in the proven worth of its diversity, the uniqueness of its ecumenical provenance and compilation, and the impact it had beyond Scotland and indeed, beyond the United Kingdom.

---

514 Edinburgh: St Andrew Press, 1998.

A Hymnal for the New Millennium

By 1998, when *Common Ground* was published, a committee was into its third year of work to produce a replacement for the 1973 *Church Hymnal Third Edition*. The proposal had been put to the General Assembly of the Church of Scotland in 1994 and approved. John Bell and Charles Robertson (then minister of the Canongate Kirk, Edinburgh) who had worked closely on the two previous volumes were appointed its Convener and Secretary.

Whereas other branches of the Reformed Church producing hymnals in the late twentieth century were having committees of around ten members with a consultant and secretarial assistance, what was to be called *CH4* was conceived and birthed by a group of 30, of whom perhaps two had a working knowledge of a hymnal other than that of their own denomination.

Like its predecessors, the hymnal came under the aegis of the Church Hymnary Trust and, accordingly, its constituent churches were represented on the committee. However, over the years first the Presbyterian Church in Ireland and, later, the Presbyterian Church in Wales withdrew their delegates, leaving membership solely in the hands of representatives of the Church of Scotland and the United Free Church of Scotland.

While the two supplements had been produced relatively quickly, a denominational hymnal, is an entirely different entity. It must, inter alia, bear witness to the tradition in which it stands, and therefore include material of proven worth from the past which still speaks to and for Christians today. It must reflect the peculiar gifts, affections and theological perspectives which the denomination holds dear. It has to take account of the diversity of peoples and places likely to use the book so that it is not merely a compilation of favoured hymns from urban churches with a good musical establishment. It must also attend to current changes in and challenges of contemporary society, particularly in the case of a national church which prides itself in serving the whole community.

The ground plan of production

Stage 1   Thoroughly peruse *RCH* and *CH3*, identifying what should be retained from both books and producing a list of items in *CH3* which were to be excluded for discussion of the churches. Similarly identify what in *Songs of God's People* and *Common Ground* had proven popular and helpful and was likely to have longevity of use.

Stage 2   Identify gaps in the current material being used and issues in Church and society which should find resonance in any new publication. With this in mind consider materials from other published sources and manuscripts which may be suitable in a new collection.

Stage 3   Have agreed materials scrutinized by parallel subgroups working on text and music with an editorial mandate.

Stage 4   Discern an appropriate ordering of the contents of the book, and arrange approved materials accordingly. Then consider whether the materials in each section show diversity in style, period and perspective and add to or subtract from accordingly.

Stage 5   Prepare copy for publishers and work on copyright information, indices, etc.

There were some other ground perspectives which emerged as the committee gelled:

1 The Psalms to be given a high profile.
2 Songs for children to be included on the basis that they could also be sung by adults and did not have a high happiness quotient as their sole effect.
3 No text to be included if it was so obscure that it would impede the integrity of worship.
4 No tune to be included which couldn't be sung *a cappella*.
5 No item to be included which was primarily for a gifted performer rather than the gathered congregation.
6 Authorship of all items to be undisclosed during selection procedure.
7 Work by consensus rather than by vote. (There were perhaps three votes in nine years.)

And, as time went on, some hitherto unarticulated desires gained common consensus:

8 The book should have an unashamedly Scottish feel to it.
9 The book should also link us to Christian communities in the developing world.
10 Strophic hymns could be supplemented by short repetitive songs and chants.

The people who committed themselves to this project were, despite their inexperience in matters of compiling a hymnal, a glorious diversity. Half were parish clergy drawn from rural and urban churches; three were prestigious choral directors, three were lecturers, a number had qualifications in music and/or were parish musicians. Most theological wings and musical stables were represented, and no one espoused that position of musical or liturgical elitism which presumes that all the best worship resources are at least a century old.

The exclusion list

The 1996 General Assemblies of the Church of Scotland and the United Free Church were presented, in the Revision Committee's Report, with a list of over 200 hymns and a similar number of tunes found in *CH3* but suggested for discontinuation. This was the result of careful scrutiny, a very positive exercise despite its intended negative result, for in the process committee members honed their understanding of what made for a good text and a good tune.

The exclusion list generated some initial waves of controversy fanned by sections of the UK press, but the consultation across the church which the exclusion list enabled was a good exercise. It enabled a sense of common ownership of the book, and generated continuing interest. The committee had agreed that if any item had ten or more letters speaking in its favour, it should be considered seriously. This, in the end, applied to only three items, principal among which was the hymn 'The Church's One Foundation'. The most persuasive argument came from a group of Aberdeen University divinity students who pointed out that it was the only hymn in *CH3* which stated a theology of the Church. So it was welcomed back, and a note taken to look for more texts with an ecclesiological emphasis.

In due course, another 100 or more items from CH3 were gradually removed as new or more convincing texts offered perspectives or language which superseded what had been sung before.

Selecting the new

With *CH4*, the landscape was very different to that for *CH3*. There were dozens of English-language hymnals which had been produced in the English-speaking world in the intervening years, hundreds of supplementary books, thousands of individual author's collections and tens of thousands of CDs promoting new material. The committee therefore must have been exposed to somewhere in the region of 4,000 different texts and tunes. The need was for material which would speak to and for worshippers today, and its provenance was secondary.

The Psalms

Until 1973, all congregations using the *Revised Church Hymnody* would have the complete 1929 revision of the 1650 Psalter at their disposal. The truth, of course, was that the number of psalm texts actually sung was considerably fewer than the 150 poems in the Bible.

The 1973 book had decided not to continue with the complete Psalter, but to take a selection of psalms and pepper them throughout the new hymn book. When this happened, around 60 different psalms were represented, some in more than one musical form and/or version of text.

The CH4 committee gradually discerned the merits of having the psalms put together as a corpus at the beginning of the new book. It was agreed that not all 150 would be represented, but that a wide spectrum in terms of emotion and content should be made available. It was further decided that while metrical versions would predominate, other forms of articulation such as responsorial should be considered. The result was a collection of 108 texts representing 78 different psalms with a diversity of musical settings. There are psalms set for antiphonal reading, as at a funeral when a small congregation may feel unwilling to sing. There is the magnificent chant for Psalm 150 by Charles Villiers Stanford. There is the tender Gaelic Lullaby *Taladh Chriosta*, set to Psalm 34, traditionally associated with St Columba.

Much of the major redrafting done by the text committee had to do with the psalms. Where the language of traditional metrical verse failed to communicate to younger generations as easily as it had to their grandparents, new or revised metricizations were substituted. But not all the ancient texts were revised. Indeed it was reckoned that some should be identified as 'icons' and rendered inviolable. So, we still can sing 'The Lord's my Shepherd' (Ps. 23), 'Now Israel May Say' (Ps. 124), 'Oh set ye open unto me' (Ps. 118) and several others, as our forebears have done for over three centuries.

The hymn texts

Charles Robertson, the secretary, was in charge of the text committee, which often met twice monthly and worked assiduously for three years in scrutinizing every jot and tittle which their precursors had approved. The twentieth century had already seen revision of some classic texts, either in the interest of gender inclusion or clarity of comprehension. Not all of these were happy. Some used language that was gender non-specific to the point where the whole text was neutralized; others so altered original and memorable words that the new product was more academic doggerel than language meant for singing.

One of the great plusses of the text committee was that it had some very experienced, strong-minded and articulate members, none of whom frequently agreed with the others. However, this ensured that the concerns of traditionalists, feminists, archaicists and modernizers all had to be offered sympathetic consideration.

Amendments in *CH4* to traditional texts are therefore more sensitive and sometimes more conservative than in other contemporary hymnals. It was agreed that where a text could be modified without prejudicing its poetic style or thought-flow too severely, the change should be made. But where an iconic text was going to be bowdlerized, it would be better either to leave it in its original and give people who find it objectionable the option not to use it; or to reconsider its inclusion in the book.

This seeming inconsistency, at the end of the day, won more friends than enemies. It allowed, for example, 'Courage, brother, do not stumble' to retain its opening line, but also allows in the last stanza for its transformation into 'Courage, sister ...' On the other hand, the revered favourite, 'Dear Lord and Father of Mankind' has its masculinity kept intact. But because the hymn was often being used at weddings on account of the tune, a new text, 'We come, dear Lord, to celebrate' allows the mellifluous 'Repton' to be sung to matrimonial rather than penitential verses.

Questions of language for God have never been addressed in Scotland with the strident protagonism and antagonism that have been present in some debates in the USA, where the last hymnal of the United Church of Christ bent over backwards to be non gender-specific regarding the Almighty. There was no clamour in any correspondence to omit the term 'Lord' or to avoid ever referring to God with a masculine pronoun, but throughout the book, there was a paring down of the prominence of gender-specific references where possible. This is complemented by the occasional song that alludes to alternative feminine images of God culled from the Scriptures. One such is a modern version of a text by Julian of Norwich:

> Mothering God, you gave me birth
> in the bright morning of this world.
> Creator, source of every breath,
> you are my rain, my wind, my sun;
> you are my rain, my wind, my sun.

The tunes

The convener, John Bell, was responsible for the tune committee, which, like its verbal counterpart, was proficient in debate, disagreement and, thankfully, discernment. For it, the main issues were appropriateness of the tune to articulate or complement the text – something which can make or break a hymn for a generation. There were also issues of pitch, given that for many people their vocal range is more limited than two generations ago, largely due to underuse of the singing voice. Decisions also had to be made about appropriate harmonization and accompaniment. While in the past, four-part harmony was the norm, tunes that come from other cultures may – as in the case of some Asian melodies – be quite unsuited to harmonized singing. But equally, some European tunes heavily harmonized in the past needed a reversal of the process in order to let them sparkle again.

Members of this group were also active in beginning to road-test materials and do pre-publication events throughout the country.

Children's materials

The committee was of a common mind that children's material was both important and a potential minefield. While many congregations may not have substantially changed their diet of hymnody in 30 years, almost every Sunday school and primary school will have dipped into a range of published material for children at assemblies or class worship.

A small group was detailed to look for texts which might endure and reflect issues of concern to children today. Consultations on children's concerns always reflected the significance of family break-up and the future of the planet, and pastoral realities which the more populist children's praise books seemed reluctant to address. The Scottish writer Stephen Fishbacher was an exception:

> When I'm feeling sad, I can call out to him.
> When I hurt inside, he feels every tear.
> When no one understands just what I'm thinking,
> *Jesus, he's always there,*
> *he's always there.*

The ordering

Every hymn book has to order its contents. *RCH* did it doctrinally, *CH3* did it liturgically. In the end for *CH4* a Trinitarian formula evolved. With the exception of the psalm section at the beginning, and small appendices at the end with short songs and liturgical responses, all the hymns and songs are gathered under the wings of the three persons of the Trinity. And because the Holy Spirit breathes life into the fledgling Church at Pentecost, the sacraments and seasons of life celebrated by the Church, appear in the third section.

The Short Songs section, which is the penultimate in the book was included because so many of these kept appearing. For some they seemed to risk on first hearing the possibility of 'vain repetition', but as people became aware that they were not substitutes for strophic hymns, but aids to developing new patterns of worship, they were warmly welcomed and accorded a place of their own. Some are useful as responses to prayer, some to enable movement in worship to happen, some to let words of Scripture permeate beyond our intellects.

Indexes and pre-publication

A huge debt is owed to the talents of Charles Robertson, the secretary of the committee. His prodigious appetite for detail and appropriateness is best recognized in the indexes at the end of the book. The categorization of hymns according to subject matter and the exhaustive list of scriptural references are his doing. They have won wide admiration and their useful-ness is fitting tribute to his labour. Similarly, the detail of copyright work was ably administered by Douglas Galbraith, then secretary to the Church of Scotland's Panel on Worship.

Significant Changes in CH4

Looking at the content of the book, it is evident that there has been a major shift in attitude towards congregational song in the last decades of the twentieth century. As work on the book proceeded and an awareness of the functions of hymnody were rehearsed within the revision commit-tee, the project evolved into something more radical than was first envis-aged. Of the 695 items in CH3, only 272 were transferred to the new book, a net loss of 400 items. Of the 527 tunes in CH3, only 230 made the journey into its twenty-first-century successor. Yet this happened without a murmur of complaint either in the church press or private correspond-ence. It suggests that for many people much of what the church had been singing was of little value or consequence. So, what may be seen as the hallmarks of the new book – a collection of 825 texts with 658 tunes?

A genuine Scottish character

In CH4, as distinct from any of its illustrious predecessors, there is clear indication that the book comes from and is primarily intended for Scot-land. That could never be due to the inclusion of a rich treasury of trad-itional Scottish hymns since there are precious few to draw on. (Of around 83 veteran Scottish texts, 42 of these come from the 1929 version of the metrical Psalter, and 21 are traditional paraphrases from the 1781 collec-tion commissioned and approved by the Church of Scotland.)

It is more the new material which is indicative of the Scottish provenance of the book. Over 100 texts in the hymnal originate from Scottish authors. A few are the metrical psalm revisions made by the text committee, but the vast majority were written by individuals, several of whom had never had texts published before. Yet each text was chosen through the rigorous and anonymous vetting process.

It would be difficult to draw up a comparative list for *CH3*. That book with 695 hymns and 530 tunes had very few original contemporary Scottish contributions. An equally stark comparison can be made with regard to native Scottish melodies. *CH3* admitted to two identifiable Gaelic folk tunes: 'Bunessan' and the unattributed 'Gaelic Melody'. Actually, there was another – 'Bonnie George Campbell', but in the interests of public decency this was rechristened 'Blessing and Honour'. By curious contrast, this paucity of Scottish folk tunes in a book which would be primarily used in Scotland was set alongside the inclusion of 4 Welsh, 15 Irish and 29 English folk tunes.

CH4 has the following Scottish folk tunes accompanying sung texts:

Ae Fond Kiss	Iona Boat Song	Solas An T'saoghail
Athchuinge	Kelvingrove	Stu Mo Run
Azair	Leaving of Lismore	Taladh Criosta
Balualow	Lewis Folk Melody	The Banks o' Doon
Bonnie Geo.	MacPherson's Rant	The Flower o' the
Campbell	Mary Morrison	Quern
Bunessan	Pulling Bracken	The Isle of Mull
Dream Angus	Reres Hill	Road and the Miles
Eriskay Love Lilt	Resignation	to Dundee
Gaelic Lullaby	Rodail	The Rowan Tree
Galloway Tam	Skye Boat Song	Tramps and Hawkers

With these tunes, Scottish hymnody aligns itself with the rest of the world, for truly there can not be a nation under the sun whose churches have so forsaken its indigenous melody – and this despite the fact that musicians from Haydn through Webern and Bruch to Kodaly and Vaughan Williams have prized Scotland's tunes and harmonized or arranged them in choral, chamber and orchestral works.

An international perspective

It is hard to know whether the increase in indigenous material reflects a heightened national consciousness within Scotland. What is less of a mystery is a growing consensus of the importance of having hymnody that represents the global Church rather than its Anglo-European axis. British churches have, by and large, seldom looked outside the local continent for liturgical resources. North American hymnody did not begin and end with 'What a Friend We Have in Jesus'. The late nineteenth and late twentieth centuries saw a tremendous output of writing, very little of which was taken up by British churches. In *CH4*, there are around 70 twentieth-century texts and as many tunes which come from the USA and Canada and have been warmly welcomed here, as was evident in the popularity of such items featured in *Common Ground*.

But more particularly, many people including Presbyterians, apprehensive of syncopation and inflexible hips, have experienced a rare joy in singing songs like 'Siyahamba' ('We are Marching in the Light of God') from South Africa. This is one of a number of songs from developing nations, which the Iona Community's Wild Goose Group began to introduce to Scottish churches in the 1980s. With an increasing awareness of the interconnectedness of the world, the campaigns for international debt relief from the most impoverished nations, and the visible presence of asylum seekers in Scottish towns and cities, there has been a new openness to owning our identity as catholic or universal Christians. And the attractiveness of many songs, particularly from African and Central/Southern American cultures has quickly endeared them to Scottish congregations.

It was therefore interesting to hear of one Glasgow congregation where people were looking forward to *CH4* because it would enable the people to sing songs which would be known to new members who had recently come from southern Africa.

A tenth of the items (84) come from Asia-Pacific, Africa or Central/South America and the Caribbean. Thus Scottish congregations are able to sing songs from their sister churches in nations as diverse as Peru, China, Romania, the Democratic Republic of Congo, Nicaragua, Korea, New Zealand, Zimbabwe, Guatemala, Tanzania and South Africa.

By contrast Professor John Barclay in *The Handbook to the Church Hymnary Third Edition*[515] commented: 'The new (1973) book has been enriched by the introduction of hymns from India (1), China (1), Ceylon (1), Africa (1) and elsewhere.'

Explicit incarnational theology

There are three major icons which feature in the majority of religious songs about Jesus – the silent baby, the dying saviour and the enthroned redeemer – all tending towards passivity. *CH4* saw a careful reassessment of the songs specific to Jesus. Not just the songs of devotion, but the songs that spoke of Christ's life and ministry were included, songs almost totally overlooked in contemporary praise collections.

---

515 Oxford: Oxford University Press, 1979.

Advent – a season only recently celebrated in Scottish Presbyterian circles – has 20 hymns to enable the season of preparation for Jesus' birth to have its own musical integrity. The public ministry of Jesus moves up from a handful of songs to having 30 texts, which reflect on the words and activity of Jesus, allowing for the incarnation to be recognized as the constant gift of God throughout Jesus' ministry rather than a momentary happening in a Bethlehem stable.

Closely allied to the songs that speak of Jesus are songs of devotion and discipleship, which allow people to commit themselves to him and to declare their affection for him. In the 1973 book, the section on personal spirituality seemed to be hidden through embarrassment in the back of the book. That may have been the perceived role for private devotions in the 1970s, but the increased interest in spirituality per se has required that this activity enjoy a higher profile, and *CH4* attempts to enable that by allying songs that speak of what we want to say to Jesus with songs that indicate what we also want to do for and with Jesus.

But is it a Contemporary Book?

To some extent being 'contemporary' is not its primary purpose. The book is not a twenty-first century supplement, but a twenty-first century hymnal, and therefore it must contain material from previous ages which had a proven worth for people living in this age.

Close on two-thirds of both texts and tunes come from the twentieth century with, as stated above, a substantial number coming from authors and composers alive at the time of publication. What they represent is the diversity of the output of today's writers. The word 'contemporary' cannot – as is sometimes the case – be solely applied to material from the 'Praise and Worship Song' stable.

All of these may be said to be contemporary hymn styles:

Praise and worship	represented by Graham Kendrick, Willow Creek, etc.
Taizé chants	repetitive songs for meditation
Global songs	most of which have emerged since the 1980s
Post Vatican II responsorials	of which Bernadette Farrell and Marty Haugen are exponents
'Celtic' songs	a term which often pertains to songs of personal spirituality
Wild Goose songs	a diverse range of material from Bell & Maule
Folk and protest	the successors to Sydney Carter

And all of these are deliberately present in the book, for the simple reason that no one new style either represents all contemporary writing, nor does any one style appeal to every worshipper.

The purpose of *CH4* is to allow the diversity of people within the churches for which it was produced to see the rich seams of Christian hymnody available from past and present sources.

The World Outside *CH4*

The great mistake about spending so much time on one book, albeit a significant benchmark publication, is that it detracts from what is happening elsewhere in church music.

While Scotland has only two full-time paid church musicians and while there has been a discernible decline in the number of trained organists and voluntary choir members, the fringes have compensated where the centre has fallen apart.

From the Street Level festivals in Dundee in the 1980s to the present Church without Walls events, there has been a showcasing of new Christian bands and their music. For almost 15 years the Late Late Service in Glasgow produced material of depth and sophistication for a largely gathered young adult evening congregation, while the Wild Goose Worship Group developed less technologically sophisticated experiences of corporate worship at monthly events in Glasgow called Last Night Out, recently superseded by Holy City.

James MacMillan, Scotland's greatest composer in 400 years, has combined excellence in sophisticated choral writing (as indicated by works such as *Seven Last Words From The Cross*) with a compassionate engagement in local church music. He is presently musician at St Columba of Iona RC parish in Glasgow where on an almost monthly basis a choir from Strathclyde University performs one of his recently written church motets. Each Sunday he leads the music, he arrives with a new responsorial written not many hours before the 11 a.m. Mass. (MacMillan's *St Anne* settting of the eucharistic texts, originally written for a school in his home diocese, is included in *CH4*.)

In Edinburgh, the Episcopal priest Steve Butler, has developed a highly participative style of congregational singing at St James' Leith. Attending that congregation is the triumvirate responsible for Fischy Music. This is a collective begun by Stephen Fishbacher to take music into schools throughout Great Britain.

The Royal School of Church Music too has seen a revival in interest. A regional organizer with Scottish responsibilities has been appointed and a number of new projects initiated.

As regards the future, no crystal balls are available. For music to improve throughout Scottish churches, it certainly will have to be afforded a higher priority. A new book can do so much, and the prophetic enterprises on the fringe may model new possibilities, but the full, conscious and active participation of congregations in the song of the Church can only happen where there is a centrally held conviction that more than historic buildings, more than the Presbyterian form of church government, more than the local church website, worship matters supremely.

CONCLUSION

Emerging Contexts for Christian Worship

Doug Gay

The essays in this volume have offered an eclectic mix of perspectives on Christian worship in a Scottish context, but we believe it is a healthy eclecticism, which reflects a living tradition of reflection, active across denominational boundaries and operative at a range of levels and intensities in both the churches and the academy. In this concluding chapter I aim to draw together some common themes, reflect on some notable absences and comment on some emerging trends.

Is the Reformation Over?

In the title of their 2005 volume, Mark Noll and Carolyn Nystrom asked *Is The Reformation Over?*[516] prompting one reviewer to write that even if they did not fully answer their own question, they made the case that the question's time had come.[517] It is a particularly poignant question to pose within Scotland and I can imagine it attracting a range of responses from those who have written in this volume.

Certainly, in a book published in the quincentenary of Calvin's birth, it is clear that we in Scotland are still pondering the legacy of the sixteenth-century Protestant Reformation. The thoroughgoing nature of Scotland's Calvinist reformation continues to mark the contemporary ecclesiastical landscape and to shape patterns of liturgical practice within Christian communities today. The Reformation was as radical in what it gave as in what it took away and both its additions and its excisions are still being debated and evaluated in the postmodern contexts of the twenty-first century. A number of waves of reception and revision have been discussed in preceding chapters and the contributions of Forrester, Yates, Macleod,

---

516 Mark Noll and Carolyn Nystrom, *Is the Reformation Over?*, Grand Rapids: Baker Academic, 2005.

517 Staff Review in *Publisher's Weekly*, January 2005.

Dawson and Brown are an eloquent testimony to the continuing crucial role of Church history in debunking myths, unsettling prevailing narratives and provoking fresh reflection on how in Lewis Namier's well-turned phrase, we all tend to 'imagine the past and remember the future'.

In fact, it is clear that contested accounts of the uses of history in narrating a 'Scottish context' relate also to pre-Reformation Church history. A number of contributors have reflected on this process in relation to the current high tide of interest in 'Celtic spirituality', an interest which has had both a direct and an indirect influence on the revision of liturgical texts. Here is an area where popular enthusiasm for 'Celtic liturgies'[518] has run ahead of academic consensus about their historical grounding. Donald Macleod's reflection offers some welcome and sobering insights here, but also interestingly raises the question of how far the recent fondness for Celtic/modern oppositions can be transposed rather directly into perceptions about Roman Catholic/Protestant oppositions? Our aim here, however, should not be simply to default to a prudish historical debunking mode. The more interesting practical theological questions need to be asked about why this accent within contemporary liturgical theology has proved so popular and currently attracts such an enthusiastic and devoted following in a wide range of international contexts, from the Nordic countries, through England, to North America.

Returning to the Reformation, the seventeenth-century mutations of the Reformation in Scotland are also of deep and continuing interest to attempts to understand liturgical currents in the present day. Bryan Spinks has written perceptively about 'The Origins of the Antipathy to Set Liturgical Forms in the English-Speaking Reformed Tradition',[519] and his observations are helpful in reading the processes of liturgical 'reduction' or 'deflation', which are crystallized in the seventeenth-century Westminster documents and exemplified in the debates around their production. These developments and their ongoing influence upon eighteenth-century Presbyterian practice within Scotland have too often been read with relentless disdain by liturgical scholars whose own preference for 'high' tradition has led them to name this era as a 'dark age' of liturgical 'decadence'.[520] The perspective of practical theology will want to show a greater interest in understanding the effects, both positive and negative, of such 'antipathy to set forms'. It will be alert to the ways in which such antipathy and the preference for the immediate and extempore which corresponds to it, have gained huge currency among Pentecostals and other low-church Protest-

---

518 See, among others, the numerous best-selling works by David Adam and Philip Newell.

519 See his chapter by that title in Lukas Vischer ed., *Christian Worship in Reformed Churches Past and Present*, Grand Rapids: Eerdmans, 2003.

520 So Millar Patrick and Charles McCrie respectively.

ants within the last century, so that today they represent key tenets of the operative liturgical theologies in many of the fastest growing sectors of the global Christian community.

Just as such a 'long' perspective on liturgical *reduction* can be fruitful in understanding current shapes of worship practice within congregations influenced by evangelical and charismatic traditions, so there is much to gain from taking a longer view of the liturgical *retrieval* that is equally noticeable within contemporary Protestant traditions. Stewart J. Brown's account of the Scoto-Catholic movement within the Church of Scotland demonstrates how, reflecting the diffuse influence of the Romantic movement and the practical exposure of certain classes of Scots to the settings and habits of Episcopalian worship, Presbyterian Scotland developed its own stream of the broader 'liturgical movement' during the Victorian era. This led to a revolution in worship practice, beginning with the return of hymn singing and musical accompaniment, which established the pipe organ as both a vast immovable presence within church architecture and a hegemonic musical standard within church song. Here too we find the roots of a retreat from the antipathy to 'set forms' and a long, slow pilgrimage back to embracing a more 'catholic' vision of how practice could be enriched by the structuring elements of the Christian year; by the distribution of liturgical voice between minister and congregation afforded by written and responsive prayer; and by a positive appreciation of the functions of ritual, symbolic action and the presence of visual symbols within worship. As we reflect on almost two centuries of the liturgical movement, this long trajectory of retrieval continues to mark the development of Protestant worship practice, bearing witness also to a century of increasing self-understanding, particularly within the main-line denominations, of their standing within a long-term ecumenical movement. Tracing the historical process here is also significant in relation to engaging contemporary debates and discussions about 'emerging church', a subject I will return to later.

Protestants and Catholics

Attention to historical context within Scotland also demands an ongoing drive to read the relationship between a dominant Protestant tradition and a Roman Catholic community, whose visibility and influence was dramatically re-established within the context of the changing socio-economic context of the nineteenth century. Large-scale immigration, overwhelmingly from Ireland, reshaped Scotland's oppressed and restricted Roman Catholic minority and led to a rapid expansion of Roman Catholic presence within lowland Scotland from the mid nineteenth century. While

Roman Catholics built churches to accommodate the needs of expanding congregations, Presbyterians in the Victorian era were also caught up in a fever of church building, fuelled by the competitive energies unleashed by the Disruption and funded by the commercial dividends of the British Empire. Many of these buildings were never to be filled and the ratio of buildings to worshippers was to become a costly and uncomfortable legacy for the Church of Scotland in the era of rapid numerical decline which began in the early 1960s and continues unabated to the present day.

The rise of the modern Roman Catholic community in Scotland was characterized in a 1998 volume as a movement 'Out of the Ghetto',[521] and the 1982 papal Mass in Bellahouston Park, Glasgow was a key symbolic exodus of Roman Catholic worship into Scotland's public spaces. With numbers regularly attending Mass in Scotland now, at least by some estimates, outnumbering those who regularly worship in Protestant churches, the context for worship in Scotland and its denominational centre of gravity has shifted radically away from the Protestant, Presbyterian hegemony of previous centuries. Owen Dudley Edwards and Michael Regan both make reference in their contributions to the way in which the Scottish hierarchy were relatively slow in recognizing the project of Vatican II and made a rather minor and conservative contribution to its deliberations. In his foreword to the *Scots People's Mass Book*, published in 1968, the then Archbishop Gordon Gray, begins his commendation of the book to Scotland's Roman Catholic worshippers with the observation that 'The day of the silent mass is now virtually over'.[522] Since the landmark publication of those first revised texts, there has indeed been a revolution in the full, conscious and active participation of the faithful called for by Vatican II. While clearly of momentous significance for Roman Catholic worshippers, the seismic changes of the Second Vatican Council have arguably been equally momentous in altering the perception of Roman Catholic worship among many Protestant observers. The shift to the vernacular liturgy, coupled with the long slow tide of liturgical reform within main-line denominations has contributed to a gradual evolution of understanding on both sides that their liturgies as well as their catechisms and creeds, share much in common. Increasing numbers of Church of Scotland worshippers using their new *Church Hymnary* 4 (whose production is detailed by John Bell in this volume) find themselves singing responses written for settings of the Mass by the leading Scots composer and lay Dominican,

---

521 Raymond Boyle and Peter Lynch, eds, *Out of the Ghetto*, Edinburgh: John Donald, 1998.

522 Gordon Gray, 'Foreword', *The Scots People's Mass Book*, London: Geoffrey Chapman, 1968.

James MacMillan.[523] The way towards this was prepared for them by the inclusion of those same liturgical items within the relevant service texts in the Church of Scotland's 1994 *Book of Common Order*.[524] In today's Scotland, when Presbyterians, Episcopalians and Roman Catholics 'visit' each other's services (whether during ecumenical events or in the course of rites of passage such as baptisms, weddings and funerals, where they attend as friends, relatives and neighbours) increasingly, they recognize many common elements within one another's liturgies, something which still seems to come with a degree of surprise. It is crucial to understand that just as there is now a generation of post Vatican II Roman Catholics in Scotland, there is also alongside them a generation of post Vatican II Protestants, who do not perceive contemporary Roman Catholic worship with the same degree of hostility and suspicion with which their parents and grandparents may have regarded the Latin Mass. It is not just Roman Catholics in Scotland who can be said to have emerged from a ghetto; Protestant culture had its own ghetto of triumphalism and suspicion to leave behind.

For all that, it would be foolish I think to suggest that the Reformation is over within Scotland. Significant differences of belief, style and understanding remain at both official and popular levels. But even here, the question asked by Noll and Nystrom may be one whose time has come, even if the answer cannot be wholly in the affirmative.

Charismatic Renewal?

One area of worship which has not been much addressed in the previous chapters, concerns the reception of the charismatic renewal in Scotland. There has been very little academic reflection on this topic, an omission which hinders our understanding of Scottish church life since the 1960s. I cannot hope to remedy that here, but it is appropriate to draw attention to some key themes and issues.

Since the charismatic renewal tended in the main to find its entry point through churches which stood in the 'evangelical' tradition, the nature of evangelicalism in Scotland and in particular, within the Church of Scotland as the largest single denomination, has some bearing on its reception. In his distinctive and groundbreaking 2005 study *Selling Worship*,[525] Pete

---

523 There is some evidence also of traffic in the opposite direction, with the music of the Iona Community, above all John Bell, gaining increasing currency within Roman Catholic worship in contemporary Scotland.

524 They had of course also been present in Communion Orders in the 1940 and 1979 books, but the 1994 book has been more widely followed in this respect than earlier versions.

525 Pete Ward, *Selling Worship*, Milton Keynes: Paternoster, 2005.

Ward sets out 'five distinctively British factors [which] came together to bring about the [post-war] evangelical resurgence in England'.[526] Ward then lists the public school 'Bash' camps; the student ministries of IVF/IVP; the children's and youth ministries of Crusaders, Pathfinders and CYFA; the growing influence of Brethren and Pentecostal churches; and finally the ministry of John Stott at All Souls Langham Place, Church of England. A parallel list for Scotland would look rather different. The influence of 'Border & Highland' camps in the private school sector was much less pronounced, although the broader Scripture Union movement of camps and school meetings was influential and groups like Crusaders had some impact. Within the Church of Scotland, the influence of the charismatic renewal did not 'take' to the same degree and leadership of the evangelical wing was taken in a different and liturgically more conservative direction by William Still of Gilcomston South Church in Aberdeen, along with other influential figures such as James and George Philip and Eric Alexander.[527] Their overwhelming emphasis was on the renewal of consecutive expository preaching[528] within a culture of traditional hymnody and minister-led extempore prayer. Liturgically this was equally hostile to the use of set forms of prayer and to the introduction of the choruses and worship songs of the charismatic renewal.[529] While their influence worked against the mainstream of evangelicalism within the Kirk being influenced by the charismatic renewal to the extent it was within the Church of England, there were others within the evangelical sector, who were more open to these influences and less persuaded by the liturgical and cultural conservatism of the 'Stillite' circle. Where their experience aligns with Ward's analysis of the English context is in the way that the main conduits for the music and theology of the charismatic renewal were evangelical youth and student organizations. Interestingly, the 'Cathedral of the Isles' in Millport on the isle of Cumbrae was home from 1975 to 1985 to members of the Community of Celebration, whose music, including that of their own 'Fisherfolk' group, shaped the influen-

---

526 It is not entirely clear why Ward mixes British and England here, although it is a common sin among English academics to be unclear how to distinguish between them!

527 This group was focused around regular gatherings of the Crieff fellowship, irreverently known to outsiders as 'the magic circle', whose style and emphases shaped the practice and ethos of a large proportion of evangelical ministers within the Church of Scotland from the 1960s to the present day.

528 A style of preaching that worked consecutively through whole books of the Bible, from start to finish, eschewing the selectivity of lectionaries and often using only one reading in each service, whether from the Old or New Testament. The passage taken up in each sermon would then also usually be worked through more or less serially, with running commentary and application woven into the sermon.

529 The group's conservatism was also marked by a lack of creativity and productivity in producing any new hymns or worship songs, so that their repertoire remained resolutely thirled to the products of previous eras.

tial renewal 'hymnals' *Sound of Living Waters* (1974) and *Fresh Sounds* (1977). Their influence was felt within a restricted network of churches, across a range of denominations, who were also linked in to the developing contemporary Christian music scene in the 1970s and 1980s. An important factor in the subsequent spread of the influence of the charismatic movement has been the role of festivals and large assemblies from Spring Harvest (whose Scottish incarnation met in Ayr from 1989) through to events such as Clan Gathering in recent years. These kinds of gatherings, along with the various tours undertaken by well-known 'worship leaders' provided key opportunities in supportive locations, for the dissemination of new songs and the acquisition of new styles, which could be taken back and introduced into local settings by those who attended.[530]

An important distinction should be registered here. The music of the charismatic renewal extended its reach and influence very widely across Scotland's churches. A thoroughgoing neo-Pentecostal/charismatic approach to the whole of worship involved incorporating exercise of the *charismata* of tongue speaking and prophecy and the introduction of 'ministry times' with prayer for healing and personal anointing. This was embraced by only a small minority of churches within Scotland as a new standard for congregational worship. However, it is certainly the case that by the 1980s, beyond the most conservative evangelical churches and the highest of 'Scoto-Catholic' churches, a wide range of congregations, across most denominations[531] were making selective use of the best known songs of Karen Lafferty, Graham Kendrick, Noel Richards and others. This pattern has continued, even as the number of churches has steadily increased, representing both independent evangelical congregations and a minority from the mainstream denominations, which embrace the more thoroughgoing 'praise and worship time' format as their main liturgical pattern. The more typical pattern remains a 'blended' worship culture, within which congregations will incorporate both traditional hymnody and newer 'praise and worship music' ranging from the early vintages of the 1960s and 1970s, through the *Songs of Fellowship* and *Jesus March* songs of the 1980s, to the *Soul Survivor* repertoire of the 1990s and the more recent influences from Matt Redman and Hillsong among others.

Such a brief survey cannot do justice to what is a complex and rather

---

530 A similar process could surely be observed within Scotland in respect of the earlier examples of Wesley in the eighteenth century, Moody and Sankey in the nineteenth century and the Billy Graham Crusades in the mid twentieth century.

531 This would also include pockets of the Roman Catholic Church, which from the 1960s had been influenced both by the charismatic renewal and by the broader cultural trend towards 'folk masses'. These pockets have continued to play a minority role within Scottish Roman Catholic worship and have increasingly aligned their repertoire with the broader contemporary 'praise and worship' movement.

'viral' movement of influences over the past four or five decades, however, Ward's work demonstrates the importance of giving serious attention to this field. It is one of the continuing weaknesses of much liturgical scholarship that it remains heavily biased towards the study of official and authorized liturgical 'texts' within main-line denominations at the expense of reflection on the explosion of new and diverse expressions of worship in local settings. Here the concerns of practical theology in respect of worship must be to reflect theologically on the full range of what congregations are doing and how and why they are doing it. This will involve deploying a broader range of methods and considering a wider range of sources than has been the norm for liturgical scholars. However, such reflective studies of the diversity of contemporary practice will be enriched by approaches which can make connections and comparisons with the longer-term liturgical memory carried by church history.[532]

Emerging Trends?

A further reason for insisting on the importance of studying the practice of independent evangelical and charismatic (neo)Pentecostal congregations is that predictions about the future shape of global Christianity and Christianity within Scotland point to a situation in which there is a continuing rise in both absolute numbers of these congregations and, linked to the continuing patterns of decline in main-line denominations, a significant rise in the proportion of the total numbers of congregations which they represent.[533]

A wide-angle look across the landscape of contemporary worship practice in Scotland will therefore register the continuing vitality and influence of charismatic evangelicalism. Despite the earlier comments about the limitations of the conservative evangelical tradition, it must also be recognized as a section of the churches, which will have significant continuing influence into the future. In particular, its stress on consecutive expository preaching continues to be pursued across a large number of congregations within the Church of Scotland and Free Church of Scotland in a way that

---

532 The textual bias of liturgical scholars has also meant that the worship traditions of 'low church' groups antipathetic towards set forms in earlier centuries have too often been given scant attention and have not been regarded as central to the discipline of studying worship and liturgy. Spinks's work cited earlier and that of Alan Sell in the same volume are important steps in this direction as is Christopher J. Ellis's volume *Gathering: A Theology and Spirituality of Worship in Free Church Tradition*, London: SCM Press, 2004.

533 See Peter Brierley, ed., *Turning The Tide: Report of the Scottish Church Census 2002*, London: Christian Research, 2003 and the ongoing series Religious Trends, esp. volumes 4 and 5, also published by Christian Research and edited by Brierley; see also ch 5 in Linda Woodhead and Paul Heelas, 2004, *The Spiritual Revolution*, Oxford: Blackwell, 2004.

is deeply valued by worshippers. In an era when homiletics scholarship has reached a very low ebb within the academy in Scotland and the UK generally, this tradition continues to prioritize the preaching task and to insist on its paramount importance within worship. In a book of essays presented to James Philip in 2002 – significantly entitled *Serving the Word of God*,[534] Ian Hamilton coined the phrase 'blood earnest experimental preaching' to describe this approach. Given the lack of sympathy with which this group's worship practice is often viewed by outsiders, Hamilton's phrase captures something of the emotional and rhetorical intensity which characterizes what insiders continue to find a compelling and transformative liturgical pattern.

In sharp contrast, our wider look will also be struck by the continuing power and influence of the 'Iona' tradition, whose global reach has been discussed here by former leader of the Iona Community Norman Shanks and also by John Bell's reflection on various contexts for his own practice.

Despite its considerable international reputation and reach, John Bell's work is not always sufficiently recognized and appreciated in his native Scotland. The concerns and emphases of the Iona Community have always had their detractors at home and the reception of Bell's work has sometimes been affected by this. However, with around three decades of prolific hymn writing to his name and the composition and creation of numerous liturgies and liturgical items over this same period, it is clear that John Bell's contribution to the worship vocabulary of the contemporary Church is almost unparalleled. Between them, the voices of first George MacLeod and then Bell have given the Iona Community a distinctive poetic theological and liturgical accent for over six decades. In addition to the hundreds of songs and hymns that Bell has composed and the many more he has collected and arranged, the slender volume known self-deprecatingly as the *Wee Worship Book*, which owes much to Bell's hand, has been a notable exemplar for the crafting of new liturgy in English since its first appearance in 1988.

Bell's work combines a number of significant features, which lend it a particular power and efficacy and have commended it so widely to an international ecumenical following. It is rooted in catholic tradition, consistently Trinitarian in its structure and striking in its capacity to hit both high and low notes in its Christology. It has a strong and pervasive pneumatological accent and is often marked by an unforced yet urgent sense of invocation of the Holy Spirit. Together with its willingness to deploy a warm and direct language of devotion and personal–communal

---

534 David Wright and David Stay, eds, *Serving the Word of God*, Fearn, Ross-shire: Mentor, 2002.

address to God, these features give Bell's work a sense of 'live' relational approach and engagement, which can be both owned by worshippers from evangelical and charismatic backgrounds and also recovered by worshippers from more liberal traditions, who were arguably in some danger of losing this dimension from their own spirituality. The capacity to offer this to such different constituencies, who often lack an appreciation of one another's preferred liturgical accents, is a major and uncommon achievement.[535] Yet Bell's language is also consistently risky and challenging and it unapologetically reflects a politicized theology with deep concerns for human liberation and ecological stewardship. While occasionally verbose and contrived, it is more often powerfully restrained and crafted in such a way as to serve the ends of liturgy rather than revel in its own virtuosity. It is this combination of fresh forms of expression with a clear understanding of classic liturgical structure which at its best works to create a classic ecumenical fusion of the reformed desire to speak a new word with the catholic concern to hold an old shape.

Bell's agenda has also been consistently directed at the ending of choral and clerical monopolies and giving new opportunities for the voices of 'lay' people to sound out within worship, whether through a reinvigorated congregational song or through a multi-vocal leadership of common worship. Although he is known through radio, television and festival/conference work as a gifted preacher, he is continually attentive to the value of creating spaces within liturgy for silent prayer and reflection and for congregational dialogue and discussion within small groups.

Finally, despite his own prodigious gifting, he is also a prodigious collaborator, who works alongside others and seeks to let their voices and insights discipline his own. Conscious of the limitations of male perspectives, he works to allow the voices and experience of women to expand his own understanding. Conscious of the limitations of white, Western and European perspectives, he has been attentive to the voices of non-Western theologians, biblical scholars, liturgists and composers and has made the quest for a postcolonial hymnody and liturgics central to his own work over three decades. His international ministry has carried his own influence widely, but has also enabled him to continually bring back to Scotland a vibrant range of resources from the world Church which have added colour and depth to the repertoire of worshippers here.

Such a paean of appreciation will no doubt embarrass Bell, but the role of practical theology in reflecting on Christian practice from within the church must surely involve a willingness to recognize good practice where it is found. Bell's work and that of the wider Iona tradition is likely to continue to grow in influence within the Scottish context alongside

---

535 The work of English liturgist Janet Morley could be seen to possess similar qualities.

that of the charismatic and conservative evangelical traditions already discussed.

Emerging Church

While these very different streams within Scottish Protestantism may seem to have little in common, there is a case for involving them all in the maternity and paternity of the hybrid phenomena being considered within twenty-first century Scotland under the term 'emerging Church'. Although it can be rightly accused of being both an elusive and an over-hyped term, 'emerging Church' is a descriptor which is fixing itself in both academic and denominational lexicons as a way to map a range of developments within contemporary worship.[536] In the UK, it was preceded by what became known from the late 1980s onwards as the 'alternative worship' movement.[537] The early paradigm here came from Sheffield's Nine O'Clock Service, based in an Anglican church in the north of England which evolved a highly visual, 'post-charismatic' worship style incorporating aspects of club culture and dance music. From 1990 to 2000, the Glasgow-based Late Late Service offered an influential example of this approach within Scotland.

The origins of alternative worship and what became known in North America from 2000 onwards as 'emerging Church' lie within low church Protestantism and in particular within the charismatic evangelical world. In terms of worship, the crucial distinctives of these projects lay in their desire to move beyond the modernist and modernizing approach of the charismatic renewal, with its performance-oriented culture of worship bands and its disdain for 'set forms'. Often self-consciously identifying as 'postmodern' in their approach, practitioners were marked by a positive attitude towards liturgical tradition, with the Taizé and Iona communities acting as crucial 'portals' into catholic tradition for those raised or formed within the mores of low church worship. Fuelled by a theological, cultural and aesthetic dissatisfaction with the deficits of their own worshipping traditions, the alt./emerging pioneers were committed to a *ressourcement*[538] of their practice, which led them to explore set forms, symbolism and iconography and the possibilities of ritual practice. Groups were variously animated by both instincts for spiritual survival, perceiving this 'depth' dimension of tradition as enabling them to achieve a new authenticity

---

536 See Ryan Gibbs and Eddie Bolger's study *Emerging Churches*, London: SPCK, 2006.

537 See the introduction to Jonny Baker, Doug Gay & Jenny Brown's volume *Alternative Worship*, London: SPCK, 2003 (Grand Rapids MI: Baker Publishing, 2004).

538 The metaphors of 're-sourcing' alongwith *aggiornamento*/supplementing mentioned below, were key metaphors of the Vatican II process in the 1960s.

in their own practice; and by more missional instincts, believing that the transmission of the gospel in the highly media-saturated contexts of their own generation required fresh examples of how to inculturate Christian spirituality. This was both more and less than a veneration of catholic tradition, since the appropriation of tradition was highly selective and it was undertaken in sync with a distinctive *aggiornamento*, which was committed to supplementing ancient practices with new technologies and new, postmodern and postcolonial theological understandings. The intention and result, was a new hybrid worship practice, a *remixing* of liturgical patterns. For those involved, their charismatic-evangelical DNA had bequeathed them a confidence about establishing new initiatives, planting new congregations and disseminating their insights and resources. I suggest that one way to read the still unfolding journey of the 'emerging churches' is to see them as a new wave of grassroots ecumenism, which is both missional and politicized, enacted primarily by low church Protestants who have little experience of or enthusiasm for official ecumenical channels or protocols.

In England, emerging themes have been 'hugged close' to the bosom of the Anglican and Methodist establishment through the 'Fresh Expressions' movement and given a theological integration into the frameworks of 'Mission-Shaped Church'[539] and what Rowan Williams has termed 'mixed-economy' church. The Church of Scotland has been slower to embrace the same themes, but its own Church Without Walls process has moved in a similar direction and in 2008, the General Assembly established an Emerging Ministries fund to support new initiatives, which were 'missional, ecclesial and experimental'.

It is too early to say whether the term 'emerging' will make an enduring contribution to discussions of worship and ecclesiology in Scotland. What seems more certain is that four key trends will be crucial in shaping future practice. First, at least for the next decade or so, continuing *decline* in attendance within the main-line denominations seems to be highly likely, given the existing demographics and the time it would take for even reasonably effective new initiatives (short of overnight mass revival) to have a broad impact. Associated with this will be a shortage of full-time stipendiary clergy, serious in the Protestant denominations and acute within the Roman Catholic Church. In addition, predictions are that the rebalancing of Protestant and Roman Catholic Scotland in terms of regular church attendance (which has been the major structural story of the twentieth century) will be offset in coming decades by the rise of evangelical congre-

---

539 Graham Cray, ed., *Mission-Shaped Church*, London: Church House Publishing, 2004, is an influential Church of England report, which has been a catalyst for Fresh Expressions and emerging Church initiatives in the years following.

gations, many within the independent sector. Taken together, this major trend of decline and minor trend of growth have changed and will continue to change the identity of the Church in Scotland.

Second, despite the major logjams that have led to official ecumenism going quiet in recent years,[540] at the level of worship practice a long-term process of ecumenical convergence is evident across Scotland's major worshipping traditions. One current sign of this within the Church of Scotland is a steady move towards more frequent Communion, which seems very likely to both continue and accelerate in the second decade of the twenty-first century, moving this church by 2020 to a situation where the typical Sunday morning service in a majority of congregations will include the Lord's Supper. This is a prospect which we can speculate would have gladdened the hearts of both Calvin and Knox, but which will have been unprecedented in the past 450 years of the Kirk's history.

By contrast, a third perceived trend, is that this process of ecumenical convergence in worship practice will be largely ignored by a significant section of low church Protestants, both conservative and charismatic evangelicals, both within and beyond the main-line denominations. The future of their practice will be driven by a different set of dynamics and theo-logics, which will include an ongoing antipathy to set forms and prescribed rituals and, in some cases, a continuing consumption of and commitment to contemporary Western praise and worship music in the tradition of the charismatic renewal. Their convictions about the cultural, aesthetic and liturgical choices involved in this will be strengthened in future by the relative success of their own congregations in attracting and maintaining members, within a broader context of decline.

Fourth, worship practice across the denominations will be increasingly altered by the rising prevalence of adult baptism upon profession of faith. This will affect both Protestant and Roman Catholic churches[541] and will follow as a direct consequence of the steep decline in rates of infant baptism within the population as a whole in recent decades. It will also be fuelled by the projected increase in independent evangelical congregations, the vast majority of which will be credo-baptist. This new trajectory in Christian initiation will be a marker of the advanced stages of transition into a post-Christendom Scotland, where birth and baptism are no longer tightly bound together for most people. It seems inevitable that it will also lead to new liturgical developments and to a changed perception of the place and significance of baptism within worship in coming years.

---

540 In particular the painful demise of the Scottish Churches Initiative for Union (SCIFU).

541 Some critics have argued that the Roman Catholic Rite of Christian Initiation for Adults (RCIA) has already implicitly conceded something like normative status to adult baptism following adult catechumenate, a position vigorously denied by the Vatican, but an example of a new rite perhaps becoming a victim of its own success.

Worship and Context

It is, of course, material to the aims of those involved in this book that it should make a contribution within both academy and churches to stimulating reflection on worship practice within Scotland. However, many of the contributors are already deeply involved in international conversations on these issues and it is our hope that this book may similarly find a place within broader global conversations about worship and context. The fact that it, like most but not all of us, has a Scottish accent should not be an obstacle to this. The miracle of Pentecost after all, is not the obliteration of difference but the practice of translation and of listening to the other. Practical theology is bound by its own self-understanding to recognize the crucial significance of context. We would argue that the fact these studies are closely related to one context is something which commends them to the global discussion. Postcolonial theology is theology which tries to hear and celebrate its own accents and that of its conversation partners and which is enabled to hear and understand itself better through the response and critique of others.

Reading through the chapters in this book, there are a number of contexts whose importance has been reinforced for me. First, I am struck by the continued importance of *historical context* and both the undesirability and the sheer impossibility of dividing practical theology rigidly from Church history. Our understanding of present practice is bound up with a series of ongoing negotiations with historical understanding: of Celtic spirituality, of Reformed identity, of c/Catholic identity, of 'Scottish' identity ...

Second, the question of *ecumenical* context remains a crucial one within a country like Scotland, where Protestant–Roman Catholic sectarianism remains a live and occasionally still violent undercurrent within wider society. A breadth of ecumenical understanding is also vital for the academy, whose areas of interest and concern can often in retrospect seem disappointingly narrow. But official ecumenism, as sponsored by the mainline churches can suffer from its own omissions and its chronic tendency to be transfixed by the classic fault lines between denominations. The Scottish context bears witness simultaneously to a powerful and continuing movement of ecumenical convergence within worship practice over almost two centuries and to the persistence alongside this of radical difference in practice over that same period, with newly divergent trajectories of practice also appearing and growing in influence in recent decades. We therefore need an understanding of *ecumenical context*, which is willing and able to address this diversity as fully as possible.

The concerns of these two contexts – the historical and the ecumenical – are mutually involving. The questions 'how did we end up here?' and 'whose story is being told/not told?' remain compelling ones for us in Scotland, pointing to a continuing agenda for research and debate.

More could be said about the salience of *social and political context* and of the way in which liturgical traditions have often been coloured by the 'high culture' concerns of 'social elites'.[542] Much more too remains to be said about how worship has and has not reflected the experience of women within Scotland. The year 2009 is (only) the fortieth anniversary of women being ordained to the ministry of Word and sacrament within the Church of Scotland; Callum Brown's controversial revisionist work on secularization theory identifies gender as a primary causal factor in the developing secularization of Scotland since the 1960s;[543] meanwhile women continue to outnumber men within Scotland's worshipping congregations – all of these and more are issues relevant to worship in context which will need to be explored in future publications.

Finally, I am convinced of the need to pay greater attention to questions of *cultural context* and for practical theology to develop a more nuanced and critical approach to reflecting on cultural difference within Western contexts. Here, there is much to learn from work in and on non-Western contexts. In two ground-breaking studies *The Eclipse of Scottish Culture* (1989)[544] and *Scotland After Enlightenment* (1997),[545] Scottish cultural studies scholars Craig Beveridge and Ronald Turnbull took up Frantz Fanon's work on 'inferiorism' and questioned a tendency on the part of Scottish as well as English scholars to devalue Scottish culture in a way which reflected patterns of domination and hegemony. They included in their critique a widespread tendency among Scottish intellectuals in the twentieth century (not least the leaders of the 1930s' Scottish literary renaissance) to indiscriminately name Calvinism as a toxic influence, which had steadily poisoned aesthetic and cultural life within Scotland over four centuries. Beveridge and Turnbull made a significant contribution to opening up a revisionist perspective on this charge and their lead has been too little followed by commentators from within theology and religious studies. The contributions here from David Fergusson, John Bell, Nigel Yates, Alison Jack and Jane Dawson all indirectly take steps of different kinds to

---

542 For an important discussion of this within contemporary theology, see Tim Gorringe's *Furthering Humanity – A Theology of Culture*, Aldershot: Ashgate, 2004; especially the discussion in chapter 3 of 'The Quality of Culture' in which Gorringe, unusually for an English theologian, makes well-informed references to Scottish folk traditions and also to the Iona Community's liturgical practice. We regret that a commissioned chapter on worship in urban priority areas was not produced in time to be included in this volume.

543 See C. Brown, *Religion and Society in Scotland Since 1707*, Edinburgh: Edinburgh University Press, 1997.

544 Edinburgh: Polygon, 1989.

545 Edinburgh: Polygon, 1997.

remedy this, but there is much more to be done in this respect, if a more nuanced and developed analysis is to be approached.

In his discussion of one of Derrida's most famous aphorisms, James K. A. Smith notes Derrida's own gloss that he means 'there is nothing outside context'.[546] As practical theologians, the editors assume there is no context-free practice and there are no context-less vantage points from which to comment on practice. We hope this volume has offered a timely contribution to developing reflection and understanding in relation to worship and liturgy and its associated settings and practices. We look forward too, to the conversations which may flow from it, in the expectation that they will expand our understanding of our own contexts and increase our attention to those of our neighbours, wherever they are in the world.

---

546 James K. A. Smith, *Who's Afraid of Postmodernism: taking Derrida, Lyotard and Foucault to Church*, Grand Rapids MI: Baker Academic, 2007, p52.

INDEX